UK Wholesalers of Soft Drinks

Profiles of the leading 1400 companies

John D Blackburn

Editor

First Edition

Spring 2019

ISBN-13: 978-1-912736-18-8

ISBN-10: 1-912736-18-7

All rights reserved. No part of this publication may be reproduced, distributed, or transmitted in any form or by any means, including photocopying, recording, or other electronic or mechanical methods, without our prior written permission, except in the case of brief quotations embodied in critical reviews and certain other non-commercial uses permitted by copyright law. For permission requests, please write to us.

Copyright © 2019 Dellam Publishing Limited

Printed in 8pt Nimbus Sans L

Designed by URW++ Design and Development GmbH

Dellam Publishing Limited

2 Heath Drive, Sutton, Surrey, SM2 5RP

Fax: 020 8770 7478   email: enquiries@dellam.com

SAN: 0177881   EAN/GLN: 5030670177882

Table of Contents

1 Acknowledgements iv

2 Introduction v

3 Total Assets League Table 1
- As a measure of size, total assets is preferable to turnover which is influenced by profit margins and whether companies are capital or labour intensive.

4 Age of Companies 7
- Each company is ranked by its date of incorporation. Newcomers are defined as those registered since 2017.

5 Geographic Distribution 17
- Each company is classed by county.

6 Company Profiles 27
- Full company name, date incorporated, net worth, total assets, registered office, activities, shareholders and parent company, directors (with date of birth, nationality and occupation) and number of employees (if available).

7 Index of Directorships 107
- Alphabetical list of directors showing their directorships. If several directors have identical names then their date of birth is shown.

8 Standard Industrial Classification 133
- These codes are used to classify businesses by the type of economic activity in which they are engaged.

9 *finis* 143

Acknowledgements

This is a long and detailed publication containing thousands of facts and figures. It is only to be expected, despite continuous and repeated editing and checking, that errors may occur. In such cases, once we are aware of any, we publish a correction on our website.

Readers are encouraged to check regularly at www.dellam.com/books for any corrections and updates.

Although we take extreme care to ensure accuracy and being up-to-date, we cannot accept responsibility for any errors or omissions.

Contains public sector information licensed under Open Government Licence v3.0. from The Charity Commission (England and Wales) and The Charity Commission for Northern Ireland. © Crown Copyright and database right (2018).

Contains information from the Scottish Charity Register supplied by the Office of the Scottish Charity Regulator and licensed under the Open Government Licence v.2.0. © Crown Copyright and database right (2018).

Contains OS data © Crown copyright and database right (2018)

Contains Royal Mail data © Royal Mail copyright and database right (2018)

Contains National Statistics data © Crown copyright and database right (2018)

Contains Office for National Statistics © Crown copyright and database right (2018)

Maps based on those produced by the Office for National Statistics Geography GIS & Mapping Unit (2012 and 2018).

Contains HM Land Registry data © Crown copyright and database right (2018).

Contains Parliamentary information licensed under the Open Parliament Licence v3.0.

House of Commons Library Briefing Papers licensed under the Open Parliament Licence v3.0.

Contains Food Standards Agency data © Crown copyright and database right (2018).

Contains Eurostat data, 1995-2018, copyright European Commission by the Decision of 12 December 2011.

Maps based on produced by ONS Geography GIS & Mapping Unit.

Contains Companies House data supplied under section 47 and 50 of the Copyright, Designs and Patents Act 1988 and Schedule 1 of the Database Regulations (SI 1997/3032).

We appreciate your interest in our publications, and your comments and suggestions are always welcome. Please contact us at enquiries@dellam.com.

Introduction

This study looks at all companies registered in the United Kingdom where they identify themselves as wholesalers of fruit and vegetable juices, mineral water and soft drinks.

This study includes companies that are dormant or non-trading some of which might be latent while others may operate under their owners' names but incorporate to protect the business name. In addition, all newly incorporated companies are included. The study will exclude those companies that do not specifically identify themselves as wholesalers of fruit and vegetable juices, mineral water and soft drinks.

The aim of this study is to provide an overview of the key movers and shakers in the UK soft drinks wholesale sector. Only key data has been isolated, particularly the company's net worth and total assets, but also its full name, date incorporated, registered office, other activities, shareholders, directors (with date of birth, occupation and nationality) and number of employees.

Two indicators of size are used: net worth and total assets. These are preferable to turnover which is influenced by profit margins and whether the companies are capital or labour intensive.

In the years 2016, 2017 and 2018, new company incorporations in the soft drinks wholesale sector were 112, 193 and 523 respectively.

The wholesale market now accounts for £27.7 billion, taking into account the removal of Palmer & Harvey PLC, which collapsed in November 2017.

Breakdown of beverages in the UK is as follows: soft drinks (28%), beer (27%), whisky (25%), cider (7%), gin (3%), mineral water (3%) and others (2%).

Carbonates remain the largest segment worth £6.9 billion.

The breadown for non-alcoholic sector is as follows: cola £1.2 billion; pure juice £851 million; juice drinks £429 million; smoothies £223 million; plain water £616 million; squashes £406 million; traditional mixers £192 million; and fruit carbonates £405 million.

The market for bottled water and fruit juice, neither of which contain added sugar, is unaffected by the sugar levy but nonetheless they do contain naturally-occurring sugars. Despite their natural sugar content, sales of freshly squeezed juices and smoothies were the fastest growing segment.

100% juice is the most important factor in choosing a product.

In terms of Gross Value Added (GVA), beverages (including soft drinks and mineral water) is the largest manufacturing group with a of £6.6 billion in 2015; contributing 23% to the total food and drink manufacturing GVA.

The percentage UK retail price increase from June 2007 to June 2016 for soft drinks was 24% with alcoholic drinks at 17% and coffee, tea, cocoa at 36%

In Great Britain, 57% of those aged 16 years and over in 2017 drank alcohol (29 million people of the population) while 20% did not drink alcohol at all.

Standard cataloguing guidelines for company names in the profile section have been used, but there will be occurrences when the name may not be strictly alphabetical. A certain licence was adopted where it was felt that strictly alphabetical could lead to improper cataloguing. Some company names have been shortened in the league tables for aesthetic reasons.

John D Blackburn
Editor

This page is intentionally left blank

UK Wholesalers of Soft Drinks   dellam

Total Assets League Table

dellam

UK Wholesalers of Soft Drinks

Company	Amount	Company	Amount
Burlingtown UK Limited	£480,930,016	Sams Fast Foods Limited	£2,499,371
Roxane UK Limited	£80,282,240	Dawsons (Wales) Limited	£2,353,234
Red Bull Company Limited	£73,608,000	Pixley Berries (Juice) Limited	£2,325,956
Vimto (Out of Home) Limited	£64,299,000	Sutaka UK Limited	£2,245,673
Leathams Limited	£59,089,000	The Berry Juice Company Limited	£2,223,799
Cobell Ltd	£18,440,732	Adrian Mecklenburgh Limited	£2,129,189
Masca Holding Limited	£17,895,648	Oranka Fruit Juices Limited	£2,069,942
Crop's Foods Ltd.	£14,288,526	Drink Warehouse UK Limited	£2,005,153
Creamline Dairies Limited	£13,913,017	Dimark Limited	£1,980,361
Swallow Holdings Limited	£13,913,017	R. & I. Jones Limited	£1,979,526
Konon Limited	£13,540,305	Seedlip Ltd	£1,870,877
MM Global Citrus Limited	£12,197,000	Camelot Chilled Foods Ltd	£1,870,487
V.A. Whitley & Co. Limited	£11,013,765	Ooberstock Limited	£1,592,134
Temple Wines (Cash & Carry) Limited	£9,808,691	Marathon Food Limited	£1,501,561
Thirsty Work Limited	£8,144,996	Veg & City Drinks Limited	£1,452,763
Ozdil UK Limited	£7,846,391	Shree Sai Trading Ltd	£1,426,703
Eda Quality Foods Limited	£7,693,200	Clarion Wines Limited	£1,361,177
D D C Foods Limited	£7,312,383	Gerrard Seel Limited	£1,341,289
Rahim Brothers Limited	£7,270,565	ATR Catering Supplies Limited	£1,335,397
Manchester Drinks Company Ltd	£6,903,282	Abevco Limited	£1,321,749
Ely & Sidney Limited	£6,741,256	Top Selection Limited	£1,316,558
Alivini Company Limited	£6,575,749	Alti's Catering Limited	£1,257,947
Aquaid Franchising Limited	£6,481,258	Urban Distribution Ltd	£1,248,184
R.A. Trading Limited	£5,374,917	Taste Merchants Ltd	£1,234,247
Anatolian Foods Ltd	£5,123,108	Shapla Cash & Carry Ltd	£1,211,535
Tydene Limited	£4,867,077	Lithuanian Beer Limited	£1,208,640
Liquidline Limited	£4,840,311	Ets Mandy SPRL Ltd.	£1,183,332
Mirpa Limited	£4,823,428	J M & D Limited	£1,122,880
Cyprofood Limited	£4,767,462	Aduna Limited	£1,116,898
Water Wellbeing Limited	£4,044,968	Grouptype Limited	£1,085,885
Wenlock Spring Water Limited	£4,027,848	Alivini (North) Limited	£1,077,817
J.C. Dudley & Co. Ltd	£3,844,353	KVC Waffles Limited	£1,068,283
Tate-Smith Limited	£3,811,111	Aquavita II UK Limited	£1,062,055
Cawston Press Limited	£3,793,469	A & A Wines Limited	£904,532
DJ Drink Solutions Limited	£3,715,638	S & M (Wholesale Supplies) Limited	£900,039
Becsco Limited	£3,707,634	Windfall Logistics Limited	£877,970
GFT Retail UK Limited	£3,678,374	Sloane Avenue Group Ltd	£867,512
Navson Ltd	£3,567,701	Thirst Quenchers (UK) Limited	£853,525
Gemini Wholesalers Limited	£3,550,427	Major Foods Limited	£824,094
Frobishers Juices Limited	£3,547,984	Kaleboard Limited	£811,531
Village Quality Products Limited	£3,473,561	Pursuit of Excellence Group Ltd	£795,827
Riddles Bros Limited	£3,361,628	GI Food Group Limited	£793,622
KSY Juice Blends UK Ltd	£3,344,185	Alfresco Drinks Limited	£788,885
Phoenix Dispensed Drinks Limited	£3,287,415	Season Harvest (NI) Limited	£784,811
Milton Sandford Wines Limited	£3,268,376	Basecamp Brews Ltd	£776,098
AFC Food (UK) Limited	£2,857,104	Watercoolers Southern Limited	£762,803
Rich Energy Limited	£2,711,662	Failte Wholesale Limited	£757,866
Adamson's Drinks Ltd.	£2,709,121	Middleton Wholesale Limited	£755,478
Supermalt UK Limited	£2,572,578	M Trading Limited	£734,681
Buffalo Refreshments Ltd	£2,532,695	C.N.A. Catering Logistics Limited	£734,271
Kaspas Distribution Ltd	£2,500,231	Caspian Foods Cash & Carry Limited	£719,039

UK Wholesalers of Soft Drinks

Company	Amount	Company	Amount
G & Y Wynne Limited	£690,024	Alancia Fruit & Vegetable Ltd	£331,481
Quando Drinks Limited	£687,103	Solerco Products Limited	£326,680
Creative Properties and Investments Ltd	£674,919	Better Tasting Drinks Co. Limited	£318,715
Ipro Sport International Limited	£662,288	Snackpax Distribution Limited	£304,809
Oasis Softdrinks Limited	£652,141	HT Sweets (UK) Limited	£304,724
Ozlem Limited	£649,019	Henry Mitchell & Sons Limited	£302,124
Sannel Foods Limited	£629,458	Total Cellar Supplies Limited	£295,655
Taj Restaurant Supplies Ltd	£613,107	Namar Limited	£294,986
More or Less Drinks Company Limited	£595,876	Ly Hong Limited	£292,856
Viserra Limited	£594,758	Bill Bean Limited	£290,807
Colemans ABC Ltd	£590,202	Continent Foods Limited	£281,958
Botanic Lab Ltd	£585,891	Natural Welsh Water Limited	£281,854
D'Auria Brothers Ice Cream and Catering Limited	£579,602	Dreams Food 1 Limited	£280,018
City Beer Limited	£566,142	Street Food Solutions UK Ltd	£279,733
Top Pops Wholesaler of Soft Drinks Limited	£553,643	Orange Be Global Ltd	£276,202
JFC Trading Limited	£546,628	Fast Food Traders Ltd	£268,321
Narayan Foods Limited	£538,079	Drink Natural Limited	£265,498
Vivid Vitality Ltd	£533,909	D.E. Scorer Limited	£259,382
Raylex Ltd	£530,375	Eatwell Catering Contractors (Norwich) Limited	£257,711
Cellar Twelve Limited	£516,459	Azka Impex (London) Limited	£254,508
Bristol Spirits Limited	£503,908	Greenme Ltd	£249,249
Direct Source Distribution Limited	£486,701	Hua Lin Trade Import Limited	£247,040
Vendit (Harrow) Limited	£485,051	Ceci-Hill Limited	£242,928
TFC Wholesale Ltd	£479,969	Soft Drink UK Limited	£239,591
Euro Globe Distributors Limited	£475,628	Rush Energy Drinks Ltd	£237,061
Cibo (London) Limited	£470,649	London Wholesale Ltd	£234,661
HDL Trading Limited	£458,912	Afrimalt UK Ltd	£226,435
Swallow Dispensed Drinks Solutions Limited	£453,365	Aspire Brands Int Ltd.	£224,086
Bucovina Cash & Carry Ltd	£453,134	Morinda UK Limited	£218,248
Superyacht Supplies Limited	£439,175	Emara Soft Drinks Ltd	£217,300
Hero Catering Supplies Limited	£427,098	Moju Ltd	£215,959
L & D Services UK Limited	£426,792	Unite Foods Trading Limited	£214,745
Mightybee Limited	£423,371	Amou Limited	£214,674
Deveron Direct Limited	£417,240	Collette International Limited	£210,977
Loughborough Student Services Limited	£414,904	Premier Pubco Limited	£209,606
Bella Refreshments Ltd.	£410,796	Toschi UK Limited	£208,573
Thremhall Limited	£407,541	Majestic Foods Limited	£207,258
Golden Fastfood Limited	£406,160	The Start-Up Drinks Lab Limited	£206,699
Storesrealm Limited	£404,033	Brand Distributors Limited	£205,743
Bloomsbury Drinks Ltd	£391,988	Eastway Cash & Carry Limited	£202,740
Zanzi Products Limited	£390,370	Thistle Foods Limited	£202,172
Merchantology Ireland Ltd	£389,460	Aberystwyth Soft Drinks Ltd	£199,298
Artisan Drinks Company Limited	£384,193	Natural Snacking Ltd	£197,705
Direct Source 2 Limited	£375,579	C S Drinks Ltd	£196,609
Total Refreshment Solutions Limited	£362,559	Unione Trading Europe Ltd	£195,160
RSS Fast Food Suppliers Ltd	£361,639	Wades & Ellie Ltd	£193,227
Ideal Lincs Limited	£354,208	Arsi Soft Drinks Limited	£192,835
Bevtec Services Limited	£353,585	Chum Bites Limited	£188,378
Lanza Foods Ltd	£351,409	Lora Trading (Europe) Ltd	£179,773
Azka Impex Limited	£350,193	Giovanni Food & Wine Limited	£177,652
Fourseasons Fruiterers Ltd	£348,022	Fresh Star Fruit & Veg Limited	£174,857

Triple R Industries Limited	£172,712	Artos Foods Limited	£98,719
Nature on Tap Limited	£171,543	Smart Buyer Wholesale Limited	£97,401
Nazar Wholesale Limited	£170,005	Zummo Central Limited	£96,186
Jeet (UK) Limited	£168,844	Noble Naturals Ltd	£95,645
E-Natural Limited	£166,035	Ravensbourne Wine Company Limited	£94,410
Suncrops UK Limited	£165,851	GM Catering Supplies Ltd	£93,753
Wobblegate Limited	£165,042	A to Z Veg Ltd	£91,541
Elderbrook Drinks Limited	£163,378	RDM Polish Food Ltd	£89,535
Shimroon Limited	£162,529	Brewed 4 U Ltd	£86,478
Afro Lanka Ltd	£156,959	Sun Exotic Wholesale Ltd	£86,360
Dodotraders UK Limited	£155,933	Czar & Co (UK) Limited	£86,123
Mezin Distribution UK Limited	£153,543	Global Sunshine Distribution Limited	£81,573
F & T Enterprise Ltd.	£152,184	Toffoc Ltd	£79,655
Cambridge Juice Co. Limited	£144,254	Merseyside Service Ltd	£77,238
MSM Foods Limited	£141,893	Alamirat Limited	£77,167
Hellenic Grocery Limited	£141,872	JR Quality Service Ltd	£76,843
Bedford Halal Meat & Grocceries Ltd	£141,804	Triumph Foodservice Limited	£76,650
Ecopure Waters International Limited	£140,609	Rocktails Drinks Limited	£76,040
N & J Wholesale Foods Limited	£139,951	Woodchester International Ltd	£75,911
Seven Bros Cookware Ltd	£138,107	London UK Star Ltd	£75,511
Vitamin Well Limited	£137,997	OK Brothers Ltd	£75,242
Jax Coco UK Ltd.	£137,508	C & M Wholesale Limited	£74,573
I S Traders Limited	£133,459	Importonics Limited	£72,237
Easy Squeeze Limited	£130,600	International Catering & Foods Limited	£71,816
Gold Star Soft Drinks Westcountry Limited	£129,558	Active Protein Limited	£70,386
Bevanda Solutions Limited	£129,557	Avic Trading Limited	£69,425
W.E.Pointon & Sons Limited	£126,385	Hi Fresh Limited	£66,710
Furze Young Limited	£125,484	The Pure Juice Company Ltd	£66,230
CBD Globe Distributors Ltd	£125,237	T & K Wholesale Ltd	£65,621
Sub Enterprises Ltd	£124,655	Kintyre Holdings Limited	£64,634
AB Trade Direct Ltd	£123,514	DWR Cerist Cyf	£63,535
Zacely Limited	£122,271	Baldwin's Sarsaparilla Limited	£62,974
Gusto Organic Ltd	£121,409	Jeeva Natural UK Ltd	£62,703
Cameron Soft Drinks Limited	£120,937	Anadolu Catering Limited	£61,984
Elegantly Spirited Limited	£120,267	Exel Distribution Ltd	£60,816
House Water Limited	£117,065	C J Canham Drinks Limited	£60,653
Thirstee Business Limited	£116,767	Altra Service Ltd	£59,721
Golden Pride Export Limited	£116,437	Organic Village Limited	£58,914
Future Generation Foods U.K. Limited	£116,029	Smoothie Fresh Ltd	£58,729
C & M Wholesale (UK) Limited	£110,096	Global Market Solutions Ltd	£57,786
AKM Trading Services Ltd	£109,015	Hamer & Perks Limited	£57,598
Hurly Burly Foods Limited	£108,371	Club Consultants Ltd	£56,652
Codex Limited	£108,352	Val Norton Ltd	£56,308
Orbit Food Ltd	£107,411	Simorgh Limited	£55,803
Ayr Brewing Company Limited	£105,871	MJ Trading (NW) Ltd	£54,900
Erbology Ltd	£105,038	Direct2door Food & Beverage Ltd.	£54,610
Choi's Trading & Co Ltd	£104,282	Flow 33 UK Limited	£53,599
Nosh Detox Delivery Limited	£102,970	Merchantology Ltd	£53,475
Global Food (Nelson) Ltd	£101,658	Astral Nutrition Limited	£53,383
JA & MD Limited	£99,192	Jasmine Direct Limited	£53,012
Classic Catering (UK) Ltd	£99,186	Sahej UK Limited	£50,982

UK Wholesalers of Soft Drinks

dellam

P & V Agents Ltd	£50,281	Aquabella London Ltd	£22,327
Verdict International Ltd	£50,000	C. J. Walls Trading UK Limited	£21,667
Alpha Aliment Ltd	£49,659	Savers Stop Wholesalers Ltd	£21,190
Global Fresh Ltd	£47,968	Alicja Food Ltd	£21,094
Acquisto Limited	£47,849	Jays Trading Ltd	£20,685
Turner Hardy & Co Limited	£46,551	West Green Supply Ltd	£20,167
L & B Foods Ltd	£46,268	Ziro Ltd	£20,047
HF Food International Ltd	£45,551	First Food Ltd	£19,504
Budget Logistics Ltd	£45,434	Organica Vita Ltd	£18,243
Fresh Fruit Direct Limited	£45,009	London Maya Sandwich Limited	£18,151
Thriftys Wholesale Limited	£44,912	CPH Games UK Limited	£18,136
D D S Food Imports Ltd	£44,892	The Magnanimous Distribution T/A Pizzeria Hut Limited	£17,709
Dan International (UK) Limited	£44,600	Big Horn UK Ltd	£17,702
K2 (Northwest) Limited	£44,434	Seagull Energy Drinks Ltd	£16,860
Amphipolis Limited	£42,801	Seasons East Ltd	£16,613
Walbrokers Limited	£41,314	Condimental Ltd	£16,550
Kadey Limited	£39,429	Prir Group Limited	£16,533
Direct Traders Ltd	£38,885	Deeti Wholesale Limited	£16,136
Zumi Natural Limited	£37,515	Tasman Bay Foods Europe Ltd	£15,692
Gabby & Bello Enterprises Ltd	£37,436	Akgun Food Ltd	£15,565
KD-Pol Ltd	£37,161	Sublime Distributors Limited	£15,063
A & H Trading Ltd	£36,392	Getfreshjuiceco Limited	£14,894
Anatolian Limited	£36,317	World Trade Values Limited	£14,787
Variety Food Fair Limited	£36,116	Zentio Limited	£14,740
Springwater Direct Ltd.	£35,302	Coconutty Ltd	£14,698
Castle Warehouse Management Limited	£35,000	Caribbean Trade Ltd	£14,560
Utku Emre Ltd	£34,798	Shu Enterprise Ltd	£14,378
Tazah Ltd	£32,510	V Wholesalers Ltd	£14,341
Fruto del Espiritu C.I.C.	£32,007	Shokers Wines & Spirits Limited	£14,210
Imran Brothers Limited	£31,793	Rex Drinks Limited	£14,205
Row & Smith Ltd	£31,391	Laspremuta Limited	£14,117
C1 Trading Ltd	£31,084	OMG Beverages Limited	£13,984
Wild Cat Energy Drink Ltd	£31,069	Capital Drinks London Limited	£13,617
Welat & Othman Limited	£30,577	Paul Berry Limited	£13,563
Babylon Foods Limited	£29,732	Racing Greens Nutraceuticals Limited	£13,276
Talbot & Barr Limited	£28,966	S & F Distribution Ltd	£13,024
Caju Drinks Ltd	£28,533	AQ Branding Ltd	£12,357
Polat International Ltd	£28,180	Pamm Beverages Limited	£12,021
SOS Hydration Limited	£27,207	Made in the States Limited	£11,582
MLI Trading Limited	£26,870	GWB Associates Limited	£10,817
Montann Limited	£26,774	Taza Food Limited	£10,123
Simex International Ltd	£26,494	CCM Enterprises Limited	£10,025
M.R.S. Supplies Limited	£26,347	Rick's Wine Ltd	£10,000
Kineta Drinks Limited	£25,655	BG Drinks Ltd	£9,903
MRU Wholesale Limited	£25,501	Nacho Juice Limited	£9,838
MS Rarytas Ltd	£25,128	Waterline (UK) Ltd	£9,699
Panton Ventures Limited	£24,604	Atlas Halal Ltd	£9,548
Bibere Ltd.	£24,552	Georgian Food and Beverages Limited	£9,425
Aspire Drinks Limited	£24,525	Cubico Limited	£9,271
Active Root 2 Ltd	£24,417	Trust in Global Food Ltd	£9,260
Globe Imex Ltd	£23,202	RMGL Ltd	£9,230

The Santa Monica Company Ltd	£9,218	Olsson Logistics Limited	£1,897
Acquire Consultancy Limited	£9,034	Potts of Goodness Limited	£1,896
Tasnim Recruiting & Consultancy Services Ltd	£8,721	Watt Energy Drink (UK) Ltd	£1,734
H2O Supplies Ltd	£8,584	Highland Cow Motor Home Ltd	£1,711
HMH Wholesale Ltd	£8,541	Atlantis Spring Water Limited	£1,678
Raw Is More Ltd.	£8,499	DH Exotic Produce Ltd	£1,663
S & B's Mart Ltd.	£8,194	Discount on Drinks Ltd	£1,356
PSB Trading Limited	£7,994	Elev8 Life Limited	£1,354
Alisha Fish Bazar Ltd	£7,636	Tongue in Peat Limited	£1,199
Squishy Drinks Limited	£7,573	Juice de Vine Limited	£1,126
Cooper & Partner Ltd	£7,200	Brighton Brew Co Ltd	£1,025
Usmoothie Ltd	£6,282	In2rehab Brands Limited	£1,000
K & E Wholesale Ltd	£5,837	Winewise Ltd	£1,000
Dragon Rise Limited	£5,638	Vittorio Ottavio Ltd	£902
Ifood Trading Ltd	£5,584	Inc. Trading Limited	£858
Samco Global Foods Ltd	£5,420	Endetrox Ltd.	£825
LB Hussan Hussain Halal Meat Superstore Ltd	£5,420	Debbie and Venky Ltd	£801
KML Home Limited	£5,225	DT Fruits Ltd	£801
Aqua Distribution Limited	£5,155	Hello Coco Limited	£800
Valley Water Limited	£5,126	GO4 Beverages Limited	£792
MBS Ventures Limited	£5,026	Meless Group Limited	£780
Bor-Tom Ltd	£4,949	Simple Nature Limited	£700
Taste of Crete Ltd	£4,760	Ferment Revolution Limited	£657
Dolphin Trading Limited	£4,674	Liverpool & Oriental Trading Company Limited	£619
Cape Crown Global Goods Limited	£4,233	Moon Lynx Ltd	£500
Foal Limited	£4,180	Premier Marketing (NW) Ltd	£471
Tropical Produce Limited	£4,090	Good Prices Ltd	£456
B4Sport Ltd.	£4,059	J.C.Davies & Hall Limited	£250
Brandin Marketing Limited	£3,901	Macedo (UK) Limited	£114
Yardely Ltd	£3,637	Biofresh Cosmos Ltd	£111
CC Trade Ltd	£3,603	Food Brands Ltd	£105
Britlines Limited	£3,525	Energy Drinks Ltd	£100
Acqua Nordica Ltd	£3,452	Freshwater Direct Limited	£100
Laz and Kol Ltd	£3,416	Gulzar Traders Ltd	£100
Monks Drinks Limited	£3,333	Printers Service Ltd	£100
Broadwater Supply and Distribution Ltd	£3,184	IR Global Service Ltd	£100
Tas Services UK Limited	£3,056	Ch@i Drinks Ltd	£60
MAS Trading Cast Ltd	£2,934	GDH Distribution Limited	£50
Govmalt & H.U.M.M.E.R. Beverages Global Co Ltd	£2,890	21st Century Nutrition Limited	£37
Adanali Limited	£2,850	Sweet Sally Limited	£26
Native Leaf Ltd	£2,818	Qahhar Drinks Ltd	£19
Xorta Global Management Limited	£2,801	Asia Direct Limited	£2
Quicklemon UK Ltd	£2,713	Wild Cat Distribution UK Limited	£2
Aura Gold Water Ltd	£2,424	Stack United Limited	£2
M & M Export Limited	£2,317	Kingsbury Wholesale Ltd	£2
Think Power Limited	£2,279	Lake Shore Distributors Ltd	£2
Jessica Worldwide Ltd	£2,168	UK Beer & Soft Drinks Ltd	£1
Log Cabin Fruits Ltd	£2,119	Ideal Trading Limited	£1
H Two Eau International Limited	£2,009		

Age of Companies

1930-1939
Henry Mitchell & Sons Limited

1940-1949
Creamline Dairies Limited
V.A. Whitley & Co. Limited

1960-1969
Cabana Soft Drinks Limited
Tate-Smith Limited
Vendit (Harrow) Limited

1970-1979 [7]
D'Auria Brothers Ice Cream and Catering
Eatwell Catering Contractors (Norwich)
W.E.Pointon & Sons Limited
D.E. Scorer Limited
Solerco Products Limited
Storesrealm Limited
Water Wellbeing Limited

1980-1989 [16]
A & A Wines Limited
Alivini Co Ltd
Crop's Foods Ltd.
Dawsons (Wales) Limited
J.C. Dudley & Co. Ltd
Ely & Sidney Limited
Gerrard Seel Limited
R. & I. Jones Limited
Kintyre Holdings Limited
Lam Cash and Carry Limited
Leathams Limited
Loughborough Student Services Ltd
Marathon Food Limited
Adrian Mecklenburgh Limited
Middleton Wholesale Limited
Ravensbourne Wine Co Ltd

1990-1994 [10]
Alivini (North) Limited
Bristol Spirits Limited
Colemans ABC Ltd
Dolphin Trading Limited
Macedo (UK) Limited
Red Bull Co Ltd
Roxane UK Limited
Supermalt UK Limited
Swallow Holdings Limited
Temple Wines (Cash & Carry) Ltd

1995
Dan International (UK) Limited
Thremhall Limited

1996
Alfresco Drinks Limited
Asia Direct Limited
Springwater Direct Ltd.
Walbrokers Limited

1997 [5]
C & M Wholesale Limited
Camelot Chilled Foods Ltd
M & M Export Limited
Shapla Cash & Carry Ltd
Total Refreshment Solutions Ltd

1998 [10]
ATR Catering Supplies Limited
Aquaid Franchising Limited
Bill Bean Limited
D D C Foods Limited
Failte Wholesale Limited
Ozlem Limited
Rivella (U.K.) Limited
S & M (Wholesale Supplies) Ltd
Sannel Foods Limited
Waterline (UK) Ltd

1999 [10]
Becsco Limited
Cobell Ltd
Collette International Limited
D D S Food Imports Ltd
Frobishers Juices Limited
GWB Associates Limited
Hamer & Perks Limited
Morinda UK Limited
Ozdil UK Limited
Season Harvest (NI) Limited

2000 [6]
Aqua Distribution Limited
Cawston Press Limited
Phoenix Dispensed Drinks Ltd
R.A. Trading Limited
Thirstee Business Limited
Top Selection Limited

2001
Fruto del Espiritu C.I.C.
Grouptype Limited
Premier Pubco Limited
Wenlock Spring Water Limited

2002 [15]
Adamson's Drinks Ltd.
Berry Juice Co Ltd
Cambridge Juice Co. Limited
Caribbean Trade Ltd
Eda Quality Foods Limited
Euro Globe Distributors Ltd
GFT Retail UK Limited
Lithuanian Beer Limited
Meless Group Limited
N & J Wholesale Foods Limited
Navson Ltd
Oranka Fruit Juices Limited
Sahej UK Limited
Shimroon Limited
Tas Services UK Limited

2003 [12]
Babylon Foods Limited
Paul Berry Limited
C J Canham Drinks Limited
City Beer Limited
Dimark Limited
Easy Squeeze Limited
Shokers Wines & Spirits Ltd
Soft Drink UK Limited
Superyacht Supplies Limited
Tydene Limited
Watercoolers Southern Limited
Wisdom of Nature Limited

2004 [11]
Alamirat Limited
Alti's Catering Limited
Baldwin's Sarsaparilla Limited
Cellar Twelve Limited
Furze Young Limited
Getfreshjuiceco Limited
Jeet (UK) Limited
Rick's Wine Ltd
Riddles Bros Limited
Toffoc Ltd
G & Y Wynne Limited

2005 [14]
BG Drinks Ltd
Ceci-Hill Limited
Cibo (London) Limited
Clarion Wines Limited
Ideal Lincs Limited
Lawton Cross Limited
Manchester Drinks Co Ltd
Natural Welsh Water Limited
OMG Beverages Limited
Sams Fast Foods Limited
TFC Wholesale Ltd
Top Pops Wholesaler of Soft Drinks
Usqueeze Limited
Zummo Central Limited

2006 [8]
Anatolian Foods Ltd
C.N.A. Catering Logistics Ltd
Cubico Limited
DJ Drink Solutions Limited
KVC Waffles Limited
MM Global Citrus Limited
Milton Sandford Wines Limited
Ubuntu Trading Co Ltd

2007 [12]
Abevco Limited
Burlingtown UK Limited
Cyprofood Limited
Giovanni Food & Wine Limited
K2 (Northwest) Limited
L & D Services UK Limited
Lanza Foods Ltd
Ly Hong Limited
Organic Village Limited
Pixley Berries (Juice) Limited
Pure Juice Co Ltd
Windfall Logistics Limited

2008 [6]
Brewed 4 U Ltd
Golden Fastfood Limited
House Water Limited
Kadey Limited
MSM Foods Limited
World Trade Values Limited

UK Wholesalers of Soft Drinks

2009 [18]
AFC Food (UK) Limited
AKM Trading Services Ltd
Afrimalt UK Ltd
Aquabella London Ltd
Ayr Brewing Co Ltd
DWR Cerist Cyf
Direct Source Distribution Ltd
Gabby & Bello Enterprises Ltd
Gold Star Soft Drinks Westcountry Ltd
H2O Supplies Ltd
In2rehab Brands Limited
J M & D Limited
Norfolk Punch Limited
Nosh Detox Delivery Limited
Rahim Brothers Limited
Thirst Quenchers (UK) Limited
Tri Star Wholesale Limited
Wades & Ellie Ltd

January-June 2010 [10]
Alancia Fruit & Vegetable Ltd
Azka Impex Limited
Drink Warehouse UK Limited
Ecopure Waters International Ltd
HDL Trading Limited
Jays Trading Ltd
Liquidline Limited
Sublime Distributors Limited
Thirsty Work Limited
Usmoothie Ltd

July-December 2010 [11]
C S Drinks Ltd
Classic Catering (UK) Ltd
Coconutty Ltd
Drink Your Fruit Limited
Gemini Wholesalers Limited
M.R.S. Supplies Limited
Oasis Softdrinks Limited
Ooberstock Limited
Sutaka UK Limited
Yardely Ltd
Zacely Limited

January-June 2011 [15]
Aduna Limited
Aroma Soft Drinks & Water Ltd
CBD Globe Distributors Ltd
Drinks R Us Limited
Energy Drinks Ltd
Fast Food Traders Ltd
Highland Cow Motor Home Ltd
Lake Shore Distributors Ltd
Narayan Foods Limited
Samco Global Foods Ltd
Shree Sai Trading Ltd
Simply Spirits Limited
Think Power Limited
Viserra Limited
Vivid Vitality Ltd

July-December 2011 [23]
AQ Branding Ltd
Bevtec Services Limited
Castle Warehouse Management Ltd
Choi's Trading & Co Ltd
DH Exotic Produce Ltd
Direct Source 2 Limited
Drink Natural Limited

Drinkslynx Limited
E-Natural Limited
Erbology Ltd
Global Market Solutions Ltd
Kurd Scot Imports & Exports Ltd
London Wholesale Ltd
Mezin Distribution UK Limited
PSB Trading Limited
Panton Ventures Limited
Premier Marketing (NW) Ltd
Qahhar Drinks Ltd
S & F Distribution Ltd
Saapos Ltd
Veg & City Drinks Limited
Wild Cat Energy Drink Ltd
Zanzi Products Limited

January-March 2012 [7]
Anadolu Catering Limited
Bor-Tom Ltd
Capital Drinks London Limited
Football Special Ltd
Hero Catering Supplies Limited
Monks Drinks Limited
P & V Agents Ltd

April-June 2012 [6]
A to Z Veg Ltd
Amou Limited
Dodotraders UK Limited
F & T Enterprise Ltd.
Global Sunshine Distribution Ltd
Gusto Organic Ltd

July-September 2012 [8]
Atlas Halal Ltd
Bucovina Cash & Carry Ltd
Cameron Soft Drinks Limited
Evoca UK Distribution Limited
Fruit Slush 'n' Shake Ltd
Jax Coco UK Ltd.
L & B Foods Ltd
Tasnim Recruiting & Consultancy Services

October-December 2012 [16]
Bibere Ltd.
Britlines Limited
C1 Trading Ltd
Direct Traders Ltd
Greenme Ltd
I S Traders Limited
KSY Juice Blends UK Ltd
Mirpa Limited
Val Norton Ltd
Orange Be Global Ltd
Prir Group Limited
Quick Constuction Ltd
Rush Energy Drinks Ltd
Unite Foods Trading Limited
Usedsoft Ltd
Zumi Natural Limited

January-March 2013 [16]
Alpha Aliment Ltd
Arab World Ltd
Bloomsbury Drinks Ltd
Cooper & Partner Ltd
Dark Night Beverages Ltd
Debbie and Venky Ltd
Inc. Trading Limited

KD-Pol Ltd
KML Home Limited
More or Less Drinks Co Ltd
Natural Snacking Ltd
OK Brothers Ltd
Rocktails Drinks Limited
Thriftys Wholesale Limited
Village Quality Products Ltd
Vittorio Ottavio Ltd

April-June 2013 [8]
Dragon Rise Limited
GDH Distribution Limited
Healthy Hydration Limited
Juice de Vine Limited
Kaleboard Limited
Quick World Service Ltd
Smoothie Fresh Ltd
Verdict International Ltd

July-September 2013 [18]
Elev8 Life Limited
Enzyme's Secret Limited
Flux Investment Ltd
Golden Pride Export Limited
H N D Trading Limited
Hellenic Grocery Limited
Hesana Ltd
Kaplan Int Limited
Lync Direct Limited
Major Foods Limited
RDM Polish Food Ltd
Raylex Ltd
Seasons East Ltd
Silvercall Limited
Sweet Sally Limited
Trust in Global Food Ltd
C. J. Walls Trading UK Ltd
Zentio Limited

October-December 2013 [19]
A & H Trading Ltd
Aspire Drinks Limited
Caspian Foods Cash & Carry Ltd
Creative Properties and Investments Ltd
Dalina Limited
Discount on Drinks Ltd
Eagle Beer Ltd
HMH Wholesale Ltd
Longstar Trading Limited
Nichols Dispense (S.W.) Ltd
Norfolk Punch (UK) Ltd
SOS Hydration Limited
Simorgh Limited
Smart Buyer Wholesale Limited
Sun Exotic Wholesale Ltd
Thistle Foods Limited
UKFast Service Ltd
Vimto (Out of Home) Limited
Ziro Ltd

January-March 2014 [14]
Artos Foods Limited
Bella Refreshments Ltd.
Bespoke Contracts (UK) Ltd
Botanic Lab Ltd
BudgetForU Limited
Ets Mandy SPRL Ltd.
Hua Lin Trade Import Limited
Ifood Trading Ltd

MLI Trading Limited
Magnanimous Distribution T/A Pizzeria Hut
Nazar Wholesale Limited
Pursuit of Excellence Group Ltd
Taj Restaurant Supplies Ltd
Watt Energy Drink (UK) Ltd

April-June 2014 [14]
Amphipolis Limited
Aquavita II UK Limited
Aspire Brands Int Ltd.
Astral Nutrition Limited
Budget Logistics Ltd
Continent Foods Limited
Foal Limited
Georgian Food and Beverages Ltd
Inspire Drinks Ltd
K & E Wholesale Ltd
Kaspas Distribution Ltd
Masca Holding Limited
Quando Drinks Limited
Seedlip Ltd

July-September 2014 [15]
Alicja Food Ltd
Brand Distributors Limited
Club Consultants Ltd
Direct2door Food & Beverage Ltd.
Flow 33 UK Limited
Fourseasons Fruiterers Ltd
Global Fresh Ltd
Liverpool & Oriental Trading Co Ltd
Majestic Wholesale Ltd
Moju Ltd
Noble Naturals Ltd
Seven Bros Cookware Ltd
Sub Enterprises Ltd
Triumph Foodservice Limited
West Green Supply Ltd

October-December 2014 [14]
Afro Lanka Ltd
Artesian Springs Limited
C & M Wholesale (UK) Limited
Crescent Moon World Project Ltd.
Global Food (Nelson) Ltd
Huma Gida UK Limited
JFC Trading Limited
Laz and Kol Ltd
Mightybee Limited
RSS Fast Food Suppliers Ltd
Sharewater Ltd
Smoothie Fresh (International) Ltd
Tazah Ltd
Triple R Industries Limited

January 2015 [5]
Africa Global Village. Com Ltd
Coot Service Ltd
DT Fruits Ltd
Glinter UK Ltd
Nature on Tap Limited

February 2015 [5]
Active Protein Limited
Codex Limited
Organica Vita Ltd
Sloane Avenue Group Ltd
Taste Merchants Ltd

March 2015 [8]
Acqua Nordica Ltd
Deeti Wholesale Limited
Elderbrook Drinks Limited
Fresh Star Fruit & Veg Limited
Ipro Sport Distribution Ltd
Mediterranean International Ltd
Tropical Produce Limited
Utku Emre Ltd

April 2015 [5]
All for You Beverages Limited
Benson International Ltd
Log Cabin Fruits Ltd
MBS Ventures Limited
Wobblegate Limited

May 2015 [10]
Aquamarine Limited
Basecamp Brews Ltd
Eastway Cash & Carry Limited
Farida Import Export Ltd
Majestic Foods Limited
Merchantology Ltd
Snackpax Distribution Limited
Super Tidy Drinks Limited
Talbot & Barr Limited
Winewise Ltd

June 2015 [6]
Freshwater Direct Limited
Squishy Drinks Limited
Street Food Solutions UK Ltd
T & K Wholesale Ltd
Tasman Bay Foods Europe Ltd
UK Beer & Soft Drinks Ltd

July 2015 [8]
Better Tasting Drinks Co. Ltd
Buy & Sales Trading Ltd
Deveron Direct Limited
House Kitchen Limited
International Catering & Foods Ltd
JR Quality Service Ltd
Moon Lynx Ltd
N & B Foods Exeter Limited

August 2015
Sweetprod Ltd

September 2015 [6]
Active Root 2 Ltd
Frutex Limited
Potts of Goodness Limited
Raw Is More Ltd.
Rich Energy Limited
Sarl Import Export Mondial Ltd

October 2015 [10]
Arsi Soft Drinks Limited
Bevanda Solutions Limited
Brighton Brew Co Ltd
Patrick Fernando & Sons UK Ltd
Lora Trading (Europe) Ltd
Merlin's Beverages Limited
Nacho Juice Limited
Suncrops UK Limited
Swallow Dispensed Drinks Solutions
Wildcat International Limited

November 2015 [5]
Buffalo Refreshments Ltd
CCM Enterprises Limited
Jeeva Natural UK Ltd
M Trading Limited
Native Leaf Ltd

December 2015
Acquisto Limited
Anatolian Limited
Emara Soft Drinks Ltd

January 2016
EWF Wine Force Ltd
Exel Distribution Ltd

February 2016 [10]
Akgun Food Ltd
Brandin Marketing Limited
GM Catering Supplies Ltd
Jasmine Direct Limited
Merchantology Ireland Ltd
Olsson Logistics Limited
Roeser Limited
Simple Nature Limited
Taza Food Limited
Total Cellar Supplies Limited

March 2016 [6]
Cape Crown Global Goods Ltd
Importonics Limited
Laspremuta Limited
MRU Wholesale Limited
PXL Drinks Ltd
Seagull Energy Drinks Ltd

April 2016 [11]
Albanblue Elementals Limited
Belgard Trading Ltd
Delta Tip Limited
Feeders Foods Wholesale Ltd
Food Brands Ltd
Hello Coco Limited
Hurly Burly Foods Limited
Netmine Technologies Ltd
Savers Stop Wholesalers Ltd
Simex International Ltd
Transgh Limited

May 2016 [7]
Govmalt & H.U.M.M.E.R. Beverages Global Co
Quench Factory Limited
Row & Smith Ltd
Sabziwala Limited
UK Star Services Limited
Wild Cat Distribution UK Ltd
Xorta Global Management Ltd

June 2016 [8]
Azka Impex (London) Limited
CPH Games UK Limited
Evogue Limited
Ipro Sport International Ltd
Order2buy Ltd
Pick N Deliver Ltd
SLB Wholesale Ltd
Tropical Ice (England) Ltd

UK Wholesalers of Soft Drinks

July 2016 [7]
AB Trade Direct Ltd
AVM UK Private Limited
Bellwether Impex (UK) Limited
GI Food Group Limited
Gulzar Traders Ltd
LB Hussan Hussain Halal Meat Superstore
Made in the States Limited

August 2016 [13]
Atlantis Spring Water Limited
Budaquelle Beverages International Ltd
Flavour Foods & Drinks Ltd
GO4 Beverages Limited
H Two Eau International Ltd
Ipro Sport Corporation Limited
Joo Soft Drinks Limited
Montann Limited
S & B's Mart Ltd.
Toschi UK Limited
Valley Water Limited
Vezlon Limited
Yorkshire Enterprise Ltd

September 2016 [17]
Altra Service Ltd
Aura Gold Water Ltd
Best Brand Food & Drinks (BBFD) Ltd
Condimental Ltd
Easy CBD Limited
First Food Ltd
Hi Fresh Limited
Ipro Sport Medical Limited
Janama Trading Co Ltd
Cooray King Holdings Limited
Nadban Limited
Quicklemon UK Ltd
RMGL Ltd
Stirling Castle Water Ltd
Turner Hardy & Co Limited
Urban Distribution Ltd
V Wholesalers Ltd

October 2016 [9]
Astra Import Ltd.
Biofresh Cosmos Ltd
Fresh Fruit Direct Limited
Future Generation Foods U.K. Ltd
MJ Trading (NW) Ltd
Orbit Food Ltd
Polat International Ltd
Primacena Ltd.
Shane's Consortium Limited

November 2016 [11]
21st Century Nutrition Limited
3BW Ltd
Aberystwyth Soft Drinks Ltd
Anya Global Limited
CC Trade Ltd
Ch@i Drinks Ltd
East Lancs Suppliers Ltd
Freedom Sale Ltd
Ladeo Limited
Panymoc Ltd
Tongue in Peat Limited

December 2016 [11]
Acquire Consultancy Limited
Bedford Halal Meat & Grocceries Ltd
Beverage Brothers Limited
Caju Drinks Ltd
Imran Brothers Limited
Jaguar Power Energy Drinks Ltd.
Lana Nai UK Co. Ltd
Namar Limited
Naturshot Limited
Racing Greens Nutraceuticals Ltd
Vidi Vici Trading Ltd

January 2017 [10]
J.C.Davies & Hall Limited
Eldoflora Limited
F.R.D Wholesale Limited
Good Prices Ltd
HF Food International Ltd
London Maya Sandwich Limited
PU Trading Ltd
Temperance Drinks Limited
Variety Food Fair Limited
Welat & Othman Limited

February 2017 [13]
Ace Incorporation Ltd
Broadwater Supply and Distribution Ltd
Chum Bites Limited
Czar & Co (UK) Limited
Dreams Food 1 Limited
Iwater Inc Ltd
JA & MD Limited
Konon Limited
Nodus International Trade Ltd
Pamm Beverages Limited
Shu Enterprise Ltd
Total Fast Food Supplies Ltd
Zayyan Foods Distribution Ltd

March 2017 [10]
Albert Altima Trade House Ltd
Artisan Drinks Co Ltd
HM Wholesale Supplies Limited
Kineta Drinks Limited
NXSK UK Ltd
Robinson Alimentation Ltd
Shack Drinks Limited
Unione Trading Europe Ltd
Winz International UK Ltd
Woodstar Limited

April 2017 [15]
Acai Express Ltd
Alisha Fish Bazar Ltd
Big Brand Distributors UK Ltd
DLG Wholesale Ltd
Geminiz Ltd
Ideal Trading Limited
Jessica Worldwide Ltd
Kingsbury Wholesale Ltd
Like Like Ltd
London UK Star Ltd
Merseyside Service Ltd
Netto Stores Limited
Paramount Food and Drink (UK) Ltd.
Stack United Limited
Wishing Tree Limited

May 2017 [15]
Adanali Limited
Aiden Service Ltd
Big Horn UK Ltd
Bri Trade Solutions Limited
Carnaby and Kingly Limited
Ferment Revolution Limited
Frosty Service Ltd
Globe Imex Ltd
HT Sweets (UK) Limited
Herbaleva Ltd
Hermes Chariot Ltd
Rex Drinks Limited
Rexcel Trading Ltd
Sotomayor Imports Limited
Taste of Crete Ltd

June 2017 [20]
A H K Wholesaler Ltd
Amedame International Ltd
Avic Trading Limited
B4Sport Ltd.
Beverages Stars Ltd
Caleno Drinks Ltd
Couto & Machado Ltd
Exoteeque Limited
GT Traders Ltd.
IR Global Service Ltd
MS Rarytas Ltd
Nor Oslo Service Ltd
Pavlinko Limited
Printers Service Ltd
Santa Monica Co Ltd
Start-Up Drinks Lab Limited
Turkish Kitchinn Wholesale Ltd
UK Cloud Business PLC
Unique Lines Ltd
Vitamin Well Limited

July 2017 [10]
All Fresh Bradford Ltd
Clean-Coco Ltd
Freshfield Exotics Ltd
Healthy Food and Drink Online Ltd
Mother Nature's Drinks Limited
No Meat No Worries Limited
Nuli Life Ltd
Suha World Ltd
TN Sales Ltd
Woodchester International Ltd

August 2017 [21]
51 Plus Ltd
Connect Waze Private Limited
Elegantly Spirited Limited
Elev8 Energy Drink Limited
Evershine Trading Limited
Innerji Ltd
Just Aqua Ltd.
M & M Emerald Ltd
MAS Trading Cast Ltd
Modern Contradiction Limited
Nar London Limited
Not Another Beer Co Ltd
One Stop Fruit & Veg Limited
Shibui Beverage Co Ltd
Skyfall Enterprise Ltd
Slurps Ice Ltd
Stonefruit Ltd
Syntex Trading Ltd

Ufton Limited
Viva Avo Ltd
Worldwide Essentials Limited

September 2017 [15]
All English Distribution Ltd.
Anytime Drinks Limited
Apna Distribution Ltd
BS and Sons London Limited
DRGN Global Ltd.
Stefan Frank Ltd
Franklin 1886 Limited
Interseel Ltd
Iturn Global Ltd
Najpol Ltd
Patson Foods Ltd
Sabroso Food UK Ltd
Stockwell Beverages Ltd
Tata Trade Ltd
UK Traders (Leics) Ltd

October 2017 [18]
815 Distributors (UK) Ltd
Anderson Beverages Ltd
Attila Martocsan Ltd
Boisson Limited
DN World Ltd
GH Brands Ltd
Global Vitality Ltd.
Haltrade UK Ltd
Juice Junkiez Limited
Knights Catering Impex Ltd
La Zgarici Ltd
Manchester Fruit and Vegetables Ltd
Pallet Price Wholesale Ltd
RMGL Trading Limited
Route 33 Limited
T & A Import and Export Trading Ltd
Tricape UK Ltd
W D L Wholesale Limited

November 2017 [25]
Alitasa Ltd
Camii Punch Ltd
Delamore Trading UK Ltd
Drinkable Ltd
E & R Fruits Limited
Fanal Ltd
Hannah & Ted Ltd
Hydra Cubed Limited
Infinite Session Ltd
Jones Bros. 1877 Ltd
Juice Junkie London Limited
Kardelen Water Limited
Neelam Traders Ltd
Neubria Limited
Orange Trading Ltd
Perfect Drinks Ltd
Platinum Group Midlands Ltd
Punchy Drinks Limited
Raji Service Ltd
Anna Seed 83 Limited
Shake It Up! The Protein Smoothie Co Ltd
Star Direct Hospitality Ltd
Super Smoo-V Co Ltd
TN Global Service Ltd
Thamby Trading Ltd

December 2017 [21]
Al Taj Al Malaki General Trading UK Ltd
Best Trading One Limited
ESL Trading Ltd
Go Fresh Ltd
Herbs 4 Healthy Living Ltd
KP Global Ltd
Kang Med Limited
L'Azur Ltd
London Drinks Supplier Ltd
NCE Trading KFT Ltd
Nature Fresh Limited
Next Gen Drinks Limited
Nobu Distribution Ltd
Oct Multi Services Limited
Polwug Trading Ltd
Pure Pom Ltd
Redgate Imports Limited
SM Supplies Ltd
Seiyas Watercoolers Ltd
Stalker U.K Limited
Zolex Global Limited

January 2018 [29]
78 Degrees Limited
A1 Best Traders Ltd
Alpha Energy Drink Limited
Avigail Limited
Birch Boost Ltd
Blue Trading International Ltd
Bot Trading Co Ltd
Discount Brands (London) UK Ltd
Doorstep Desserts Distribution Ltd
Elan Import and Export Limited
Estelon Holdings Limited
Fevertree Europe Limited
Fevertree Row Limited
Fevertree UK Limited
Fevertree US Limited
Fresh Produce Deliveries Ltd
Fresh Produce Imports UK Ltd
Ibiza Recharge Limited
Jascera UK Ltd
KG Wholesale Ltd
Lord Eden Beverages Ltd
MKM Group Trading & Investment Ltd
Nexgen 2018 Ltd
Nile Minar Enterprise Limited
Premier Soft Drinks Ltd
Rarewood (London) Limited
Tradinguk55 Limited
Tronika Traders Limited
ZSlush Ltd

February 2018 [30]
2 Brothers Birmingham Ltd
AFZ Trade Ltd
Al Pixel Points Limited
Bakhta Moroccan Mint Iced Tea Ltd
Dollshouse Childrens Drinks Ltd
Endetrox Ltd.
Europol Trade Ltd.
Priya Even Limited
Gorog Trading Limited
Jonsen International Ltd
MBW Traders Ltd
Medina Food World Ltd
Mesh Facilities Limited
N'ife Limited
Noble Smokehouse Ltd
Notgin Ltd

Numidia Taste Ltd
One Up Beverages Corporation (1 Up)
Orpheus Tea Ltd
PMI Management Limited
MD Rahma Ltd
Sunspice UK Limited
TSK Trade Limited
Tatry Trade Ltd
Theodore Global Limited
Vinroe Distribution Ltd
Vitamor Limited
Wolf Wholesale Limited
Zero Options Ltd
Zoop Up Energy Ltd

March 2018 [38]
Angel Global Export Ltd
Apollo Fruit & Veg UK Ltd
Asi Wholesale & Retail Ltd
Bedrock Trade Ltd
Cane Press Ltd
Carpatica International Ltd
Dutch Delight UK Limited
Eda Quality Foods North UK Ltd
Fast Car Sales Services Ltd
Five Star Cash & Carry Ltd
Fruity Cards Ltd
Harp & Crown Cider Co Ltd
Jaden Wholesale Limited
Luella Malmesbury Ltd
Marco Polo Exotics Ltd
Mashmoom International Limited
Matlowone Limited
Mithun MM Limited
Musielski Wholesale Ltd
NBA Wholesale Ltd
Nalla Sales Ltd
Newton Soft Drinks Wholesale Ltd
Organix Ltd
Paddy and Scotts Launch Pad Ltd
Passa Distribution Ltd
Passa Wholesale Ltd
Pro Nutrition Ltd
RTH Healthcare PLC
Red Baron Beverages Limited
Slimsters Sports Drinks Ltd
Stockwell Wholesalers Limited
Syon Distributors Ltd
Thailand 11234501 International Trade Co.,
Tolmid International Ltd
Trade HQ Ltd
Vivo Viva Beverages Limited
WGTSS Ltd
Yorkshire Exports Limited

April 2018 [40]
AMG Wholesale Ltd
Agrofresh Ltd
All in One Household Ltd
Amsterdam Taste Ltd
Aquacoll UK Ltd
Bioactive Live Ltd
Bukhari and Tanweer Limited
Cheti & Co Holdings Limited
Clear Drinks Limited
DYoung and Son Limited
Dining Capital Limited
Dua Enterprises Limited
Eurozone Limited
Ewid Ltd
FMCG Enterprises Limited

UK Wholesalers of Soft Drinks

dellam

Flavours of Sardinia Limited
Fruit & Veg 2 U Ltd
Glitter Service Ltd
Global Food Wholesalers Ltd
Going Ahead Ltd
Great Wins Ltd
K.M Food & Drinks Ltd
KKS Fresh Fruits Ltd
KPN Wholesale Ltd
Klomar Ltd
Moringa Superfoods UK Limited
Oneway Trading Ltd
Oneworlddistribution Ltd
Paradigm Red Limited
Peregrine Welsh Water Limited
Pinnacle Drinks Limited
Pure Organic Drinks Limited
Rio Mata Atlantica Limited
Sepandero Venturi UK Limited
Sris International Ltd
UK Wings Limited
Under The Sun Europe Ltd
WLL Wholesale Ltd
Wine City Limited
ZSM Traders Ltd

May 2018 [43]
5of5 Juices Ltd
901WD Ltd
Agrotrade International Trading Ltd
Ammart Ltd
Bargain Food and Wine Ltd
Bio Icecream Ltd
Boomshakes Ltd
Claddagh Food and Drink Ltd
DSA Frozen Foods Ltd
Dark Invest Ltd
Emaya Foods Limited
FS Wholesale Distributors (UK) Ltd
Fernhill Wholesale Ltd
Fresh N Green Ltd
Frutex UK PVT Limited
Gloucester Wholesale Ltd
Gohir Soft Drinks Ltd
Hubit General Trading Ltd
I Star Wholesale Limited
J & D Wholesalers Ltd
KT Wholesale Ltd
Link International Ltd
Liquid Brand Exports Limited
Maira Trade Ltd
Manteo Trading Co Ltd
Meadow Harvest Ltd
Natures Vitality Limited
Nextgen Distribution Limited
PP Cash & Carry Ltd
Patrik Trading Ltd
Prestwich Catering & Wholesale Ltd
Primacy Trade Ltd
Reineta Limited
Rejuveu Ltd
JJ Sis Limited
Smith & Munden Ltd
Source 360 Ltd
Ultimum Drinks Limited
WLH Food Ltd
Waltrix Publishing Ireland Ltd
Your Water Ltd
YummyColombia Ltd
Zaid & Besher Ltd

June 2018 [41]
7 Star Trading Ltd
AB Catering (Blackburn) Ltd
Ahara Ventures Ltd
Ariana International Ltd
Artathlon Beverages Limited
Artathlon Water Limited
Asta Barista Baby Ltd
Beverages Group Limited
Brilliant Beverage Co Ltd
Buzbees Beverages Limited
Domore Imports Ltd
Drinks Bay Limited
Emperor Trades Limited
Fruitex Limited
GSTWholesale Limited
A Gohir Soft Drinks UK Ltd
Hell Beverages UK Ltd
Hellenic Agora Limited
MSK Halal Ltd
MTS Export Import Ltd
Magna Juice Ltd
Mercado Da Saudade Ltd
Mirza Trading Limited
Moreton Sweets (Wholesale) Ltd
My Smoothies Co Limited
Naturally Fresh Drink Limited
Nawab Traders Limited
New Kumasi Market 2 Ltd
Paisley Drinks Co. Ltd
Panda Rolls Ltd
Panopoulos Forest Ltd
Panymocc Limited
Quinton Trading Ltd
R.A.W. Goods Co Ltd
Arif Rahim Ltd
Starburst Hub Ltd
Surprisingly Treaty Ltd
Syphony Water Limited
TTS Private Ltd
Topmost Foods Distribution Ltd.
Vild Water Limited

July 2018 [38]
AJ Fruit & Vegetable Enterprises Ltd
Al Kass General Trading Ltd
Aqua Carpatica UK Ltd
Assala Limited
Bassen Ltd
Chosen Enterprises Limited
DNG Group Ltd
DNG Trading Ltd
Drink Free Ltd
Ever-Tree Wholesale & Retail Ltd
FIBM Wholesale Ltd
First Fruits Drinks Ltd
Fusecutter Ltd
Gone Fresh Limited
Healthy Hit Ltd
Herbarium Limited
Humble Bumble Ltd
J & H Global UK Ltd
Jacksons Milk Deliveries Ltd
Juicydee Ltd
K.A Top Traders Limited
Luso Shop Ltd
Miwater Ltd
PVS Trading Ltd
Panopoulos Waters Ltd
Parkway UK Wholesale Ltd
Premier Food & Beverage Ltd

Rabia Food & Drinks Ltd
Riverroll Limited
SS Midland Ltd
Secspirits Ltd
T's Dazzling Delicious Sweets Ltd
TVS Private Ltd
Tastebuds Trading Ltd
Vision Global Enterprise Ltd
Warren Farm Shop Ltd
J Water Disabled Children Ltd
Zeyroj Soft Drinks Ltd

August 2018 [49]
AG Fresh Produce Limited
AKKG Enterprise Limited
Abantu Moringa Ltd
Abel Service Ltd
After Eight Alcohol Concierge Ltd
Alicia's Coffee House Limited
Aliss UK Limited
Alpine Water Coolers Ltd
Ana Express Ltd
Bazaar Store Ltd
Bi Fa Limited
Burrows & Sturgess Ltd
Carmine Ciao & Co Ltd
Choise Group Ltd
Desi Trading Ltd
Drinks International Birmingham Ltd
Earths Greatest Ltd
Epson Trading Limited
Fresh Produce International Ltd
GVK Wholesale Ltd
Geema Service Ltd
Great British Beverages Ltd
HP Juicery Ltd
Hayat Supermarket Ltd
Jamarec UK Limited
Jameson's Trading Ltd
Juicery Ltd
Lore & Truth Ltd
MX365 Energy Ltd
Merlin Distribution Limited
Milky Milkshakes Ltd
Monrone Health Ltd
Moudine Trade Ltd
Nova Wholesale Ltd
Ombre Drinks Limited
One Grace LMT Ltd
Polski Wholesale Limited
Premium Jacks Limited
Realmix Beverage Ltd
Saga Trading Ltd
SmsZee Limited
Sublime Corporation Limited
Supreme Links Limited
Syed Drinks Limited
Third Eye Nutrition Ltd
UK Brighton Food & Nutrition Research Centre
Unicorn Foodline Ltd
Venkat Ltd
Welldrinks Ltd

September 2018 [46]
AZ Health Food Center Ltd
Apex Sourcing International Ltd
BVG Distributors Limited
Bambu Drinks Limited
Bornova Import Export Limited
Canafizz Ltd

China Cambrian Limited
Dora Distribution Ltd
Drinks2u Ltd
Drinksparadies Ltd
Driver's Drinks Co Ltd
Eqoob Limited
Eren Catering Ltd
Eurotrade Supply Limited
Faqir Billionaire Ltd
Farm Shop at Ombersley Limited
Feel Group Limited
Funbella Ltd
GB Heritage Ltd
GCA Foods Edinburgh Ltd
Gibraltar Gin Co Ltd
Golden Eagle Foods Edinburgh Ltd
Golden Eagle Trade Edinburgh Ltd
Green Ambition Limited
Green Warehouse Hodge Hill Ltd
Green Warehouse Washwood Ltd
Harsimran K Ltd
S Jee Enterprises Ltd
Kaz Enterprise Limited
Lep Food & Wine Ltd
Lifting Spirits Ltd
Nootrilix Limited
Northern Food Services Limited
O & E Food Ltd
Ola Acai Ltd
PTP Enterprise Limited
RJ Traders Ltd
Sasa Super Foods Ltd
Shac International Limited
Sheikh Super Store Ltd
Sunugal Trading Limited
Super Food Base Ltd
Sweet Caroline Ltd
Tomatelios UK Ltd
U.D.C. Wholesale Ltd
Vitte Nutrition Ltd

October 2018 [55]
413 Limited
AWA Water Ltd
Abijah Global Limited
Abukor Ltd
Alchemy Biotics Limited
All Vending Services Limited
Allure International Ltd
Arthur's Juice Co Ltd
Aur'a Natural Gold Water Ltd
BV Group UK Limited
Bluetech Marketing Ltd
Said Boukhebelt Ltd
Remy Cazabet Ltd
Cybel Ltd
Daneisa Ltd
Drayton Limited
Emmunity Limited
Eurodrinks Ltd
FMCG Express Limited
Falcos Food Ltd
Fletcher's Fruit & Veg Ltd
Fresh Pal Ltd
Georgian Wine Co Ltd
Green Foods International Ltd
Hatton Wholesale Ltd
Hoversy Technologies Ltd
Indigo Traders Ltd
Ital World Ltd
Jaguar Beverage Ltd
Jalkhushi Fresh & Frozen Fish Ltd

Jojo Best Coffee Ltd
JustGeneralTradingServices Ltd
KKR Wine Ltd
Kakkar Enterprises Ltd
Kepenek Food Ltd
Loyal Trader Ltd
MU Distributors Ltd
Mani Mathi Trading Ltd
Menon Naturals Ltd
Nile Nutrients Ltd
Nirajen Ltd
P N New Ltd
PMahesh Trading Limited
Pirm Trading Limited
Punjab Masala Ltd
RHM Trading UK Limited
Rahims Trading Ltd
Real Natural UK Ltd
Rook Trading Ltd
Sativatech Ltd
Symphony Fine Foods Ltd
Tomato Tantrum Ltd
Yachinelyaoui Limited
Yashrab Ltd
Youngs Vintage Management Ltd

November 2018 [47]
420 Beverages Ltd
5S Import Ltd
A A Suppliers Ltd
AB (Cheshire) Group Ltd
AWA Nature Ltd
Afromax Ltd
Al-Shahba Ltd
Apollo Distribution Limited
Artis Trade Ltd
Bia Trade Ltd
Bogazici Ltd
Bravocservices Ltd
Browett & Fair Ltd
Cheti & Co Limited
Chiltern Mix Limited
Drinx Division Ltd
East2west Traders Ltd
Fearis Beverages Ltd
Forward Moving Limited
Huskiblu Ltd
Ilie Cash & Carry Ltd
Imperial House of 3 Kings Ltd
Inside Out Life Drinks Ltd
Ion Distribution Ltd
Juice on the Go Ltd
Kaluwa Ltd
Kasgo Limited
Kheira Ltd
LBSM Limited
MEA Health and Wellness Ltd
MK Bazaar Ltd
Mane and Rose Limited
Manor Wholesale Ltd
Northern Lights Ltd.
Number One Water Ltd
Paynesbb Limited
Platinum Packaging Ltd
Platinum UK Drinks Ltd
Rayan Cash & Carry Ltd
Regal Trade Limited
Social Drinking Co Ltd
Thass Ltd
Tiqle Global Limited
Topstop Wholesalers Limited
White World Service Ltd

Zauq Services Ltd
Zeroholic Ltd

December 2018 [67]
ABNN Fresh UK Ltd
Afterall Ltd
Alpha Neno Limited
Ammy Trading Ltd
Arollo Trade Ltd
Aster Service Ltd
Bare Drinks Limited
Bossco Headland Ltd
Britannia International Wholesalers Ltd
Castleton International Ltd
Crux Energy Drinks Ltd
DMK Wholesale Ltd
Darkhorse Universal Limited
Discover Health Ltd
Drea Ltd
Drinks Europe Ltd
Exoshell UK Ltd
Falafel Factory Ltd
Fexty Ltd
Freestar Drinks Ltd
Fruit & Veg Imports Ltd
GSKB Ltd
Gentian Global Ltd
Gladiator Nutrition Supplements Ltd
Global Sports Trade Ltd
Glow Penny Ltd
Good Gut Guys Ltd
Hillcrest WM Ltd
IMH Traders Limited
Indigo Private Ltd
Intercontinental Trade Solutions Ltd
Jasmine Blue Ltd
Leoba Service Ltd
M & M European Merchants Ltd
MCIA Ltd
MD Investgroupp Ltd
MK Inter Ltd
Madina Drinks Ltd
Majit Drinks Ltd
Marcin & Son Ltd
McBerries Ltd
Mocktail Company (2018) Ltd
J Mullens Ltd
Nohew Trade Ltd
Pem Trade Sales Ltd
Pound Hill Ltd
Premium Drinks Distribution Ltd
Pres & Co. Limited
Refribrit Ltd
Regency Traders Ltd
Risco Service Ltd
Rolan Excel Limited
S & B Wholesale Limited
S K Enteprises Ltd
SVM Trading Ltd
Sanus Foods Ltd
Shopocus Ltd
Star International Ltd
Strong Pound Ltd
Thirst Call Ltd
Vinz Ltd
Whiskey and Bourbon Club Ltd
Wholesale Your Way Ltd
Winnack and Hart Industries Ltd
Y Acay Berry Ltd
Yourchoice Wholesale Ltd
Z & Z Global Ltd

UK Wholesalers of Soft Drinks

January 2019 [51]
A2Z Fruit & Veg Ltd
ABZ Food Ltd
Avigail Dairies Limited
Basil World Ltd
Beeston General Store & Off Licences Ltd
Bennu Rising Ltd.
Big Star Trader Ltd
Blackbird Trader Ltd
Boukashka Ltd
Brands Nexus Ltd
Bubra Drinks Ltd
Cafe Collective UK Trading Co Ltd
Cali Juices Limited
Cityfresh Limited
Crab Trading Ltd
Dessert Makers Limited
Drink Fitness Ltd
ERE Igga Ltd
Eagle Drinks Ltd
Elham Elliethy Ltd
Elias Trading Limited
Eslan Lookray Ltd
Evo Fit Ltd
Fitness Prostar Ltd
Fresh Food Concepts Ltd
Fruitfullest Ltd.
Global Food (Ashton) Ltd
H & F Export Limited
JSJuices Ltd
Janere UK Limited
Juicer Ltd
KU Bargin Deals Ltd
KU Supplies Ltd
Kanpes G Ltd
Kristals Trading Limited
Loris Wholesale Ltd
M & S Trading (London) Limited
MB Drinks Ltd
Massafood Ltd
NQN Enterprises Limited
New Drinking Ltd
Noah Brothers Ltd
Numba UK Limited
Onofrei Cash & Carry Ltd
Rimpex-UK Limited
Saravanan Traders (UK) Ltd
Suntrack Ltd
Thames Wholesale Ltd
Uddin Discount Ltd
Vangoo Enterprise Holding Ltd
Willow World Ltd

February 2019 [57]
ADA Beverages Ltd
Agencia Ltd
Birch Sales Ltd
Bongo Sale Ltd
Bright Smoothies Ltd
Buddthi Ltd
Budgie Juices Ltd
Butterfly Foods and Packaging Ltd
Caspian Black Limited
Choice Asia Ltd
Colbury Limited
Cordus Ltd
East and West Foods Cash and Carry
Eliya Europe Ltd
Eltrados Ltd
Essential Juices Ltd
Eurostar HRK Ltd
Evrywater Ltd
Export and Import Trading Ltd
Firewater Merchants Ltd
Fruits & Vegetables Ltd.
Good News International Trading Ltd
Green Cash & Carry Ltd
Grillburger Holdings Limited
Haggard.Grb Ltd
Janos Horvath Ltd
Ice Guys Ltd
JCW Foods Ltd
JJ Import/Export Ltd
JK Manchester Ltd
Juice Warrior Ltd
Key Traders Ltd
Lanex Ltd
Luckova Ltd
Magna Carta Drinks Limited
Mercury Wholesale Ltd
Mock Drink Co Ltd
Natural Enzymes Limited
Nekta Food & Juice Bar Ltd
New Global Ltd
Nippon Trading Ltd
Nordic Life Water UK Limited
Oriental Express London Ltd
Pick Pedal Pour Ltd
Prod Act Ltd.
RB Beverages Ltd
Rozana Foods Limited
Seafire Brewing Co. Ltd
Shark Trading Ltd
Shelby Co Vending Limited
Shruthinaya Ltd
Simple Brands Ltd
Sips MCR Ltd
Snacks Dist Limited
Sow Limited
Sylvy Glosry Limited
Thusi Wholesale Ltd

This page is intentionally left blank

Geographic Distribution by County

Co Antrim
Merchantology Ireland Ltd
Sylvy Glosry Limited

Co Armagh
Paramount Food and Drink (UK) Ltd.
Parkway UK Wholesale Ltd
Waltrix Publishing Ireland Ltd
Zero Options Ltd

Co Down
Lake Shore Distributors Ltd

Co Londonderry
Aroma Soft Drinks & Water Ltd
Football Special Ltd

Co Tyrone
AWA Water Ltd
BG Drinks Ltd
Riddles Bros Limited
Season Harvest (NI) Limited

Aberdeenshire
ABZ Food Ltd
Deveron Direct Limited
Val Norton Ltd
Premium Drinks Distribution Ltd

Angus
Eurodrinks Ltd

Argyll
Kintyre Holdings Limited

Ayrshire
Ayr Brewing Co Ltd

Clackmannanshire
Stirling Castle Water Ltd

Fife
Adamson's Drinks Ltd.
MX365 Energy Ltd
Seafire Brewing Co. Ltd
Springwater Direct Ltd.

Isle of Lewis
Grillburger Holdings Limited

Lanarkshire [17]
AG Fresh Produce Limited
Africa Global Village. Com Ltd
AI Pixel Points Limited
Apollo Distribution Limited
Clean-Coco Ltd
Eslan Lookray Ltd
Evershine Trading Limited
Failte Wholesale Limited
Foal Limited
Fresh Produce Deliveries Ltd
Ideal Trading Limited
Jonsen International Ltd
Kurd Scot Imports & Exports Ltd
Lifting Spirits Ltd
PMI Management Limited
Rabia Food & Drinks Ltd
Thistle Foods Limited

Renfrewshire
Highland Cow Motor Home Ltd
Paisley Drinks Co. Ltd
Start-Up Drinks Lab Limited
Tongue in Peat Limited

Roxburghshire
Norfolk Punch Limited

Stirlingshire
B4Sport Ltd.
One Grace LMT Ltd

Anglesey
Toffoc Ltd

Bedfordshire [13]
Bedford Halal Meat & Grocceries Ltd
Crop's Foods Ltd.
Dark Invest Ltd
Dora Distribution Ltd
Exel Distribution Ltd
Global Sunshine Distribution Ltd
Gorog Trading Limited
HMH Wholesale Ltd
Iwater Inc Ltd
KT Wholesale Ltd
Merlin Distribution Limited
Seven Bros Cookware Ltd
Theodore Global Limited

Berkshire [12]
Asia Direct Limited
Chiltern Mix Limited
Elderbrook Drinks Limited
GT Traders Ltd.
Haltrade UK Ltd
LB Hussan Hussain Halal Meat Superstore
Laspremuta Limited
Milton Sandford Wines Limited
Ooberstock Limited
Panda Rolls Ltd
Platinum Packaging Ltd
Rex Drinks Limited

Buckinghamshire [15]
Ace Incorporation Ltd
Bespoke Contracts (UK) Ltd
Bornova Import Export Limited
J.C. Dudley & Co. Ltd
Elev8 Life Limited
Hatton Wholesale Ltd
Herbarium Limited
JCW Foods Ltd
K & E Wholesale Ltd
Lora Trading (Europe) Ltd
N & J Wholesale Foods Limited
Oranka Fruit Juices Limited
Triple R Industries Limited
Tropical Produce Limited
Unite Foods Trading Limited

Cambridgeshire [10]
Afromax Ltd
Attila Martocsan Ltd
Ecopure Waters International Ltd
Geminiz Ltd
Global Food Wholesalers Ltd
Global Market Solutions Ltd
Jojo Best Coffee Ltd
Kepenek Food Ltd
Moringa Superfoods UK Limited
Rayan Cash & Carry Ltd

Cardiganshire
Aberystwyth Soft Drinks Ltd

Cheshire [19]
Acquisto Limited
Bevanda Solutions Limited
Canafizz Ltd
Collette International Limited
Drea Ltd
Elham Elliethy Ltd
Feeders Foods Wholesale Ltd
GB Heritage Ltd
GDH Distribution Limited
Gerrard Seel Limited
Kheira Ltd
Neubria Limited
RMGL Trading Limited
Racing Greens Nutraceuticals Ltd
Rook Trading Ltd
Solerco Products Limited
Tatry Trade Ltd
Tomatelios UK Ltd
Yardely Ltd

Cleveland [9]
Basil World Ltd
Bossco Headland Ltd
Eqoob Limited
IR Global Service Ltd
Leoba Service Ltd
Log Cabin Fruits Ltd
Onofrei Cash & Carry Ltd
Printers Service Ltd
Raji Service Ltd

Clwyd
Energy Drinks Ltd
UK Star Services Limited

Co Durham
Astral Nutrition Limited
Evo Fit Ltd
WLH Food Ltd

Cornwall
Condimental Ltd
Fruit Slush 'n' Shake Ltd
Rocktails Drinks Limited
Sow Limited

Cumbria
C S Drinks Ltd
McBerries Ltd

Denbighshire
W D L Wholesale Limited

UK Wholesalers of Soft Drinks

Derbyshire [19]
ADA Beverages Ltd
Abevco Limited
Bargain Food and Wine Ltd
Boisson Limited
Burrows & Sturgess Ltd
Emaya Foods Limited
Flavour Foods & Drinks Ltd
Franklin 1886 Limited
Hannah & Ted Ltd
Hydra Cubed Limited
Liquid Brand Exports Limited
Luso Shop Ltd
Order2buy Ltd
PXL Drinks Ltd
Pallet Price Wholesale Ltd
Prir Group Limited
Pro Nutrition Ltd
Regal Trade Limited
SS Midland Ltd

Devon [10]
Beverage Brothers Limited
Botanic Lab Ltd
Cobell Ltd
Frobishers Juices Limited
Gold Star Soft Drinks Westcountry Ltd
Kineta Drinks Limited
N & B Foods Exeter Limited
Notgin Ltd
Thirsty Work Limited
Total Cellar Supplies Limited

Dorset [7]
DH Exotic Produce Ltd
Imran Brothers Limited
Natural Snacking Ltd
S & B's Mart Ltd.
Shimroon Limited
Whiskey and Bourbon Club Ltd
Zacely Limited

Dyfed
Alicja Food Ltd
Enzyme's Secret Limited

Essex [76]
AB Trade Direct Ltd
Afrimalt UK Ltd
Alancia Fruit & Vegetable Ltd
Ammy Trading Ltd
Aquamarine Limited
Artesian Springs Limited
Azka Impex (London) Limited
Big Star Trader Ltd
Blackbird Trader Ltd
Broadwater Supply and Distribution Ltd
Buzbees Beverages Limited
Cambridge Juice Co. Limited
Carmine Ciao & Co Ltd
Cellar Twelve Limited
Classic Catering (UK) Ltd
DMK Wholesale Ltd
Discount on Drinks Ltd
Eagle Beer Ltd
Eastway Cash & Carry Limited
Easy Squeeze Limited
Euro Globe Distributors Ltd
Export and Import Trading Ltd
FMCG Enterprises Limited

Fast Car Sales Services Ltd
Five Star Cash & Carry Ltd
Fruto del Espiritu C.I.C.
Furze Young Limited
Gibraltar Gin Co Ltd
Great Wins Ltd
H2O Supplies Ltd
Harsimran K Ltd
Healthy Hydration Limited
Hi Fresh Limited
Huma Gida UK Limited
Ipro Sport Corporation Limited
Ipro Sport Distribution Ltd
Ipro Sport International Ltd
Ipro Sport Medical Limited
JustGeneralTradingServices Ltd
Lep Food & Wine Ltd
Lithuanian Beer Limited
MBW Traders Ltd
MK Bazaar Ltd
MLI Trading Limited
Magnanimous Distribution T/A Pizzeria Hut
Majit Drinks Ltd
Major Foods Limited
Manor Wholesale Ltd
Marco Polo Exotics Ltd
Matlowone Limited
Mezin Distribution UK Limited
Mirza Trading Limited
My Smoothies Co Limited
Nar London Limited
Narayan Foods Limited
Nile Minar Enterprise Limited
Ozdil UK Limited
PSB Trading Limited
MD Rahma Ltd
S & B Wholesale Limited
SVM Trading Ltd
Sheikh Super Store Ltd
Shree Sai Trading Ltd
Silvercall Limited
Sris International Ltd
Sublime Distributors Limited
Sun Exotic Wholesale Ltd
Sweet Sally Limited
Thremhall Limited
Tolmid International Ltd
Top Selection Limited
Transgh Limited
V Wholesalers Ltd
Variety Food Fair Limited
Warren Farm Shop Ltd
ZSM Traders Ltd

Flintshire
G & Y Wynne Limited

Glamorgan [12]
Al-Shahba Ltd
GM Catering Supplies Ltd
JFC Trading Limited
KML Home Limited
Lore & Truth Ltd
Made in the States Limited
Premier Soft Drinks Ltd
SmsZee Limited
Street Food Solutions UK Ltd
Super Tidy Drinks Limited
Top Pops Wholesaler of Soft Drinks
Total Fast Food Supplies Ltd

Gloucestershire [9]
Asta Barista Baby Ltd
Clear Drinks Limited
Cubico Limited
Direct Source Distribution Ltd
GH Brands Ltd
Gloucester Wholesale Ltd
Just Aqua Ltd.
Luella Malmesbury Ltd
Woodchester International Ltd

Gwynedd
DWR Cerist Cyf
Dawsons (Wales) Limited
R. & I. Jones Limited
Zeroholic Ltd

Hampshire [11]
Assala Limited
First Food Ltd
Fresh Produce International Ltd
Hellenic Grocery Limited
Jamarec UK Limited
Kanpes G Ltd
Merlin's Beverages Limited
Nordic Life Water UK Limited
Turner Hardy & Co Limited
Usmoothie Ltd
Zaid & Besher Ltd

Herefordshire [5]
J.C.Davies & Hall Limited
Lawton Cross Limited
Pixley Berries (Juice) Limited
Real Natural UK Ltd
Shack Drinks Limited

Hertfordshire [26]
Active Protein Limited
Apollo Fruit & Veg UK Ltd
Bogazici Ltd
Buddthi Ltd
Ch@i Drinks Ltd
D D S Food Imports Ltd
Delamore Trading UK Ltd
Dodotraders UK Limited
Ever-Tree Wholesale & Retail Ltd
Food Brands Ltd
Gemini Wholesalers Limited
Golden Pride Export Limited
House Water Limited
Kasgo Limited
Marathon Food Limited
Mashmoom International Limited
Miwater Ltd
Noble Smokehouse Ltd
Panymocc Limited
Simple Brands Ltd
Smoothie Fresh (International) Ltd
Smoothie Fresh Ltd
Source 360 Ltd
Storesrealm Limited
Sutaka UK Limited
Windfall Logistics Limited

dellam UK Wholesalers of Soft Drinks

Kent [28]
Aur'a Natural Gold Water Ltd
Bot Trading Co Ltd
Cordus Ltd
DT Fruits Ltd
Dan International (UK) Limited
Drink Free Ltd
Drink Warehouse UK Limited
Elegantly Spirited Limited
Ets Mandy SPRL Ltd.
Firewater Merchants Ltd
Flux Investment Ltd
Fresh Fruit Direct Limited
Inspire Drinks Ltd
MM Global Citrus Limited
Nadban Limited
Natural Welsh Water Limited
OMG Beverages Limited
Pavlinko Limited
Quench Factory Limited
Refribrit Ltd
Rolan Excel Limited
Row & Smith Ltd
Tas Services UK Limited
Triumph Foodservice Limited
Water Wellbeing Limited
Watercoolers Southern Limited
Wisdom of Nature Limited
Yourchoice Wholesale Ltd

Lancashire [68]
AB (Cheshire) Group Ltd
AB Catering (Blackburn) Ltd
AQ Branding Ltd
Al Taj Al Malaki General Trading UK Ltd
All Fresh Bradford Ltd
Avic Trading Limited
Avigail Dairies Limited
Avigail Limited
Bellwether Impex (UK) Limited
Bravocservices Ltd
Butterfly Foods and Packaging Ltd
C & M Wholesale (UK) Limited
Creamline Dairies Limited
Czar & Co (UK) Limited
Darkhorse Universal Limited
ESL Trading Ltd
East Lancs Suppliers Ltd
Evoca UK Distribution Limited
Exoshell UK Ltd
Fast Food Traders Ltd
Fernhill Wholesale Ltd
Fresh Food Concepts Ltd
Freshwater Direct Limited
Gabby & Bello Enterprises Ltd
Global Food (Ashton) Ltd
Global Food (Nelson) Ltd
Gone Fresh Limited
Hamer & Perks Limited
J & H Global UK Ltd
J M & D Limited
JK Manchester Ltd
Jays Trading Ltd
Juicer Ltd
K2 (Northwest) Limited
Kaleboard Limited
L & B Foods Ltd
Lanex Ltd
Luckova Ltd
MJ Trading (NW) Ltd
MTS Export Import Ltd

Maira Trade Ltd
Manchester Drinks Co Ltd
Marcin & Son Ltd
Middleton Wholesale Limited
Montann Limited
Musielski Wholesale Ltd
No Meat No Worries Limited
Nodus International Trade Ltd
Northern Food Services Limited
Orange Trading Ltd
Passa Distribution Ltd
Passa Wholesale Ltd
Pick N Deliver Ltd
Premier Marketing (NW) Ltd
Prestwich Catering & Wholesale Ltd
RMGL Ltd
Rush Energy Drinks Ltd
Samco Global Foods Ltd
Shelby Co Vending Limited
Sips MCR Ltd
Swallow Holdings Limited
Syphony Water Limited
Taste of Crete Ltd
Think Power Limited
Tradinguk55 Limited
Unicorn Foodline Ltd
Vidi Vici Trading Ltd
V.A. Whitley & Co. Limited

Leicestershire [32]
Ammart Ltd
Bor-Tom Ltd
Doorstep Desserts Distribution Ltd
F.R.D Wholesale Limited
Falafel Factory Ltd
Green Warehouse Hodge Hill Ltd
Green Warehouse Washwood Ltd
S Jee Enterprises Ltd
Kaz Enterprise Limited
Lord Eden Beverages Ltd
Loughborough Student Services Ltd
MAS Trading Cast Ltd
MB Drinks Ltd
Patrik Trading Ltd
Pure Organic Drinks Limited
SM Supplies Ltd
Seiyas Watercoolers Ltd
Slurps Ice Ltd
Syntex Trading Ltd
TSK Trade Limited
Tata Trade Ltd
Toschi UK Limited
Trade HQ Ltd
UK Traders (Leics) Ltd
Utku Emre Ltd
Valley Water Limited
Wild Cat Distribution UK Ltd
Wild Cat Energy Drink Ltd
Wildcat International Limited
Wine City Limited
Winnack and Hart Industries Ltd
World Trade Values Limited

Lincolnshire
Best Brand Food & Drinks (BBFD) Ltd
Brilliant Beverage Co Ltd
Ideal Lincs Limited
Quick World Service Ltd

London [452]
21st Century Nutrition Limited
3BW Ltd
413 Limited
420 Beverages Ltd
51 Plus Ltd
78 Degrees Limited
815 Distributors (UK) Ltd
901WD Ltd
A & H Trading Ltd
A to Z Veg Ltd
A1 Best Traders Ltd
AKM Trading Services Ltd
AMG Wholesale Ltd
AVM UK Private Limited
AWA Nature Ltd
AZ Health Food Center Ltd
Abijah Global Limited
Abukor Ltd
Acai Express Ltd
Acqua Nordica Ltd
Adanali Limited
Aduna Limited
After Eight Alcohol Concierge Ltd
Agencia Ltd
Agrofresh Ltd
Agrotrade International Trading Ltd
Alamirat Limited
Alchemy Biotics Limited
Alisha Fish Bazar Ltd
Aliss UK Limited
Alitasa Ltd
Alivini (North) Limited
Alivini Co Ltd
All for You Beverages Limited
Allure International Ltd
Alpha Energy Drink Limited
Alti's Catering Limited
Amphipolis Limited
Ana Express Ltd
Anadolu Catering Limited
Anatolian Foods Ltd
Anatolian Limited
Angel Global Export Ltd
Anya Global Limited
Anytime Drinks Limited
Apna Distribution Ltd
Aqua Carpatica UK Ltd
Aquacoll UK Ltd
Aquavita II UK Limited
Arab World Ltd
Ariana International Ltd
Arollo Trade Ltd
Artathlon Beverages Limited
Artathlon Water Limited
Arthur's Juice Co Ltd
Artis Trade Ltd
Artos Foods Limited
Aspire Brands Int Ltd.
Aspire Drinks Limited
Atlantis Spring Water Limited
Atlas Halal Ltd
Aura Gold Water Ltd
BV Group UK Limited
BVG Distributors Limited
Babylon Foods Limited
Bakhta Moroccan Mint Iced Tea Ltd
Baldwin's Sarsaparilla Limited
Bambu Drinks Limited
Basecamp Brews Ltd
Bedrock Trade Ltd
Berry Juice Co Ltd

UK Wholesalers of Soft Drinks

Best Trading One Limited
Bia Trade Ltd
Bibere Ltd.
Big Brand Distributors UK Ltd
Big Horn UK Ltd
Bill Bean Limited
Bioactive Live Ltd
Biofresh Cosmos Ltd
Bloomsbury Drinks Ltd
Bluetech Marketing Ltd
Boukashka Ltd
Brand Distributors Limited
Britannia International Wholesalers Ltd
Browett & Fair Ltd
Bubra Drinks Ltd
Bucovina Cash & Carry Ltd
Budgie Juices Ltd
Buffalo Refreshments Ltd
Burlingtown UK Limited
C & M Wholesale Limited
C.N.A. Catering Logistics Ltd
CBD Globe Distributors Ltd
CC Trade Ltd
CCM Enterprises Limited
Caju Drinks Ltd
Camii Punch Ltd
Cane Press Ltd
Cape Crown Global Goods Ltd
Capital Drinks London Limited
Carnaby and Kingly Limited
Carpatica International Ltd
Caspian Black Limited
Cheti & Co Holdings Limited
Cheti & Co Limited
China Cambrian Limited
Choi's Trading & Co Ltd
Choise Group Ltd
Chosen Enterprises Limited
Cibo (London) Limited
Cityfresh Limited
Colbury Limited
Couto & Machado Ltd
Creative Properties and Investments Ltd
Crescent Moon World Project Ltd.
Crux Energy Drinks Ltd
Cybel Ltd
Cyprofood Limited
D'Auria Brothers Ice Cream and Catering
DLG Wholesale Ltd
DRGN Global Ltd.
DYoung and Son Limited
Dalina Limited
Deeti Wholesale Limited
Dessert Makers Limited
Dimark Limited
Dining Capital Limited
Direct Traders Ltd
Direct2door Food & Beverage Ltd.
Discount Brands (London) UK Ltd
Dragon Rise Limited
Drink Fitness Ltd
Drinkable Ltd
Drinks Bay Limited
Drinks Europe Ltd
E & R Fruits Limited
Earths Greatest Ltd
East2west Traders Ltd
Elev8 Energy Drink Limited
Elias Trading Limited
Ely & Sidney Limited
Emmunity Limited
Emperor Trades Limited

Endetrox Ltd.
Epson Trading Limited
Erbology Ltd
Eren Catering Ltd
Estelon Holdings Limited
Eurotrade Supply Limited
Eurozone Limited
Evogue Limited
Evrywater Ltd
Ewid Ltd
F & T Enterprise Ltd.
Falcos Food Ltd
Fanal Ltd
Faqir Billionaire Ltd
Feel Group Limited
Ferment Revolution Limited
Fevertree Europe Limited
Fevertree Row Limited
Fevertree UK Limited
Fevertree US Limited
Fitness Prostar Ltd
Flavours of Sardinia Limited
Flow 33 UK Limited
Forward Moving Limited
Fresh N Green Ltd
Fresh Pal Ltd
Fresh Produce Imports UK Ltd
Frosty Service Ltd
Fruit & Veg Imports Ltd
Fruitex Limited
Fruitfullest Ltd.
Fruity Cards Ltd
Funbella Ltd
Future Generation Foods U.K. Ltd
GI Food Group Limited
GSKB Ltd
GVK Wholesale Ltd
GWB Associates Limited
Geema Service Ltd
Gentian Global Ltd
Georgian Wine Co Ltd
Gladiator Nutrition Supplements Ltd
Global Vitality Ltd.
Globe Imex Ltd
Go Fresh Ltd
Good News International Trading Ltd
Govmalt & H.U.M.M.E.R. Beverages Global Co
Greenme Ltd
H Two Eau International Ltd
HDL Trading Limited
Healthy Hit Ltd
Hellenic Agora Limited
Herbaleva Ltd
Herbs 4 Healthy Living Ltd
Hero Catering Supplies Limited
Hesana Ltd
House Kitchen Limited
Hoversy Technologies Ltd
Huskiblu Ltd
Ibiza Recharge Limited
Ice Guys Ltd
Ifood Trading Ltd
Imperial House of 3 Kings Ltd
Inc. Trading Limited
Indigo Private Ltd
Indigo Traders Ltd
Infinite Session Ltd
Innerji Ltd
Inside Out Life Drinks Ltd
International Catering & Foods Ltd
Interseel Ltd

Ion Distribution Ltd
Iturn Global Ltd
J & D Wholesalers Ltd
JJ Import/Export Ltd
JSJuices Ltd
Jacksons Milk Deliveries Ltd
Jaguar Beverage Ltd
Jaguar Power Energy Drinks Ltd.
Jameson's Trading Ltd
Janama Trading Co Ltd
Janere UK Limited
Jasmine Blue Ltd
Jax Coco UK Ltd.
Jones Bros. 1877 Ltd
Juice Junkie London Limited
Juice Junkiez Limited
Juice Warrior Ltd
Juice on the Go Ltd
Juicydee Ltd
K.A Top Traders Limited
KD-Pol Ltd
KKS Fresh Fruits Ltd
KPN Wholesale Ltd
KSY Juice Blends UK Ltd
KVC Waffles Limited
Kaluwa Ltd
Kang Med Limited
Kaplan Int Limited
Kardelen Water Limited
Cooray King Holdings Limited
Konon Limited
L & D Services UK Limited
L'Azur Ltd
La Zgarici Ltd
Ladeo Limited
Lam Cash and Carry Limited
Lana Nai UK Co. Ltd
Lanza Foods Ltd
Leathams Limited
Like Like Ltd
London Drinks Supplier Ltd
London Maya Sandwich Limited
London UK Star Ltd
London Wholesale Ltd
Longstar Trading Limited
Ly Hong Limited
M & M Emerald Ltd
M & S Trading (London) Limited
M Trading Limited
M.R.S. Supplies Limited
MD Investgroupp Ltd
MKM Group Trading & Investment Ltd
MSK Halal Ltd
MU Distributors Ltd
Madina Drinks Ltd
Magna Juice Ltd
Mane and Rose Limited
Mani Mathi Trading Ltd
Manteo Trading Co Ltd
Masca Holding Limited
Meadow Harvest Ltd
Mediterranean International Ltd
Menon Naturals Ltd
Mesh Facilities Limited
Mightybee Limited
Mirpa Limited
Mocktail Company (2018) Ltd
Modern Contradiction Limited
Moju Ltd
Monks Drinks Limited
Monrone Health Ltd
Moon Lynx Ltd

Moreton Sweets (Wholesale) Ltd
Morinda UK Limited
Mother Nature's Drinks Limited
Moudine Trade Ltd
N'ife Limited
NBA Wholesale Ltd
NCE Trading KFT Ltd
NQN Enterprises Limited
NXSK UK Ltd
Nacho Juice Limited
Namar Limited
Natural Enzymes Limited
Nature on Tap Limited
Natures Vitality Limited
Naturshot Limited
Neelam Traders Ltd
New Drinking Ltd
New Kumasi Market 2 Ltd
Newton Soft Drinks Wholesale Ltd
Next Gen Drinks Limited
Nile Nutrients Ltd
Nippon Trading Ltd
Northern Lights Ltd.
Nova Wholesale Ltd
Nuli Life Ltd
Number One Water Ltd
O & E Food Ltd
OK Brothers Ltd
Oct Multi Services Limited
Ola Acai Ltd
Olsson Logistics Limited
Oneway Trading Ltd
Orange Be Global Ltd
Organic Village Limited
Organica Vita Ltd
Organix Ltd
Oriental Express London Ltd
Orpheus Tea Ltd
Ozlem Limited
P & V Agents Ltd
PMahesh Trading Limited
PTP Enterprise Limited
PVS Trading Ltd
Panopoulos Forest Ltd
Panopoulos Waters Ltd
Paynesbb Limited
Polat International Ltd
Premier Food & Beverage Ltd
Premium Jacks Limited
Pres & Co. Limited
Punchy Drinks Limited
Qahhar Drinks Ltd
Quick Constuction Ltd
Quicklemon UK Ltd
R.A.W. Goods Co Ltd
RHM Trading UK Limited
RTH Healthcare PLC
Rahim Brothers Limited
Rahims Trading Ltd
Rarewood (London) Limited
Ravensbourne Wine Co Ltd
Raw Is More Ltd.
Raylex Ltd
Red Bull Co Ltd
Redgate Imports Limited
Reineta Limited
Rejuveu Ltd
Rexcel Trading Ltd
Rich Energy Limited
Rick's Wine Ltd
Rio Mata Atlantica Limited
Rivella (U.K.) Limited

Riverroll Limited
Route 33 Limited
S & F Distribution Ltd
S & M (Wholesale Supplies) Ltd
SOS Hydration Limited
Sabziwala Limited
Saga Trading Ltd
Sams Fast Foods Limited
Sannel Foods Limited
Sasa Super Foods Ltd
Seagull Energy Drinks Ltd
Secspirits Ltd
Anna Seed 83 Limited
Seedlip Ltd
Sepandero Venturi UK Limited
Shac International Limited
Sharewater Ltd
Shibui Beverage Co Ltd
Shruthinaya Ltd
Simex International Ltd
Simorgh Limited
Sloane Avenue Group Ltd
Sotomayor Imports Limited
Star International Ltd
Stockwell Beverages Ltd
Stockwell Wholesalers Limited
Stonefruit Ltd
Sublime Corporation Limited
Suha World Ltd
Suncrops UK Limited
Suntrack Ltd
Sunugal Trading Limited
Supermalt UK Limited
Supreme Links Limited
Sweet Caroline Ltd
Sweetprod Ltd
Syed Drinks Limited
Symphony Fine Foods Ltd
Syon Distributors Ltd
T & A Import and Export Trading Ltd
T's Dazzling Delicious Sweets Ltd
TTS Private Ltd
TVS Private Ltd
Taj Restaurant Supplies Ltd
Talbot & Barr Limited
Tazah Ltd
Temple Wines (Cash & Carry) Ltd
Thailand 11234501 International Trade Co.,
Thames Wholesale Ltd
Thass Ltd
Third Eye Nutrition Ltd
Thirst Quenchers (UK) Limited
Tiqle Global Limited
Topmost Foods Distribution Ltd.
Topstop Wholesalers Limited
Tricape UK Ltd
Tronika Traders Limited
Turkish Kitchinn Wholesale Ltd
Tydene Limited
UK Brighton Food & Nutrition Research Centre
UK Cloud Business PLC
UK Wings Limited
Ufton Limited
Under The Sun Europe Ltd
Usedsoft Ltd
Veg & City Drinks Limited
Vendit (Harrow) Limited
Venkat Ltd
Vezlon Limited
Vild Water Limited
Village Quality Products Ltd

Vinroe Distribution Ltd
Viserra Limited
Vision Global Enterprise Ltd
Vitamin Well Limited
Vitamor Limited
Vitte Nutrition Ltd
Viva Avo Ltd
WGTSS Ltd
Wades & Ellie Ltd
C. J. Walls Trading UK Ltd
Watt Energy Drink (UK) Ltd
Welldrinks Ltd
West Green Supply Ltd
Willow World Ltd
Winz International UK Ltd
Worldwide Essentials Limited
Y Acay Berry Ltd
Yachinelyaoui Limited
Yashrab Ltd
YummyColombia Ltd
Zayyan Foods Distribution Ltd
Zolex Global Limited
Zoop Up Energy Ltd

Merseyside [47]
Akgun Food Ltd
Alpine Water Coolers Ltd
Altra Service Ltd
Asi Wholesale & Retail Ltd
Aster Service Ltd
Birch Sales Ltd
Bongo Sale Ltd
Boomshakes Ltd
Budaquelle Beverages International Ltd
BudgetForU Limited
Cabana Soft Drinks Limited
Crab Trading Ltd
DJ Drink Solutions Limited
Discover Health Ltd
Drinks R Us Limited
Drinkslynx Limited
Europol Trade Ltd.
Glitter Service Ltd
HP Juicery Ltd
Haggard.Grb Ltd
Healthy Food and Drink Online Ltd
Hua Lin Trade Import Limited
Hubit General Trading Ltd
Ilie Cash & Carry Ltd
Juicery Ltd
Liverpool & Oriental Trading Co Ltd
Adrian Mecklenburgh Limited
Mercury Wholesale Ltd
Merseyside Service Ltd
Milky Milkshakes Ltd
New Global Ltd
Nichols Dispense (S.W.) Ltd
Numba UK Limited
PP Cash & Carry Ltd
PU Trading Ltd
Pem Trade Sales Ltd
Pinnacle Drinks Limited
Robinson Alimentation Ltd
Shark Trading Ltd
Simply Spirits Limited
TN Global Service Ltd
TN Sales Ltd
Thriftys Wholesale Limited
Ultimum Drinks Limited
Vimto (Out of Home) Limited
White World Service Ltd
Wishing Tree Limited

UK Wholesalers of Soft Drinks

Middlesex [101]
A A Suppliers Ltd
Afro Lanka Ltd
Ahara Ventures Ltd
Al Kass General Trading Ltd
Albanblue Elementals Limited
All in One Household Ltd
Amou Limited
Aqua Distribution Limited
Aquabella London Ltd
Arsi Soft Drinks Limited
BS and Sons London Limited
Brandin Marketing Limited
Britlines Limited
Budget Logistics Ltd
Bukhari and Tanweer Limited
Buy & Sales Trading Ltd
Castleton International Ltd
Claddagh Food and Drink Ltd
Club Consultants Ltd
Connect Waze Private Limited
D D C Foods Limited
DN World Ltd
DNG Group Ltd
DNG Trading Ltd
Direct Source 2 Limited
Drayton Limited
Dreams Food 1 Limited
Dutch Delight UK Limited
E-Natural Limited
Eda Quality Foods Limited
Eda Quality Foods North UK Ltd
Eldoflora Limited
Eltrados Ltd
Essential Juices Ltd
Patrick Fernando & Sons UK Ltd
Fresh Star Fruit & Veg Limited
Fruit & Veg 2 U Ltd
Frutex Limited
Frutex UK PVT Limited
GO4 Beverages Limited
Global Fresh Ltd
Going Ahead Ltd
Golden Fastfood Limited
Good Gut Guys Ltd
Grouptype Limited
Gulzar Traders Ltd
HM Wholesale Supplies Limited
Hello Coco Limited
Hermes Chariot Ltd
Humble Bumble Ltd
Ital World Ltd
Jalkhushi Fresh & Frozen Fish Ltd
Jeet (UK) Limited
Jeeva Natural UK Ltd
Jessica Worldwide Ltd
KP Global Ltd
Kadey Limited
Kakkar Enterprises Ltd
Klomar Ltd
Knights Catering Impex Ltd
LBSM Limited
Loyal Trader Ltd
M & M Export Limited
MCIA Ltd
Massafood Ltd
Meless Group Limited
Naturally Fresh Drink Limited
Ombre Drinks Limited
Pamm Beverages Limited
Panton Ventures Limited
Patson Foods Ltd
Prod Act Ltd.
Pure Pom Ltd
Quinton Trading Ltd
R.A. Trading Limited
SLB Wholesale Ltd
Saapos Ltd
Sabroso Food UK Ltd
Sahej UK Limited
Sanus Foods Ltd
JJ Sis Limited
Smart Buyer Wholesale Limited
Smith & Munden Ltd
Social Drinking Co Ltd
Star Direct Hospitality Ltd
Super Food Base Ltd
Super Smoo-V Co Ltd
Thusi Wholesale Ltd
Tri Star Wholesale Limited
U.D.C. Wholesale Ltd
UKFast Service Ltd
Unique Lines Ltd
Vangoo Enterprise Holding Ltd
Vinz Ltd
Vittorio Ottavio Ltd
Winewise Ltd
Woodstar Limited
Zanzi Products Limited
Zentio Limited
Zeyroj Soft Drinks Ltd
Ziro Ltd

Midlothian [10]
Active Root 2 Ltd
Anderson Beverages Ltd
FIBM Wholesale Ltd
GCA Foods Edinburgh Ltd
Global Sports Trade Ltd
Golden Eagle Foods Edinburgh Ltd
Golden Eagle Trade Edinburgh Ltd
MBS Ventures Limited
RDM Polish Food Ltd
Total Refreshment Solutions Ltd

Norfolk [8]
Albert Altima Trade House Ltd
Alicia's Coffee House Limited
Artisan Drinks Co Ltd
C1 Trading Ltd
C J Canham Drinks Limited
Eatwell Catering Contractors (Norwich)
Mercado Da Saudade Ltd
Rimpex-UK Limited

Northamptonshire [9]
Better Tasting Drinks Co. Ltd
Bio Icecream Ltd
Cawston Press Limited
City Beer Limited
Easy CBD Limited
Fusecutter Ltd
Mithun MM Limited
Norfolk Punch (UK) Ltd
Thirstee Business Limited

Nottinghamshire [11]
Beeston General Store & Off Licences Ltd
Paul Berry Limited
Fearis Beverages Ltd
Green Cash & Carry Ltd
H & F Export Limited
In2rehab Brands Limited
More or Less Drinks Co Ltd
Perfect Drinks Ltd
Squishy Drinks Limited
Stalker U.K Limited
WLL Wholesale Ltd

Oxfordshire [6]
Bassen Ltd
Fourseasons Fruiterers Ltd
MS Rarytas Ltd
Merchantology Ltd
Noah Brothers Ltd
Numidia Taste Ltd

Powys
Peregrine Welsh Water Limited
Taste Merchants Ltd

Shropshire [6]
Kristals Trading Limited
Nootrilix Limited
Potts of Goodness Limited
Snacks Dist Limited
Wenlock Spring Water Limited
Zummo Central Limited

Somerset [15]
7 Star Trading Ltd
A2Z Fruit & Veg Ltd
Alfresco Drinks Limited
Bristol Spirits Limited
Cafe Collective UK Trading Co Ltd
Caleno Drinks Ltd
First Fruits Drinks Ltd
Great British Beverages Ltd
JA & MD Limited
Juice de Vine Limited
Oneworlddistribution Ltd
Pick Pedal Pour Ltd
Ubuntu Trading Co Ltd
Vivid Vitality Ltd
Your Water Ltd

Staffordshire [11]
Abantu Moringa Ltd
Dolphin Trading Limited
Fletcher's Fruit & Veg Ltd
Hayat Supermarket Ltd
MEA Health and Wellness Ltd
Nexgen 2018 Ltd
Not Another Beer Co Ltd
W.E.Pointon & Sons Limited
Premier Pubco Limited
Roxane UK Limited
Shake It Up! The Protein Smoothie Co Ltd

Suffolk [8]
Aquaid Franchising Limited
Hurly Burly Foods Limited
Liquidline Limited
Magna Carta Drinks Limited
Paddy and Scotts Launch Pad Ltd
Roeser Limited
Snackpax Distribution Limited
Waterline (UK) Ltd

Surrey [59]
A & A Wines Limited
ABNN Fresh UK Ltd
AFC Food (UK) Limited
AJ Fruit & Vegetable Enterprises Ltd
Aiden Service Ltd
Alpha Neno Limited
Astra Import Ltd.
Bare Drinks Limited
Said Boukhebelt Ltd
Brands Nexus Ltd
Remy Cazabet Ltd
Choice Asia Ltd
Chum Bites Limited
Coot Service Ltd
Debbie and Venky Ltd
Domore Imports Ltd
Drinksparadies Ltd
Drinx Division Ltd
EWF Wine Force Ltd
Eliya Europe Ltd
Priya Even Limited
Exoteeque Limited
FS Wholesale Distributors (UK) Ltd
Farida Import Export Ltd
Stefan Frank Ltd
Freedom Sale Ltd
Fruits & Vegetables Ltd.
GFT Retail UK Limited
Georgian Food and Beverages Ltd
H N D Trading Limited
Jasmine Direct Limited
KG Wholesale Ltd
Kaspas Distribution Ltd
MK Inter Ltd
Macedo (UK) Limited
Nature Fresh Limited
Navson Ltd
Nextgen Distribution Limited
Nirajen Ltd
Nor Oslo Service Ltd
Paradigm Red Limited
Polwug Trading Ltd
Punjab Masala Ltd
Pure Juice Co Ltd
RJ Traders Ltd
RSS Fast Food Suppliers Ltd
Rozana Foods Limited
Savers Stop Wholesalers Ltd
Stack United Limited
Starburst Hub Ltd
Sunspice UK Limited
T & K Wholesale Ltd
Tasman Bay Foods Europe Ltd
Tasnim Recruiting & Consultancy Services
Tomato Tantrum Ltd
UK Beer & Soft Drinks Ltd
Unione Trading Europe Ltd
Usqueeze Limited
ZSlush Ltd

Sussex [21]
All English Distribution Ltd.
Alpha Aliment Ltd
Bevtec Services Limited
Brighton Brew Co Ltd
Camelot Chilled Foods Ltd
Cameron Soft Drinks Limited
Colemans ABC Ltd
Driver's Drinks Co Ltd
Giovanni Food & Wine Limited

Green Ambition Limited
Gusto Organic Ltd
Joo Soft Drinks Limited
KKR Wine Ltd
Noble Naturals Ltd
Nosh Detox Delivery Limited
Surprisingly Treaty Ltd
Walbrokers Limited
Wobblegate Limited
Xorta Global Management Ltd
Youngs Vintage Management Ltd
Zumi Natural Limited

Tyne & Wear [14]
Afterall Ltd
Importonics Limited
KU Bargin Deals Ltd
KU Supplies Ltd
Mock Drink Co Ltd
J Mullens Ltd
Nekta Food & Juice Bar Ltd
D.E. Scorer Limited
Strong Pound Ltd
TFC Wholesale Ltd
Thirst Call Ltd
Uddin Discount Ltd
J Water Disabled Children Ltd
Wholesale Your Way Ltd

Warwickshire [27]
AKKG Enterprise Limited
Abel Service Ltd
Amedame International Ltd
Birch Boost Ltd
Brewed 4 U Ltd
Caribbean Trade Ltd
Delta Tip Limited
Drinks2u Ltd
ERE Igga Ltd
Eagle Drinks Ltd
Elan Import and Export Limited
JR Quality Service Ltd
Jaden Wholesale Limited
Key Traders Ltd
Loris Wholesale Ltd
Majestic Foods Limited
Medina Food World Ltd
Nalla Sales Ltd
Nazar Wholesale Limited
Panymoc Ltd
Platinum UK Drinks Ltd
Risco Service Ltd
Sarl Import Export Mondial Ltd
Shane's Consortium Limited
Simple Nature Limited
Temperance Drinks Limited
Thamby Trading Ltd

West Midlands [76]
2 Brothers Birmingham Ltd
A H K Wholesaler Ltd
All Vending Services Limited
Amsterdam Taste Ltd
Apex Sourcing International Ltd
Azka Impex Limited
Belgard Trading Ltd
Bennu Rising Ltd.
Benson International Ltd
Beverages Group Limited
Beverages Stars Ltd
Bri Trade Solutions Limited

Cali Juices Limited
Caspian Foods Cash & Carry Ltd
Castle Warehouse Management Ltd
Codex Limited
Continent Foods Limited
Cooper & Partner Ltd
Dark Night Beverages Ltd
Desi Trading Ltd
Drink Your Fruit Limited
Drinks International Birmingham Ltd
Dua Enterprises Limited
East and West Foods Cash and Carry
FMCG Express Limited
Fexty Ltd
Freshfield Exotics Ltd
GSTWholesale Limited
Glinter UK Ltd
Glow Penny Ltd
Gohir Soft Drinks Ltd
A Gohir Soft Drinks UK Ltd
Good Prices Ltd
Green Foods International Ltd
HT Sweets (UK) Limited
Hell Beverages UK Ltd
Hillcrest WM Ltd
I S Traders Limited
I Star Wholesale Limited
IMH Traders Limited
Jascera UK Ltd
K.M Food & Drinks Ltd
Kingsbury Wholesale Ltd
Laz and Kol Ltd
Link International Ltd
Lync Direct Limited
M & M European Merchants Ltd
MRU Wholesale Limited
Netmine Technologies Ltd
Netto Stores Limited
Nohew Trade Ltd
Orbit Food Ltd
Phoenix Dispensed Drinks Ltd
Pirm Trading Limited
Platinum Group Midlands Ltd
Pound Hill Ltd
Primacy Trade Ltd
Pursuit of Excellence Group Ltd
RB Beverages Ltd
Arif Rahim Ltd
Realmix Beverage Ltd
Regency Traders Ltd
S K Enteprises Ltd
Shapla Cash & Carry Ltd
Shokers Wines & Spirits Ltd
Shopocus Ltd
Shu Enterprise Ltd
Skyfall Enterprise Ltd
Swallow Dispensed Drinks Solutions
Taza Food Limited
Tropical Ice (England) Ltd
Trust in Global Food Ltd
Urban Distribution Ltd
Welat & Othman Limited
Z & Z Global Ltd
Zauq Services Ltd

Wiltshire
Clarion Wines Limited
Freestar Drinks Ltd
Intercontinental Trade Solutions Ltd

Worcestershire
5of5 Juices Ltd

UK Wholesalers of Soft Drinks

CPH Games UK Limited
Ceci-Hill Limited
Farm Shop at Ombersley Limited

Yorkshire [51]
5S Import Ltd
AFZ Trade Ltd
ATR Catering Supplies Limited
Acquire Consultancy Limited
Bazaar Store Ltd
Becsco Limited
Bella Refreshments Ltd.
Bi Fa Limited
Blue Trading International Ltd
Bright Smoothies Ltd
Coconutty Ltd
DSA Frozen Foods Ltd
Daneisa Ltd

Dollshouse Childrens Drinks Ltd
Drink Natural Limited
Emara Soft Drinks Ltd
Eurostar HRK Ltd
Getfreshjuiceco Limited
HF Food International Ltd
Harp & Crown Cider Co Ltd
Janos Horvath Ltd
MSM Foods Limited
Majestic Wholesale Ltd
Manchester Fruit and Vegetables Ltd
Henry Mitchell & Sons Limited
Najpol Ltd
Native Leaf Ltd
Nawab Traders Limited
Nobu Distribution Ltd
Oasis Softdrinks Limited
One Stop Fruit & Veg Limited
One Up Beverages Corporation (1 Up)

P N New Ltd
Polski Wholesale Limited
Quando Drinks Limited
Red Baron Beverages Limited
Santa Monica Co Ltd
Saravanan Traders (UK) Ltd
Sativatech Ltd
Seasons East Ltd
Slimsters Sports Drinks Ltd
Soft Drink UK Limited
Sub Enterprises Ltd
Superyacht Supplies Limited
Tastebuds Trading Ltd
Tate-Smith Limited
Verdict International Ltd
Vivo Viva Beverages Limited
Wolf Wholesale Limited
Yorkshire Enterprise Ltd
Yorkshire Exports Limited

This page is intentionally left blank

Company Profiles

2 Brothers Birmingham Ltd
Incorporated: 23 February 2018
Registered Office: 21 Stony Street, Smethwick, W Midlands, B67 7QL
Major Shareholder: Brijmohan Singh
Officers: Brijmohan Singh [1969] Director/General Operature [Indian]

21st Century Nutrition Limited
Incorporated: 2 November 2016 *Employees:* 1
Net Worth Deficit: £7,763 *Total Assets:* £37
Registered Office: 140 Buckingham Palace Road, London, SW1W 9SA
Shareholders: Marcus Clive Newby; Simon William David Feather
Officers: Adam Starr [1967] Director

3BW Ltd
Incorporated: 22 November 2016
Registered Office: 33 Holborn, London, EC1N 2HT
Shareholders: WBE Limited; Sainsbury's Supermarkets Ltd
Officers: James Bailey [1974] Director; Oliver Bowden [1982] Director; Tim Buttimore [1960] Director; Jonathan Peter Wilkinson [1979] Director

413 Limited
Incorporated: 30 October 2018
Registered Office: 20 Ledbury House, East Dulwich, London, SE22 8AN
Major Shareholder: Adebowale Johnson
Officers: Adebowale Johnson [1984] Director/Business Executive

420 Beverages Ltd
Incorporated: 7 November 2018
Registered Office: 14 David Mews, London, W1U 6EQ
Parent: Raylex Ltd
Officers: Raymond Pang [1987] Director

51 Plus Ltd
Incorporated: 7 August 2017
Registered Office: 85 Great Portland Street, London, W1W 7LT
Shareholders: Adryan Martinelli; Chantal Lara Francesca Martinelli
Officers: Adryan Martinelli [1983] Director/Manager [Italian]; Chantal Lara Francesca Martinelli [1988] Director/Manager

5of5 Juices Ltd
Incorporated: 10 May 2018
Registered Office: 31 Sidbury, Worcester, WR1 2HT
Shareholders: Antoan Lyubomirov Dimitrov; Nikolay Penkov Tsvetkov
Officers: Antoan Lyubomirov Dimitrov [1997] Director/Student [Bulgarian]; Nikolay Penkov Tsvetkov [1997] Director/Student [Bulgarian]

5S Import Ltd
Incorporated: 5 November 2018
Registered Office: Above Shops, Flat 1, Mill Lane, Adwick-le-Street, Doncaster, S Yorks, DN6 7AG
Major Shareholder: Velupillai Sajikumar
Officers: Velupillai Sajikumar [1976] Director

7 Star Trading Ltd
Incorporated: 22 June 2018
Registered Office: 283 Speedwell Road, Bristol, BS5 7SY
Shareholders: Muhammad Asif; Naznin Iqbal
Officers: Muhammad Asif, Secretary; Muhammad Asif [1984] Director/Sales Executive

78 Degrees Limited
Incorporated: 29 January 2018
Registered Office: 71-75 Shelton Street, Covent Garden, London, WC2H 9JQ
Major Shareholder: Andrew Fishburn
Officers: Andrew Fishburn [1986] Director

815 Distributors (UK) Ltd
Incorporated: 31 October 2017
Registered Office: 71-75 Shelton Street, London, WC2H 9JK
Officers: Garnet George Grayson, Secretary; Chelsea Alexa Singh [1990] Director [Jamaican/British]; Courtney Montrose Singh [1962] Managing Director; Suzanne Oliviene Singh [1963] Director [Jamaican]

901WD Ltd
Incorporated: 11 May 2018
Registered Office: Kemp House, 160 City Road, London, EC1V 2NX
Major Shareholder: Shahid Hussain
Officers: Shahid Hussain [1964] Director

A & A Wines Limited
Incorporated: 26 July 1984 *Employees:* 11
Net Worth: £369,074 *Total Assets:* £904,532
Registered Office: Unit 13 Manfield Park, Cranleigh, Surrey, GU6 8PT
Shareholders: Andrew Philip Bickerton; Andrew Paul Connor
Officers: Vachirawan Connor, Secretary; Andrew Philip Bickerton [1958] Director; Andrew Paul Connor [1959] Director

A & H Trading Ltd
Incorporated: 3 December 2013 *Employees:* 2
Previous: H & N Enterprises Limited
Net Worth Deficit: £5,802 *Total Assets:* £36,392
Registered Office: 88-90 High Street, Yiewsley, West Drayton, London, UB7 7DS
Shareholders: Mohammed Abdulgalil Radman Radman; Abubaker Abood Alhagri; Mohamed Hasme Mohamed Haleeldeen
Officers: Abubaker Abood Alhagri [1976] Director; Mohamed Hasme Mohamed Haleeldeen [1975] Director [Sri Lankan]; Mohammed Abdulgalil Radman Radman [1978] Director [Yemeni]

A A Suppliers Ltd
Incorporated: 16 November 2018
Registered Office: 83 Hayes End Drive, Hayes, Middlesex, UB4 8HE
Major Shareholder: Azrar Ahmed Ghuman Begum
Officers: Azrar Ahmed Ghuman Begum [1981] Director [Spanish]

A H K Wholesaler Ltd
Incorporated: 12 June 2017
Registered Office: Unit 3 Upper Chapel Street, Tividale, Oldbury, W Midlands, B69 2HS
Major Shareholder: Saika Tehzim Ahmed
Officers: Saika Tehzim Ahmed [1978] Director

A to Z Veg Ltd
Incorporated: 21 June 2012 *Employees:* 5
Net Worth: £8,028 *Total Assets:* £91,541
Registered Office: Arch 406-407 St Pauls Way, London, E3 4AQ
Major Shareholder: Afruz Mahbubul Hoque
Officers: Mahbubul Hoque Afruz [1964] Director/Businessman

A1 Best Traders Ltd
Incorporated: 2 January 2018
Registered Office: 20-22 Wenlock Road, London, N1 7GU
Shareholder: Timothy Reginald Stevens
Officers: Timothy Reginald Stevens [1962] Director/Driver

A2Z Fruit & Veg Ltd
Incorporated: 28 January 2019
Registered Office: Unit C, 126 Albert Road, Bristol, BS2 0YA
Major Shareholder: Mustafa Polat
Officers: Olcay Kaplan [1987] Director/Businessman [Turkish]; Mustafa Polat [1980] Director/Businessman

AB (Cheshire) Group Ltd
Incorporated: 20 November 2018
Registered Office: 67 Watling Street, Preston, Lancs, PR2 8EA
Major Shareholder: Zunaira Maiwish
Officers: Zunaira Maiwish [1993] Director

AB Catering (Blackburn) Ltd
Incorporated: 21 June 2018
Registered Office: 455 Whalley New Road, Blackburn, BB1 9SP
Officers: Abid Hussain [1958] Director/Manager; Ibrar Hussain [1976] Director

AB Trade Direct Ltd
Incorporated: 21 July 2016
Net Worth: £2,167 *Total Assets:* £123,514
Registered Office: 555-557 Cranbrook Road, Ilford, Essex, IG2 6HE
Officers: Alex Frederick Mechell [1986] Director

Abantu Moringa Ltd
Incorporated: 9 August 2018
Registered Office: 53 Dundee Road, Stoke on Trent, Staffs, ST1 4BS
Shareholders: Kondwa Thawethe; Joshua Hordell
Officers: Joshua Hordell [1990] Director/Student; Kondwa Thawethe [1994] Director/Administrator [Zambian]

Abel Service Ltd
Incorporated: 15 August 2018
Registered Office: 231 Lower Hillmorton Road, Rugby, Warwicks, CV21 4AA
Major Shareholder: Visvanadane Frarenganadaayer
Officers: Visvanadane Frarenganadaayer [1958] Director/Manager [French]

Aberystwyth Soft Drinks Ltd
Incorporated: 2 November 2016 *Employees:* 5
Net Worth: £4,906 *Total Assets:* £199,298
Registered Office: Aberystwyth Soft Drinks, Pen Y Garn, Bow Street, Ceredigion, SY24 5BQ
Shareholders: Catherine Elizabeth Howard; Christopher Frank Howard
Officers: Catherine Elizabeth Howard [1971] Director/Business Owner; Christopher Frank Howard [1969] Director/Business Owner

Abevco Limited
Incorporated: 2 October 2007 *Employees:* 18
Net Worth: £962,247 *Total Assets:* £1,321,749
Registered Office: Unit 3 Container Terminal, Belper Road, Kilburn, Derbys, DE56 0LQ
Shareholders: Hussam Attieh; Nidal Attieh
Officers: Susan Margaret Payne, Secretary; Nidal Attieh [1973] Director

Abijah Global Limited
Incorporated: 2 October 2018
Registered Office: 43 Pincott Place, Brockley, London, SE4 2ER
Major Shareholder: Adesola Adelowo
Officers: Adesola Adelowo [1959] Director/Carer

ABNN Fresh UK Ltd
Incorporated: 4 December 2018
Registered Office: 145 Gander Green Lane, Sutton, Surrey, SM1 2EZ
Shareholder: Prakash Ambekar
Officers: Prakash Ambekar [1977] Director

Abukor Ltd
Incorporated: 11 October 2018
Registered Office: Waheen Group, 175 Hillside, London, NW10 8LL
Officers: Edil Abdi Abukor [1993] Director/Nurse

ABZ Food Ltd
Incorporated: 25 January 2019
Registered Office: 43 Modley Place, Ellon, Aberdeenshire, AB41 9BB
Major Shareholder: Steven James Main
Officers: Steven Main, Secretary; Steven James Main [1991] Director

Acai Express Ltd
Incorporated: 7 April 2017
Registered Office: SJPR Accountants Ltd, Suite 4, Charan House, 18 Union Road, London, SW4 6JP
Major Shareholder: Weuber Lacerda Santana
Officers: Weuber Lacerda Santana [1979] Director [Brazilian]

Ace Incorporation Ltd
Incorporated: 15 February 2017
Registered Office: Tree Tops, Burtons Lane, Chalfont St Giles, Bucks, HP8 4BD
Officers: Seema Ganatra, Secretary; Mahek Ganatra [1996] Director/Economist

Acqua Nordica Ltd
Incorporated: 26 March 2015
Net Worth: £1,902 *Total Assets:* £3,452
Registered Office: 17 Ensign House, Admirals Way, Canary Wharf, London, E14 9XQ
Shareholder: Birgir Loftsson
Officers: Andrew Fomychov [1966] Director/Manager; Birgir Loftsson [1967] Director/Manager [Icelander]

Acquire Consultancy Limited
Incorporated: 8 December 2016
Net Worth: £4,365 *Total Assets:* £9,034
Registered Office: Park House, Wilmington Street, Leeds, LS7 2BP
Officers: Hamza Sethi, Secretary; Hamza Sethi [1984] Commercial Director; Nadia Sethi [1984] Director

Acquisto Limited
Incorporated: 14 December 2015
Net Worth Deficit: £2,151 *Total Assets:* £47,849
Registered Office: Whitewell House, 69 Crewe Road, Nantwich, Cheshire, CW5 6HX
Officers: Lesley Jane Clarke, Secretary; Lesley Jane Clarke [1963] Financial Director; Darren Paul Goldney [1970] Director; Ross McLean Gourlay [1962] Director; John Schofield [1954] Director

Active Protein Limited
Incorporated: 25 February 2015 *Employees:* 4
Net Worth: £33,355 *Total Assets:* £70,386
Registered Office: Croft Chambers, 11 Bancroft, Hitchin, Herts, SG5 1JQ
Shareholders: Catherine Colman; Max Colman
Officers: Catherine Colman [1987] Director; Max Colman [1989] Director; Brian Daniel [1964] Sales Director; Stephen Michael Draisey [1959] Director/Consultant

Active Root 2 Ltd
Incorporated: 14 September 2015 *Employees:* 3
Net Worth Deficit: £34,493 *Total Assets:* £24,417
Registered Office: 8 Glengyle Terrace, Edinburgh, EH3 9LL
Shareholders: William Townsend; George Ashley
Officers: Dr George Ashley [1982] Director; William Townsend [1982] Director

ADA Beverages Ltd
Incorporated: 13 February 2019
Registered Office: Flat 63, Parker Street, Derby, DE1 3HX
Major Shareholder: Andrew Atkin
Officers: Andrew Atkin, Secretary; Andrew Atkin [1984] Director/Self Employed

Adamson's Drinks Ltd.
Incorporated: 17 July 2002 *Employees:* 48
Net Worth: £954,564 *Total Assets:* £2,709,121
Registered Office: Balfour House, 2 Pitreavie Drive, Pitreavie Business Park, Dunfermline, Fife, KY11 8US
Shareholders: Andrew Gregor Wylie; Anastassis Christos Georgiades
Officers: Pauline Wylie, Secretary; Anastassis Christos Georgiades [1955] Director/Manager; Andrew Gregor Wylie [1970] Director

Adanali Limited
Incorporated: 16 May 2017
Net Worth: £1,579 *Total Assets:* £2,850
Registered Office: Demsa Accounts, 278 Langham Road, London, N15 3NP
Major Shareholder: Mutlu Karakilcik
Officers: Mutlu Karakilcik [1980] Director/Businessman [Turkish]

Aduna Limited
Incorporated: 20 May 2011 *Employees:* 10
Net Worth: £574,857 *Total Assets:* £1,116,898
Registered Office: Chester House, Kennington Business Park, 1-3 Brixton Road, London, SW9 6DE
Shareholder: Andrew David Hunt
Officers: Angus James Davison [1965] Director; Andrew David Hunt [1977] Director; Nicholas Kyffin Salter [1962] Director

AFC Food (UK) Limited
Incorporated: 8 December 2009
Net Worth: £1,041,899 *Total Assets:* £2,857,104
Registered Office: 275 King Henry Drive, New Addington, Croydon, Surrey, CR0 0AE
Major Shareholder: Muhammad Wahid
Officers: Muhammad Wahid [1974] Director [Pakistani]

Africa Global Village. Com Ltd
Incorporated: 8 January 2015
Registered Office: 381 Great Western Road, Glasgow, G4 9HY
Major Shareholder: Mohammad Sohail Rafique
Officers: Mohammad Sohail Rafique [1952] Director

Afrimalt UK Ltd
Incorporated: 2 June 2009
Net Worth: £126,669 *Total Assets:* £226,435
Registered Office: 43a High Street, Barkingside, Ilford, Essex, IG6 2AD
Major Shareholder: Ibrahim Kanamia
Officers: Faruk Kanamia [1965] Director; Hanif Kanamia [1967] Director; Ibrahim Kanamia [1935] Managing Director

Afro Lanka Ltd
Incorporated: 16 December 2014
Net Worth: £64,097 *Total Assets:* £156,959
Registered Office: 129 Lynton Road, Harrow, Middlesex, HA2 9NH
Major Shareholder: Sharmala Pirapatharan
Officers: Sharmala Pirapatharan [1978] Director

Afromax Ltd
Incorporated: 16 November 2018
Registered Office: 124-126 Gladstone Street, Peterborough, Cambs, PE1 2BS
Shareholders: Telmo Monteiro Correia; Belisa Enide de Oliveira Correia
Officers: Belisa Enide de Oliveira Correia [1978] Director/Domestic Assistant [Portuguese/Bissau Guinean]; Telmo Monteiro Correia [1978] Director/Butcher [Portuguese/Bissau Guinean]

After Eight Alcohol Concierge Ltd
Incorporated: 31 August 2018
Registered Office: 20-22 Wenlock Road, London, N1 7GU
Major Shareholder: Zavon Miller
Officers: Zavon Miller [1990] Director/Self Employed [Zimbabwean]

Afterall Ltd
Incorporated: 3 December 2018
Registered Office: 2 Greenlands, Boldon Lane, Cleadon Village, Tyne & Wear, SR6 7RH
Major Shareholder: Stuart John Ashman
Officers: Rebecca Frances Ashman, Secretary; Stuart John Ashman [1966] Director/Chief Executive

AFZ Trade Ltd
Incorporated: 27 February 2018
Registered Office: 16 Hall Avenue, Huddersfield, W Yorks, HD1 3NL
Major Shareholder: Sonam Arora
Officers: Sonam Arora [1990] Company Secretary/Director [Indian]; Asmat Fayyaz [1986] Director

AG Fresh Produce Limited
Incorporated: 16 August 2018
Registered Office: 95 Gateside Road, Wishaw, N Lanarks, ML2 7RZ
Officers: Ali Gafsi [1957] Director/Trader

Agencia Ltd
Incorporated: 11 February 2019
Registered Office: 20-22 Wenlock Road, London, N1 7GU
Major Shareholder: Shamsher Singh
Officers: Shamsher Singh [1964] Director

Agrofresh Ltd
Incorporated: 7 April 2018
Registered Office: Kemp House, 160 City Road, London, EC1V 2NX
Officers: Derrick Mubiru [1979] Director/Occupational Psychologist; Fiona Mubiru [1982] Director/Teacher

Agrotrade International Trading Ltd
Incorporated: 16 May 2018
Registered Office: First Floor, 85 Great Portland Street, London, W1W 7LT
Officers: Lajos Balog [1994] Director [Hungarian]

Ahara Ventures Ltd
Incorporated: 15 June 2018
Registered Office: Rubicon House, Unit 5 Second Way, Wembley, Middlesex, HA9 0YJ
Major Shareholder: Neel Naresh Nagrecha
Officers: Radha Nagrecha Gagneja [1982] Director/Accountant; Davendra Parbat Khimani [1972] Director; Neel Naresh Nagrecha [1980] Director

Aiden Service Ltd
Incorporated: 12 May 2017
Registered Office: 10 Hazelwood House, 4 Brunswick Road, Sutton, Surrey, SM1 4DQ
Officers: Ishara Buddika Samarasena [1987] Director/General Manager [Sri Lankan]

AJ Fruit & Vegetable Enterprises Ltd
Incorporated: 13 July 2018
Registered Office: 39 Frithwald Road, Chertsey, Surrey, KT16 9EZ
Major Shareholder: Suresh Parmar
Officers: Suresh Parmar [1976] Director

Akgun Food Ltd
Incorporated: 2 February 2016
Net Worth: £8,752 *Total Assets:* £15,565
Registered Office: 66 Back Market Street, Newton-le-Willows, St Helens, Merseyside, WA12 9BW
Major Shareholder: Ramazan Akgun
Officers: Ramazan Akgun [1969] Director

AKKG Enterprise Limited
Incorporated: 1 August 2018
Registered Office: 57 Harnal Lane West, Coventry, Warwicks, CV1 4EY
Major Shareholder: Avtar Gill
Officers: Avtar Gill, Secretary; Avtar Gill [1990] Director/Store Occupier

AKM Trading Services Ltd
Incorporated: 17 September 2009 *Employees:* 2
Net Worth Deficit: £25,623 *Total Assets:* £109,015
Registered Office: Churchill House, 120 Bunns Lane, London, NW7 2AS
Shareholders: Costas Symeou; Andrew Anastasi Symeou
Officers: Constantine Symeou, Secretary; Andrew Symeou [1981] Director/Logistics Manager; Constantine Symeou [1984] Director/Buyer

Al Kass General Trading Ltd
Incorporated: 17 July 2018
Registered Office: Flat 1-3, 660B London Road, Hounslow, Middlesex, TW3 1PG
Major Shareholder: Mohamud Somalia Dirie
Officers: Mohamud Somalia Dirie [1956] Director/Businessman

Al Pixel Points Limited
Incorporated: 1 February 2018
Registered Office: Pixel Points Ltd, 272 Bath Street, Glasgow, G2 4JR
Major Shareholder: Hardeep Singh
Officers: Hardeep Singh, Secretary; Hardeep Singh [1982] Director/Salesman

Al Taj Al Malaki General Trading UK Ltd
Incorporated: 7 December 2017
Registered Office: Flat 5, Milwain Road, Manchester, M19 2PT
Parent: Al Taj Al Malaki General Trading LLC
Officers: Rahat Rizvi [1977] Director/Marketing Manager [Pakistani]

Al-Shahba Ltd
Incorporated: 21 November 2018
Registered Office: 231 Woolaston Avenue, Cardiff, CF23 6EX
Shareholders: Ali Mirzo; Wajih Derbas
Officers: Wajih Derbas [1969] Director/Civil Engineer [Syrian]; Ali Mirzo [1969] Director/Businessman [Syrian]

Alamirat Limited
Incorporated: 6 September 2004
Net Worth: £22,557 *Total Assets:* £77,167
Registered Office: 73 High Road, London, NW10 2SU
Major Shareholder: Sabah Ziyagham
Officers: Sabah Ziyagham [1963] Director [Iranian]

Alancia Fruit & Vegetable Ltd
Incorporated: 28 June 2010
Net Worth: £116,805 *Total Assets:* £331,481
Registered Office: 54 New Road, Seven Kings, Essex, IG3 8AT
Major Shareholder: Mohammed Ali Sheikh
Officers: Mohammed Ali Sheikh [1990] Director/Manager

Albanblue Elementals Limited
Incorporated: 6 April 2016
Registered Office: Freeman Lawrence & Partners, Amba House, Harrow, Middlesex, HA1 1BA
Parent: Albangreen Enterprises Limited
Officers: Richard Neville Ogden [1951] Director/Consultant

Albert Altima Trade House Limited
Incorporated: 6 March 2017
Registered Office: 21 Pinder Road, Norwich, NR3 2EG
Major Shareholder: Vladislav Cudalb
Officers: Vladislav Cudalb [1986] Director/General Manager [Romanian]

Alchemy Biotics Limited
Incorporated: 4 October 2018
Registered Office: 114 Colindale Avenue, London, NW9 5GX
Major Shareholder: Kai Man Liu
Officers: Kai Man Liu [1961] Director/Importer

Alfresco Drinks Limited
Incorporated: 15 November 1996 *Employees:* 4
Net Worth: £236,506 *Total Assets:* £788,885
Registered Office: 12 Old Mills Industrial Estate, Paulton, Bristol, BS39 7SU
Shareholder: Robin Michael Philpot Sheppard
Officers: John Stewart Fuller, Secretary; Sally Godley-Maynard [1964] Director/Investment Manager; Richard Gay Maude-Roxby [1947] Director/Consultant; Robin Michael Philpot Sheppard [1954] Director/Hotelier

Alicia's Coffee House Limited
Incorporated: 23 August 2018
Registered Office: 3 Howlett Drive, Norwich, NR5 9BZ
Shareholders: Jhasen Adam; Abdul-Fattah Ghassan Mustafa Hussein
Officers: Jhasen Adam [1972] Director/Businessman; Abdul-Fattah Ghassan Mustafa Hussein [1975] Director/Marketing Consultant [Jordanian]

Alicja Food Ltd
Incorporated: 18 September 2014 *Employees:* 6
Net Worth: £900 *Total Assets:* £21,094
Registered Office: 25 Blue Street, Carmarthen, Dyfed, SA31 3LE
Major Shareholder: Alicja Olszewska
Officers: Alicja Olszewska [1983] Director/Shop [Polish]

Alisha Fish Bazar Ltd
Incorporated: 19 April 2017
Net Worth: £1,261   *Total Assets:* £7,636
Registered Office: 41 Queens Market, Green Street, London, E13 9BA
Shareholders: Ashfa Rahman; Ashfa Rahman; Atikur Rahman
Officers: Ashfa Rahman, Secretary; Ashfa Rahman, Secretary; Ashfa Rahman [1982] Director; Ashfa Rahman [1982] Director; Atikur Rahman [1985] Director [Bangladeshi]

Aliss UK Limited
Incorporated: 2 August 2018
Registered Office: Unit 13, 2 Artichoke Hill, London, E1W 2DE
Major Shareholder: Edgar Alexander Zerpa Torres
Officers: Edgar Alexander Zerpa Torres [1975] Director/Entrepreneur [Venezuelan]

Alitasa Ltd
Incorporated: 23 November 2017
Registered Office: 13 Benwick Close, London, SE16 2HE
Major Shareholder: Juste Juozapaityte
Officers: Juste Juozapaityte, Secretary; Juste Juozapaityte [1990] Director [Lithuanian]

Alivini (North) Limited
Incorporated: 14 December 1993   *Employees:* 13
Net Worth: £303,136   *Total Assets:* £1,077,817
Registered Office: Units 2 and 3, 199 Eade Road, London, N4 1DN
Parent: Franciacorta Limited
Officers: Stephen Dennis Bridgeman, Secretary; Stephen Dennis Bridgeman [1942] Director; Custudio Jose Dos Santos [1957] Director/Wine & Food Importer [Portuguese]; Jose de Nobrega Pires [1956] Director/Wine & Food Importer [Portuguese]; Antonio Pirozzi [1943] Director; Maria Vitoria Santos-Pires [1960] Director/Financier [Portuguese]; Gianni Segatta [1945] Director

Alivini Company Limited
Incorporated: 12 February 1985   *Employees:* 84
Net Worth: £4,616,283   *Total Assets:* £6,575,749
Registered Office: Units 2 and 3, 199 Eade Road, London, N4 1DN
Parent: Franciacorta Limited
Officers: Stephen Dennis Bridgeman, Secretary; Stephen Dennis Bridgeman [1942] Director; Custudio Jose Dos Santos [1957] Director/Wine & Food Importer [Portuguese]; Jose de Nobrega Pires [1956] Director/Wine & Food Importer [Portuguese]; Antonio Pirozzi [1943] Director; Maria Vitoria Santos-Pires [1960] Director/Financier [Portuguese]; Gianni Segatta [1945] Director/Wine & Food Importer

All English Distribution Ltd.
Incorporated: 25 September 2017
Registered Office: Flat 3, 31 The Avenue, Eastbourne, E Sussex, BN21 3YD
Officers: Patrick Guy Armstrong Carey [1972] Director/Entrepreneur

All for You Beverages Limited
Incorporated: 20 April 2015
Registered Office: Office 4, 219 Kensington High Street, Kensington, London, W8 6BD
Shareholders: Fabian Videloup; Wlodzimierz Lesniowski
Officers: Fabian Videloup, Secretary; Fabian Videloup [1972] Director [French]

All Fresh Bradford Ltd
Incorporated: 3 July 2017
Registered Office: Greengate Business Centre, 2 Greengate Street, Oldham, Lancs, OL4 1FN
Major Shareholder: Amir Rasul
Officers: Amir Rasul [1981] Director

All in One Household Ltd
Incorporated: 28 April 2018
Registered Office: 108 Ashford Avenue, Hayes, Middlesex, UB4 0NB
Major Shareholder: Alin Grigoras Busuioc
Officers: Alin Grigoras Busuioc [1997] Director [Romanian]

All Vending Services Limited
Incorporated: 24 October 2018
Registered Office: Realtone House, Cliveland Street, Birmingham, B19 3SH
Major Shareholder: Curtis Armstrong
Officers: Curtis Armstrong [1961] Director/Retail Assistant

Allure International Ltd
Incorporated: 30 October 2018
Registered Office: 27 Old Gloucester Street, London, WC1N 3AX
Major Shareholder: Basant Sigdyal
Officers: Basant Sigdyal [1959] Director [Nepalese]

Alpha Aliment Ltd
Incorporated: 22 January 2013   *Employees:* 3
Net Worth: £46,305   *Total Assets:* £49,659
Registered Office: 39 Withypitts, Turners Hill, Crawley, W Sussex, RH10 4PJ
Major Shareholder: Gusztav Jozsef Hatsek
Officers: Gusztav Jozsef Hatsek [1969] Director [Hungarian]

Alpha Energy Drink Limited
Incorporated: 31 January 2018
Registered Office: Kemp House, 160 City Road, London, EC1V 2NX
Officers: Arnon Satayaprakorb [1971] Director/Businessman [American]

Alpha Neno Limited
Incorporated: 21 December 2018
Registered Office: Brooklands Business Park, Abbey House, Wellington Way, Weybridge, Surrey, KT13 0TT
Major Shareholder: Vellautham Sivaloganathan
Officers: Vellautham Sivaloganathan [1958] Director/Manager

Alpine Water Coolers Ltd
Incorporated: 6 August 2018
Registered Office: 5 Column Road, West Kirby, Wirral, Merseyside, CH48 7EA
Major Shareholder: Jack Desmond Hazelhurst
Officers: Jack Desmond Hazelhurst [1987] Director

Alti's Catering Limited
Incorporated: 4 October 2004   *Employees:* 27
Net Worth: £744,110   *Total Assets:* £1,257,947
Registered Office: 291 Green Lanes, London, N13 4XS
Shareholders: Musamettin Alti; Huseyin Alti
Officers: Huseyin Alti, Secretary; Musamettin Alti [1968] Director/Business Manager

UK Wholesalers of Soft Drinks   dellam

Altra Service Ltd
Incorporated: 9 September 2016
Net Worth: £44,622 Total Assets: £59,721
Registered Office: 106 New Chester Road, Wirral, Merseyside, CH62 5AG
Officers: Rameskumar Sivapatham, Secretary; Rameskumar Sivapatham [1975] Director/Manager [Norwegian]

Amedame International Ltd
Incorporated: 29 June 2017
Registered Office: 126 Clay Lane, Coventry, Warwicks, CV2 4LT
Major Shareholder: Mariusz Pechta
Officers: Mariusz Pechta [1980] Director/Economist [Polish]

AMG Wholesale Ltd
Incorporated: 24 April 2018
Registered Office: 24 Hockley Avenue, Eastham, London, E6 3AN
Major Shareholder: Asokkumar Mylvaganam
Officers: Asokkumar Mylvaganam [1974] Director [Swiss]

Ammart Ltd
Incorporated: 16 May 2018
Registered Office: 1 Caroline Court, Leicester, LE2 8QW
Major Shareholder: Artur Dyttwach
Officers: Artur Dyttwach [1988] Director/Manager [Polish]

Ammy Trading Ltd
Incorporated: 31 December 2018
Registered Office: 48 Pembroke Road, Ilford, Essex, IG3 8PH
Major Shareholder: Gurpreet Singh
Officers: Gurpreet Singh [1990] Director/Builder [Indian]

Amou Limited
Incorporated: 19 April 2012
Net Worth: £2,364 Total Assets: £214,674
Registered Office: Unit 3 Chiltern Business Village, Arundel Road, Uxbridge, Middlesex, UB8 2SN
Shareholders: Ahmad Jawid Ismat; Naqibullah Ismat; Ehsanullah Asmatpoor
Officers: Naqibullah Ismat, Secretary; Ehsanullah Asmatpoor [1958] Director; Ahmad Jawid Ismat [1974] Director

Amphipolis Limited
Incorporated: 16 May 2014 Employees: 2
Net Worth: £24,299 Total Assets: £42,801
Registered Office: First Floor, 677 High Road, North Finchley, London, N12 0DA
Major Shareholder: Paschalis Polyzos
Officers: Paschalis Polyzos [1968] Director [Greek]

Amsterdam Taste Ltd
Incorporated: 12 April 2018
Registered Office: Dutch Taste, 37 Gibbins Road, Selly Oak, Birmingham, B29 6PQ
Officers: Hassan Chikhi [1986] Director [Dutch]

Ana Express Ltd
Incorporated: 25 August 2018
Registered Office: 89 Tooting High Street, London, SW17 0SP
Major Shareholder: Elena Crecan
Officers: Elena Crecan [1968] Director [Romanian]

Anadolu Catering Limited
Incorporated: 16 February 2012 Employees: 8
Net Worth: £5,473 Total Assets: £61,984
Registered Office: First Floor South, 332-336 Holloway Road, London, N7 6NJ
Major Shareholder: Tahsin Karatay
Officers: Pinar Karatay, Secretary; Tahsin Karatay [1980] Director/Caterer

Anatolian Foods Ltd
Incorporated: 18 May 2006 Employees: 37
Net Worth: £1,250,045 Total Assets: £5,123,108
Registered Office: 1 Kings Avenue, Winchmore Hill, London, N21 3NA
Shareholders: Yildiray Donmez; Murat Gec
Officers: Murat Gec, Secretary; Yildiray Donmez [1974] Managing Director [Turkish]; Murat Gec [1975] Director

Anatolian Limited
Incorporated: 8 December 2015 Employees: 2
Net Worth Deficit: £1,355 Total Assets: £36,317
Registered Office: 22 Eastbury Road, Beckton, London, E6 6LP
Shareholders: Murat Gec; Yildiray Donmez
Officers: Murat Gec, Secretary; Yildiray Donmez [1974] Director [Turkish]; Murat Gec [1975] Director

Anderson Beverages Ltd
Incorporated: 17 October 2017
Registered Office: 38 Sloan Street, Edinburgh, EH6 8PH
Shareholders: Caitlin Sian Anderson; Chloe Dawn Anderson
Officers: Caitlin Sian Anderson [1990] Director/Sales; Chloe Dawn Anderson [1998] Director/Administration

Angel Global Export Ltd
Incorporated: 16 March 2018
Registered Office: 71-75 Shelton Street, Covent Garden, London, WC2H 9JQ
Major Shareholder: Bernadette Mahinc
Officers: Bernadette Mahinc [1959] Director/Contractor [French]

Anya Global Limited
Incorporated: 15 November 2016
Registered Office: 3rd Floor, 207 Regent Street, London, W1B 3HH
Major Shareholder: Yashpal Singh Yadav
Officers: Dr Arun Kumar Chauhan [1971] Director/Doctor; Yashpal Singh Yadav [1984] Director [Indian]

Anytime Drinks Limited
Incorporated: 4 September 2017
Registered Office: 12 Tadmor Street, London, W12 8AH
Shareholders: Edward John Henry Dallas; Charles Murray Crawley; Felix Ferdinand von Hurter
Officers: Charles Murray Crawley [1987] Director; Edward John Henry Dallas [1984] Director; Felix Ferdinand Von Hurter [1986] Director

Apex Sourcing International Ltd
Incorporated: 7 September 2018
Registered Office: 97 Unett Street, Smethwick, W Midlands, B66 3TA
Major Shareholder: Kulwant Sohal
Officers: Kulwant Sohal [1981] Director

Apna Distribution Ltd
Incorporated: 13 September 2017
Registered Office: Kemp House, 160 City Road, London, EC1V 2NX
Major Shareholder: Mohammed Nabil Nazir

Apollo Distribution Limited
Incorporated: 9 November 2018
Registered Office: Spiersbridge Business Park, 1 Spiersbridge Way, Glasgow, G46 8NG
Shareholders: Amer Shah; Saeed Mohammed
Officers: Saeed Mohammed [1965] Director; Amer Shah [1966] Director

Apollo Fruit & Veg UK Ltd
Incorporated: 12 March 2018
Registered Office: 14 Sutherland Close, High Barnet, Herts, EN5 2JL
Major Shareholder: Sakthivel Karuppiah
Officers: Sakthivel Karuppiah [1973] Director

AQ Branding Ltd
Incorporated: 26 September 2011
Net Worth Deficit: £15,263 *Total Assets:* £12,357
Registered Office: 41 Bridgeman Terrace, Wigan, Lancs, WN1 1TT
Shareholders: Ruth Elizabeth Brookes; Nicholas Anthony Brookes
Officers: Nicholas Anthony Brookes [1965] Director; Ruth Elizabeth Brookes [1965] Director

Aqua Carpatica UK Ltd
Incorporated: 25 July 2018
Registered Office: Unit 4, 303 Holloway Road, London, N7 8HS
Major Shareholder: Jean Valvis
Officers: Jean Valvis [1954] President and General Director [Swiss]

Aqua Distribution Limited
Incorporated: 2 May 2000
Net Worth Deficit: £15,912 *Total Assets:* £5,155
Registered Office: 27 Gonville Crescent, Northolt, Middlesex, UB5 4SH
Major Shareholder: Talal Abdul Rahim Alaywan
Officers: Talal Abdul Rahim Alaywan [1966] Director/Sales

Aquabella London Ltd
Incorporated: 18 May 2009
Net Worth Deficit: £152,501 *Total Assets:* £22,327
Registered Office: 13 Abbey Mews, Isleworth, Middlesex, TW7 5BJ
Major Shareholder: Anabella de Barros
Officers: Anabella de Barros [1969] Director/Manager [Portuguese]; David Wilson Barros Mendes Da Silva [1987] Director [Portuguese]; Edson Luis Barros Mendes Da Silva [1987] Director [Portuguese]

Aquacoll UK Ltd
Incorporated: 24 April 2018
Registered Office: 71-75 Shelton Street, London, WC2H 9JQ
Major Shareholder: Janos Varga
Officers: Janos Varga [1984] Director/Software Engineer [Hungarian]

Aquaid Franchising Limited
Incorporated: 5 February 1998 *Employees:* 90
Net Worth: £1,824,387 *Total Assets:* £6,481,258
Registered Office: 10 Kings Court, Willie Snaith Road, Newmarket, Suffolk, CB8 7SG
Major Shareholder: Paul Melville Searle
Officers: Uffe Fodgaard Hansen, Secretary; David Paul Fremel [1961] Director; Aidan Anthony Geraghty [1961] Finance Director; Uffe Fodgaard Hansen [1978] Joint Managing Director [Danish]; Michael O'Donoghue [1970] Operations Director; Kirsten Ronsholt Searle [1967] Director [Danish]; Paul Melville Searle [1959] Joint Managing Director

Aquamarine Limited
Incorporated: 22 May 2015
Registered Office: 1 New Mossford Way, Barkingside, Ilford, Essex, IG6 1FB
Major Shareholder: Kirubanandam Swayamprakasam
Officers: Paramagurusamy Mohanaraj [1974] Director; Kirubanandam Swayamprakasam [1977] Director

Aquavita II UK Limited
Incorporated: 4 June 2014
Net Worth: £312,673 *Total Assets:* £1,062,055
Registered Office: Acre House, 11-15 William Road, London, NW1 3ER
Officers: Jane Nakalanzi Kaggwa [1974] Director [American]

Arab World Ltd
Incorporated: 7 February 2013
Registered Office: c/o Osama Abdel Rahman, 2b Gowlett Road, London, SE15 4HY
Major Shareholder: Osama Abdel Rahman
Officers: Osama Abdel Rahman [1969] Director

Ariana International Ltd
Incorporated: 1 June 2018
Registered Office: 3-3a Ascot Parade, Clapham Park Road, London, SW4 7EY
Shareholders: Shazia Rasul; Amrit Gogar; Haji Ghulam Nabi Dost
Officers: Amrit Gogar [1962] Director [Afghan]; Shazia Rasul [1979] Director

Arollo Trade Ltd
Incorporated: 3 December 2018
Registered Office: 27 Old Gloucester Street, London, WC1N 3AX
Officers: George Henderson [1994] Director/Partner; Thomas Lever [1988] Director

Aroma Soft Drinks & Water Limited
Incorporated: 3 February 2011
Registered Office: 12a North Edward Street, Londonderry, BT48 7EW
Officers: Kazim Demirarslan [1953] Director [Irish]

Arsi Soft Drinks Limited
Incorporated: 3 October 2015
Net Worth Deficit: £4,040 *Total Assets:* £192,835
Registered Office: Unit 19 Pop In Commercial Centre, South Way, Wembley, Middlesex, HA9 0HF
Major Shareholder: Sitwat Jahan
Officers: Arshad Ali [1981] Director/Businessman [Pakistani]; Sitwat Jahan [1979] Director [Pakistani]

Artathlon Beverages Limited
Incorporated: 29 June 2018
Registered Office: 22 Naylor House, 10 John Fearon Walk, London, W10 4NX
Major Shareholder: Panayiotis Neufelt
Officers: Panayiotis Neufelt [1967] Director [Greek]

Artathlon Water Limited
Incorporated: 29 June 2018
Registered Office: 22 Naylor House, 10 John Fearon Walk, London, W10 4NX
Major Shareholder: Panayiotis Neufelt
Officers: Panayiotis Neufelt [1967] Director [Greek]

Artesian Springs Limited
Incorporated: 6 October 2014
Registered Office: Morello Quater, 669 Cherrydown East, Basildon, Essex, SS16 5GS
Major Shareholder: Arpad Nemeth
Officers: Ildiko Szentesi, Secretary; Arpad Nemeth [1977] Director [Hungarian]

Arthur's Juice Company Limited
Incorporated: 19 October 2018
Registered Office: 49 South Molton Street, London, W1K 5LH
Major Shareholder: Max Hastings
Officers: Max Hastings [1974] Director

Artis Trade Ltd
Incorporated: 5 November 2018
Registered Office: Kemp House, 160 City Road, London, EC1V 2NX
Major Shareholder: Thomas Oliver Ellwood Lever
Officers: Andrew Phillip Holt, Secretary; Thomas Oliver Ellwood Lever [1988] Director

Artisan Drinks Company Limited
Incorporated: 9 March 2017 Employees: 2
Net Worth: £345,506 Total Assets: £384,193
Registered Office: 22-26 King Street, King's Lynn, Norfolk, PE30 1HJ
Major Shareholder: Steven William Cooper
Officers: Michael John Andrews [1969] Director; Steven William Cooper [1970] Director; Mark Davidson [1960] Director [South African]; Alan Walsh [1982] Director

Artos Foods Limited
Incorporated: 18 February 2014 Employees: 2
Net Worth: £76,805 Total Assets: £98,719
Registered Office: 239-241 Kennington Lane, London, SE11 5QU
Parent: Masca Holding Limited
Officers: Cetin Agcagul [1985] Director; Suleyman Cagin [1966] Director

Asi Wholesale & Retail Ltd
Incorporated: 13 March 2018
Registered Office: 256 Oldchester Road, Birkenhead, Merseyside, CH42 3TF
Major Shareholder: Antony Sayanthan Inpanathan
Officers: Antony Sayanthan Inpanathan [1989] Director/Sales Manager [French]

Asia Direct Limited
Incorporated: 22 August 1996
Net Worth: £2 Total Assets: £2
Registered Office: 3 Marfleet Close, Lower Earley, Reading, Berks, RG6 3XL
Officers: Kerminder Kaur Ahluwalia, Secretary; Prabhsharan Singh Ahluwalia [1959] Director/Insurance Consultant

Aspire Brands Int Ltd.
Incorporated: 25 June 2014 Employees: 4
Net Worth Deficit: £117,806 Total Assets: £224,086
Registered Office: 60 Windsor Avenue, London, SW19 2RR
Shareholders: Darren Keith Linnell; Neil David Blewitt
Officers: Neil Blewitt [1986] Director; Darren Keith Linnell [1984] Director

Aspire Drinks Limited
Incorporated: 22 October 2013
Net Worth: £24,525 Total Assets: £24,525
Registered Office: 60 Windsor Avenue, London, SW19 2RR
Officers: Neil David Blewitt [1986] Director; Darren Keith Linnell [1984] Director

Assala Limited
Incorporated: 16 July 2018
Registered Office: 76 The Avenue, Bournemouth, BH9 2US
Officers: Sid Ahmed Khirani [1981] Director

Asta Barista Baby Ltd
Incorporated: 14 June 2018
Registered Office: Green Hay, The Green, Churchdown, Glos, GL3 2LF
Officers: Daphne Brett [1971] Director/Change Manager; Jason Mortimer [1970] Director/Security Consultant

Aster Service Ltd
Incorporated: 18 December 2018
Registered Office: 106 New Chester Road, Wirral, Merseyside, CH62 5AG
Major Shareholder: Anthony Alfred John Leonard
Officers: Anthony Alfred John Leonard [1986] Director/Sales Assistant [Sri Lankan]

Astra Import Ltd.
Incorporated: 6 October 2016
Registered Office: 3 Brookside Avenue, Ashford, Surrey, TW15 3NH
Officers: Nicolae Buza [1991] Director/Entrepreneur [Romanian]

Astral Nutrition Limited
Incorporated: 9 June 2014
Net Worth Deficit: £18,725 Total Assets: £53,383
Registered Office: 8 Picktree Terrace, Chester-le-Street, Co Durham, DH3 3ST
Major Shareholder: Gary Jonathan Ward
Officers: Gary Jonathan Ward [1989] Director

Atlantis Spring Water Limited
Incorporated: 1 August 2016
Net Worth Deficit: £5,672 Total Assets: £1,678
Registered Office: Unit 304, 110 Pennington Street, London, E1W 2BB
Officers: Abdul Basith Chowdhury, Secretary; Shumon Ali [1987] Director

Atlas Halal Ltd
Incorporated: 27 July 2012
Net Worth Deficit: £3,937 Total Assets: £9,548
Registered Office: Ground Floor, 203 The Vale, London, W3 7QS
Major Shareholder: Arjun Patel
Officers: Arjun Patel [1985] Director [Indian]

ATR Catering Supplies Limited
Incorporated: 28 October 1998
Net Worth: £379,023 Total Assets: £1,335,397
Registered Office: Pride Buildings, Hall Lane, Bradford, W Yorks, BD4 7AB
Major Shareholder: Mohammed Rafiq
Officers: Mohamed Shaffiq, Secretary; Mohammed Rafiq [1965] Director; Mohammed Shaffiq [1967] Director

Attila Martocsan Ltd
Incorporated: 24 October 2017
Registered Office: 50 Saltersgate, Peterborough, Cambs, PE1 4YA
Major Shareholder: Attila Martocsan
Officers: Attila Martocsan [1957] Director [Hungarian]

Aur'a Natural Gold Water Ltd
Incorporated: 1 October 2018
Registered Office: Raven House, 291 Watling Street, Dartford, Kent, DA2 6EP
Major Shareholder: Claudiu Dobrik
Officers: Claudiu Dobrik [1976] Director [Romanian]

Aura Gold Water Ltd
Incorporated: 17 September 2016
Net Worth Deficit: £4,757 *Total Assets:* £2,424
Registered Office: 29 Woodfield Avenue, London, NW9 6PR
Major Shareholder: Corneliu Alin Carcu
Officers: Corneliu Alin Carcu [1983] Director [Romanian]

Avic Trading Limited
Incorporated: 26 June 2017
Net Worth: £32,847 *Total Assets:* £69,425
Registered Office: Unit 37 Phoenix Industrial Estate, Cheetham Street, Failsworth, Manchester, M35 9DS
Major Shareholder: Cristian Perez Lopez
Officers: Cristian Perez Lopez [1991] Director/Manager [Spanish]

Avigail Dairies Limited
Incorporated: 24 January 2019
Registered Office: 31 Ambrose Street, Manchester, M12 5DD
Major Shareholder: Mian Salahuddin Anjum
Officers: Mian Salahuddin Anjum, Secretary; Mian Salahuddin Anjum [1964] Director; Mohammad Jameel [1973] Director/Manager [Pakistani]

Avigail Limited
Incorporated: 16 January 2018
Registered Office: 31 Ambrose Street, Manchester, M12 5DD
Major Shareholder: Mian Salahuddin Anjum
Officers: Mian Salahuddin Anjum, Secretary; Mian Salahuddin Anjum [1964] Director; Mohammad Jameel [1973] Director/Manager [Pakistani]

AVM UK Private Limited
Incorporated: 22 July 2016
Registered Office: 439 High Street North, London, E12 6TJ
Major Shareholder: Marian Bogdan
Officers: Marian Bogdan, Secretary; Marian Bogdan [1981] Director [Romanian]

AWA Nature Ltd
Incorporated: 26 November 2018
Registered Office: 39 Park West, Kendal Street, London, W2 2QG
Major Shareholder: Houssein Awada
Officers: Houssein Awada, Secretary; Houssein Awada [1975] Director

AWA Water Ltd
Incorporated: 30 October 2018
Registered Office: 12 Killyman Road, Dungannon, Co Tyrone, BT71 6DH
Major Shareholder: Maciej Smuczynski
Officers: Maciej Smuczynski [1983] Director [Polish]

Ayr Brewing Company Limited
Incorporated: 28 May 2009
Net Worth: £32,922 *Total Assets:* £105,871
Registered Office: 17 Scaur O'Doon Road, Ayr, KA7 4EP
Shareholders: Paul Rossi; Anthony Valenti
Officers: Anthony Valenti, Secretary; Paul Rossi [1954] Director/Hotelier; Anthony Valenti [1961] Director/Restaurateur

AZ Health Food Center Ltd
Incorporated: 21 September 2018
Registered Office: 192 Woodseer Street, London, E1 5HQ
Major Shareholder: Anh Dao Carrick
Officers: Anh Dao Carrick [1981] Director/Accountant

Azka Impex (London) Limited
Incorporated: 8 June 2016
Net Worth: £20,524 *Total Assets:* £254,508
Registered Office: Unit 10 Lyon Business Park, River Road, Barking, Essex, IG11 0JS
Shareholder: Lutfur Rahman Belal
Officers: Lutfur Rahman Belal [1969] Director; Mohammad Kaykous Molla [1967] Director [Austrian]

Azka Impex Limited
Incorporated: 15 April 2010 *Employees:* 16
Net Worth: £13,494 *Total Assets:* £350,193
Registered Office: 94 Soho Hill, Hockley, Birmingham, B19 1AD
Shareholder: Lutfur Rahman Belal
Officers: Lutfur Rahman Belal [1969] Director/Wholesaler; Syeda Amrana Hasin [1976] Director/Wholesaler

B4Sport Ltd.
Incorporated: 5 June 2017
Net Worth Deficit: £206 *Total Assets:* £4,059
Registered Office: Suite 3, Scion House, Stirling University, Innovation Park, Stirling, FK9 4NF
Major Shareholder: Mohsin Laginaf
Officers: Mohsin Laginaf [1988] Director

Babylon Foods Limited
Incorporated: 5 March 2003
Net Worth: £2,888 *Total Assets:* £29,732
Registered Office: 396 Edgware Road, London, W2 1ED
Major Shareholder: Mohammed Ali Mahmoud
Officers: Sabah Abdulasool Abdulmahdi, Secretary; Mohammed Ali Mahmoud [1959] Director

Bakhta Moroccan Mint Iced Tea Limited
Incorporated: 8 February 2018
Registered Office: 433 Clarence Lane, London, SW15 5QD
Officers: El Houssain Sghir [1972] Director/Plumber [Moroccan]

Baldwin's Sarsaparilla Limited
Incorporated: 13 October 2004
Net Worth: £31,191 *Total Assets:* £62,974
Registered Office: 171-173 Walworth Road, London, SE17 1RW
Major Shareholder: Stephen Howard Dagnell
Officers: Tracey Caroline Robertson, Secretary; Stephen Howard Dagnell [1954] Director/Health Food Retailer

Bambu Drinks Limited
Incorporated: 4 September 2018
Registered Office: 71-75 Shelton Street, London, WC2H 9JQ
Major Shareholder: Parmjit Mattu
Officers: Parmjit Mattu [1965] Director

Bare Drinks Limited
Incorporated: 24 December 2018
Registered Office: 1 The Old Forge, South Road, Weybridge, Surrey, KT13 9DZ
Shareholders: Adam Roy Melrose; Samuel James Wright
Officers: Adam Roy Melrose [1981] Director; Samuel James Wright [1985] Director

Bargain Food and Wine Ltd
Incorporated: 24 May 2018
Registered Office: 89 Brackens Lane, Alvaston, Derby, DE24 0AN
Officers: Shameem Raja [1975] Director

Basecamp Brews Ltd
Incorporated: 5 May 2015 *Employees:* 14
Previous: Team Tenzing Ltd
Net Worth Deficit: £540,109 *Total Assets:* £776,098
Registered Office: Second Floor, Windsor House, 40-41 Great Castle Street, London, W1W 8LU
Major Shareholder: Huib Van Bockel
Officers: Rob Rijnders [1968] Director/Chief International Business Officer [Dutch]; Huib Van Bockel [1973] Director/Marketing [Dutch]; Petrus Wilhelmus Van Groeningen [1983] Director/Head of Sales [Dutch]

Basil World Ltd
Incorporated: 18 January 2019
Registered Office: 46 Alphonsus Street, Middlesbrough, Cleveland, TS3 6EA
Major Shareholder: Inpanathan Inparaji
Officers: Inpanathan Inparaji [1983] Director/Sales Manager [French]

Bassen Ltd
Incorporated: 25 July 2018
Registered Office: 75 Gainsborough Green, Abingdon, Oxon, OX14 5JL
Shareholders: Gkor Tovmasian; Hayk Tovmasyan
Officers: Gkor Tovmasian [1991] Director/Self Employed [Greek]

Bazaar Store Ltd
Incorporated: 28 August 2018
Registered Office: Unit 7A-7B, Parkway Drive, Sheffield, S9 4WN
Major Shareholder: Gunel Zaidova
Officers: Cihan Cocelli, Secretary; Gunel Zaidova [1986] Managing Director

Becsco Limited
Incorporated: 28 October 1999
Net Worth: £1,590,801 *Total Assets:* £3,707,634
Registered Office: Unit 2-5 Carlton Industrial Estate, Albion Road, Carlton, Barnsley, S Yorks, S71 3HW
Major Shareholder: Scott Padgett
Officers: Cassandra Lianne Padgett, Secretary; Scott Padgett, Secretary; Cassandra Lianne Padgett [1981] Director/Administrator; Scott Padgett [1971] Director/Technical Representative

Bedford Halal Meat & Grocceries Ltd
Incorporated: 12 December 2016
Net Worth Deficit: £29,792 *Total Assets:* £141,804
Registered Office: 30 London Road, Bedford, MK42 0NS
Major Shareholder: Ashar Noman
Officers: Ashar Noman, Secretary; Shaukat Mehmood [1984] Director; Ashar Noman [1984] Director [Pakistani]

Bedrock Trade Ltd
Incorporated: 19 March 2018
Registered Office: 71-75 Shelton Street, Covent Garden, London, WC2H 9JQ
Major Shareholder: Andrea Faure Rolland
Officers: Andrea Faure Rolland, Secretary; Andrea Faure Rolland [1977] Director [Italian]

Beeston General Store & Off Licences Ltd
Incorporated: 31 January 2019
Registered Office: 42 Chiwell Road, Beeston, Nottingham, NG9 1EJ
Major Shareholder: Thurairajan Vajigaran
Officers: Thurairajan Vajigaran [1976] Director/Sales Assistant

Belgard Trading Ltd
Incorporated: 8 April 2016
Registered Office: 3 Bream Close, Wolverhampton, W Midlands, WV10 0TJ
Officers: Gurchetan Singh Kooner [1971] Director/Self Employed

Bella Refreshments Ltd.
Incorporated: 31 March 2014
Net Worth Deficit: £39,138 *Total Assets:* £410,796
Registered Office: Units 2-5 Albion Road, Carlton Industrial Estate, Carlton, Barnsley, S Yorks, S71 3HW
Shareholders: David Jonathan Lockwood; Scott Padgett
Officers: David Jonathan Lockwood [1973] Director/Self Employed; Chris Marshall [1977] Director; Scott Padgett [1971] Director/Self Employed

Bellwether Impex (UK) Limited
Incorporated: 19 July 2016
Registered Office: 21 Goldcraft Close, Heywood, Lancs, OL10 2QW
Major Shareholder: Moses Adedoyin Adegbite
Officers: Moses Adedoyin Adegbite [1975] Director/Business Person [Ghanaian]

Bennu Rising Ltd.
Incorporated: 31 January 2019
Registered Office: Fort Dunlop, Fort Parkway, Birmingham, B24 9FE
Shareholders: Joseph Burris; Mizani Bennu
Officers: Joseph Burris [1988] Director/Entrepreneur

Benson International Ltd
Incorporated: 13 April 2015
Registered Office: 41 Runnymede Road, Birmingham, B11 3BN
Major Shareholder: Muhammad Akmal
Officers: Muhammad Akmal [1973] Director

The Berry Juice Company Limited
Incorporated: 20 March 2002 *Employees:* 5
Net Worth: £958,229 *Total Assets:* £2,223,799
Registered Office: 1a St Mary Abbots Place, High Street Kensington, London, W8 6LS
Officers: Mohamed Iqbal Asaria, Secretary; Khaled El-Yafi [1979] Director/Manager of The Berry Company; Ghias Elyafi [1949] Director/Businessman; Zayd Zahid [1981] Director/Investment Manager [Saudi Arabian]

Paul Berry Limited
Incorporated: 6 July 2003 *Employees:* 1
Net Worth: £5,533 *Total Assets:* £13,563
Registered Office: 42 Mays Avenue, Carlton, Nottingham, NG4 1AU
Major Shareholder: Paul Andrew Berry
Officers: Karen Eveline Berry, Secretary; Paul Andrew Berry [1962] Director/Dairy Retail

Bespoke Contracts (UK) Ltd
Incorporated: 11 March 2014
Registered Office: GPG House, Walker Avenue, Wolverton Mill, Milton Keynes, Bucks, MK12 5TW
Major Shareholder: Guiseppe John Oliva
Officers: Guiseppe John Oliva [1977] Director

Best Brand Food & Drinks (BBFD) Limited
Incorporated: 28 September 2016
Registered Office: 13 Wendover Road, Scunthorpe, N Lincs, DN17 3SN
Major Shareholder: Omer Salem
Officers: Omer Babakar Salem [1967] Director

Best Trading One Limited
Incorporated: 12 December 2017
Registered Office: 1st Floor, Roxburghe House, 273-287 Regent Street, London, W1B 2HA
Major Shareholder: Mahesh Devshi Dhanji
Officers: Mahesh Devshi Dhanji [1983] Director

Better Tasting Drinks Co. Limited
Incorporated: 22 July 2015 *Employees:* 6
Net Worth: £245,089 *Total Assets:* £318,715
Registered Office: Timsons Business Centre, Bath Road, Kettering, Northants, NN16 8NQ
Officers: Mary Louise Avery [1979] Director/Brewer & Business Owner; William Bruce Kendall [1961] Director; Mark Richard Palmer [1973] Director

Bevanda Solutions Limited
Incorporated: 22 October 2015 *Employees:* 3
Net Worth: £70,088 *Total Assets:* £129,557
Registered Office: 27 Saltmeadows, Nantwich, Cheshire, CW5 5HF
Shareholders: Gregory Keith Holtham; Margaret Elizabeth Holtham
Officers: Gregory Keith Holtham [1959] Director/Sales and Marketing; Margaret Elizabeth Holtham [1958] Director/Sales and Marketing

Beverage Brothers Limited
Incorporated: 6 December 2016
Registered Office: 4 Kingswood Court, Long Meadow, South Brent, Devon, TQ10 9YS
Major Shareholder: Philip Clark
Officers: Philip Clark [1959] Director

The Beverages Group Limited
Incorporated: 15 June 2018
Registered Office: Monway Buildings, Portway Road, Wednesbury, W Midlands, WS10 7EQ
Officers: Wojciech Marek Nowak [1981] Director [Polish]

Beverages Stars Ltd
Incorporated: 30 June 2017
Registered Office: Unit 4 Tat Bank Road, Oldbury, W Midlands, B69 4NB
Officers: Mustakim Azharbhai Saiyed [1990] Director/Wholesaler [Indian]

Bevtec Services Limited
Incorporated: 4 November 2011 *Employees:* 10
Net Worth: £229,819 *Total Assets:* £353,585
Registered Office: Unit 6 Graylands Estate, Langhurstwood Road, Horsham, W Sussex, RH12 4QD
Shareholders: Paul Lindfield; Naomi Nichollette Lindfield
Officers: Naomi Lindfield, Secretary; Naomi Nichollette Lindfield [1968] Director/Soft Drinks Wholesale; Paul Lindfield [1965] Director/Soft Drinks Wholesale; Roger Smalley [1960] Director/Business Development

BG Drinks Ltd
Incorporated: 26 January 2005
Net Worth: £3,035 *Total Assets:* £9,903
Registered Office: 34 Skreen Road, Omagh, Co Tyrone, BT78 1SR
Shareholders: Patrick Gracey; Cecil Brown
Officers: Patrick Gracey, Secretary; Cecil Brown [1946] Director/Salesman; Patrick Gracey [1968] Director/Sales Manager

Bi Fa Limited
Incorporated: 28 August 2018
Registered Office: 3-5 Wood Street, Huddersfield, W Yorks, HD1 1BT
Major Shareholder: Yi Zhang
Officers: Yi Zhang [1960] Director

Bia Trade Ltd
Incorporated: 22 November 2018
Registered Office: 123 Jeremys Green, London, N18 2ND
Major Shareholder: Bojidar Jichev
Officers: Bojidar Jichev [1969] Director [Bulgarian]

Bibere Ltd.
Incorporated: 20 December 2012
Net Worth Deficit: £57,922 *Total Assets:* £24,552
Registered Office: First Floor, Universal House, Unit 10, 88-94 Wentworth Street, London, E1 7SA
Major Shareholder: Andrea Amici
Officers: Andrea Amici [1968] Director

Big Brand Distributors UK Limited
Incorporated: 3 April 2017
Registered Office: 78 Katherine Road, London, E6 1EN
Officers: Nazar Hussain [1989] Director [Pakistani]

Big Horn UK Ltd
Incorporated: 10 May 2017
Net Worth Deficit: £20,895 *Total Assets:* £17,702
Registered Office: 40 Heyworth Road, London, E15 1ST
Major Shareholder: Lyubomir Enchev
Officers: Lyubomir Enchev [1971] Director/Manager [Bulgarian]; Gergana Encheva [1976] Director/General Manager

Big Star Trader Ltd
Incorporated: 25 January 2019
Registered Office: Flat 14, Chartwell Court, Woodford Green, Essex, IG8 9HF
Major Shareholder: Abdul Rauf Mughal
Officers: Abdul Rauf Mughal [1974] Director

Bill Bean Limited
Incorporated: 27 February 1998 *Employees:* 16
Net Worth: £20,758 *Total Assets:* £290,807
Registered Office: Acre House, 11-15 William Road, London, NW1 3ER
Shareholders: Dennis John Warrington; Sally Ann Warrington
Officers: Sally Ann Warrington, Secretary/Administration & Financial Director; Dennis John Warrington [1960] Managing Director; Sally Ann Warrington [1961] Administration & Financial Director

Bio Icecream Ltd
Incorporated: 10 May 2018
Registered Office: 94 Yelvertoft Road, Northampton, NN2 7TG
Major Shareholder: Constantin Pandele
Officers: Constantin Pandele [1952] Director/Long Distance Lorry Driver [Romanian]

UK Wholesalers of Soft Drinks

Bioactive Live Ltd
Incorporated: 18 April 2018
Registered Office: 85 Great Portland Street, London, W1W 7LT
Officers: Lajos Balog [1994] Director [Hungarian]

Biofresh Cosmos Ltd
Incorporated: 21 October 2016
Net Worth Deficit: £9,859 *Total Assets:* £111
Registered Office: 258 Merton Road, London, SW18 5JL
Major Shareholder: Muhammad Saad Khan
Officers: Muhammad Saad Khan [1984] Director/Certified Chartered Accountant; Christos Papadimitrakopoulos [1970] Director [Greek]

Birch Boost Ltd
Incorporated: 8 January 2018
Registered Office: 1st Floor, Packwood House, Guild Street, Stratford upon Avon, Warwicks, CV37 6RP
Major Shareholder: Patrick Birch
Officers: Dr Patrick Birch [1990] Director/Founder

Birch Sales Ltd
Incorporated: 22 February 2019
Registered Office: 58 Muirhead Avenue East, Liverpool, L11 1EL
Major Shareholder: Ponneswaran Ponnuthurai
Officers: Ponneswaran Ponnuthurai [1970] Director/Sales Assistant [Norwegian]

Blackbird Trader Ltd
Incorporated: 25 January 2019
Registered Office: Flat 14, Chartwell Court, Woodford Green, Essex, IG8 9HF
Major Shareholder: Abdul Rauf Mughal
Officers: Abdul Rauf Mughal [1974] Director

Bloomsbury Drinks Ltd
Incorporated: 26 March 2013
Net Worth: £171,569 *Total Assets:* £391,988
Registered Office: Basement of Tavistock Hotel, Bedford Way, London, WC1H 9EU
Officers: Jonathan Charles Dalton [1973] Director [Australian]; Mark Corin Walton [1973] Director

Blue Trading International Limited
Incorporated: 10 January 2018
Registered Office: 91 Nether Hall Road, Doncaster, S Yorks, DN1 2QA
Major Shareholder: Erkan Eren
Officers: Erkan Eren [1965] Director/Manager

Bluetech Marketing Ltd
Incorporated: 22 October 2018
Registered Office: 20-22 Wenlock Road, London, N1 7GU
Major Shareholder: Igor Krisztian Tokarev
Officers: Igor Krisztian Tokarev [1996] Director [Hungarian]

Bogazici Ltd
Incorporated: 6 November 2018
Registered Office: 14 Clarance Lodge, Taverners Way, Hoddesdon, Herts, EN11 8TH
Major Shareholder: Metin Kuzu
Officers: Metin Kuzu [1979] Finance Director [Turkish]

Boisson Limited
Incorporated: 19 October 2017
Registered Office: 653 London Road, Wilmorton, Derby, DE24 8UQ
Major Shareholder: Hardeep Singh Matto
Officers: Hardeep Singh Matto [1976] Director/Business Manager

Bongo Sale Ltd
Incorporated: 20 February 2019
Registered Office: 106 New Chester Road, Wirral, Merseyside, CH62 5AG
Major Shareholder: Rameskumar Sivapatham
Officers: Rameskumar Sivapatham [1975] Director/Sales Assistant [Norwegian]

Boomshakes Ltd
Incorporated: 23 May 2018
Registered Office: 20 Kirkburn Close, Liverpool, L8 9YA
Major Shareholder: Kieron Keith
Officers: Kieron Keith [1996] Director

Bor-Tom Ltd
Incorporated: 27 March 2012
Net Worth Deficit: £10,377 *Total Assets:* £4,949
Registered Office: 5 Juno Close, Hinckley, Leics, LE10 0WH
Major Shareholder: Tomasz Bortacki
Officers: Tomasz Bortacki [1981] Director [Polish]

Bornova Import Export Limited
Incorporated: 17 September 2018
Registered Office: c/o 21 Icentre Howard Way, Interchange Park, Newport Pagnell, Milton Keynes, Bucks, MK16 9PY
Major Shareholder: Mustafa Kochan
Officers: Mustafa Kochan [1969] Managing Director [Turkish]

Bossco Headland Ltd
Incorporated: 10 December 2018
Registered Office: 1 Wilson Street, Hartlepool, Cleveland, TS26 8JX
Major Shareholder: Suvaissan Savarimuthu
Officers: Suvaissan Savarimuthu [1982] Director/Manager [Sri Lankan]; Sinthupiriya Suvaissan [1993] Director/Self Employed [Sri Lankan]

Bot Trading Company Ltd
Incorporated: 4 January 2018
Registered Office: Linden House, Linden Close, Tunbridge Wells, Kent, TN4 8HH
Parent: Trifin Partners Ltd
Officers: Andrew Marcus Fox [1963] Director

Botanic Lab Ltd
Incorporated: 2 January 2014 *Employees:* 8
Net Worth Deficit: £127,616 *Total Assets:* £585,891
Registered Office: 28 Alexandra Terrace, Exmouth, Devon, EX8 1BD
Shareholder: Rebekah Marie Hall
Officers: Simon Peter Bamber [1964] Director; Rebekah Marie Hall [1981] Director

Boukashka Ltd
Incorporated: 22 January 2019
Registered Office: Kemp House, 160 City Road, London, EC1V 2NX
Officers: Alexis Le Morellec [1980] Director/Manager [French]

Said Boukhebelt Ltd
Incorporated: 15 October 2018
Registered Office: 6 Sheridan Court, 99 Coombe Road, Croydon, Surrey, CR0 5SP
Major Shareholder: Said Boukhebelt
Officers: Said Boukhebelt [1966] Director [French]

Brand Distributors Limited
Incorporated: 14 July 2014 *Employees:* 3
Net Worth Deficit: £44,692 *Total Assets:* £205,743
Registered Office: 3 Pentland Close, Edmonton, London, N9 0XN
Major Shareholder: Nakash Ghani
Officers: Nakash Ghani [1990] Director

Brandin Marketing Limited
Incorporated: 19 February 2016
Net Worth: £1,299 *Total Assets:* £3,901
Registered Office: 337 Athlon Road, Wembley, Middlesex, HA0 1EF
Major Shareholder: Bimalkumar Shah
Officers: Bhavesa Popatlal Shah [1971] Director [Indian]; Bimalkumar Shah [1962] Director

Brands Nexus Ltd
Incorporated: 16 January 2019
Registered Office: 11a Upper Mulgrave Road, Cheam, Sutton, Surrey, SM2 7AY
Major Shareholder: Tahir Mehmood Younes
Officers: Tahir Mehmood Younes [1972] Director/Design Consultant

Bravocservices Ltd
Incorporated: 13 November 2018
Registered Office: 7 Walters Drive, Oldham, Lancs, OL8 2LX
Officers: Cary Grant [1972] Director/Electrical Engineer

Brewed 4 U Ltd
Incorporated: 7 May 2008
Net Worth Deficit: £85,624 *Total Assets:* £86,478
Registered Office: The Railway Hotel, Boston Place, Coventry, Warwicks, CV6 5NN
Officers: Ana Magdalena Sumra [1976] Director [Romanian]

Bri Trade Solutions Limited
Incorporated: 23 May 2017
Registered Office: Innovation Campus, Faraday Wharf, Holt Street, Birmingham Science Park, Birmingham, B7 4BB
Shareholder: Khalid Aziz
Officers: Khalid Aziz [1972] Managing Director

Bright Smoothies Ltd
Incorporated: 21 February 2019
Registered Office: 49 Westfield Road, Leeds, LS3 1DF
Major Shareholder: Lewis Dan Challinor
Officers: Lewis Dan Challinor [1994] Director/Student

Brighton Brew Co Ltd
Incorporated: 7 October 2015
Net Worth Deficit: £19,149 *Total Assets:* £1,025
Registered Office: 70 New Church Road, Hove, E Sussex, BN3 4FL
Major Shareholder: Max Danin
Officers: Max Danin [1991] Director

Brilliant Beverage Company Limited
Incorporated: 7 June 2018
Registered Office: 2 Lakeside Drive, Silica Lodge, Scunthorpe, N Lincs, DN17 2AG
Major Shareholder: Musthafa Thiruvoth Peedikayil Moidu
Officers: Musthafa Thiruvoth Peedikayil Moidu [1972] Director

Bristol Spirits Limited
Incorporated: 12 March 1993
Net Worth: £438,899 *Total Assets:* £503,908
Registered Office: Albion Dockside Building, Hanover Place, Bristol, BS1 6UT
Major Shareholder: John Andrew Barrett
Officers: Helen Susan Kent, Secretary; John Andrew Barrett [1948] Director/Wine and Spirit Merchant; Dorothy Anne Cameron [1946] Director/Accommodation Manager; Helen Susan Kent [1960] Director/Accountant

Britannia International Wholesalers Ltd
Incorporated: 24 December 2018
Registered Office: 71-75 Shelton Street, London, WC2H 9JQ
Major Shareholder: Mohit Pabbi
Officers: Mohit Pabbi [1987] Director

Britlines Limited
Incorporated: 11 October 2012
Net Worth: £1,025 *Total Assets:* £3,525
Registered Office: 158 Nestle Avenue, Hayes, Middlesex, UB3 4QF
Officers: Harminder Singh [1983] Director/Businessman [Indian]

Broadwater Supply and Distribution Ltd
Incorporated: 6 February 2017
Net Worth: £3,184 *Total Assets:* £3,184
Registered Office: 11 Du Cane Place, The Grove, Witham, Essex, CM8 2UQ
Major Shareholder: James Carl William Smith
Officers: Simon Anthony Slater [1972] Sales Director; James Carl William Smith [1980] Director

Browett & Fair Ltd
Incorporated: 7 November 2018
Registered Office: 2 Pickle Mews, London, SW9 0FJ
Shareholders: Nicholas William Fair; Ben David Hulton Browett
Officers: Ben David Hulton Browett [1992] Director/Wine Merchant; Nicholas William Fair [1993] Director/Accounts Manager

BS and Sons London Limited
Incorporated: 21 September 2017
Registered Office: 19 Brent Road, Southall, Middlesex, UB2 5JY
Major Shareholder: Narender Singh Chahal
Officers: Narender Singh Chahal [1976] Director/Businessman [Indian]; Mukesh Kumar [1983] Director/Businessman [Indian]

Bubra Drinks Ltd
Incorporated: 21 January 2019
Registered Office: 86 Clarson House, 3 Midnight Avenue, London, SE5 0AF
Major Shareholder: Dennis Paul Tuffour-Kensah
Officers: Dennis Paul Tuffour-Kensah [1976] Director/Operational Manager

Bucovina Cash & Carry Ltd
Incorporated: 24 August 2012
Net Worth: £25,472 *Total Assets:* £453,134
Registered Office: Unit B, Colindale Business Park, Carlisle Road, London, NW9 0HN
Major Shareholder: Costica Hrisca
Officers: Irina Calota, Secretary; Costica Hrisca [1984] Director [Romanian]; Gabriela Vasilache [1988] Commercial Director [Romanian]

UK Wholesalers of Soft Drinks   dellam

Budaquelle Beverages International Ltd
Incorporated: 18 August 2016
Registered Office: Unit 42 Price Street Business Centre, Price Street, Birkenhead, Merseyside, CH41 4JQ
Major Shareholder: Laszlo Ficsor
Officers: Laszlo Ficsor [1956] Director/Businessman [German]

Buddthi Ltd
Incorporated: 13 February 2019
Registered Office: 41 Redhall Drive, Hatfield, Herts, AL10 9EG
Major Shareholder: Buddhika de Alwis
Officers: Buddhika de Alwis, Secretary; Buddhika de Alwis [1985] Director [Sri Lankan]

Budget Logistics Ltd
Incorporated: 18 June 2014
Previous: London Spice Exotica Limited
Net Worth: £2,522 *Total Assets:* £45,434
Registered Office: 62 Vicarage Farm Road, Hounslow, Middlesex, TW5 0AB
Officers: Rosh Ladhar [1976] Director/Import and Accounts Clerk

BudgetForU Limited
Incorporated: 20 January 2014
Registered Office: 61a Walton Road, Liverpool, L4 4AF
Major Shareholder: Jeyakumar Rajaratnam
Officers: Jeyakumar Rajaratnam [1972] Sales Director [Norwegian]

Budgie Juices Ltd
Incorporated: 19 February 2019
Registered Office: 71-75 Shelton Street, London, WC2H 9JQ
Major Shareholder: Aneesa Patel
Officers: Aneesa Patel [1984] Director

Buffalo Refreshments Ltd
Incorporated: 3 November 2015
Net Worth: £574,879 *Total Assets:* £2,532,695
Registered Office: 1a Clive Avenue, London, N18 2RW
Major Shareholder: Joardar Heydon
Officers: Joardar Heydon [1999] Director; Stephen Lesley Heydon [1970] Director

Bukhari and Tanweer Limited
Incorporated: 3 April 2018
Registered Office: 58 Sussex Avenue, Isleworth, Middlesex, TW7 6LB
Major Shareholder: Syed Muhammed Ali Bukhari
Officers: Syed Muhammed Ali Bukhari, Secretary; Syed Muhammed Ali Bukhari [1980] Director

Burlingtown UK Limited
Incorporated: 12 November 2007 *Employees:* 9
Net Worth: £380,213,920 *Total Assets:* £480,930,016
Registered Office: 3rd Floor, 25 Park Lane, London, W1K 1RA
Shareholders: Jose Luis Cutrale; Rosana Cutrale
Officers: Philip John Warner, Secretary; Graziela Cutrale [1975] Director/Operations Manager [Italian]; Jose Luis Cutrale [1946] Director [Italian]; Jose Henrique Cutrale [1974] Director [Italian]; Rosana Cutrale F [1950] Director [Italian]; Jose Luis Cutrale Junior [1973] Director [Italian]

Burrows & Sturgess Ltd
Incorporated: 16 August 2018
Registered Office: Oakhurst House, 57 Ashbourne Road, Derby, DE22 3FS
Shareholders: Charles Edward Martin; Emma Elizabeth Martin
Officers: Charles Edward Martin [1978] Director/Head of Pricing; Emma Elizabeth Martin [1978] Director/Teacher

Butterfly Foods and Packaging Ltd
Incorporated: 15 February 2019
Registered Office: Maden Fold, Gannow Lane, Burnley, Lancs, BB12 6JJ
Shareholders: Shoaib Patel; Konstancija Petraviciute
Officers: Shoaib Patel [1966] Managing Director

Buy & Sales Trading Ltd
Incorporated: 8 July 2015
Registered Office: Grant House, Grant Road, Harrow, Middlesex, HA3 7SB
Major Shareholder: Sooppaiya Pillayar
Officers: Sooppaiya Pillayar [1985] Director/Sales Manager

Buzbees Beverages Limited
Incorporated: 20 June 2018
Registered Office: Amshold House, Goldings Hill, Loughton, Essex, IG10 2RW
Shareholder: Amsvest Limited
Officers: Michael Ray, Secretary; Mark Anthony Busby [1971] Director; Lord Alan Michael Sugar [1947] Director

The BV Group UK Limited
Incorporated: 12 October 2018
Registered Office: 1 Berkeley Street, London, W1J 8DJ
Major Shareholder: Harshit Mishra
Officers: Harshit Mishra [1995] Director/Distributor [Indian]

BVG Distributors Limited
Incorporated: 6 September 2018
Registered Office: 1 Berkeley Street, London, W1J 8DJ
Major Shareholder: Harshit Mishra
Officers: Harshit Mishra [1995] Director [Indian]

C & M Wholesale (UK) Limited
Incorporated: 3 December 2014
Net Worth: £35,060 *Total Assets:* £110,096
Registered Office: 61 Wellington Street East, Salford, M7 4DN
Major Shareholder: Yoel Elimelech Friedman
Officers: Yoel Elimelech Friedman [1981] Director/Secretary

C & M Wholesale Limited
Incorporated: 12 June 1997
Net Worth: £73,246 *Total Assets:* £74,573
Registered Office: 206 High Road, London, N15 4NP
Shareholder: Menachem Michael Friedman
Officers: Menucha Friedman, Secretary; Menachem Michael Friedman [1950] Director

C S Drinks Ltd
Incorporated: 13 December 2010 *Employees:* 4
Net Worth: £158,332 *Total Assets:* £196,609
Registered Office: Broughton Lodge Mews, Field Broughton, Grange-Over-Sands, Cumbria, LA11 6HL
Major Shareholder: Stephen Bernard Page
Officers: Stephen Bernard Page, Secretary; Dianne Lesley Page [1954] Director; Stephen Bernard Page [1956] Director

C.N.A. Catering Logistics Limited
Incorporated: 2 May 2006 *Employees:* 12
Net Worth: £360,262 *Total Assets:* £734,271
Registered Office: 50-51 Cromwell Industrial Estate, Argall Avenue, London, E10 7QE
Shareholder: Ahmet Turgay Simsek
Officers: Ahmet Turgay Simsek [1962] Director/Manager

C1 Trading Ltd
Incorporated: 17 October 2012
Net Worth: £13,296 *Total Assets:* £31,084
Registered Office: The Old Post Office, North Burlingham, Norwich, NR13 4SU
Shareholder: Susan Ann Judd
Officers: Susan Anne Judd [1951] Director/Self Employed

Cabana Soft Drinks Limited
Incorporated: 10 September 1968
Registered Office: Laurel House, Woodlands Park, Ashton Road, Newton-le-Willows, St Helens, Merseyside, WA12 0HH
Parent: Nichols PLC
Officers: Timothy John Croston, Secretary; Timothy John Croston [1963] Director

The Cafe Collective UK Trading Company Ltd
Incorporated: 17 January 2019
Registered Office: The Lock House, Brassmill Lane, Bath, BA1 3JW
Shareholders: Charlotte Heynen; Ashley Bailey; Veronica Ganan Burgoa; Jhampoll Gutierrez Gomez
Officers: Ashley Bailey [1988] Director; Veronica Ganan Burgoa [1978] Director [Spanish]; Jhampoll Gutierrez Gomez [1986] Director; Charlotte Heynen [1993] Director

Caju Drinks Ltd
Incorporated: 7 December 2016
Net Worth: £15,622 *Total Assets:* £28,533
Registered Office: 3rd Floor, 207 Regent Street, London, W1B 3HH
Officers: Weaam Kodoud [1986] Director [Belgian]

Caleno Drinks Ltd
Incorporated: 29 June 2017
Registered Office: 1 Orchard Road, St George, Bristol, BS5 7HS
Officers: Natalie Antonina Bucceri [1987] Director/Corporate Strategy Manager [Italian/Australian]; Eleanor Roxanne Webb [1990] Director

Cali Juices Limited
Incorporated: 30 January 2019
Registered Office: 320 Warstones Road, Penn, Wolverhampton, W Midlands, WV4 4JZ
Major Shareholder: Inderjit Singh Dadial
Officers: Inderjit Singh Dadial [1990] Director/Wholesaler

Cambridge Juice Co. Limited
Incorporated: 11 April 2002 *Employees:* 3
Net Worth: £55,993 *Total Assets:* £144,254
Registered Office: Lewis House, Great Chesterford Court, Great Chesterford, Saffron Walden, Essex, CB10 1PF
Major Shareholder: Matthew Gray
Officers: Paula Ann Sykes, Secretary; Matthew Gray [1953] Director/Manager

Camelot Chilled Foods Ltd
Incorporated: 18 February 1997 *Employees:* 65
Net Worth: £1,103,146 *Total Assets:* £1,870,487
Registered Office: Units 1-5 Camelot Business Centre, Whitworth Road, Crawley, W Sussex, RH11 7RY
Shareholder: Atul Kantibhai Patel
Officers: Atul Kantibhai Patel, Secretary/Engineer; Arju Atul Patel [1963] Director; Atul Kantibhai Patel [1961] Director/Engineer

Cameron Soft Drinks Limited
Incorporated: 14 August 2012
Net Worth: £30,269 *Total Assets:* £120,937
Registered Office: 41b Beach Road, Littlehampton, W Sussex, BN17 5JA
Shareholders: Jared Alexander Hugill; Nicholas Mark Cameron
Officers: Nicholas Mark Cameron [1971] Director/Vending Machine Engineer; Jared Alexander Hugill [1969] Director/Vending Machine Engineer

Camii Punch Ltd
Incorporated: 16 November 2017
Registered Office: 20-22 Wenlock Road, London, N1 7GU
Major Shareholder: Janine Camille
Officers: Janine Camille [1991] Director

Canafizz Ltd
Incorporated: 19 September 2018
Registered Office: 55 Bloomsbury Lane, Timperley, Altrincham, Cheshire, WA15 6LU
Major Shareholder: Simon Rainey
Officers: Simon Rainey [1974] Director/General Manager

The Cane Press Ltd
Incorporated: 12 March 2018
Registered Office: 20-22 Wenlock Road, London, N1 7GU
Major Shareholder: Dawn Wilson
Officers: Dawn Wilson [1984] Director

C J Canham Drinks Limited
Incorporated: 7 November 2003
Net Worth: £24,386 *Total Assets:* £60,653
Registered Office: 29 Mahoney Green, Green Lane West, Rackheath, Norwich, NR13 6JY
Shareholders: Christopher James Canham; Gina Canham
Officers: Gina Frances Canham, Secretary; Christopher James Canham [1960] Director/Soft Drinks Wholesaler; Gina Frances Canham [1961] Director/Company Secretary

Cape Crown Global Goods Limited
Incorporated: 7 March 2016 *Employees:* 1
Net Worth Deficit: £7,139 *Total Assets:* £4,233
Registered Office: Collingham House, 10-12 Gladstone Road, Wimbledon, London, SW19 1QT
Major Shareholder: Richard Patrick Wynne
Officers: Richard Patrick Wynne [1978] Director

Capital Drinks London Limited
Incorporated: 6 March 2012
Net Worth: £5,692 *Total Assets:* £13,617
Registered Office: Unit 2 County House, 2 Conway Mews, London, W1T 6AA
Major Shareholder: Nasima Aktar
Officers: Nasima Aktar [1990] Director

Caribbean Trade Ltd
Incorporated: 13 June 2002
Net Worth Deficit: £31,705 *Total Assets:* £14,560
Registered Office: 171 Bell Green Road, Bell Green, Coventry, Warwicks, CV6 7GW
Officers: Fiona Quaynor, Secretary; Osbourne Victor Frank [1951] Director/Proprietor

Carmine Ciao & Co Ltd
Incorporated: 21 August 2018
Registered Office: 23 Vincent Close, Ilford, Essex, IG6 2SZ
Major Shareholder: Carmine Langella
Officers: Carmine Langella, Secretary; Carmine Langella [1968] Director [Italian]

Carnaby and Kingly Limited
Incorporated: 10 May 2017
Registered Office: Second Floor Flat, 2 Fernshaw Road, London, SW10 0TF
Shareholders: Luca Giorgio Maggiora; Jordan Rocca
Officers: Luca Giorgio Maggiora [1980] Director [Italian]; Jordan Rocca [1981] Director/Events Promoter [Italian]

Carpatica International Limited
Incorporated: 8 March 2018
Registered Office: 71-75 Shelton Street, London, WC2H 9JQ
Major Shareholder: Robert Ovidiu Negru
Officers: Robert Ovidiu Negru, Secretary; Robert Ovidiu Negru [1990] Director/Transport Manager [Romanian]

Caspian Black Limited
Incorporated: 8 February 2019
Registered Office: 76 Barry Road, London, SE22 0HP
Shareholders: Nicholas Charles Vedat Hitchins; Alasdair Hitchins
Officers: Nicholas Charles Vedat Hitchins [1988] Director/Chartered Engineer

Caspian Foods Cash & Carry Limited
Incorporated: 29 October 2013
Net Worth: £202,791 *Total Assets:* £719,039
Registered Office: Unit 4 Port Hope Road Industrial Estate, Port Hope Road, Birmingham, B11 1JT
Officers: Rzgar Ahmed [1976] Director

Castle Warehouse Management Limited
Incorporated: 24 October 2011
Previous: Castle Facility Management Limited
Net Worth Deficit: £81,514 *Total Assets:* £35,000
Registered Office: 1-3 Winkle Street, West Bromwich, W Midlands, B70 9SA
Officers: Peter Goggins [1967] Director

Castleton International Limited
Incorporated: 14 December 2018
Registered Office: Building A, 108 Mandeville Road, Enfield, Middlesex, EN3 6SH
Officers: Patrick Maragh [1960] Director

Cawston Press Limited
Incorporated: 21 June 2000 *Employees:* 21
Previous: Cawston Vale Limited
Net Worth: £456,978 *Total Assets:* £3,793,469
Registered Office: Timsons Business Centre, Bath Road, Kettering, Northants, NN16 8NQ
Officers: Alyson Dunn, Secretary; Nicholas Anthony Beart [1963] Director; Stephen Kearns [1974] Director; William Bruce Kendall [1961] Director; Mark Richard Palmer [1973] Director; Stephen Edward Unwin [1956] Director

Remy Cazabet Ltd
Incorporated: 15 October 2018
Registered Office: 6 Sheridan Court, 99 Coombe Road, Croydon, Surrey, CR0 5SP
Major Shareholder: Remy Cazabet
Officers: Remy Cazabet [1985] Director [French]

CBD Globe Distributors Ltd
Incorporated: 7 April 2011
Previous: Lionstone Developments Limited
Net Worth Deficit: £150,988 *Total Assets:* £125,237
Registered Office: Calder & Co, 16 Charles II Street, London, SW1Y 4NW
Shareholders: Ferrelyn Folkes; Patrick John Surtees Folkes
Officers: Patrick John Surtees Folkes [1960] Director

CC Trade Ltd
Incorporated: 21 November 2016
Net Worth Deficit: £624 *Total Assets:* £3,603
Registered Office: 71-75 Shelton Street, Covent Garden, London, WC2H 9JQ
Major Shareholder: David Nagy
Officers: David Nagy [1988] Director [Slovak]

CCM Enterprises Limited
Incorporated: 27 November 2015
Net Worth Deficit: £38,554 *Total Assets:* £10,025
Registered Office: 20-22 Wenlock Road, London, N1 7GU
Shareholders: Eduardo Jose Clavijo; Kevin Meehan
Officers: Kevin Meehan, Secretary; Eduardo Jose Clavijo [1972] Director [Spanish]; Kevin Andrew Meehan [1966] Director

Ceci-Hill Limited
Incorporated: 22 September 2005
Net Worth: £146,085 *Total Assets:* £242,928
Registered Office: 6 Link Way, Malvern, Worcs, WR14 1UQ
Major Shareholder: Matthew Hill
Officers: Jane Hill, Secretary; Matthew Hill [1977] Director/Retailer

Cellar Twelve Limited
Incorporated: 26 March 2004
Net Worth: £10,515 *Total Assets:* £516,459
Registered Office: Unit 6 Reeds Farm Estate, Cow Watering Lane, Writtle, Chelmsford, Essex, CM1 3SB
Shareholders: Damian Paul Barrett; David Graeme MacDonald
Officers: Damian Paul Barrett, Secretary/Wine Merchant; Damian Paul Barrett [1971] Director/Wine Merchant; David Graeme MacDonald [1970] Director/Wine Merchant

Ch@i Drinks Ltd
Incorporated: 4 November 2016
Net Worth Deficit: £825 *Total Assets:* £60
Registered Office: Windfall House, D1, The Courtyard, Alban Park, St Albans, Herts, AL4 0LA
Shareholder: Angelos Panayiotou
Officers: Angelos Panayiotou, Secretary; Mudassar Aziz [1979] Director/Accountant; Omair Mateen Chawla [1980] Director [Pakistani]; Angelos Panayiotou [1975] Director/Accountants

Cheti & Co Holdings Limited
Incorporated: 27 April 2018
Registered Office: 153-155 Hoxton Street, London, N1 6PJ
Shareholders: Ryan Chetiyawardana; Jonathan Charles Jackson; Grow Partners Limited
Officers: Ryan Chetiyawardana [1984] Director/Mixologist; Jonathan Charles Jackson [1982] Director/Consultant

Cheti & Co Limited
Incorporated: 12 November 2018
Registered Office: 153-155 Hoxton Street, London, N1 6PJ
Parent: Cheti & Co Holdings Limited
Officers: Ryan Chetiyawardana [1984] Director/Mixologist; Jonathan Charles Jackson [1982] Director/Consultant

The Chiltern Mix Limited
Incorporated: 19 November 2018
Registered Office: 14 Whittle Parkway, Progress Business Centre, Slough, SL1 6DQ
Shareholders: Melanie Joanne McNelly; Ross Gordon Smethurst
Officers: Melanie Joanne McNelly [1968] Director

China Cambrian Limited
Incorporated: 3 September 2018
Registered Office: 36b Denbigh Road, London, W13 8NH
Major Shareholder: Ruan Jiabing
Officers: Nehal Mangrio [1984] Director/Trainee Solicitor; Yanyan Yang [1986] Director/Manager [Chinese]

Choi's Trading & Co Ltd
Incorporated: 30 August 2011
Net Worth: £11,651 *Total Assets:* £104,282
Registered Office: Office 3, Unit 4 Dorma Trading Estate, Staffa Road, London, E10 7QX
Major Shareholder: Yuk Lam Choi
Officers: Yuk Lam Choi [1966] Director/Businessman

Choice Asia Ltd
Incorporated: 20 February 2019
Registered Office: 102d-1, Peel House, 34-44 London Road, Morden, Surrey, SM4 5BX
Officers: Krishco Fernando [1989] Director

Choise Group Ltd
Incorporated: 28 August 2018
Registered Office: 71-75 Shelton Street, London, WC2H 9JQ
Major Shareholder: Serkan Aksakal
Officers: Serkan Aksakal, Secretary; Serkan Aksakal [1981] Director/Self Employed

Chosen Enterprises Limited
Incorporated: 31 July 2018
Registered Office: 2 Cherry Lodge, Southview Avenue, London, NW10 1RG
Major Shareholder: Isac Muwanguzi
Officers: Arthur Chosen [2001] Director; Rose Kisakye [1973] Finance Director; Isac Muwanguzi [1964] Managing Director

Chum Bites Limited
Incorporated: 8 February 2017
Net Worth: £158,017 *Total Assets:* £188,378
Registered Office: 6th Floor, Times House, Throwley Way, Sutton, Surrey, SM41 4JQ
Major Shareholder: John Colin Bartley
Officers: Grant Keen Rushmere [1970] Director/Entrepreneur [South African]; Thomas Fokko Van Lambaart [1968] Director [Dutch]

Cibo (London) Limited
Incorporated: 1 September 2005
Net Worth: £188,940 *Total Assets:* £470,649
Registered Office: Unit 1-8 Low Profile House, 94 Vale Road, London, N4 1PZ
Major Shareholder: Franco Turano
Officers: Clare Buckle, Secretary; Clare Turano [1969] Director; Franco Turano [1975] Director/Manager [Italian]

City Beer Limited
Incorporated: 25 July 2003
Net Worth: £319,107 *Total Assets:* £566,142
Registered Office: 2 Everitt Close, Denington Industrial Estate, Wellingborough, Northants, NN8 2QE
Shareholders: Ketan Shah; Binny Shah
Officers: Binny Shah, Secretary/Director; Binny Shah [1963] Director; Kavit Shah [1988] Director; Ketan Shah [1959] Director

Cityfresh Limited
Incorporated: 2 January 2019
Registered Office: 261 Romford Road, London, E7 9HJ
Major Shareholder: Ahmed Khan
Officers: Ahmed Khan [1980] Director

Claddagh Food and Drink Limited
Incorporated: 29 May 2018
Registered Office: 92 Halifax Road, Enfield, Middlesex, EN2 0PJ
Shareholders: Beau Christopher O'Niel; Fiona McSharry
Officers: Beau Christopher O'Niel [1972] Director/Transport Manager

Clarion Wines Limited
Incorporated: 17 February 2005 *Employees:* 3
Net Worth: £329,958 *Total Assets:* £1,361,177
Registered Office: Zion Hill House, Cuffs Lane, Tisbury, Wilts, SP3 6LG
Officers: Richard John Berkley Matthews, Secretary; Patrick Robin Barran [1959] Director/Wine Trader; Richard John Berkley Matthews [1968] Director/Wine Buyer; Toby William Crowther l'anson [1984] Director/Wine Merchant

Classic Catering (UK) Ltd
Incorporated: 24 August 2010 *Employees:* 2
Net Worth: £2,725 *Total Assets:* £99,186
Registered Office: Cumberland House, 24-28 Baxter Avenue, Southend on Sea, Essex, SS2 6HZ
Shareholders: Angela Margaret Gollu; Dursun Gollu
Officers: Angela Margaret Gollu, Secretary; Dursun Gollu [1964] Director/Wholesaler [Turkish]

Clean-Coco Ltd
Incorporated: 20 July 2017
Registered Office: Flat 0/1, 138 Dorchester Avenue, Glasgow, G12 0EA
Major Shareholder: Gillian Jones
Officers: Gillian Jones [1993] Director

Clear Drinks Limited
Incorporated: 10 April 2018
Registered Office: Malvern View Business Park, Stella Way, Bishops Cleeve, Cheltenham, Glos, GL52 7DQ
Officers: Jenna Zoe Barclay [1987] Director

Club Consultants Ltd
Incorporated: 17 July 2014
Net Worth Deficit: £27,854 *Total Assets:* £56,652
Registered Office: c/o 447 Kenton Road, Harrow, Middlesex, HA3 0XY
Officers: Timothy Lawrence Luscombe [1957] Director/Consultant; Russell Paul West [1968] Director/IT Consultant

Cobell Ltd
Incorporated: 12 November 1999 *Employees:* 54
Net Worth: £6,220,997 *Total Assets:* £18,440,732
Registered Office: The Juice House, 1 Leigham Business Units, Silverton Road, Matford Park, Exeter, Devon, EX2 8HY
Parent: Symrise Limited
Officers: Nicholas Russell [1963] Director; Heinrich Friedrich Ludwig Schaper [1956] Director/President Flavour Division [German]

Coconutty Ltd
Incorporated: 10 November 2010
Net Worth Deficit: £6,429 *Total Assets:* £14,698
Registered Office: 26 Cambrian Bar, Low Moor, Bradford, BD12 0EB
Major Shareholder: Matthew Colin Stockwell
Officers: Matthew Colin Stockwell [1968] Director

Codex Limited
Incorporated: 24 February 2015
Net Worth: £95,752 *Total Assets:* £108,352
Registered Office: Metalcraft Estate, Ezekiel Lane, Willenhall, W Midlands, WV12 5QU
Officers: Gavin Michael Haystead [1980] Sales Director

Colbury Limited
Incorporated: 18 February 2019
Registered Office: 37 Bowline Court, 15 Telegraph Avenue, London, SE10 0TF
Shareholders: Erfan Abdollahei; Thilanka Isuru Jayasekera
Officers: Erfan Abdollahei [1994] Director/Founder; Thilanka Isuru Jayasekera [1994] Director/Co - Founder [Sri Lankan]

Colemans ABC Ltd
Incorporated: 17 November 1993 *Employees:* 15
Net Worth: £24,137 *Total Assets:* £590,202
Registered Office: The Old Tram Depot, Bexhill Road, St Leonards on Sea, E Sussex, TN38 8BG
Officers: Teresa Ann Coleman, Secretary; David John Coleman [1956] Director/Soft Drinks Distributor; Teresa Ann Coleman [1956] Director/Company Secretary

Collette International Limited
Incorporated: 1 July 1999 *Employees:* 3
Net Worth: £201,829 *Total Assets:* £210,977
Registered Office: Hill House Farm, Barbers Lane, Antrobus, Cheshire, CW9 6JT
Major Shareholder: David Ian Lavender
Officers: David Lavender, Secretary; Stephen Paul Chamberlain [1951] Director; David Lavender [1959] Director; Kathryn Mary Lavender [1979] Director

Condimental Ltd
Incorporated: 19 September 2016
Net Worth: £392 *Total Assets:* £16,550
Registered Office: St Denys House, 22 East Hill, St Austell, Cornwall, PL25 4TR
Shareholders: Christopher John Gordon; Kristian Richard Fleming
Officers: Kristian Richard Fleming [1974] Director; Christopher John Gordon [1979] Director

Connect Waze Private Limited
Incorporated: 31 August 2017
Registered Office: 78 Hutton Lane, Harrow, Middlesex, HA3 6RD
Major Shareholder: Rajamohan Kathiresan
Officers: Rajamohan Kathiresan, Secretary; Rajamohan Kathiresan [1970] Director

Continent Foods Limited
Incorporated: 19 June 2014
Net Worth: £82,423 *Total Assets:* £281,958
Registered Office: Unit 19 Small Heath Trading Estate, Armoury Road, Birmingham, B11 2RJ
Major Shareholder: Nadira Shaheen
Officers: Humza Haroon [1997] Director/Businessman

Cooper & Partner Ltd
Incorporated: 8 February 2013
Net Worth: £4,247 *Total Assets:* £7,200
Registered Office: 17 Mace Street, Cradley Heath, W Midlands, B64 6HL
Major Shareholder: Syed Haider Ali Naqvi
Officers: Syed Haider Ali Naqvi [1983] Director/Consultancy [Pakistani]

Coot Service Ltd
Incorporated: 26 January 2015
Registered Office: 102d-1, Peel House, 34-44 London Road, Morden, Surrey, SM4 5BX
Major Shareholder: Michel Dennis
Officers: Michel Dennis [1993] Director/Sales Manager [French]

Cordus Ltd
Incorporated: 1 February 2019
Registered Office: Frogs Hole Farm, Sissinghurst Road, Biddenden, Ashford, Kent, TN27 8EY
Major Shareholder: Alexander Gregor Norwood Hill
Officers: Alexander Gregor Norwood Hill [1972] Managing Director

Couto & Machado Ltd
Incorporated: 5 June 2017
Registered Office: 1-3 Britannia Way, Park Royal, London, NW10 7PR
Shareholders: Lino Escorcio Machado; Alexandre Alan de Santana Pereira Couto
Officers: Alexandre Alan de Santana Pereira Couto [1979] Director [Brazilian]; Lino Escorcio Machado [1982] Director [Portuguese]

CPH Games UK Limited
Incorporated: 15 June 2016
Net Worth: £159 *Total Assets:* £18,136
Registered Office: 12 Minton Mews, Carlyle Road, Bromsgrove, Worcs, B60 2PN
Major Shareholder: Mette Marie Feildorf
Officers: Mette Marie Feildorf [1968] Director/Educational Resources [Danish]

Crab Trading Ltd
Incorporated: 30 January 2019
Registered Office: 80 Ince Avenue, Liverpool, L4 7UY
Major Shareholder: Thevachandran Veerakathipillai
Officers: Thevachandran Veerakathipillai [1976] Director/Sales Assistant [Norwegian]

Creamline Dairies Limited
Incorporated: 21 June 1945 *Employees:* 267
Net Worth: £8,757,747 *Total Assets:* £13,913,017
Registered Office: Creamline Dairies, Mellors Road, Trafford Park, Manchester, M17 1PB
Parent: Swallow Holdings Limited
Officers: Christopher David Swallow, Secretary/Management Executive; Robert Kenneth Berry Purvis [1969] Director/Management Executive; Anthony David Swallow [1940] Director/Executive; Christopher David Swallow [1970] Director/Management Executive; Helga Hildegard Gertrud Swallow [1935] Director/Housewife [German]

Creative Properties and Investments Ltd
Incorporated: 27 November 2013
Net Worth: £674,618 *Total Assets:* £674,919
Registered Office: 15 Stratton Street, London, W1J 8LQ
Major Shareholder: Andreas Yanakopoulos
Officers: Georgios Chondrorizos [1967] Director [Greek]; Andreas Yanakopoulos [1963] Director [Greek]

Crescent Moon World Project Ltd.
Incorporated: 20 October 2014
Net Worth Deficit: £706
Registered Office: c/o JSA Partners Accountants, 41 Skylines Village, Limeharbour, London, E14 9TS
Shareholders: Zsolt Koszegi; Melinda Tiber
Officers: Zsolt Koszegi [1974] Director [Hungarian]; Melinda Tiber [1973] Director [Hungarian]

Crop's Foods Ltd.
Incorporated: 6 April 1989 *Employees:* 26
Previous: M D C Foods Limited
Net Worth: £1,906,713 *Total Assets:* £14,288,526
Registered Office: 254 Capability Green, Luton, Beds, LU1 3LU
Parent: Crop's & Partners UK Limited
Officers: Michael Dennis Cullinane, Secretary; Michael Dennis Cullinane [1948] Director; Michel Delbaere [1953] Director [Belgian]; Pieter Anthony Delbaere [1979] Director/Business Unit Manager [Belgian]; Paul Andrew Weatherby [1973] Managing Director

Crux Energy Drinks Ltd
Incorporated: 24 December 2018
Registered Office: 20-22 Wenlock Road, London, N1 7GU
Major Shareholder: Gareth Rhys Griffiths
Officers: Gareth Rhys Griffiths [1980] Director

Cubico Limited
Incorporated: 15 November 2006
Net Worth Deficit: £486 *Total Assets:* £9,271
Registered Office: 61 The Street, Uley, Dursley, Glos, GL11 5SL
Major Shareholder: Paul Chillingworth
Officers: Jacqueline Frances Chillingworth, Secretary; Paul Chillingworth [1958] Director/CAD Consultant

Cybel Ltd
Incorporated: 4 October 2018
Registered Office: First Floor, 85 Great Portland Street, London, W1W 7LT
Shareholders: Ntsimba Monica Elvire Massamba; Nzouzi Julia Trecy Massamba
Officers: Ntsimba Monica Elvire Massamba [1995] Director/Chief Executive [French/Congolese]; Nzouzi Julia Trecy Massamba [1995] Director/Dietitian-Nutritionist [French/Congolese]

Cyprofood Limited
Incorporated: 4 January 2007 *Employees:* 43
Net Worth: £2,960,578 *Total Assets:* £4,767,462
Registered Office: 239-241 Kennington Lane, London, SE11 5QU
Parent: Masca Holding Limited
Officers: Suleyman Cagin, Secretary; Cetin Agcagul [1985] Director; Suleyman Cagin [1966] Director/Marketing

Czar & Co (UK) Limited
Incorporated: 17 February 2017 *Employees:* 2
Net Worth Deficit: £50,372 *Total Assets:* £86,123
Registered Office: 21 Navigation Business Village, Navigation Way, Ashton on Ribble, Preston, Lancs, PR2 2YP
Shareholders: Cristian Czar; Simon Harcourt Johnson
Officers: Cristian Czar [1966] Director [Croatian]; Simon Harcourt Johnson [1948] Director

D D C Foods Limited
Incorporated: 5 November 1998 *Employees:* 84
Net Worth: £1,535,771 *Total Assets:* £7,312,383
Registered Office: 166 College Road, Harrow, Middlesex, HA1 1RA
Shareholders: Christopher Christofi; Polly Christofi
Officers: Polly Christofi, Secretary; Christopher Christofi [1965] Director; Polly Christophi [1972] Director; Jack David Morgan [1990] Director; Stephen John Morgan [1961] Operations Director; Steven John Tyler [1966] Director

D D S Food Imports Ltd
Incorporated: 7 June 1999
Net Worth Deficit: £35,443 *Total Assets:* £44,892
Registered Office: Raydean House, Western Parade, Great North Road, New Barnet, Barnet, Herts, EN5 1AH
Shareholders: Michele Brazza; Eleonora Brazza
Officers: Michele Brazza [1960] Director [Italian]

D'Auria Brothers Ice Cream and Catering Limited
Incorporated: 20 December 1979 *Employees:* 29
Net Worth: £159,340 *Total Assets:* £579,602
Registered Office: Hyde House, The Hyde, Edgware Road, London, NW9 6LA
Major Shareholder: Alberto D'Auria
Officers: Nubia Malta D'Auria, Secretary; Alberto D'Auria [1946] Director [Italian]; Alfonso D'Auria [1976] Director

Dalina Limited
Incorporated: 19 November 2013
Registered Office: 8 Clock House Parade, North Circular Road, London, N13 6BG
Major Shareholder: Ebru Turk
Officers: Ebru Turk [1987] Director

Dan International (UK) Limited
Incorporated: 10 April 1995
Net Worth Deficit: £7,832 *Total Assets:* £44,600
Registered Office: Unit F1, Larkfield Trading Estate, New Hythe Lane, Larkfield, Aylesford, Kent, ME20 6SW
Parent: D & D Snack Foods Limited
Officers: Steven Charles Dussek [1960] Director/MD

Daneisa Ltd
Incorporated: 9 October 2018
Registered Office: 7 Bracken Park, Scarcroft, Leeds, LS14 3HZ
Major Shareholder: Zafar Khan
Officers: Zafar Khan [1972] Director

Dark Invest Ltd
Incorporated: 1 May 2018
Registered Office: First Floor, Woburn Court, 2 Railton Road, Woburn Road Industrial Estate, Kempston, Beds, MK42 7PN
Shareholders: Devinder Singh Chahal; Kamaldeep Kaur Chahal
Officers: Devinder Singh Chahal [1969] Director; Kamaldeep Kaur Chahal [1971] Director

Dark Night Beverages Ltd
Incorporated: 15 January 2013
Registered Office: 91-92 Charles Henry Street, Highgate, Birmingham, B12 0SJ
Major Shareholder: Asif Hussain
Officers: Asif Hussain [1983] Director

Darkhorse Universal Limited
Incorporated: 28 December 2018
Registered Office: 39 Harling Road, Preston, Lancs, PR1 5YR
Major Shareholder: Ishtiaq Ahmed
Officers: Ishtiaq Ahmed [1978] Director/Entrepreneur

J.C.Davies & Hall Limited
Incorporated: 10 January 2017
Net Worth Deficit: £136 *Total Assets:* £250
Registered Office: The Townsend Farm, Stretton Grandison, Ledbury, Herefords, HR8 2TS
Officers: Malcolm Davies [1955] Director/Farmer; James Hall [1987] Director/Wholesale

Dawsons (Wales) Limited
Incorporated: 6 December 1985
Net Worth: £820,232 *Total Assets:* £2,353,234
Registered Office: Unit 10 Penamser Industrial Estate, Porthmadog, Gwynedd, LL49 9NZ
Major Shareholder: Peter Maxwell Dawson
Officers: Peter Maxwell Dawson, Secretary; Peter Maxwell Dawson [1951] Director/Businessman

Debbie and Venky Ltd
Incorporated: 28 January 2013
Net Worth Deficit: £27,661 *Total Assets:* £801
Registered Office: 48 Claremont Avenue, New Malden, Surrey, KT3 6QN
Shareholders: Venkatesh Nathan Sankaran; Poonam Pathak
Officers: Venkatesh Nathan Sankaran [1975] Director; Poonam Pathak [1975] Director

Deeti Wholesale Limited
Incorporated: 4 March 2015
Net Worth: £1,422 *Total Assets:* £16,136
Registered Office: Area A23, 7-11 Minerva Road, Park Royal, London, NW10 6HJ
Major Shareholder: Maulikkumar Ashokbhai Patel
Officers: Maulikkumar Ashokbhai Patel [1980] Director

Delamore Trading UK Ltd
Incorporated: 9 November 2017
Registered Office: 85a Shenley Road, Borehamwood, Herts, WD6 1AG
Shareholders: Parag Vinodbhai Vora; Sunil Soman Pillai
Officers: Sunil Soman Pillai [1970] Director [Indian]; Parag Vinodbhai Vora [1969] Director [Indian]

Delta Tip Limited
Incorporated: 21 April 2016
Registered Office: Flat 80, Wheelwright Lane, Coventry, Warwicks, CV6 4HH
Major Shareholder: Thushyanthan Navarasalingam
Officers: Thushyanthan Navarasalingam [1988] Director/Sales Assistant [French]

Desi Trading Ltd
Incorporated: 2 August 2018
Registered Office: 538 Bordesley Green, Birmingham, B9 5PD
Major Shareholder: Shazia Aroleeb
Officers: Shazia Aroleeb [1971] Director

Dessert Makers Limited
Incorporated: 25 January 2019
Registered Office: 5 Pendley House, Whiston Road, Hackney, London, E2 8SF
Major Shareholder: Naghman Hussain
Officers: Naghman Hussain [1989] Director/Biomedical Scientist

Deveron Direct Limited
Incorporated: 6 July 2015 *Employees:* 5
Net Worth: £236,725 *Total Assets:* £417,240
Registered Office: Station Brae, Macduff, Aberdeenshire, AB44 1UL
Shareholders: Kenneth Milne West; Desmond Victor James Cheyne
Officers: Desmond Victor James Cheyne [1974] Director; Kenneth Milne West [1965] Director

DH Exotic Produce Ltd
Incorporated: 12 September 2011
Net Worth Deficit: £12,267 *Total Assets:* £1,663
Registered Office: 33 Emerson Road, Poole, Dorset, BH15 1QS
Major Shareholder: Dac Huu Vu
Officers: Hanh Nguyen, Secretary; Dac Huu Vu [1967] Director

Dimark Limited
Incorporated: 16 December 2003 *Employees:* 32
Net Worth: £691,013 *Total Assets:* £1,980,361
Registered Office: Unit 4 & 5 Advent Business Park, 14 Advent Way, Edmonton, London, N18 3AL
Shareholders: Ali Hidir Caktu; Ibrahim Yucesoy
Officers: Ali Hidir Caktu [1963] Director/Businessman

Dining Capital Limited
Incorporated: 23 April 2018
Registered Office: The St Botolph Building, 138 Houndsditch, London, EC3A 7AR
Major Shareholder: Mohamed Nabil Hayel Saeed Anam
Officers: Hayel Nabil Hayel Saeed Anam [1992] Director/Investor [Canadian]; Mohamed Nabil Hayel Saeed Anam [1993] Director/Investor [Kittitian]

Direct Source 2 Limited
Incorporated: 24 August 2011 *Employees:* 25
Net Worth: £117,930 *Total Assets:* £375,579
Registered Office: Unit 5 Craufurd Business Park, Silverdale Road, Hayes, Middlesex, UB3 3BN
Parent: Beriwal International Limited
Officers: Anil Ram Kumar Beriwal [1959] Director; Meena Anil Beriwal [1961] Director; Pushpak Anil Beriwal [1990] Director

Direct Source Distribution Limited
Incorporated: 22 June 2009 *Employees:* 40
Net Worth: £147,786 *Total Assets:* £486,701
Registered Office: 37 High Street, Tewkesbury, Glos, GL20 5BB
Shareholder: Sohail Azam
Officers: Sohail Azam [1966] Director

Direct Traders Ltd
Incorporated: 14 November 2012
Net Worth: £1,819 *Total Assets:* £38,885
Registered Office: 52 Sebert Road, London, E7 0NQ
Major Shareholder: Nadeem Guffoor Iqbal
Officers: Nadeem Guffoor Iqbal [1982] Director

Direct2door Food & Beverage Ltd.
Incorporated: 11 August 2014
Net Worth: £16,053 *Total Assets:* £54,610
Registered Office: 72 Atkinson Road, London, E16 3LS
Major Shareholder: Silmara Piagno
Officers: Silmara Piagno [1977] Director [Italian]

Discount Brands (London) UK Limited
Incorporated: 23 January 2018
Registered Office: 42a Stanlake Road, London, W12 7HL
Officers: Andrew Wilkinson [1977] Director/Consultant

Discount on Drinks Ltd
Incorporated: 14 October 2013
Net Worth: £1,356 *Total Assets:* £1,356
Registered Office: 24 Cooke Street, Barking, Essex, IG11 7AF
Major Shareholder: Ola Alabede
Officers: Alessandra Alabede, Secretary; Ola Alabede [1973] Managing Director

Discover Health Ltd
Incorporated: 17 December 2018
Registered Office: 4 Beldale Park, Kirkby, Merseyside, L32 2DE
Shareholder: Matthew Anthony Robb

DJ Drink Solutions Limited
Incorporated: 20 April 2006 *Employees:* 38
Net Worth: £1,102,492 *Total Assets:* £3,715,638
Registered Office: Laurel House, Woodlands Park, Ashton Road, Newton-le-Willows, Merseyside, WA12 0HH
Parent: Nichols PLC
Officers: Timothy John Croston [1963] Director

DLG Wholesale Ltd
Incorporated: 21 April 2017
Registered Office: 20 Westerham Avenue, London, N9 9BU
Major Shareholder: Dogan Ucar
Officers: Dogan Ucar [1974] Director

DMK Wholesale Ltd
Incorporated: 31 December 2018
Registered Office: 27 Sovereign Road, Barking, Essex, IG11 0XQ
Major Shareholder: Malik Mauro Ferreira Falcao Chantre
Officers: Malik Mauro Ferreira Falcao Chantre [1994] Director [Portuguese]

DN World Ltd
Incorporated: 13 October 2017
Registered Office: 11 Elmore Road, Enfield, Middlesex, EN3 5QA
Officers: Ambika Chandramohan [1984] Director

DNG Group Ltd
Incorporated: 30 July 2018
Registered Office: 509 Kenton Road, Harrow, Middlesex, HA3 0UL
Major Shareholder: Dev Dhingra
Officers: Dev Dhingra [2000] Director [Indian]

DNG Trading Ltd
Incorporated: 2 July 2018
Registered Office: 509 Kenton Road, Harrow, Middlesex, HA3 0UL
Major Shareholder: Priya Dhingra
Officers: Priya Dhingra [1994] Director [Indian]

Dodotraders UK Limited
Incorporated: 9 May 2012
Net Worth: £58,953 *Total Assets:* £155,933
Registered Office: 4 Hanover Walk, Hatfield, Herts, AL10 9EL
Major Shareholder: Baboo Taukoor
Officers: Baboo Oomeshwarsingh Taukoor [1973] Director

Dollshouse Childrens Drinks Ltd
Incorporated: 28 February 2018
Registered Office: Bridge House, 64-72 Mabgate, Leeds, LS9 7DZ
Major Shareholder: Diane Robert Wilson
Officers: Diane Wilson [1944] Director/Company Formation Agent Semi-Retired

Dolphin Trading Limited
Incorporated: 11 April 1994 *Employees:* 1
Net Worth Deficit: £42,465 *Total Assets:* £4,674
Registered Office: 177-179 Newcastle Street, Burslem, Stoke on Trent, Staffs, ST6 3QJ
Major Shareholder: Anastasis Televantidis
Officers: Andriani Anastasi, Secretary; Andriani Anastasi [1932] Secretary & Director; Anastasis Televantidis [1966] Sales Director

Domore Imports Ltd
Incorporated: 11 June 2018
Registered Office: 170 Parchmore Road, Thornton Heath, Surrey, CR7 8HA
Shareholders: Jennifer Patricia Warner; Joanne Elizabeth Josephs
Officers: Joanne Elizabeth Josephs [1964] Director/Home Maker; Jennifer Patricia Warner [1971] Director/Ambulance Driver

Doorstep Desserts Distribution Limited
Incorporated: 30 January 2018
Registered Office: 34 Northcote Road, Leicester, LE2 3FH
Parent: Doorstep Desserts (Holdings) Limited
Officers: Ahtesham Nazir Moosa [1987] Managing Director; Oubed Nazir Moosa [1989] Finance Director

Dora Distribution Ltd
Incorporated: 1 September 2018
Registered Office: 158 Buckingham Drive, Luton, Beds, LU2 9RE
Major Shareholder: Petrica Iliesiu
Officers: Petrica Iliesiu [1983] Director [Romanian]

Dragon Rise Limited
Incorporated: 9 May 2013 *Employees:* 2
Net Worth Deficit: £15,189 *Total Assets:* £5,638
Registered Office: 30 Charing Cross Road, London, WC2H 0DE
Major Shareholder: Ruiming Duan
Officers: Rui Ming Duan [1983] Director [Chinese]

Drayton Limited
Incorporated: 30 October 2018
Registered Office: 45 Cherry Orchard, West Drayton, Middlesex, UB7 7JR
Major Shareholder: Surinder Kaur Bal
Officers: Surinder Kaur Bal [1989] Director/Health and Safety

Drea Ltd
Incorporated: 19 December 2018
Registered Office: 3 Kendal Close, Timperley, Altrincham, Cheshire, WA15 7EU
Shareholders: Kishor Ganpatrao Pawar; Disha Avinash Ahaley
Officers: Purushottam Pandurang Desai [1974] Director

Dreams Food 1 Limited
Incorporated: 8 February 2017
Net Worth Deficit: £8,319 *Total Assets:* £280,018
Registered Office: Unit 99 Green Lane, Hounslow, Middlesex, TW4 6BW
Shareholders: Abdulhadi Alyouseff; Ammar Mohammad Al-Saeed
Officers: Ammar Mohammad Al-Saeed [1979] Director [Syrian]; Abdulhadi Alyouseff [1989] Director [Syrian]

DRGN Global Ltd.
Incorporated: 26 September 2017
Registered Office: 47 Marylebone Lane, London, W1U 2NT
Major Shareholder: Vishal Sodha
Officers: Vishal Sodha [1978] Director

Drink Fitness Ltd
Incorporated: 15 January 2019
Registered Office: 35b Halliford Street, London, N1 3EL
Major Shareholder: Billie Georgina Davies
Officers: Billie Georgina Davies [1989] Director/Entrepreneur

Drink Free Ltd
Incorporated: 20 July 2018
Registered Office: Unit 1 High House Lane, Kenardington, Ashford, Kent, TN26 2LF
Major Shareholder: Andrew Iain Stewart Laughland
Officers: Andrew Iain Stewart Laughland [1965] Director

Drink Natural Limited
Incorporated: 19 September 2011 *Employees:* 4
Net Worth: £68,607 *Total Assets:* £265,498
Registered Office: Archways, Spartan Road, Low Moor, Bradford, W Yorks, BD12 0RY
Major Shareholder: John Hodgson
Officers: John Hodgson [1959] Director

Drink Warehouse UK Limited
Incorporated: 23 February 2010 *Employees:* 32
Net Worth: £429,241 *Total Assets:* £2,005,153
Registered Office: Unit 5 Old Timber Yard Industrial Estate, Manston Road, Ramsgate, Kent, CT12 6HJ
Shareholders: Leanne Farley; Michael James Curtis
Officers: Michael James Curtis [1981] Director; Leanne Farley [1980] Director

Drink Your Fruit Limited
Incorporated: 20 August 2010
Registered Office: 39 Thistle Down Close, Sutton Coldfield, W Midlands, B74 3EE
Major Shareholder: John Ivar Peter Hofstedt
Officers: Valerie June Hofstedt, Secretary; John Ivar Peter Hofstedt [1946] Sales Director

Drinkable Ltd
Incorporated: 20 November 2017
Registered Office: 53a Selborne Road, London, N14 7DD
Officers: Sokol Veselaj [1971] Director

The Drinks Bay Limited
Incorporated: 5 June 2018
Registered Office: Unit A3, Connaught Business Centre, Hyde Estate Road, London, NW9 6JL
Major Shareholder: Victoria Ibidun Ogunniyi
Officers: Victoria Ibidun Ogunniyi [1970] Director/Businesswoman

Drinks Europe Ltd
Incorporated: 4 December 2018
Registered Office: Kemp House, 160 City Road, London, EC1V 2NX
Officers: Rahim Khalid [1980] Managing Director

Drinks International Birmingham Ltd
Incorporated: 24 August 2018
Registered Office: 149 Spon Lane, West Bromwich, W Midlands, B70 6AS
Major Shareholder: Sukhvinder Singh Uppal
Officers: Sukhvinder Singh Uppal [1991] Director

Drinks R Us Limited
Incorporated: 8 March 2011
Registered Office: 48-52 Penny Lane, Mossley Hill, Liverpool, L18 1DG
Major Shareholder: Rakesh Ishwar Daryanani
Officers: Rakesh Ishwar Daryanani [1982] Director

Drinks2u Ltd
Incorporated: 5 September 2018
Registered Office: 113 Maidavale Crescent, Coventry, Warwicks, CV3 6GE
Major Shareholder: Gurdip Singh Manak
Officers: Gurdip Singh Manak [1983] Director/Salesman

Drinkslynx Limited
Incorporated: 22 July 2011
Registered Office: 48-52 Penny Lane, Mossley Hill, Liverpool, L18 1DG
Major Shareholder: Rakesh Ishwar Daryanani
Officers: Rakesh Ishwar Daryanani [1982] Director

Drinksparadies Ltd
Incorporated: 7 September 2018
Registered Office: 68A Tolworth Broadway, Surbiton, Surrey, KT6 7JB
Major Shareholder: Saravanan Palanivel
Officers: Saravanan Palanivel [1982] Director/Chef [Indian]

Drinx Division Ltd
Incorporated: 30 November 2018
Registered Office: 33 The Market, Wrythe Lane, Carshalton, Surrey, SM5 1AG
Major Shareholder: Cowthom Amurtherajan
Officers: Cowthom Amurtherajan [1992] Director/Store Manager

The Driver's Drinks Company Limited
Incorporated: 13 September 2018
Registered Office: Yew Tree House, Lewes Road, Forest Row, E Sussex, RH18 5AA
Major Shareholder: Hamish Christian Gordon
Officers: Hamish Christian Gordon [1971] Director

DSA Frozen Foods Ltd
Incorporated: 15 May 2018
Registered Office: 41 Abbotside Close, Bradford, BD10 8DL
Officers: Adrian Damian Szachniewicz [1999] Director and Company Secretary [Polish]

DT Fruits Ltd
Incorporated: 28 January 2015
Net Worth Deficit: £417 *Total Assets:* £801
Registered Office: 3 Turner Avenue, Biggin Hill, Westerham, Kent, TN16 3GL
Major Shareholder: Danny Lee Tucker
Officers: Danny Lee Tucker [1981] Director/Trader

Dua Enterprises Limited
Incorporated: 7 April 2018
Registered Office: 211 Swanshurst Lane, Birmingham, B13 0AR
Officers: Aamir Zulfiqar [1980] Managing Director [Pakistani]

J.C. Dudley & Co. Ltd
Incorporated: 13 April 1983 *Employees:* 13
Net Worth: £465,758 *Total Assets:* £3,844,353
Registered Office: Cheyney House, Francis Yard, East Street, Chesham, Bucks, HP5 1DG
Officers: Andrea Mary Allen [1960] Financial Director; Mark Jonathon Cheyney Dudley [1965] Director; Michael Richard Cheyney Dudley [1955] Director

Dutch Delight UK Limited
Incorporated: 20 March 2018
Registered Office: 16 Harrow View, Hayes, Middlesex, UB3 2DW
Officers: Faisal Roya [1995] Director/Self Employed [Dutch]

DWR Cerist Cyf
Incorporated: 19 March 2009 *Employees:* 3
Net Worth Deficit: £137,740 *Total Assets:* £63,535
Registered Office: 2 Victoria Place, Bethesda, Bangor, Gwynedd, LL57 3AG
Shareholder: Agoriad Cyf
Officers: Arthur Edward Beechey, Secretary; David Austin [1955] Director/Assistant Bank Manager; Michael John Barlow [1947] Director/Training Contracts Manager

DYoung and Son Limited
Incorporated: 4 April 2018
Registered Office: 103 Wandsworth Road, London, SW8 2LX
Major Shareholder: Gordon Young

E & R Fruits Limited
Incorporated: 14 November 2017
Registered Office: Office A132, New Covent Garden Market, Nine Elms Lane, London, SW8 5EE
Major Shareholder: Mohamed Rachidi
Officers: Mohamed Rachidi [1978] Director [Moroccan]

E-Natural Limited
Incorporated: 24 August 2011
Net Worth: £30,485 *Total Assets:* £166,035
Registered Office: 201 Whitchurch Lane, Edgware, Middlesex, HA8 6QT
Shareholder: Rakhee Thakorlal
Officers: Praneal Thakorlal, Secretary; Praneal Jitendra Thakorlal [1979] Director/Businessman; Rakhee Thakorlal [1979] Director/Sales Advisor

Eagle Beer Ltd
Incorporated: 7 November 2013
Registered Office: 147 Cranbrook Road, Ilford, Essex, IG1 4PU
Major Shareholder: Fatma Akkaya
Officers: Fatma Akkaya [1970] Director

Eagle Drinks Ltd
Incorporated: 30 January 2019
Registered Office: 27 Rollason Road, Coventry, Warwicks, CV6 4AP
Officers: Arun Arulsothy [1991] Director/Sales Assistant [French]

Earths Greatest Ltd
Incorporated: 10 August 2018
Registered Office: 11 Woodside Road, London, E13 8RX
Major Shareholder: Tyrell Neil Langlais
Officers: Tyrell Neil Langlais [1988] Director

East and West Foods Cash and Carry Limited
Incorporated: 6 February 2019
Registered Office: 61b Caroline Street, Birmingham, B3 1UF
Officers: Surinder Singh [1974] Director/Wholesaler

East Lancs Suppliers Ltd
Incorporated: 24 November 2016
Registered Office: 153 Buncer Lane, Blackburn, BB2 6SY
Major Shareholder: Zabir Mohammed Patel
Officers: Dr Aadil Patel [1991] Director/Doctor; Dr Aaishah Patel [1993] Director/Dentist; Shahina Patel [1966] Director; Zabir Mohammed Patel [1963] Director

East2west Traders Ltd
Incorporated: 15 November 2018
Registered Office: 22 Dombey House, Wolseley Street, London, SE1 2BL
Major Shareholder: Semaan Harb
Officers: Semaan Harb [1989] Director

Eastway Cash & Carry Limited
Incorporated: 26 May 2015
Previous: Crescent Trading Solutions Limited
Net Worth: £74,007 *Total Assets:* £202,740
Registered Office: Unit Q1, Pegasus Works, 8-10 Roebuck Road, Hainault Business Park, Ilford, Essex, IG6 3UF
Officers: Anilbai Ramgharya [1956] Director/Investor

Easy CBD Limited
Incorporated: 17 September 2016
Registered Office: Bramleys, High Street, Scaldwell, Northants, NN6 9JS
Officers: Adam Richard Bates [1968] Director

Easy Squeeze Limited
Incorporated: 19 November 2003
Net Worth: £106,421 *Total Assets:* £130,600
Registered Office: 114 Hamlet Court Road, Westcliff on Sea, Essex, SS0 7LP
Shareholders: Dunneese Horscroft; William James Horscroft
Officers: William James Horscroft, Secretary; Dunneese Horscroft [1956] Director; William James Horscroft [1953] Director

Eatwell Catering Contractors (Norwich) Limited
Incorporated: 31 January 1972
Net Worth: £173,310 *Total Assets:* £257,711
Registered Office: Hollyhocks, Church Road, Yelverton, Norwich, NR14 7PB
Major Shareholder: Alan John Fuller
Officers: Janice Pamela Page, Secretary; Alan John Fuller [1949] Director/Caterer

Ecopure Waters International Limited
Incorporated: 4 May 2010 *Employees:* 3
Net Worth: £39,903 *Total Assets:* £140,609
Registered Office: Mill House, Mill Court, Great Shelford, Cambridge, CB22 5LD
Major Shareholder: John Michael Shirley-Beavan
Officers: John Michael Shirley-Beavan [1956] Director; Sophia Elinor Shirley-Beavan [1960] Director [Irish]; Jonathan Edward Hedderly Ward [1956] Director

Eda Quality Foods Limited
Incorporated: 3 September 2002 *Employees:* 85
Net Worth: £1,926,170 *Total Assets:* £7,693,200
Registered Office: Unit 1-8 Centenary Industrial Estate, Jeffreys Road, Enfield, Middlesex, EN3 7UD
Parent: TFC Holdings London Limited
Officers: Eran Ucur, Secretary; Ercan Ucur [1970] Director; Huseyin Ucur [1945] Director

Eda Quality Foods North UK Limited
Incorporated: 23 March 2018
Registered Office: Unit 1-8 Centenary Estate, Centenary Road, Enfield, Middlesex, EN3 7UD
Shareholders: Eda Quality Foods North UK Ltd; Victoria Dincer
Officers: Victoria Dincer [1970] Director; Ercan Ucur [1970] Director

Elan Import and Export Limited
Incorporated: 8 January 2018
Registered Office: 45 Wallace Road, Coventry, Warwicks, CV6 2LW
Officers: Elenchezhiyan Shanmugasundaram [1979] Director/Production Line Worker

Elderbrook Drinks Limited
Incorporated: 6 March 2015 *Employees:* 5
Net Worth: £75,212 *Total Assets:* £163,378
Registered Office: Prince Albert House, 20 King Street, Maidenhead, Berks, SL6 1DT
Shareholders: David Thomas Folkman; Craig Ian Jones
Officers: David Thomas Folkman [1975] Director/Commercial Manager; Justin Hicklin [1960] Director/Chairman; Craig Ian Jones [1986] Director/Commercial Manager; Lynn Catherine Woodward [1969] Director

Eldoflora Limited
Incorporated: 16 January 2017
Registered Office: Unit 2 Pop In Business Centre, South Way, Wembley, Middlesex, HA9 0HB
Major Shareholder: Tushar Dodhia
Officers: Tushar Dodhia [1963] Director/Businessman

Elegantly Spirited Limited
Incorporated: 23 August 2017 *Employees:* 1
Net Worth: £85,510 *Total Assets:* £120,267
Registered Office: Waterworks House, Pluckley Road, Charing, Kent, TN27 0AH
Officers: Martin George Pullen, Secretary; Alexander Jonathan Carlton [1973] Director; Andrew Saulez King [1966] Director/Consultant

Elev8 Energy Drink Limited
Incorporated: 16 August 2017
Registered Office: Level 1, Devonshire House, One Mayfair Place, London, W1J 8AJ
Parent: Pan 1 Limited
Officers: Dejphon Chansiri [1968] Director [Thai]

Elev8 Life Limited
Incorporated: 9 July 2013
Net Worth Deficit: £1,098 *Total Assets:* £1,354
Registered Office: Magnolia Cottage, Whaddon Road, Little Horwood, Milton Keynes, Bucks, MK17 0PR
Major Shareholder: Steven Adam Morley
Officers: Steven Adam Morley [1972] Director Sales

Elham Elliethy Ltd
Incorporated: 22 January 2019
Registered Office: 3 Meadow Street, Northwich, Cheshire, CW9 5BF
Major Shareholder: Martins Bonders
Officers: Awais Ahmad [1976] Director; Martins Bonders [1989] Director [Latvian]

Elias Trading Limited
Incorporated: 14 January 2019
Registered Office: 64 Constantine House, 14 Boulevard Drive, London, NW9 5XD
Major Shareholder: Oluyemisi Tolani Abioye
Officers: Richard Ayomide Oyegbami, Secretary; Oluyemisi Tolani Abioye [1966] Director

Eliya Europe Ltd
Incorporated: 28 February 2019
Registered Office: 15 The Borough, Brockham, Betchworth, Surrey, RH3 7NB
Major Shareholder: Bjorn Filip Botvid Johansson
Officers: Bjorn Filip Botvid Johansson [1978] Director [Swedish]

Eltrados Ltd
Incorporated: 5 February 2019
Registered Office: 2nd Floor, College House, 17 King Edwards Road, Ruislip, Middlesex, HA4 7AE
Major Shareholder: Ahmed Aly
Officers: Ahmed Aly [1980] Director/BA Information System [Egyptian]; Katarzyna Aly [1983] Director/Teacher [Polish]

Ely & Sidney Limited
Incorporated: 30 June 1981 *Employees:* 3
Net Worth: £811,735 *Total Assets:* £6,741,256
Registered Office: 91 Brick Lane, London, E1 6QL
Shareholder: Ely & Sidney Holdings Limited
Officers: Jason Zeloof, Secretary; Jason Zeloof [1974] Director

Emara Soft Drinks Ltd
Incorporated: 14 December 2015
Net Worth Deficit: £128,126 *Total Assets:* £217,300
Registered Office: Unit 2 Stevenson Road, Sheffield, S9 3XG
Major Shareholder: Ibrahim El-Hamdoon
Officers: Ibrahim El-Hamdoon [1981] Managing Director

Emaya Foods Limited
Incorporated: 1 May 2018
Registered Office: 52 Alonso Close, Chellaston, Derby, DE73 5AX
Officers: Dr Raguraman Munusamy [1979] Director/Engineer

Emmunity Limited
Incorporated: 10 October 2018
Registered Office: c/o Freuds, 1 Stephen Street, London, W1T 1AL
Major Shareholder: George Freud
Officers: George Freud [1995] Director

Emperor Trades Limited
Incorporated: 25 June 2018
Registered Office: Flat 4, Parnham House, Parnham Street, London, E14 7TX
Officers: Jamil Ahmed [1992] Director/Business Sales

Endetrox Ltd.
Incorporated: 15 February 2018
Net Worth Deficit: £564 *Total Assets:* £825
Registered Office: 4 Ryhope Road, London, N11 1BX
Major Shareholder: Laszlo Horvath
Officers: Laszlo Horvath [1986] Director [Hungarian]

Energy Drinks Ltd
Incorporated: 19 January 2011
Net Worth Deficit: £52,792 *Total Assets:* £100
Registered Office: Office Suite, Paxton Workshops, Llewelyn Road, Tanyfron, Wrexham, Clwyd, LL11 5TL
Major Shareholder: Howard Ian Edwards
Officers: Howard Ian Edwards [1963] Director

Enzyme's Secret Limited
Incorporated: 9 September 2013
Registered Office: Unit 107 Dale, Haverfordwest, Dyfed, SA62 3QU
Major Shareholder: Po Hsin Huang
Officers: Po Hsin Huang [1983] Director

Epson Trading Limited
Incorporated: 2 August 2018
Registered Office: Kemp House, 160 City Road, London, EC1V 2NX
Major Shareholder: Shabir Mohammed
Officers: Shabir Mohammed, Secretary; Shabir Mohammed [1974] Director/Businessman

Eqoob Limited
Incorporated: 19 September 2018
Registered Office: Unit 3H, Warelands Way, Middlesbrough, Cleveland, TS4 2JY
Major Shareholder: Abdelhamid Salih
Officers: Adem Bekhiet Adem, Secretary; Abdelhamid Salih [1986] Director/General Manager

Erbology Ltd
Incorporated: 28 September 2011 *Employees:* 2
Previous: Swiss Laboratories Ltd
Net Worth: £47,720 *Total Assets:* £105,038
Registered Office: 20-22 Wenlock Road, London, N1 7GU
Shareholders: Victor Turcan; Irina Turcan
Officers: Irina Turcan [1986] Director/Entrepreneur; Ludmila Turcan [1963] Director/Entrepreneur [Czech]; Victor Turcan [1989] Director/Entrepreneur [Czech]

ERE Igga Ltd
Incorporated: 8 January 2019
Registered Office: 139 Avon Street, Coventry, Warwicks, CV2 3GQ
Major Shareholder: Hawa Bari
Officers: Koko Tanoh, Secretary; Hawa Bari [1983] Director/Sales Professional

Eren Catering Ltd
Incorporated: 27 September 2018
Registered Office: 151 West Green Road, London, N15 5EA
Major Shareholder: Ahmet Ozgur
Officers: Ahmet Ozgur [1973] Director [Turkish]

ESL Trading Ltd
Incorporated: 28 December 2017
Registered Office: 1 Curzon Road, Salford, M7 2EG
Major Shareholder: Eliyohu Simchoh Leech
Officers: Eliyohu Simchoh Leech [1986] Director/Salesman

Eslan Lookray Ltd
Incorporated: 8 January 2019
Registered Office: 9 George Square, Glasgow, G2 1QQ
Major Shareholder: Vellautham Sivaloganathan
Officers: Vellautham Sivaloganathan [1958] Director/Manager

Essential Juices Ltd
Incorporated: 14 February 2019
Registered Office: 129a Southbury Road, Enfield, Middlesex, EN1 1PN
Major Shareholder: Ricci Francesca Gowland
Officers: Ricci Francesca Gowland [1986] Director

Estelon Holdings Limited
Incorporated: 5 January 2018
Registered Office: Broad Water Lodge, Higham Road, London, N17 6NN
Officers: Uzaifa Katende [1989] Director

Ets Mandy SPRL Ltd.
Incorporated: 31 January 2014 *Employees:* 1
Previous: Cheillon Limited
Net Worth: £1,092,009 *Total Assets:* £1,183,332
Registered Office: Unit 7 Pickhill Business Centre, Smallhythe Road, Tenterden, Kent, TN30 7LZ
Major Shareholder: Francois Mandy
Officers: Francois Mandy, Secretary; Francois Mandy [1948] Director [Belgian]

Euro Globe Distributors Limited
Incorporated: 18 March 2002
Net Worth: £310,656 *Total Assets:* £475,628
Registered Office: Unit D, Hainault Works, Hainault Road, Romford, Essex, RM6 5NF
Major Shareholder: Kulwant Singh Panessar
Officers: Kulwant Singh Panessar [1954] Director

Eurodrinks Ltd
Incorporated: 4 October 2018
Registered Office: 123 Bridge Street, Brechin, Angus, DD9 6HU
Major Shareholder: Andrzej Pawel Abratkiewicz
Officers: Andrzej Pawel Abratkiewicz [1966] Director [Polish]

Europol Trade Ltd.
Incorporated: 19 February 2018
Registered Office: 15 Stonegate Drive, Liverpool, L8 4YS
Major Shareholder: Anna Kuhn-Zowada
Officers: Anna Kuhn-Zowada [1981] Managing Director [Polish]

Eurostar HRK Ltd
Incorporated: 13 February 2019
Registered Office: 25 Bellbrooke Place, Leeds, LS9 6AR
Shareholder: Habib Ur Rehman Khan
Officers: Habib Ur Rehman Khan [1961] Director [Belgian]

Eurotrade Supply Limited
Incorporated: 20 September 2018
Registered Office: Kemp House, City Road, London, EC1V 2NX
Major Shareholder: Dennis Michael Dennis Michael Obrien
Officers: Dennis Michael Obrien [1964] Director

Eurozone Limited
Incorporated: 17 April 2018
Registered Office: 130 Old Street, London, EC1V 9BD
Officers: Murad Habiboglu, Secretary; Murad Habiboglu [1974] Director [Turkish]

Priya Even Limited
Incorporated: 22 February 2018
Registered Office: 9b Sanderstead Road, South Croydon, Surrey, CR2 0PH
Officers: Gnanapriya Seenivasan [1987] Director [Indian]

Ever-Tree Wholesale & Retail Limited
Incorporated: 4 July 2018
Registered Office: Unit 7-10 Station Approach, Hitchin, Herts, SG4 9UW
Major Shareholder: Sercihan Yusuf Ucur
Officers: Sercihan Yusuf Ucur [1995] Director

Evershine Trading Limited
Incorporated: 2 August 2017
Registered Office: 30 Kingshill Drive, Glasgow, G44 4QY
Major Shareholder: Sheikh Sabir Mahmood
Officers: Sheikh Sabir Mahmood [1953] Director/Manager

UK Wholesalers of Soft Drinks   dellam

Evo Fit Ltd
Incorporated: 7 January 2019
Registered Office: Old Co-op Buildings, West Parade, Leadgate, Consett, Co Durham, DH8 7PL
Shareholders: Fraser David Neill; Callum Robert William Dixon
Officers: Callum Robert William Dixon [1993] Director/Fitness Trainer; Fraser David Neill [1995] Director/Fitness Trainer

Evoca UK Distribution Limited
Incorporated: 16 July 2012
Registered Office: Unit 3, 200 Gorton Road, Gorton, Manchester, M12 5DX
Officers: Waqas Ahmed [1990] Director

Evogue Limited
Incorporated: 14 June 2016
Registered Office: 38 Park Street, Mayfair, London, W1K 2JF
Major Shareholder: Andreas Yanakopoulos
Officers: Georgios Chondrorizos [1967] Director [Greek]

Evrywater Ltd
Incorporated: 6 February 2019
Registered Office: 7 Worlds End Estate, Upper Blantyre Walk, London, SW10 0DX
Major Shareholder: Amin Elwerfalli
Officers: Amin Elwerfalli [1991] Director/Plumber

EWF Wine Force Ltd
Incorporated: 27 January 2016
Registered Office: KR121, Kingspark Business Centre, 152-178 Kingston Road, New Malden, Surrey, KT3 3ST
Major Shareholder: Thirudan Kalavady
Officers: Thirudan Kalavady, Secretary; Thirudan Kalavady [1989] Director/Manager

Ewid Ltd
Incorporated: 10 April 2018
Registered Office: 99a Cricklewood Brodway, London, NW2 3JG
Major Shareholder: Malika Sadedine
Officers: Malika Sadedine [1982] Sales Director [French]

Exel Distribution Ltd
Incorporated: 15 January 2016
Net Worth Deficit: £39,249 *Total Assets:* £60,816
Registered Office: 30 Beverley Road, Luton, Beds, LU4 8EU
Major Shareholder: Rahim Khalid
Officers: Rahim Khalid, Secretary; Rahim Khalid [1980] Director/Property Manager

Exoshell UK Ltd
Incorporated: 31 December 2018
Registered Office: Peter House, Oxford Street, Manchester, M1 5AN
Major Shareholder: Talat Mahmood
Officers: Talat Mahmood [1974] Director

Exoteeque Limited
Incorporated: 12 June 2017
Net Worth Deficit: £7,808
Registered Office: 118-120 London Road, Mitcham, Surrey, CR4 3LB
Major Shareholder: Connie Petronella Parillon
Officers: Connie Petronella Parillon [1967] Director/Administrator

Export and Import Trading Ltd
Incorporated: 15 February 2019
Registered Office: 1 Bowden Terminal, Luckyn Lane, Basildon, Essex, SS14 3AX
Major Shareholder: Richard John Hull
Officers: Richard John Hull [1959] Director

F & T Enterprise Ltd.
Incorporated: 20 June 2012
Net Worth Deficit: £166,476 *Total Assets:* £152,184
Registered Office: 83 Balham High Road, Balham, London, SW12 9AP
Shareholders: Faisal Adnan; Muhammad Tayyab
Officers: Faysal Shaikh, Secretary; Faisal Adnan [1982] Director/Entrepreneur [Pakistani]; Muhammad Tayyab [1988] Director/Entrepreneur [Pakistani]

F.R.D Wholesale Limited
Incorporated: 19 January 2017
Registered Office: 17 Herald Way, Hinckley, Leics, LE10 2NX
Officers: Jagdeep Singh Dhami [1981] Director/Sales Manager

Failte Wholesale Limited
Incorporated: 22 October 1998 *Employees:* 2
Net Worth: £645,313 *Total Assets:* £757,866
Registered Office: East Warehouse, Glasgow Fruit Market, 130 Blochairn Road, Glasgow, G21 2DU
Shareholders: James Cummiskey; Margaret Cummiskey
Officers: James Cummiskey, Secretary/Grocery Retailer; James Cummiskey [1960] Director; Margaret Cummiskey [1960] Director

Falafel Factory Ltd
Incorporated: 20 December 2018
Registered Office: 161 Evington Road, Leicester, LE2 1QL
Major Shareholder: Hanan Al-Kawamleh
Officers: Hanan Al-Kawamleh [1977] Director [Jordanian]

Falcos Food Ltd
Incorporated: 24 October 2018
Registered Office: Suite 63, 22 Notting Hill Gate, London, W11 3JE
Major Shareholder: Salvatore Falconetti
Officers: Salvatore Falconetti [1987] Director [Italian]

Fanal Ltd
Incorporated: 14 November 2017
Registered Office: Flat 7, 61 Marlborough Place, London, NW8 0PT
Shareholders: Faraz Rezazadeh Helmi; Alborz Monzavi
Officers: Faraz Rezazadeh Helmi [1988] Director and Company Secretary [Iranian]

Faqir Billionaire Ltd
Incorporated: 10 September 2018
Registered Office: Four Kings Avenue, London, W5 2SH
Major Shareholder: Ameed Faqir Zada
Officers: Ameed Faqir Zada [1978] Director/Chief Executive

Farida Import Export Ltd
Incorporated: 5 May 2015
Registered Office: 302 Thornton Road, Croydon, Surrey, CR0 3EU
Major Shareholder: Omar El Basyouni
Officers: Omar El Basyouni [1982] Director/Entrepreneur

The Farm Shop at Ombersley Limited
Incorporated: 13 September 2018
Registered Office: Knotts Field Nurserys, Holt Fleet Road, Ombersley, Droitwich, Worcs, WR9 0HG
Major Shareholder: Alan Wilkinson
Officers: Alan Wilkinson [1954] Director/Businessman

Fast Car Sales Services Ltd
Incorporated: 9 March 2018
Registered Office: Ajaxworks, Movement House, Hertford Road, Barking, Essex, IG11 8DY
Officers: Abdul Hak Maljee [1969] Managing Director; Muhammad Maljee [1997] Director

Fast Food Traders Ltd
Incorporated: 8 March 2011 *Employees:* 10
Net Worth: £81,201 *Total Assets:* £268,321
Registered Office: Unit 3 Crofton Street, Old Trafford, Manchester, M16 9LY
Major Shareholder: Khalid Balaam
Officers: Khalid Balaam [1975] Director [Libyan]

Fearis Beverages Ltd
Incorporated: 19 November 2018
Registered Office: Unit 1973, 19 Vernon House, Friar Lane, Nottingham, NG1 6DQ
Major Shareholder: Amy Louise Fearis
Officers: Amy Louise Fearis [1992] Director/Administrator

Feeders Foods Wholesale Ltd
Incorporated: 28 April 2016
Registered Office: Deanway Technology Centre, 2 Wilmslow Road, Wilmslow, Cheshire, SK9 3FB
Officers: Adil Jabbar [1993] Director

Feel Group Limited
Incorporated: 27 September 2018
Registered Office: 20 Montrose Crescent, London, N12 0ED
Major Shareholder: Firat Helvacioglu
Officers: Firat Helvacioglu [1967] Director/Salesman [Turkish]

Ferment Revolution Limited
Incorporated: 12 May 2017 *Employees:* 3
Net Worth Deficit: £3,181 *Total Assets:* £657
Registered Office: 86a Yerbury Road, London, N19 4RS
Shareholders: Nicole Schubert-Nicolas; Clare Susannah Gerrard; Teresa Elizabeth Franke
Officers: Teresa Elizabeth Franke [1974] Director/Entrepreneur; Clare Susannah Gerrard [1963] Director/Entrepreneur; Nicole Schubert-Nicolas [1977] Director/Entrepreneur [German]

Patrick Fernando & Sons UK Ltd
Incorporated: 9 October 2015
Registered Office: 935 Harrow Road, Wembley, Middlesex, HA0 2RX
Shareholder: Joseph Reginold Fernando
Officers: Joseph Reginold Fernando [1968] Director

Fernhill Wholesale Ltd
Incorporated: 18 May 2018
Registered Office: Unit 2 Hornby Street, Bury, Lancs, BL9 5BL
Major Shareholder: Christopher Dore
Officers: Christopher Dore, Secretary; Christopher Dore [1945] Director

Fevertree Europe Limited
Incorporated: 2 January 2018
Registered Office: Kildare House, 3 Dorset Rise, London, EC4Y 8EN
Parent: Fevertree Limited
Officers: Andrew Branchflower [1979] Finance Director; Timothy Daniel Gray Warrillow [1975] Director

Fevertree Row Limited
Incorporated: 2 January 2018
Registered Office: Kildare House, 3 Dorset Rise, London, EC4Y 8EN
Parent: Fevertree Limited
Officers: Andrew Branchflower [1979] Finance Director; Timothy Daniel Gray Warrillow [1975] Director

Fevertree UK Limited
Incorporated: 2 January 2018
Registered Office: Kildare House, 3 Dorset Rise, London, EC4Y 8EN
Parent: Fevertree Limited
Officers: Andrew Branchflower [1979] Finance Director; Timothy Daniel Gray Warrillow [1975] Director

Fevertree US Limited
Incorporated: 2 January 2018
Registered Office: Kildare House, 3 Dorset Rise, London, EC4Y 8EN
Parent: Fevertree Limited
Officers: Andrew Branchflower [1979] Finance Director; Timothy Daniel Gray Warrillow [1975] Director

Fexty Ltd
Incorporated: 1 December 2018
Registered Office: 63a Blakeland Street, Birmingham, B9 5XQ
Major Shareholder: Zaheer Ahmad
Officers: Zaheer Ahmad [1960] Director

FIBM Wholesale Ltd
Incorporated: 4 July 2018
Registered Office: 354 Leith Walk, Edinburgh, EH6 5BR
Major Shareholder: Faisal Mahmood
Officers: Faisal Mahmood [1989] Director/IT Manager [Pakistani]

Firewater Merchants Ltd
Incorporated: 25 February 2019
Registered Office: 23 Craddock Road, Canterbury, Kent, CT1 1YP
Shareholders: Kofo Olaniyan; Laurenzay Beckford-Miller
Officers: Laurenzay Beckford-Miller [1997] Director/Self Employed; Kofo Olaniyan [1997] Director/Self Employed

First Food Ltd
Incorporated: 15 September 2016
Net Worth Deficit: £11,201 *Total Assets:* £19,504
Registered Office: 11a Meyrick Park Crescent, Bournemouth, BH3 7AG
Major Shareholder: Ilker Cimenlik
Officers: Ilker Cimenlik [1990] Director/Businessman [Turkish]

First Fruits Drinks Ltd
Incorporated: 6 July 2018
Registered Office: 2 Copes Lane, Ilton, Ilminster, Somerset, TA19 9HQ
Shareholders: Mark James Clydesdale; Kathryn Jane Maggs
Officers: Mark James Clydesdale [1987] Director/Engineer; Kathryn Jane Maggs [1990] Director/Waiter

Fitness Prostar Ltd
Incorporated: 17 January 2019
Registered Office: 83 Chobham Road, London, E15 1LX
Major Shareholder: Mark Cordwell
Officers: Mark Cordwell [1978] Director/Fitness Trainer

Five Star Cash & Carry Ltd
Incorporated: 16 March 2018
Registered Office: 27a Beehive Lane, Ilford, Essex, IG1 3RG
Major Shareholder: Salman Javed
Officers: Salman Javed [1956] Director

Flavour Foods & Drinks Ltd
Incorporated: 10 August 2016
Registered Office: 28 Bonsall Avenue, Derby, DE23 6JW
Officers: Sandeep Shinde [1974] Director

Flavours of Sardinia Limited
Incorporated: 4 April 2018
Registered Office: 9 Seagrave Road, London, SW6 1RP
Major Shareholder: Mauro Battista Ibba
Officers: Mauro Battista Ibba [1988] Director [Italian]

Fletcher's Fruit & Veg Ltd
Incorporated: 8 October 2018
Registered Office: 1a-1b Market Hall Street, Cannock, Staffs, WS11 1EB
Shareholders: Gillian Fletcher; Madeline Fletcher; Joseph James Fletcher
Officers: Gillian Fletcher [1962] Director; Joseph James Fletcher [1997] Director; Madeline Fletcher [1993] Director

Flow 33 UK Limited
Incorporated: 16 September 2014 *Employees:* 1
Net Worth Deficit: £111,448 *Total Assets:* £53,599
Registered Office: 63 Hampstead House, 176 Finchley Road, London, NW3 6BT
Major Shareholder: Ilan Azouri
Officers: Ilan Azouri [1969] Director [Israeli]

Flux Investment Ltd
Incorporated: 9 July 2013
Registered Office: 114a Bellegrove Road, Welling, Kent, DA16 3QR
Officers: Tripty Gurung Carpenter [1987] Director

FMCG Enterprises Limited
Incorporated: 23 April 2018
Registered Office: 5 Oakwood Estate, South Road, Harlow, Essex, CM20 2BZ
Officers: Hakan Akin [1976] Director [Turkish]

FMCG Express Limited
Incorporated: 16 October 2018
Registered Office: 28 Park Avenue, Oldbury, W Midlands, B68 8ET
Shareholders: Ranjit Singh; Jaswant Malhi
Officers: Jaswant Malhi [1977] Director; Ranjit Singh [1965] Director

Foal Limited
Incorporated: 16 April 2014
Net Worth Deficit: £17,623 *Total Assets:* £4,180
Registered Office: Flat 1/1, 2 Hanson Park, Glasgow, G31 2HA
Major Shareholder: Craig Robert Strachan
Officers: Craig Robert Strachan [1988] Managing Director

Food Brands Ltd
Incorporated: 26 April 2016
Net Worth Deficit: £15,470 *Total Assets:* £105
Registered Office: 192 Queens Road, Watford, Herts, WD17 2NT
Major Shareholder: Rabia Sherwani
Officers: Rabia Sherwani [1983] Director

Football Special Ltd
Incorporated: 20 January 2012
Previous: James McDaid & Sons Limited
Registered Office: c/o John Kennedy, 77 Butlers Wharf, Enagh, Derry, BT47 6SR
Major Shareholder: Edward McDaid
Officers: Desmond Doherty [1946] Director/Operations [Irish]; Seamus McDaid [1989] Director/Manager [Irish]; Edward McDaid [1949] Director [Irish]

Forward Moving Limited
Incorporated: 5 November 2018
Registered Office: Flat 2, 7 Rayners Road, London, SW15 2AY
Major Shareholder: Gianfranco Cianti
Officers: Gianfranco Cianti [1987] Director [Italian]

Fourseasons Fruiterers Ltd
Incorporated: 20 August 2014 *Employees:* 7
Net Worth Deficit: £286,359 *Total Assets:* £348,022
Registered Office: Victoria House, 10 Broad Street, Abingdon, Oxon, OX14 3LH
Shareholders: Nicola Ventriglia; Franco Ventriglia
Officers: Franco Ventriglia, Secretary; Franco Ventriglia [1974] Director [Italian]; Nicola Ventriglia Senior [1947] Director [Italian]

Stefan Frank Ltd
Incorporated: 12 September 2017
Registered Office: 105 Bond Road, Mitcham, Surrey, CR4 3HG
Shareholders: Fukhera Khalid; Stefan Poleon
Officers: Fukhera Khalid [1968] Director/Businessman; Stefan Poleon [1984] Director/Businessman

Franklin 1886 Limited
Incorporated: 23 September 2017
Registered Office: 5th Floor, CASA, Lockoford Lane, Chesterfield, Derbys, S41 7JB
Major Shareholder: Steven James Garcia Perez
Officers: Julian Atkins [1974] Sales Director; Shaun Bacon [1965] Finance Director; Sebastian Garcia Perez [1999] Director; Mark Peter James [1971] Sales Director; Steven James Garcia Perez [1956] Director

Freedom Sale Ltd
Incorporated: 8 November 2016
Registered Office: 102d-1, Peel House, 34-44 London Road, Morden, Surrey, SM4 5BX
Major Shareholder: Krishco Fernando
Officers: Krishco Fernando [1989] Director/General Manager

Freestar Drinks Ltd
Incorporated: 20 December 2018
Registered Office: The Old Mill, Ramsbury, Marlborough, Wilts, SN8 2PN
Major Shareholder: Matilda Charlotte Dallas
Officers: Matilda Charlotte Dallas [1988] Director/Gardener

Fresh Food Concepts Ltd
Incorporated: 14 January 2019
Registered Office: Harrisons, Blackgate Lane, Preston, Lancs, PR4 6JJ
Major Shareholder: Antony Thomas Harrison
Officers: Lord Antony Thomas Harrison [1961] Director

Fresh Fruit Direct Limited
Incorporated: 6 October 2016 *Employees:* 1
Net Worth: £24,878 *Total Assets:* £45,009
Registered Office: 5 London Road, Rainham, Gillingham, Kent, ME8 7RG
Major Shareholder: Mariusz Wojciech Szatkowski
Officers: Mariusz Wojciech Szatkowski [1979] Director [Polish]

Fresh N Green Ltd
Incorporated: 1 May 2018
Registered Office: Kemp House, 160 City Road, London, EC1V 2NX
Shareholders: Hawwa Nuzhath; Hassan Khalid
Officers: Hawwa Nuzhath, Secretary; Hassan Khalid [1965] Director [Maldivian]; Hawwa Nuzhath [1982] Director [Maldivian]

Fresh Pal Ltd
Incorporated: 22 October 2018
Registered Office: Kemp House, 160 City Road, London, EC1V 2NX
Officers: Catalina Balan [1982] Director [Romanian]

Fresh Produce Deliveries Limited
Incorporated: 17 January 2018
Registered Office: Glasgow Fruit Market, 210 Kennedy Street, Lister Street, Glasgow, G4 0BQ
Major Shareholder: David Bilsland
Officers: Joan Campbell Alexander [1958] Director/Office Manageress; David Bilsland [1956] Director

Fresh Produce Imports UK Ltd
Incorporated: 3 January 2018
Registered Office: Kemp House, 160 City Road, London, EC1V 2NX
Major Shareholder: Joy Ellingham
Officers: Joy Ellingham [1963] Director

Fresh Produce International Limited
Incorporated: 9 August 2018
Registered Office: 9 Reynolds Street, Fleet, Hants, GU51 1LG
Shareholder: Gideon William Chataika Chimuchere
Officers: Gideon William Chataika Chimuchere [1969] Director [Zimbabwean]

Fresh Star Fruit & Veg Limited
Incorporated: 19 March 2015 *Employees:* 2
Net Worth: £150,122 *Total Assets:* £174,857
Registered Office: 1-8 Centenary Estate, Jeffreys Road, Enfield, Middlesex, EN3 7UD
Parent: TFC Holdings London Limited
Officers: Ercan Ucur [1970] Director

Freshfield Exotics Ltd
Incorporated: 19 July 2017
Registered Office: 70 Kendal Road, Birmingham, B11 1HA
Major Shareholder: Samaera Khan
Officers: Samaera Khan [1974] Director/Business Manager

Freshwater Direct Limited
Incorporated: 29 June 2015
Net Worth: £100 *Total Assets:* £100
Registered Office: Flexi Spaces, 40 Ashton Old Road, Manchester, M12 6LP
Major Shareholder: Heath Donnelly
Officers: Heath Donnelly, Secretary; Heath Donnelly [1971] Director

Frobishers Juices Limited
Incorporated: 23 March 1999 *Employees:* 23
Net Worth: £1,903,931 *Total Assets:* £3,547,984
Registered Office: 6a Cranmere Court, Lustleigh Close, Matford Business Park, Marsh Barton Trading Estate, Exeter, Devon, EX2 8PW
Parent: Frobishers Juices (Holdings) Limited
Officers: Steven Carter [1960] Director; Andrew Clark [1963] Director; Graham Paget Holland [1969] Director; David Michael Pearce [1964] Managing Director; Nicholas Simon Sprague [1967] Director/Commodities Trader; Ian Charles Taylor [1972] Director

Frosty Service Ltd
Incorporated: 12 May 2017
Registered Office: 65 Coburg Road, London, N22 6UB
Major Shareholder: Sooppaiya Pillayar
Officers: Sooppaiya Pillayar [1985] Director/Sales Manager

Fruit & Veg 2 U Ltd
Incorporated: 27 April 2018
Registered Office: 1 Grenville Cottages, Winnington Road, Enfield, Middlesex, EN3 5RW
Major Shareholder: Ali Maraslioglu
Officers: Ali Maraslioglu [1983] Director

Fruit & Veg Imports Ltd
Incorporated: 11 December 2018
Registered Office: 71-75 Shelton Street, Covent Garden, London, WC2H 9JQ
Major Shareholder: Darius Rimkus
Officers: Darius Rimkus, Secretary; Darius Rimkus [1960] Director [Lithuanian]

Fruit Slush 'n' Shake Ltd
Incorporated: 12 September 2012
Registered Office: The Old School, The Stennack, St Ives, Cornwall, TR26 1QU
Major Shareholder: Ronald Peter John Battersbee
Officers: Ronald Peter John Battersbee [1945] Director/Refrigeration Engineer

Fruitex Limited
Incorporated: 7 June 2018
Registered Office: 291 Romford Road, London, E7 9HJ
Officers: Jacqueline Karen Johnson [1973] Director

Fruitfullest Ltd.
Incorporated: 22 January 2019
Registered Office: 27 Hartington Road, Walthamstow, London, E17 8AS
Major Shareholder: Mohamed Saber Khemdoudi
Officers: Mohamed Saber Khemdoudi [1989] Director/Security Guard

Fruits & Vegetables Ltd.
Incorporated: 7 February 2019
Registered Office: 75 Walton Green, New Addington, Croydon, Surrey, CR0 0TY
Major Shareholder: Dantwo Kyofa Matovu
Officers: Dantwo Kyofa Matovu [1986] Director

Fruity Cards Ltd
Incorporated: 6 March 2018
Registered Office: 58 Henry Cooper Way, London, SE9 4JF
Major Shareholder: Anita Sharpe
Officers: Anita Sharpe [1985] Director

Frutex Limited
Incorporated: 11 September 2015
Registered Office: 646 Hanworth Road, Whitton, Hounslow, Middlesex, TW4 5NR
Major Shareholder: Harjit Singh Lakman
Officers: Harjit Singh Lakman [1964] Director

Frutex UK PVT Limited
Incorporated: 2 May 2018
Registered Office: 50 Salisbury Road, Hounslow, Middlesex, TW4 6JQ
Major Shareholder: Endrit Palushi
Officers: Endrit Palushi [1998] Director/Businessman

Fruto del Espiritu C.I.C.
Incorporated: 25 January 2001
Previous: Fruto del Espiritu (UK) Ltd
Net Worth: £13,184 *Total Assets:* £32,007
Registered Office: Trees, 75 Fyfield Road, Ongar, Essex, CM5 0AL
Officers: Frances Harris, Secretary; Ruth Mary Stranack de Ballestas [1967] Managing Director

FS Wholesale Distributors (UK) Ltd
Incorporated: 1 May 2018
Registered Office: 174 Canterbury Road, Croydon, Surrey, CR0 3HE
Officers: Faysal Shaikh [1973] Director/Businessman; Muhammad Tayyab [1988] Director/Entrepreneur [Pakistani]

Funbella Ltd
Incorporated: 11 September 2018
Registered Office: 1 Erwood Road, London, SE7 8DR
Officers: Margaret Olubunmi Adepegba [1965] Director

Furze Young Limited
Incorporated: 14 December 2004
Net Worth: £84,096 *Total Assets:* £125,484
Registered Office: 10-12 Mulberry Green, Old Harlow, Essex, CM17 0ET
Major Shareholder: James Robert Furze
Officers: James Robert Furze, Secretary; James Robert Furze [1954] Director

Fusecutter Ltd
Incorporated: 25 July 2018
Registered Office: Unit 3 Trinity Centre, Park Farm Industrial Estate, Wellingborough, Northants, NN8 6ZB
Major Shareholder: Jenna Williams
Officers: Rose Anne Guimba [1994] Director [Filipino]

Future Generation Foods U.K. Limited
Incorporated: 10 October 2016 *Employees:* 1
Net Worth Deficit: £13,323 *Total Assets:* £116,029
Registered Office: Crowe Clark Whitehill LLP, St Brides House, 10 Salisbury Square, London, EC4Y 8EH
Major Shareholder: Matthew William Bailey
Officers: Matthew William Bailey [1968] Director [Australian]

Gabby & Bello Enterprises Ltd
Incorporated: 14 July 2009
Net Worth Deficit: £20,350 *Total Assets:* £37,436
Registered Office: 10 Fourth Avenue, Clayton, Manchester, M11 4LZ
Major Shareholder: Gbola Daud Bello
Officers: Gbola Daud Bello [1961] Director [Nigerian]

GB Heritage Ltd
Incorporated: 21 September 2018
Registered Office: Beck House, King Street, Knutsford, Cheshire, WA16 6DX
Major Shareholder: Siobhan Cathrina Maria Brady
Officers: Siobhan Cathrina Maria Brady [1972] Sales Director

GCA Foods Edinburgh Ltd
Incorporated: 13 September 2018
Registered Office: Unit 1a Poltonhall Industrial Estate, Lasswade, Edinburgh, EH18 1BW
Major Shareholder: Giray Karsli
Officers: Giray Karsli [1979] Director

GDH Distribution Limited
Incorporated: 5 April 2013
Net Worth Deficit: £9,820 *Total Assets:* £50
Registered Office: Ollerbarrow House, 209-211 Ashley Road, Hale, Cheshire, WA15 9SQ
Major Shareholder: Gary David Hymanson
Officers: Gary David Hymanson [1966] Director

Geema Service Ltd
Incorporated: 14 August 2018
Registered Office: 24 Little Ilford Lane, London, E12 5PW
Major Shareholder: Jansan Sivalingam
Officers: Jansan Sivalingam [1987] Director

Gemini Wholesalers Limited
Incorporated: 19 July 2010
Net Worth: £110,769 *Total Assets:* £3,550,427
Registered Office: Unit 14 Wedgwood Court, off Wedgwood Way, Stevenage, Herts, SG1 4QR
Major Shareholder: Nileshkumar Agrawal
Officers: Nileshkumar Agrawal, Secretary; Nileshkumar Agrawal [1976] Director [Indian]

Geminiz Ltd
Incorporated: 6 April 2017
Registered Office: 32 Storrington Way, Werrington, Peterborough, Cambs, PE4 6QW
Major Shareholder: Miguel Angel Soto Mercado
Officers: Sebastian Bolliger Villalobos [1976] Director/Investor [Mexican]; Miguel Angel Soto Mercado [1975] Managing Director [Mexican]

Gentian Global Ltd
Incorporated: 7 December 2018
Registered Office: 27 Old Gloucester Street, London, WC1N 3AX
Shareholders: Rowan Smith; Reginald Lascaris; Kenneth Kinsey-Quick
Officers: Kenneth Kinsey-Quick, Secretary; Kenneth Kinsey-Quick [1966] Director; Reginald Lascaris [1947] Director; Rowan Smith [1964] Director [South African]

Georgian Food and Beverages Limited
Incorporated: 7 April 2014
Net Worth Deficit: £20,271 *Total Assets:* £9,425
Registered Office: 23 Consfield Avenue, New Malden, Surrey, KT3 6HB
Major Shareholder: Ioseb Natenadze
Officers: Ioseb Natenadze [1983] Director [Georgian]

Georgian Wine Company Ltd
Incorporated: 10 October 2018
Registered Office: 122 Boundary Road, London, NW8 0RH
Major Shareholder: Zura Kokorashvili
Officers: Zura Kokorashvili [1983] Director/Businessman

Gerrard Seel Limited
Incorporated: 4 May 1984 Employees: 12
Net Worth: £873,963 Total Assets: £1,341,289
Registered Office: 31 Melford Court, Hardwick Grange, Woolston, Warrington, Cheshire, WA1 4RZ
Shareholder: Philip Roger Barlow
Officers: Richard Louis Hales, Secretary; Philip Roger Barlow [1954] Director; Richard Louis Hales [1959] Director

Getfreshjuiceco Limited
Incorporated: 15 March 2004
Net Worth: £13,619 Total Assets: £14,894
Registered Office: 23 Queen Street, Mosborough, Sheffield, S20 5BP
Shareholder: Paul John Renwick
Officers: Nicola Ruth Strafford [1971] Director/Pharmacist

GFT Retail UK Limited
Incorporated: 24 September 2002 Employees: 4
Net Worth: £2,766,019 Total Assets: £3,678,374
Registered Office: Ormond House, 162 Park Close, Ashley Park, Walton on Thames, Surrey, KT12 1EW
Shareholders: Susan Dawn Pezzack; Stephen Pezzack
Officers: Susan Dawn Pezzack, Secretary; Stephen Robert Pezzack [1963] Director [Canadian]

GH Brands Ltd
Incorporated: 24 October 2017
Registered Office: 2 Court Mews, 268 London Road, Cheltenham, Glos, GL52 6HS
Shareholders: Mark Andrew Herbert; Martin William Gulliver
Officers: Martin William Gulliver [1986] Director; Mark Andrew Herbert [1985] Director

GI Food Group Limited
Incorporated: 21 July 2016
Net Worth: £244,693 Total Assets: £793,622
Registered Office: Gable House, 239 Regents Park Road, London, N3 3LF
Major Shareholder: Daniela Yordanova Yordanova Ivanova
Officers: Daniela Yordanova Ivanova [1979] Director [Bulgarian]; Keith Robert Ridgway [1950] Director

The Gibraltar Gin Company Limited
Incorporated: 21 September 2018
Registered Office: Morants Hall, Colchester Road, Great Bromley, Colchester, Essex, CO7 7TN
Major Shareholder: Michael Joseph Volf
Officers: Michael Joseph Volf [1959] Director/Owner Care Group

Giovanni Food & Wine Limited
Incorporated: 21 June 2007 Employees: 14
Net Worth: £50,704 Total Assets: £177,652
Registered Office: Premier House, 36-48 Queen Street, Horsham, W Sussex, RH13 5AD
Shareholders: Franco James Barozzi; Maurizia Ascani
Officers: Maurizia Ascani [1975] Director/Manager of Cafe [Italian]; Franco James Barozzi [1986] Director

Gladiator Nutrition Supplements Limited
Incorporated: 20 December 2018
Registered Office: 14 Lewes House, Friary Estate, London, SE15 1RP
Major Shareholder: Adam Edward Sealey
Officers: Adam Edward Sealey [1983] Director/Entrepreneur

Glinter UK Ltd
Incorporated: 27 January 2015
Net Worth Deficit: £52,614
Registered Office: Dolphin House, 54 Coventry Road, Birmingham, B10 0RX
Shareholders: Abdiaziz Omar Nur; Abdulkadir Mohamed Ali
Officers: Abdulkadir Mohamed Ali [1985] Director/Accountant; Abdiaziz Omar Nur [1985] Director/Accountant [Danish]

Glitter Service Ltd
Incorporated: 26 April 2018
Registered Office: 109 Alderwood Avenue, Speke, Liverpool, L24 7RB
Major Shareholder: Gajan Selvan
Officers: Gajan Selvan [1983] Director/Sales Assistant

Global Food (Ashton) Ltd
Incorporated: 18 January 2019
Registered Office: Yacoob Malik & Co Accountants, 2 Brighton Range, Manchester, M18 7LP
Major Shareholder: Shaban Hussain
Officers: Shaban Hussain [1975] Director

Global Food (Nelson) Ltd
Incorporated: 23 December 2014
Net Worth Deficit: £12,384 Total Assets: £101,658
Registered Office: Trafalgar Hotel, Railway Street, Nelson, Lancs, BB9 0SE
Shareholder: Qadeer Hussain
Officers: Qadeer Hussain [1980] Director

Global Food Wholesalers Ltd
Incorporated: 25 April 2018
Registered Office: c/o RH & Co, 1st Floor, 254-256 Lincoln Road, Peterborough, Cambs, PE1 2ND
Shareholders: Farhad Khalnd Bilbas; Arkad Amirramathan
Officers: Arkad Amirramathan [1996] Director; Farhad Khalnd Bilbas [1969] Director

Global Fresh Ltd
Incorporated: 7 August 2014
Net Worth Deficit: £17,922 Total Assets: £47,968
Registered Office: MPS Business Centre, Fourth Way, Wembley, Middlesex, HA9 0HQ
Major Shareholder: Sami Mozil
Officers: Sami Mozil [1969] Director

Global Market Solutions Ltd
Incorporated: 24 October 2011
Net Worth: £41,326 Total Assets: £57,786
Registered Office: 48 Bath Road, Eye, Peterborough, PE6 7PY
Major Shareholder: Younes Tajer
Officers: Emma Victoria Tajer, Secretary; Younes Tajer [1978] Director/Student

Global Sports Trade Ltd
Incorporated: 20 December 2018
Registered Office: Summit House, 4-5 Mitchell Street, Edinburgh, EH6 7BD
Major Shareholder: John Bradley Carless
Officers: John Bradley Carless [1988] Director/IT Support

Global Sunshine Distribution Limited
Incorporated: 8 May 2012
Net Worth: £28,345 Total Assets: £81,573
Registered Office: 144 London Road, Dunstable, Beds, LU6 3EX
Major Shareholder: Samuel Oteng
Officers: Paulina Nti-Appiah [1967] Director/Carer [Ghanaian]; Samuel Oteng [1966] Director/Trader [Ghanaian]

UK Wholesalers of Soft Drinks

Global Vitality Ltd.
Incorporated: 5 October 2017
Registered Office: 27 Russell Road, London, N20 0TN
Shareholder: Anar Mammadov
Officers: Anar Mammadov [1977] Director

Globe Imex Ltd
Incorporated: 31 May 2017
Net Worth: £15,302 *Total Assets:* £23,202
Registered Office: 20-22 Wenlock Road, London, N1 7GU
Shareholders: Narrinder Singh; Ravinder Kaur
Officers: Ravinder Kaur [1955] Director; Narrinder Singh [1980] Director

Gloucester Wholesale Ltd
Incorporated: 8 May 2018
Registered Office: 13-19 Stroud Road, Gloucester, GL1 5AA
Major Shareholder: Qiuji Lim
Officers: Qiuji Lim, Secretary; Qiuji Lim [1988] Director [Irish]

Glow Penny Ltd
Incorporated: 17 December 2018
Registered Office: 22 Amberley Grove, Birmingham, B6 7AN
Major Shareholder: Saqib Suleman
Officers: Saqib Suleman [1983] Director

GM Catering Supplies Ltd
Incorporated: 2 February 2016
Net Worth: £51,329 *Total Assets:* £93,753
Registered Office: The Gate Business Centre, Keppoch Street, Cardiff, CF24 3JW
Shareholder: Mian Gul
Officers: Mian Gul [1987] Director

Go Fresh Ltd
Incorporated: 14 December 2017
Registered Office: 20-22 Wenlock Road, London, N1 7GU
Major Shareholder: Jesvinder Devi
Officers: Jesvinder Devi [1970] Director/Project Manager

GO4 Beverages Limited
Incorporated: 15 August 2016
Net Worth: £344 *Total Assets:* £792
Registered Office: 8 Eastmead Avenue, Greenford, Middlesex, UB6 9RA
Officers: Nathanael Lasme [1959] Director [Ivorian]

Gohir Soft Drinks Ltd
Incorporated: 22 May 2018
Registered Office: 116 Aylesford Road, Handsworth, W Midlands, B21 8DG
Major Shareholder: Amandeep Gohir
Officers: Amandeep Gohir, Secretary; Amandeep Gohir [1983] Director

A Gohir Soft Drinks UK Limited
Incorporated: 8 June 2018
Registered Office: 116 Aylesford Road, Handsworth, Birmingham, B21 8DG
Major Shareholder: Amandeep Gohir
Officers: Amandeep Gohir, Secretary; Amandeep Gohir [1983] Director

Going Ahead Ltd
Incorporated: 9 April 2018
Registered Office: 10 District Road, Wembley, Middlesex, HA0 2LD
Major Shareholder: Seweryn Stefan Gonera
Officers: Seweryn Stefan Gonera [1968] Director [Polish]

Gold Star Soft Drinks Westcountry Limited
Incorporated: 18 December 2009
Net Worth: £6,977 *Total Assets:* £129,558
Registered Office: 15 Bradfield Close, Leigham, Plymouth, PL6 8NG
Major Shareholder: Roger Melville Jolly
Officers: Roger Melville Jolly [1959] Director/Manager

Golden Eagle Foods Edinburgh Ltd
Incorporated: 13 September 2018
Registered Office: Unit 1b Poltonhall Industrial Estate, Lasswade, Edinburgh, EH18 1BW
Major Shareholder: Caroline Mary Bennett
Officers: Caroline Mary Bennett [1978] Director

Golden Eagle Trade Edinburgh Ltd
Incorporated: 13 September 2018
Registered Office: Unit 1b Poltonhall Industrial Estate, Lasswade, Edinburgh, EH18 1BW
Major Shareholder: Caroline Mary Bennett
Officers: Caroline Mary Bennett [1978] Director

Golden Fastfood Limited
Incorporated: 21 October 2008
Net Worth: £9,292 *Total Assets:* £406,160
Registered Office: Unit 6F, Chancery Gate Business Centre, Brent Road, Southall, Middlesex, UB2 5DB
Major Shareholder: Mehmet Demirkaya
Officers: Mehmet Demirkaya [1975] Director/Businessman

Golden Pride Export Limited
Incorporated: 27 September 2013 *Employees:* 1
Net Worth Deficit: £68,451 *Total Assets:* £116,437
Registered Office: 55 High Street, Hoddesdon, Herts, EN11 8TQ
Officers: David Elias Fine [1952] Director; Brett Levin [1981] Director

Gone Fresh Limited
Incorporated: 24 July 2018
Registered Office: 183 Leeds Road, Nelson, Lancs, BB9 8EQ
Officers: Abdul Rahim Rana [1981] Director

The Good Gut Guys Ltd
Incorporated: 4 December 2018
Registered Office: 23d Queens Road, Twickenham, Middlesex, TW1 4EZ
Major Shareholder: Hayley Louise Ford
Officers: Hayley Louise Ford [1988] Director/Administrator

Good News International Trading Ltd
Incorporated: 1 February 2019
Registered Office: 71-75 Shelton Street, Covent Garden, London, WC2H 9JQ
Major Shareholder: Dakun Wang
Officers: Dakun Wang, Secretary; Dakun Wang [1976] Director/Manager

Good Prices Ltd
Incorporated: 27 January 2017
Net Worth: £456 *Total Assets:* £456
Registered Office: Unit 7 Rea Industrial State, Inkerman Street, Birmingham, B7 4SH
Officers: Robert Marius Roth [1984] Director [Romanian]

Gorog Trading Limited
Incorporated: 6 February 2018
Registered Office: 77 Dewsbury Road, Luton, Beds, LU3 2HJ
Major Shareholder: Ferenc Gorog
Officers: Ferenc Gorog [1956] Director [Hungarian]

Govmalt & H.U.M.M.E.R. Beverages Global Company Limited
Incorporated: 26 May 2016
Net Worth: £1,740 *Total Assets:* £2,890
Registered Office: 117 Bostall Lane, Abbeywood, London, SE2 0JY
Major Shareholder: Victoria Umoru
Officers: Sharon Umoru, Secretary; Lawrence Umoru [1994] Director/Business Analyst; Victoria Umoru [1971] Director

Great British Beverages Limited
Incorporated: 9 August 2018
Registered Office: Martins, Wootton Courtenay, Minehead, Somerset, TA24 8RL
Major Shareholder: Christopher Mark Davenport
Officers: Christopher Mark Davenport [1962] Director

Great Wins Ltd
Incorporated: 19 April 2018
Registered Office: 21 Ripley Road, Ilford, Essex, IG3 9HA
Major Shareholder: Navaradnam Thuvaraganathan
Officers: Navaradnam Thuvaraganathan [1962] Director

Green Ambition Limited
Incorporated: 6 September 2018
Registered Office: 10a-12a High Street, East Grinstead, W Sussex, RH19 3AW
Shareholders: Vince Fox; William Spice
Officers: Vincent James Fox [1979] Director/Project Manager; William Edward Spice [1983] Director/Procurement Consultant

Green Cash & Carry Ltd
Incorporated: 8 February 2019
Registered Office: 15 Herbert Road, Kirkby in Ashfield, Nottingham, NG17 9DD
Major Shareholder: Octavian Rusu
Officers: Octavian Rusu [1988] Director [Romanian]

Green Foods International Ltd
Incorporated: 30 October 2018
Registered Office: 40 Parliament Street, Small Heath, Birmingham, B10 0QJ
Major Shareholder: Sheikh Mohammed Goyas Uddin
Officers: Sheikh Mohammed Goyas Uddin [1970] Director/Businessman

Green Warehouse Hodge Hill Ltd
Incorporated: 28 September 2018
Registered Office: 1 Camden Street, Leicester, LE1 2AP
Major Shareholder: Mohamed Korakkottil
Officers: Mohamed Korakkottil [1961] Director/Manager [Indian]

Green Warehouse Washwood Ltd
Incorporated: 27 September 2018
Registered Office: 1 Camden Street, Leicester, LE1 2AP
Major Shareholder: Mohamed Mohamed
Officers: Mohamed Korakkottil [1961] Director/Manager [Indian]

Greenme Ltd
Incorporated: 11 December 2012
Net Worth Deficit: £3,922,085 *Total Assets:* £249,249
Registered Office: 1a Crown Lane, London, SW16 3DJ
Officers: Johanna Elizabeth Snyman [1969] Director/Consultant [South African]

Grillburger Holdings Limited
Incorporated: 13 February 2019
Registered Office: 29 Inaclete Road, Stornoway, Isle of Lewis, HS1 2RB
Major Shareholder: Sean Clark
Officers: Sean Clark, Secretary; Sean Clark [1980] Director/Fish Merchant; Alistair MacLennan [1958] Director/Self Employed

Grouptype Limited
Incorporated: 9 October 2001
Net Worth: £1,010,885 *Total Assets:* £1,085,885
Registered Office: 81 Pinner View, Harrow, Middlesex, HA1 4RZ
Shareholders: Sonia Majithia; Sarjool Majithia
Officers: Chunilal Shah, Secretary; Sarjool Majithia [1968] Managing Director; Sonia Majithia [1968] Director

GSKB Ltd
Incorporated: 3 December 2018
Registered Office: Flat 4, 32 Clifton Gardens, London, NW11 7EL
Major Shareholder: Richard George Hurst
Officers: Richard George Hurst [1972] Director [Portuguese]

GSTWholesale Limited
Incorporated: 18 June 2018
Registered Office: 10 Sabell Road, Smethwick, W Midlands, B67 7PN
Officers: Gurpreet Sahota [1992] Director

GT Traders Ltd.
Incorporated: 21 June 2017
Registered Office: 7 Burlington Avenue, Slough, SL1 2JY
Major Shareholder: Shazad Hussain Choudry
Officers: Shazad Hussain Choudry [1974] Director/Management; Mohammed Omair Javed [1986] Director/Manager

Gulzar Traders Ltd
Incorporated: 14 July 2016
Net Worth: £100 *Total Assets:* £100
Registered Office: Flat 11, 85 Sudbury Avenue, Wembley, Middlesex, HA0 3BL
Major Shareholder: Abdul Azim
Officers: Abdul Azim [1979] Director/Business Person

Gusto Organic Ltd
Incorporated: 10 April 2012 *Employees:* 1
Net Worth Deficit: £190,134 *Total Assets:* £121,409
Registered Office: Midways, Freezeland Lane, Bexhill on Sea, E Sussex, TN39 5JD
Shareholders: William Fugard; Craig Lynn Sams
Officers: William Fugard [1970] Sales Director; Craig Lynn Sams [1944] Director/Writer

GVK Wholesale Ltd
Incorporated: 23 August 2018
Registered Office: 13 Opal Close, London, E16 3TT
Major Shareholder: Balasomasuntharam Karunarajah
Officers: Balasomasuntharam Karunarajah [1966] Director [Swiss]

GWB Associates Limited
Incorporated: 12 August 1999
Net Worth Deficit: £21,873 *Total Assets:* £10,817
Registered Office: 8 Luffman Road, London, SE12 9SX
Major Shareholder: Graham William Beever
Officers: Patricia Beever, Secretary; Graham William Beever [1952] Director

UK Wholesalers of Soft Drinks

H & F Export Limited
Incorporated: 8 January 2019
Registered Office: 35 Sherwood Street, Warsop, Mansfield, Notts, NG20 0JR
Officers: Francis Austin O'Neill [1983] Director/Consultant; Xiangyu Wei [1990] Director [Chinese]

H N D Trading Limited
Incorporated: 12 August 2013
Registered Office: 117 Station Crescent, Ashford, Surrey, TW15 3HN
Major Shareholder: Srinivasa Rao Rao
Officers: Harsha Vardhan Babu Vajja [1991] Director/Entrepreneur [Indian]; Srinivasa Rao Vajja [1964] Director/Entrepreneur [Indian]

H Two Eau International Limited
Incorporated: 19 August 2016
Net Worth: £3 *Total Assets:* £2,009
Registered Office: Flat 1, 75 Egerton Gardens, London, SW3 2BY
Shareholders: Brigidino Fiordilino; Andreas Breijs; Levico Acque SRL.
Officers: Andreas Breijs, Secretary; Brigidino Fiordilino [1964] Director/Trade Agent [Italian]

H2O Supplies Ltd
Incorporated: 11 March 2009
Net Worth: £1,040 *Total Assets:* £8,584
Registered Office: 2 Mowbrays Road, Romford, Essex, RM5 3ET
Major Shareholder: Shoaib Awan
Officers: Shoaib Awan [1982] Director

Haggard.Grb Ltd
Incorporated: 26 February 2019
Registered Office: 128 Field Street, Liverpool, L3 8BY
Major Shareholder: Ghaith Imad Ismat
Officers: Ghaith Imad Ismat [1991] Director/Salesman [Slovak]

Haltrade UK Ltd
Incorporated: 2 October 2017
Registered Office: Unit 19 Observatory Mall, Deen, High Street, Slough, Berks, SL1 1LE
Shareholders: Zahid Sharif Butt; Tengku Rozidar
Officers: Zahid Sharif Butt [1976] Director; Maximiliana Theresia Henrica Hendrickx-Butt [1982] Director and Company Secretary [Dutch]; Tengku Rozidar [1968] Director [Malaysian]

Hamer & Perks Limited
Incorporated: 8 April 1999 *Employees:* 2
Net Worth Deficit: £20,731 *Total Assets:* £57,598
Registered Office: Unit D, Constellation Mill, Higher Ainsworth Road, Radcliffe, Bury, Lancs, M26 4AD
Major Shareholder: Frederick John Thomas Rushton
Officers: Frederick Johnthomas Rushton [1966] Director/Salesman

Hannah & Ted Ltd
Incorporated: 28 November 2017
Registered Office: 39 Clamp Drive, Swadlincote, Derbys, DE11 9BP
Major Shareholder: Marcin Taton
Officers: Marcin Taton [1981] Director [Polish]

Harp & Crown Cider Company Limited
Incorporated: 5 March 2018
Registered Office: Bridge House, 64-72 Mabgate, Leeds, LS9 7DZ
Major Shareholder: Robert (Elias) Wilson
Officers: Robert Wilson [1941] Director (CEO)

Harsimran K Ltd
Incorporated: 28 September 2018
Registered Office: 6 Natal Road, Ilford, Essex, IG1 2HA
Major Shareholder: Jaipreet Singh Bath
Officers: Jaipreet Singh Bath [1977] Director [Indian]

Hatton Wholesale Ltd
Incorporated: 9 October 2018
Registered Office: 24 Crossland, Milton Keynes, Bucks, MK14 6AX
Officers: Antony Suthagaran Jeyaseelan [1981] Director

Hayat Supermarket Ltd
Incorporated: 8 August 2018
Registered Office: 36-40 Snow Hill, Stoke on Trent, Staffs, ST1 4LY
Officers: Asif Mahmood Mirza [1957] Director; Atif Arslan Mirza [1988] Director/Manager; Yousaf Islam Mirza [1991] Director/Manager; Ramazan Ozturk [1991] Director/Manager [Turkish]

HDL Trading Limited
Incorporated: 2 June 2010 *Employees:* 1
Previous: Heaven Drinks Limited
Net Worth: £133,108 *Total Assets:* £458,912
Registered Office: 132 Burnt Ash Road, Lee, London, SE12 8PU
Major Shareholder: Giosue Guglielmi
Officers: Giosue Guglielmi [1971] Director [Italian]

Healthy Food and Drink Online Limited
Incorporated: 18 July 2017
Registered Office: Flat 37, 20 Henry Street, Liverpool, L1 5BS
Officers: Seyed Ali Shojaee [1984] Director [Iranian]

Healthy Hit Ltd
Incorporated: 16 July 2018
Registered Office: 114 Orbis Wharf, Bridge Court Road, London, SW11 3GX
Major Shareholder: Roeiner Santos Batista
Officers: Roeiner Santos Batista [1980] Director/Chief Executive [British/Brazilian]

Healthy Hydration Limited
Incorporated: 25 April 2013
Previous: Ipro Sport Management Limited
Registered Office: Suite E2, 2nd Floor, The Octagon, Middleborough, Colchester, Essex, CO1 1TG
Officers: Thomas Edward Garrad [1991] Director

Hell Beverages UK Ltd
Incorporated: 12 June 2018
Registered Office: Waterside House, Unit 3 Waterside Business Park, 1649 Pershore Road, Kings Norton, Birmingham, B30 3DR
Major Shareholder: Tomas Grosch
Officers: Tomas Grosch [1970] Director [Slovak]

Hellenic Agora Limited
Incorporated: 27 June 2018
Registered Office: 178 Seven Sisters Road, London, N7 7PX
Major Shareholder: Panagiotis Soiledis
Officers: Panagiotis Soiledis [1963] Director [Greek]

Hellenic Grocery Limited
Incorporated: 9 July 2013
Net Worth: £54,772 *Total Assets:* £141,872
Registered Office: Unit 15 Hilsea Business Estate, Limberline Spur, Portsmouth, PO3 5JW
Major Shareholder: Evangelos Elykidis
Officers: Evangelos Lykidis [1978] Director [Greek]

Hello Coco Limited
Incorporated: 28 April 2016
Net Worth: £100 *Total Assets:* £800
Registered Office: 110 Viglen House, Alperton Lane, Wembley, Middlesex, HA0 1HD
Major Shareholder: Hemanth Patak
Officers: Heman Pathak [1959] Director/Businessman

Herbaleva Ltd
Incorporated: 16 May 2017
Registered Office: Flat D, 290 Dollis Hill Lane, London, NW2 5HH
Major Shareholder: Abdelrahman Traboulssi Barake
Officers: Abdelrahman Traboulssi Barake, Secretary; Abdelrahman Traboulssi Barake [1968] Director [Swedish]

Herbarium Limited
Incorporated: 4 July 2018
Registered Office: Kings Head House, 15 London End, Beaconsfield, Bucks, HP9 2HN
Major Shareholder: Andrew Clive Stacey
Officers: Andrew Clive Stacey [1967] Director

Herbs 4 Healthy Living Ltd
Incorporated: 6 December 2017
Registered Office: 20-22 Wenlock Road, London, N1 7GU
Officers: Dawn Patricia Ramsay [1961] Director/Teacher

Hermes Chariot Ltd
Incorporated: 30 May 2017
Registered Office: 25 West End Road, Southall, Middlesex, UB1 1JQ
Officers: Rohit Ratra [1994] Director; Sunil Rattu [1993] Director

Hero Catering Supplies Limited
Incorporated: 11 January 2012
Net Worth: £12,630 *Total Assets:* £427,098
Registered Office: 2a Stacey Avenue, London, N18 3PL
Major Shareholder: Ferdi Kahraman
Officers: Ferdi Kahraman [1984] Director/Caterer [Turkish]

Hesana Ltd
Incorporated: 9 July 2013
Registered Office: International House, 24 Holborn Viaduct, London, EC1A 2BN
Officers: Kolawole Hakeem Alabi [1979] Director/Sales Officer [Nigerian]; Birahim M'bow [1983] Director/Strategy Officer [French]; Lamine M'bow [1985] Director/Marketing Officer [French]

HF Food International Ltd
Incorporated: 3 January 2017
Net Worth: £10,921 *Total Assets:* £45,551
Registered Office: 236 Cranbrook Avenue, Hull, HU6 7TY
Major Shareholder: Suleyman Haji
Officers: Suleyman Haji [1976] Director/Car Parts Dealer; Hicham Wahbi [1978] Director/Teacher [French]

Hi Fresh Limited
Incorporated: 7 September 2016
Net Worth: £2,783 *Total Assets:* £66,710
Registered Office: 8 Thatches Grove, Chadwell Heath, Romford, Essex, RM6 5LA
Officers: Rajinder Singh [1986] Director [Indian]

Highland Cow Motor Home Ltd
Incorporated: 20 May 2011
Net Worth: £1,008 *Total Assets:* £1,711
Registered Office: 8 Low Road, Castlehead, Paisley, Renfrewshire, PA2 6AG
Officers: Hilary McCusker, Secretary; Ronald Mark Hounsell [1961] Director; Hilary McCusker [1959] Director/Editor

Hillcrest WM Ltd
Incorporated: 1 December 2018
Registered Office: 63a Blakeland Street, Birmingham, B9 5XQ
Major Shareholder: Zaheer Ahmad
Officers: Zaheer Ahmad [1960] Director

HM Wholesale Supplies Limited
Incorporated: 24 March 2017
Registered Office: 12 Kingshill Drive, Harrow, Middlesex, HA3 8TF
Major Shareholder: Hasanali Pyaralli Musani
Officers: Hasanali Pyaralli Musani [1957] Director

HMH Wholesale Ltd
Incorporated: 12 November 2013 *Employees:* 1
Net Worth: £2,845 *Total Assets:* £8,541
Registered Office: 52 Trinity Road, Luton, Beds, LU3 2LW
Major Shareholder: Halm Henry Micheal
Officers: Henry Michael Halm [1970] Director/Wholesale

Janos Horvath Ltd
Incorporated: 14 February 2019
Registered Office: 21 Cambridge Street, Bradford, BD7 3BX
Major Shareholder: Janos Richard Horvath
Officers: Janos Richard Horvath [1998] Director [Hungarian]

House Kitchen Limited
Incorporated: 9 July 2015
Registered Office: 72-74 Dean Street, London, W1D 3SG
Parent: Quentin Restaurants Holdco No.2 Limited
Officers: Nicholas Keith Arthur Jones [1963] Director; Enrique Lax Banon [1975] Director/Financial Services [Spanish]; Peter Jonathan McPhee [1975] Director [American]; Svend Christoffer Stael Thykier [1972] Director/Film Producer [Danish]

House Water Limited
Incorporated: 20 February 2008
Net Worth Deficit: £97,017 *Total Assets:* £117,065
Registered Office: Fiveways, 57-59 Hatfield Road, Potters Bar, Herts, EN6 1HS
Shareholders: Christine Francis Turness; Peter Laurence Turness
Officers: Richard Glyn Davies [1954] Director; Peter Laurence Turness [1951] Director

Hoversy Technologies Ltd
Incorporated: 23 October 2018
Registered Office: 70 Carmen Street, London, E14 6NW
Major Shareholder: Domenico de Ruosi
Officers: Domenico de Ruosi [1988] Director/Entrepreneur [Italian]

HP Juicery Ltd
Incorporated: 28 August 2018
Registered Office: 111 High Park Street, Liverpool, L8 3UF
Major Shareholder: Justin Yun
Officers: Justin Yun [1992] Director/Concierge

UK Wholesalers of Soft Drinks   dellam

HT Sweets (UK) Limited
Incorporated: 18 May 2017
Net Worth: £28,423 *Total Assets:* £304,724
Registered Office: Haider House, 35 Auckland Road, Birmingham, B11 1RH
Major Shareholder: Mahroof Ullah
Officers: Shazia Maroof [1975] Director; Maroof Ullah [1967] Managing Director

Hua Lin Trade Import Limited
Incorporated: 10 March 2014 *Employees:* 18
Net Worth Deficit: £36,462 *Total Assets:* £247,040
Registered Office: 25 Boundary Street, Liverpool, L5 9UB
Major Shareholder: Xin Zhang
Officers: Jason Yao, Secretary; Rong Li [1977] Director [Chinese]; Yao Sun [1980] Director; Xin Zhang [1983] Director [Chinese]

Hubit General Trading Ltd
Incorporated: 16 May 2018
Registered Office: Mitchell Carlesworth, 5 Temple Square, Temple Street, Liverpool, L2 5RH
Major Shareholder: Davide Di Costanzo
Officers: Davide di Costanzo [1989] Director [Italian]

Huma Gida UK Limited
Incorporated: 10 October 2014
Registered Office: 7 The Chase, Newhall, Harlow, Essex, CM17 9JA
Major Shareholder: Simge Uygun
Officers: Simge Uygun [1984] Director

Humble Bumble Ltd
Incorporated: 13 July 2018
Registered Office: 2nd Floor, College House, 17 King Edwards Road, Ruislip, Middlesex, HA4 7AE
Major Shareholder: Ian Scarborough
Officers: Ian Scarborough [1988] Director/Graphic Design

Hurly Burly Foods Limited
Incorporated: 11 April 2016
Net Worth: £14,600 *Total Assets:* £108,371
Registered Office: Providence House, 141-145 Princes Street, Ipswich, Suffolk, IP1 1QJ
Major Shareholder: Robert Hugo Chamberlain
Officers: Robert Hugo Chamberlain [1984] Director

Huskiblu Ltd
Incorporated: 27 November 2018
Registered Office: Kemp House, 160 City Road, London, EC1V 2NX
Officers: Michael Lipman [1960] Director/Solicitor

Hydra Cubed Limited
Incorporated: 10 November 2017
Registered Office: 57 Ashbourne Road, Derby, DE22 3FS
Major Shareholder: Anthony Philip Royston Salway
Officers: George Andrew Fotheringham [1957] Director/Chartered Accountant; Anthony Philip Royston Salway [1975] Director; Adam Whitchurch [1975] Director

I S Traders Limited
Incorporated: 26 November 2012
Net Worth: £376 *Total Assets:* £133,459
Registered Office: 521 Green Lane, Small Heath, Birmingham, B9 5PT
Major Shareholder: Zishan Saad Ayub
Officers: Zishan Saad Ayub [1981] Director

I Star Wholesale Limited
Incorporated: 29 May 2018
Registered Office: 69 Waldrons Moor, Birmingham, B14 6RT
Major Shareholder: Riaz Hussain
Officers: Riaz Hussain [1970] Director/Driver

Ibiza Recharge Limited
Incorporated: 18 January 2018
Registered Office: 27 Old Gloucester Street, London, WC1N 3AX
Major Shareholder: Andreas Sundbom
Officers: Andreas Sundbom [1973] Director [Swedish]

Ice Guys Ltd
Incorporated: 1 February 2019
Registered Office: 20-22 Wenlock Road, London, N1 7GU
Major Shareholder: Jason Marcelin
Officers: Jason Marcelin [1987] Director

Ideal Lincs Limited
Incorporated: 20 June 2005 *Employees:* 7
Net Worth Deficit: £56,144 *Total Assets:* £354,208
Registered Office: Grange Offices, Girsby Grange, Burgh on Bain, Market Rasen, Lincs, LN8 6LA
Major Shareholder: Paul MacKenzie Davey
Officers: Emma Caroline Davey, Secretary; Paul MacKenzie Davey, Secretary/Farmer; Emma Caroline Davey [1977] Company Secretary/Director; Paul MacKenzie Davey [1970] Director/Farmer; Richard MacKenzie Davey [1937] Director/Farmer

Ideal Trading Limited
Incorporated: 3 April 2017
Net Worth: £1 *Total Assets:* £1
Registered Office: Unit 22, 198 Swanston Street, Glasgow, G40 4HW
Major Shareholder: Sheikh Sabir Mahmood
Officers: Sheikh Sabir Mahmood, Secretary; Sheikh Sabir Mahmood [1953] Director/Manager

Ifood Trading Ltd
Incorporated: 20 February 2014
Previous: Joud Ltd
Net Worth Deficit: £9,849 *Total Assets:* £5,584
Registered Office: Suite 10, West Africa House, Ashbourne Road, Ealing, London, W5 3QP
Major Shareholder: Sheekh Aly Mohamad Anas
Officers: Mohamad Anas Sheekh Aly [1979] Director [Syrian]

Ilie Cash & Carry Ltd
Incorporated: 12 November 2018
Registered Office: 77a Bagot Street, Liverpool, L15 0HT
Major Shareholder: Petrut Vili Ilie
Officers: Petrut Vili Ilie [1994] Director [Romanian]

IMH Traders Limited
Incorporated: 7 December 2018
Registered Office: 92 Cromwell Lane, Birmingham, B31 1AS
Officers: Irina-Maria Hreniuc [1979] Director/Owner [Romanian]

Imperial House of 3 Kings Ltd
Incorporated: 5 November 2018
Registered Office: 34 New House, 67-68 Hatton Garden, London, EC1N 8JY
Major Shareholder: Yolanda Toussaint
Officers: Yolanda Toussaint [1979] Director

Importonics Limited
Incorporated: 9 March 2016
Net Worth: £20,325 *Total Assets:* £72,237
Registered Office: Jarrow Business Centre, Viking Business Park, Jarrow, Tyne & Wear, NE32 3DT
Shareholders: Antonio Jose Almiron-Martinez; Joan Targas Marcilla
Officers: Antonio Jose Almiron Martinez [1968] Director [Spanish]; Joan Targas Marcilla [1983] Director [Spanish]

Imran Brothers Limited
Incorporated: 21 December 2016
Net Worth Deficit: £17,507 *Total Assets:* £31,793
Registered Office: Unit 12, 18-26 Fancy Road, Poole, Dorset, BH12 4PZ
Major Shareholder: Mohammed Imran Abdal Talukder
Officers: Mohammed Imran Abdal Talukder [1986] Director

In2rehab Brands Limited
Incorporated: 3 December 2009
Net Worth Deficit: £3,948 *Total Assets:* £1,000
Registered Office: Harcourt House, Crab Lane, North Muskham, Newark, Notts, NG23 6HH
Major Shareholder: Antony Richard Harrison
Officers: Antony Richard Harrison [1965] Director

Inc. Trading Limited
Incorporated: 3 January 2013
Net Worth Deficit: £43,407 *Total Assets:* £858
Registered Office: 11 Greystoke House, 150 Brunswick Road, Ealing, London, W5 1AW
Major Shareholder: Laxman Nandwani
Officers: Laxman Nandwani [1966] Director/Wholesale and Retail

Indigo Private Ltd
Incorporated: 17 December 2018
Registered Office: 439 High Street North, London, E12 6TJ
Major Shareholder: Mohanasegaram Kandasamy
Officers: Mohanasegaram Kandasamy [1971] Director [Swiss]

Indigo Traders Ltd
Incorporated: 9 October 2018
Registered Office: 120 Hatherley Gardens, London, E6 3HB
Major Shareholder: Jose Pedro Rocha de Andrade
Officers: Jose Pedro Rocha de Andrade [1973] Director [Portuguese]

Infinite Session Ltd
Incorporated: 1 November 2017
Registered Office: 32 Chroma Mansions, 14 Penny Brookes Street, London, E20 1BP
Shareholders: Christopher John Hannaway; Thomas Eamon Hannaway
Officers: Christopher John Hannaway [1989] Director; Thomas Eamon Hannaway [1987] Director

Innerji Ltd
Incorporated: 25 August 2017
Registered Office: 272 Regents Park Road, Finchley Central, London, N3 3HN
Major Shareholder: Parham Sassooni
Officers: Parham Sassooni [1967] Director

Inside Out Life Drinks Ltd
Incorporated: 9 November 2018
Registered Office: 6 Pulton Place, Fulham, London, SW6 1EF
Major Shareholder: Ornel Emanuel Downer
Officers: Ornel Emanuel Downer [1972] Director/Sports Coach

Inspire Drinks Ltd
Incorporated: 7 May 2014
Net Worth Deficit: £4,166
Registered Office: Hilden Park House, 79 Tonbridge Road, Hildenborough, Tonbridge, Kent, TN11 9BH
Major Shareholder: Lisa Lee
Officers: Lisa Lee [1986] Director/Wholesaler

Intercontinental Trade Solutions Limited
Incorporated: 18 December 2018
Registered Office: 76 Padstow Road, Churchward, Swindon, Wilts, SN2 2EG
Officers: Samwel Maina [1989] Director

International Catering & Foods Limited
Incorporated: 13 July 2015 *Employees:* 1
Net Worth: £6,577 *Total Assets:* £71,816
Registered Office: 632 Green Lanes, London, N8 0SD
Major Shareholder: Huseyin Kilic
Officers: Huseyin Kilic [1961] Director

Interseel Ltd
Incorporated: 26 September 2017
Registered Office: 20-22 Wenlock Road, London, N1 7GU
Major Shareholder: Laszlo Szilagyi
Officers: Laszlo Szilagyi [1974] Director [Hungarian]

Ion Distribution Ltd
Incorporated: 14 November 2018
Registered Office: 20-22 Wenlock Road, London, N1 7GU
Major Shareholder: Martin Giles
Officers: Martin Giles [1987] Director/Horticulturist [Irish]

Ipro Sport Corporation Limited
Incorporated: 12 August 2016
Registered Office: 2nd Floor, Suite E2, The Octagon, Middleborough, Colchester, Essex, CO1 1TG
Parent: Ipro Sport Holdings Limited
Officers: Sophie Louise Christy [1975] Commercial Director

Ipro Sport Distribution Ltd
Incorporated: 20 March 2015
Net Worth Deficit: £412,377
Registered Office: 2nd Floor, Suite E2, The Octagon, Middleborough, Colchester, Essex, CO1 1TG
Officers: Sophie Louise Christy [1975] Commercial Director; Thomas Edward Garrad [1991] Director

Ipro Sport International Limited
Incorporated: 15 June 2016 *Employees:* 5
Net Worth: £601,397 *Total Assets:* £662,288
Registered Office: 2nd Floor, Suite E2, The Octagon, Middleborough, Colchester, Essex, CO1 1TG
Officers: Sophie Louise Christy [1975] Commercial Director

Ipro Sport Medical Limited
Incorporated: 20 September 2016
Registered Office: 2nd Floor, Suite E2, The Octagon, Middleborough, Colchester, Essex, CO1 1TG
Parent: Ipro Sport Holdings Limited
Officers: Sophie Louise Christy [1975] Commercial Director

IR Global Service Ltd
Incorporated: 30 June 2017
Net Worth: £100 Total Assets: £100
Registered Office: 46 Alphonsus Street, Middlesbrough, Cleveland, TS3 6EA
Officers: Inpanathan Inparaji, Secretary; Inpanathan Inparaji [1983] Director/Sales Assistant [French]

Ital World Ltd
Incorporated: 15 October 2018
Registered Office: 66 Hindes Road, Harrow, Middlesex, HA1 1SL
Major Shareholder: Brian Francis McKay
Officers: Brian Francis McKay [1974] Director/Artist

Iturn Global Ltd
Incorporated: 5 September 2017
Registered Office: Kemp House, 160 City Road, London, EC1V 2NX
Officers: Sankalp Rajen Sikka [1997] Director/Self Employed [Indian]

Iwater Inc Ltd
Incorporated: 6 February 2017
Registered Office: 72 Cardigan Street, Luton, Beds, LU1 1RR
Officers: Shamila Chaudhry [1980] Director

J & D Wholesalers Ltd
Incorporated: 30 May 2018
Registered Office: Kemp House, 160 City Road, London, EC1V 2NX
Officers: Luxan Sriskantharajah [1994] Director [Sri Lankan]

J & H Global UK Ltd
Incorporated: 27 July 2018
Registered Office: Calico House, Printworks Lane, Manchester, M19 3JP
Major Shareholder: Jude Nwokoro
Officers: Jude Nwokoro [1978] Director/Trader

J M & D Limited
Incorporated: 20 February 2009 Employees: 8
Net Worth: £81,929 Total Assets: £1,122,880
Registered Office: The Chancery, 58 Spring Gardens, Manchester, M2 1EW
Major Shareholder: Daniel Michael Hassall
Officers: Daniel Michael Hassall [1984] Director/FMCS Sales

JA & MD Limited
Incorporated: 9 February 2017
Net Worth: £96,143 Total Assets: £99,192
Registered Office: The Lodge, Park Road, Shepton Mallet, Somerset, BA4 5BS
Officers: Nicola Claydon, Secretary; John Haydon Jackson [1943] Director

Jacksons Milk Deliveries Ltd
Incorporated: 25 July 2018
Registered Office: 71-75 Shelton Street, London, WC2H 9JQ
Major Shareholder: Shelley Jackson
Officers: Shelley Jackson, Secretary; Shelley Jackson [1973] Director/Milk Lady

Jaden Wholesale Limited
Incorporated: 26 March 2018
Registered Office: Unit 5 Woodbarn Farm, Ansley, Nuneaton, Warwicks, CV10 0QP
Major Shareholder: Richard Arthurs
Officers: Richard Arthurs [1972] Director/Commodities Trader

Jaguar Beverage Ltd
Incorporated: 5 October 2018
Registered Office: Kemp House, 160 City Road, London, EC1V 2NX
Officers: Saeed Mohammadi [1971] Director [Canadian]

Jaguar Power Energy Drinks Ltd.
Incorporated: 5 December 2016
Registered Office: 132 Barking Road, London, E6 3BD
Major Shareholder: Zulfiqar Butt
Officers: Zulfiqar Butt [1982] Director/Businessman [Pakistani]

Jalkhushi Fresh & Frozen Fish Ltd
Incorporated: 14 October 2018
Registered Office: 13 Clayton Avenue, Wembley, Middlesex, HA0 4JU
Major Shareholder: Laxmibai China
Officers: Laxmibai China [1984] Director/Office Assistant Work [British/Portuguese]

Jamarec UK Limited
Incorporated: 14 August 2018
Registered Office: 6 Arnhem Close, Aldershot, Hants, GU11 1RJ
Shareholders: Ebrima Mboob; Oumie Adams
Officers: Ebrima Mboob, Secretary; Oumie Adams [1987] Managing Director [Danish]; Ebrima Mboob [1988] Managing Director

Jameson's Trading Ltd
Incorporated: 15 August 2018
Registered Office: 71-75 Shelton Street, London, WC2H 9JQ
Major Shareholder: Louis Jameson-Card
Officers: Louis Jameson-Card [1988] Director/Traffic Warden

Janama Trading Co Ltd
Incorporated: 9 September 2016
Registered Office: 5 Cedars Avenue, Walthamstow, London, E17 7QL
Major Shareholder: Javed Azam
Officers: Javed Azam [1962] Director

Janere UK Limited
Incorporated: 28 January 2019
Registered Office: 67 Luffield Road, Abbey Wood, London, SE2 9JN
Major Shareholder: Benedicta Janere
Officers: Benedicta Janere [1961] Director/Health Care Administrator

Jascera UK Ltd
Incorporated: 16 January 2018
Registered Office: 39 Richards House, Burrowes Street, Walsall, W Midlands, WS2 8NN
Major Shareholder: Ogonna Solomon Anolue
Officers: Ogonna Solomon Anolue [1975] Director/Entrepreneur [Nigerian]

Jasmine Blue Ltd
Incorporated: 10 December 2018
Registered Office: 82 Claremont Road, London, NW2 1AP
Major Shareholder: Sharron Constantine Palathis
Officers: Sharron Constantine Palathis [1994] Director/Sales Manager [French]

Jasmine Direct Limited
Incorporated: 17 February 2016
Net Worth: £16,815 *Total Assets:* £53,012
Registered Office: 214 Lower Addiscombe Road, Croydon, Surrey, CR0 7AB
Major Shareholder: Mete Ibis
Officers: Mete Ibis [1987] Director/Businessman [Turkish]

Jax Coco UK Ltd.
Incorporated: 17 September 2012 *Employees:* 2
Net Worth Deficit: £1,473,770 *Total Assets:* £137,508
Registered Office: 4th Floor, 21 Knightsbridge, London, SW1X 7LY
Parent: Jing Holdings Limited
Officers: Jane Elizabeth Gottschalk [1973] Director; Andreas Ruben Keijsers [1966] Director

Jays Trading Ltd
Incorporated: 16 June 2010
Net Worth: £10,945 *Total Assets:* £20,685
Registered Office: 299 Littleton Road, Salford, M7 3TA
Officers: Kevin Green [1955] Director/Self Employed

JCW Foods Ltd
Incorporated: 13 February 2019
Registered Office: Wycombe Timber Packing Co Ltd, 15 Haddenham Business Park, Aylesbury, Bucks, HP17 8LJ
Officers: Julian Woodley [1953] Director

S Jee Enterprises Ltd
Incorporated: 6 September 2018
Registered Office: 34 Deancourt Road, Leicester, LE2 6GH
Major Shareholder: Sanjeev Singh
Officers: Sanjeev Singh, Secretary; Sanjeev Singh [1979] Director

Jeet (UK) Limited
Incorporated: 9 July 2004
Net Worth: £77,789 *Total Assets:* £168,844
Registered Office: Unit 23 Phoenix Distribution Park, Phoenix Way, Hounslow, Middlesex, TW5 9NB
Major Shareholder: Salinder Kaur Gill
Officers: Salinder Kaur Gill [1979] Director/Sales Manager

Jeeva Natural UK Ltd
Incorporated: 19 November 2015
Net Worth Deficit: £40,540 *Total Assets:* £62,703
Registered Office: Regus, Stockley Park Lakeside House, 1 Furzeground Way, Stockley Park East, Uxbridge, Middlesex, UB11 1BD
Major Shareholder: Bhavana Sanchez Kanadia
Officers: Kaliya Perumal Servoo Ravishanker, Secretary; Bhavna Sanchez Kanadia [1980] Director; Harphjan Singh Rooprah [1963] Director

Jessica Worldwide Ltd
Incorporated: 3 April 2017
Net Worth Deficit: £380 *Total Assets:* £2,168
Registered Office: 180 Mansell Road, Greenford, Middlesex, UB6 9EH
Officers: Kamaljit Singh [1976] Director/Self Employed

JFC Trading Limited
Incorporated: 10 October 2014
Net Worth: £524,281 *Total Assets:* £546,628
Registered Office: Companies House, Default Address, Cardiff, CF14 8LH
Parent: James Harry Holmes
Officers: James Harry Holmes, Secretary; James Harry Holmes [1948] Director

JJ Import/Export Ltd
Incorporated: 12 February 2019
Registered Office: 46 Haven Lane, London, W5 2HN
Major Shareholder: Jurate Jasinskaite
Officers: Jurate Jasinskaite [1984] Director [Lithuanian]

JK Manchester Ltd
Incorporated: 6 February 2019
Registered Office: 10 Earlswood Walk, Bolton, Lancs, BL3 2SE
Major Shareholder: Javed Khalid
Officers: Javed Khalid [1972] Director [Spanish]

Jojo Best Coffee Ltd
Incorporated: 16 October 2018
Registered Office: 244 Hammonds Drive, Peterborough, Cambs, PE1 5AX
Major Shareholder: Jozef Rac
Officers: Jozef RAC [1976] Director/Retailer [Slovak]

Jones Bros. 1877 Ltd
Incorporated: 14 November 2017
Registered Office: 16c Blount Street, London, E14 7BZ
Officers: Catherine Susan Marian Jones [1954] Director; Henry David Jones [1988] Director; Henry Llewellyn Michael Jones [1955] Director; Lucy Catherine O'Rourke [1986] Director; Stephen Terence O'Rourke [1984] Director

R. & I. Jones Limited
Incorporated: 4 May 1989 *Employees:* 24
Net Worth: £1,320,631 *Total Assets:* £1,979,526
Registered Office: Old Bank Buildings, Bank Quay, Caernarfon, Gwynedd, LL55 1SU
Major Shareholder: Aled Roberts
Officers: Dorothy Roberts, Secretary; Aled Roberts [1970] Director; Dorothy Roberts [1946] Director; Meirion Roberts [1940] Director

Jonsen International Ltd
Incorporated: 13 February 2018
Registered Office: Flat 1/2 Govan Hill, 239 Langside Road, Glasgow, G42 8XX
Major Shareholder: Mirza Saeed Ahmed Baig
Officers: Mirza Saeed Ahmed Baig [1962] Director

Joo Soft Drinks Limited
Incorporated: 8 August 2016
Registered Office: Wilson House, 48 Brooklyn Road, Seaford, E Sussex, BN25 2DX
Major Shareholder: Praful Patel
Officers: Praful Patel [1959] Director

JR Quality Service Ltd
Incorporated: 20 July 2015
Net Worth: £60,348 *Total Assets:* £76,843
Registered Office: 82 Humber Avenue, Coventry, Warwicks, CV1 2AT
Major Shareholder: Jeyakumar Rajaratnam
Officers: Jeyakumar Rajaratnam, Secretary; Jeyakumar Rajaratnam [1972] Director/Sale Assistant [Norwegian]

JSJuices Ltd
Incorporated: 2 January 2019
Registered Office: 71-75 Shelton Street, London, WC2H 9JQ
Major Shareholder: Javan Simpson
Officers: Javan Simpson [1994] Director

Juice de Vine Limited
Incorporated: 2 April 2013
Net Worth Deficit: £33,218 Total Assets: £1,126
Registered Office: Wesley Offices, 74 Silver Street, Nailsea, Bristol, BS48 2DS
Major Shareholder: Ivan Morgan
Officers: Ivan Percival Morgan [1960] Director/Family Support Worker

Juice Junkie London Limited
Incorporated: 9 November 2017
Registered Office: 68 Ulster Gardens, London, N13 5DW
Officers: Mahmut Dede [1983] Director

Juice Junkiez Limited
Incorporated: 13 October 2017
Registered Office: 100 Dartmouth Road, London, NW2 4HB
Officers: Jermaine Thompson [1986] Director

Juice on the Go Ltd
Incorporated: 21 November 2018
Registered Office: 1 Whitehall Gardens, London, W3 9RD
Major Shareholder: Michael Nathan Brown
Officers: Michael Nathan Brown [1989] Director/Entrepreneur

The Juice Warrior Ltd
Incorporated: 6 February 2019
Registered Office: First Floor, Beaumont House, Lambton Road, London, SW20 0LW
Major Shareholder: Rachael Godinet
Officers: Rachael Godinet [1974] Director [British/New Zealander]

Juicer Ltd
Incorporated: 29 January 2019
Registered Office: 74a Randal Street, Blackburn, BB1 7LG
Major Shareholder: Naouar Sqarou
Officers: Naouar Sqarou [1986] Director/Manager [Moroccan]

The Juicery Ltd
Incorporated: 25 August 2018
Registered Office: 124 High Park Street, Liverpool, L8 3UQ
Major Shareholder: Mark McDonagh
Officers: Mark McDonagh [1989] Director/Self Employed

Juicydee Ltd
Incorporated: 18 July 2018
Registered Office: 72-74 Loughborough Road, London, SW9 7SB
Major Shareholder: Omari Aidoo
Officers: Omari Aidoo [1995] Director/Student

Just Aqua Ltd.
Incorporated: 25 August 2017
Registered Office: c/o Grosvenor House, Practice Avening, Priory Park, London Road, Tetbury, Glos, GL8 8HZ
Shareholders: Karel Albert Jagtenberg; Maria Rika Christiana Jagtenberg-Bakker
Officers: Karel Albert Jagtenberg [1957] Director [Dutch]; Maria Rika Christiana Jagtenberg-Bakker [1959] Director [Dutch]

JustGeneralTradingServices Limited
Incorporated: 3 October 2018
Registered Office: 30 Wythfield Road, Pitsea, Essex, SS13 3EN
Major Shareholder: Reece Garner
Officers: Reece Garner [1994] Director/Business Owner

K & E Wholesale Ltd
Incorporated: 25 April 2014
Net Worth: £3,889 Total Assets: £5,837
Registered Office: 9 Maxwell Road, Beaconsfield, Bucks, HP9 1RG
Major Shareholder: Krzysztof Zalewski
Officers: Krzysztof Zalewski [1978] Director/Driver [Polish]

K.A Top Traders Limited
Incorporated: 17 July 2018
Registered Office: Suite 23, Fifth Floor, 63-66 Hatton Garden, London, EC1N 8LE
Major Shareholder: Khudeza Begum Ahmed
Officers: Khudeza Begum Ahmed [1990] Director/Administrator

K.M Food & Drinks Ltd
Incorporated: 10 April 2018
Registered Office: 9 Warmley Close, Wolverhampton, W Midlands, WV6 0XF
Major Shareholder: Walentyna Oliwia Kunicka-Michalak
Officers: Walentyna Oliwia Kunicka-Michalak [1996] Director/Nurse [Polish]

K2 (Northwest) Limited
Incorporated: 5 January 2007
Net Worth: £4,341 Total Assets: £44,434
Registered Office: 10 Netherfield Close, Oldham, Lancs, OL8 4ER
Major Shareholder: Mahmood Qadir Sheikh
Officers: Nadia Irum Sheikh, Secretary; Mahmood Qadir Sheikh [1966] Director

Kadey Limited
Incorporated: 29 December 2008 Employees: 1
Net Worth Deficit: £49,907 Total Assets: £39,429
Registered Office: 8 Pinner View, Harrow, Middlesex, HA1 4QA
Shareholders: Nisha Dholakia; Kirit Dholakia
Officers: Nisha Dholakia, Secretary; Kirit Dholakia [1960] Director/Business Person

Kakkar Enterprises Ltd
Incorporated: 8 October 2018
Registered Office: 18 Lister House, Croyde Avenue, Hayes, Middlesex, UB3 4EP
Major Shareholder: Harmit Singh Kakkar
Officers: Harmit Singh Kakkar [1979] Director/Businessman

Kaleboard Limited
Incorporated: 17 June 2013
Net Worth: £728,284 Total Assets: £811,531
Registered Office: 124-126 Littleton Road, Salford, M7 3TW
Major Shareholder: Ranjeev Singh
Officers: Ranjeev Singh [1972] Director

Kaluwa Ltd
Incorporated: 7 November 2018
Registered Office: Kemp House, 160 City Road, London, EC1V 2NX
Major Shareholder: Anthony Manoj Rajaratnam
Officers: Anthony Manoj Rajaratnam, Secretary; Anthony Manoj Rajaratnam [1978] Director

Kang Med Limited
Incorporated: 8 December 2017
Registered Office: 8 Standard Road, London, NW10 6EU
Major Shareholder: Fei Yang
Officers: Fei Yang, Secretary; Fei Yang [1981] Director [Chinese]

Kanpes G Ltd
Incorporated: 24 January 2019
Registered Office: 28 Northumberland Road, Southampton, SO14 0FB
Major Shareholder: Rajinder Pal Singh
Officers: Rajinder Pal Singh [1966] Director/Manager [Portuguese]

Kaplan Int Limited
Incorporated: 26 September 2013
Registered Office: 121 Somerford Grove Estate, London, N16 7TN
Major Shareholder: Mehmet Bakir
Officers: Mehmet Bakir [1986] Director

Kardelen Water Limited
Incorporated: 10 November 2017
Registered Office: 71-75 Shelton Street, Covent Garden, London, WC2H 9JQ
Major Shareholder: Eksandra Arlauskaite
Officers: Eksandra Arlauskaite [1984] Director [Lithuanian]

Kasgo Limited
Incorporated: 15 November 2018
Registered Office: 15 Butterwick, Watford, Herts, WD25 9SD
Shareholders: Malgorzata Malinowska; Kasun Tharindu Madushanka Karunakara Arachchige
Officers: Kasun Tharindu Madushanka Karunakara Arachchige, Secretary; Malgorzata Malinowska, Secretary; Kasun Tharindu Madushanka Karunakara Arachchige [1987] Director/Postman [Sri Lankan]; Malgorzata Malinowska [1985] Director/Assistant Manager [Polish]

Kaspas Distribution Ltd
Incorporated: 1 May 2014 *Employees:* 14
Net Worth: £1,820,370 *Total Assets:* £2,500,231
Registered Office: Unit 22 Silverwing Industrial Estate, Imperial Way, Croydon, Surrey, CR0 4RR
Shareholders: Azhar Rehman; Mazhar Rehman
Officers: Azhar Rehman [1975] Director; Mazhar Rehman [1977] Director; Qasim Ali Rehman [1989] Director

Kaz Enterprise Limited
Incorporated: 1 September 2018
Registered Office: 149 Heacham Drive, Leicester, LE4 0LL
Major Shareholder: Mindaugas Kazilionis
Officers: Mindaugas Kazilionis, Secretary; Mindaugas Kazilionis [1981] Director [Lithuanian]

KD-Pol Ltd
Incorporated: 25 February 2013
Net Worth: £12,991 *Total Assets:* £37,161
Registered Office: 45 Princes Avenue, London, N13 6HA
Shareholders: Katarzyna Calka; Daniel Calka
Officers: Daniel Calka [1985] Director/Import and Sale [Polish]; Katarzyna Calka [1984] Director/Import and Sale [Polish]

Kepenek Food Ltd
Incorporated: 12 October 2018
Registered Office: 22 Wulfric Square, Bretton, Peterborough, Cambs, PE3 8RF
Major Shareholder: Kamal Jalil
Officers: Kamal Jalil [1976] Director [Iraqi]

Key Traders Ltd
Incorporated: 18 February 2019
Registered Office: 102 Clay Lane, Coventry, Warwicks, CV2 4LN
Major Shareholder: Gaurav Kukar Kumar
Officers: Gaurav Kukar Kumar [1986] Director [Indian]

KG Wholesale Ltd
Incorporated: 3 January 2018
Registered Office: 10 Montacute Road, Morden, Surrey, SM4 6RL
Major Shareholder: Gajendran Kalaiyarasan
Officers: Gajendran Kalaiyarasan [1994] Director/Sale Assistant [French]

Kheira Ltd
Incorporated: 5 November 2018
Registered Office: Carpenter Court, 1 Maple Road, Bramhall, Stockport, Cheshire, SK7 2DH
Major Shareholder: Eddib Nabil
Officers: Eddib Nabil [1989] Director/Manager [Swedish]

Kineta Drinks Limited
Incorporated: 15 March 2017 *Employees:* 1
Net Worth Deficit: £35,904 *Total Assets:* £25,655
Registered Office: The Quadrangle, Seale Hayne, Howton Road, Newton Abbot, Devon, TQ12 6NQ
Major Shareholder: Leane Bramhall
Officers: Leane Bramhall [1982] Managing Director

Cooray King Holdings Limited
Incorporated: 21 September 2016
Registered Office: Level 3, 207 Regent Street, London, W1B 3HH
Shareholder: Justin Francis St Clair King
Officers: Julian King [1973] Director; Justin Francis St Clair King [1970] Director

Kingsbury Wholesale Ltd
Incorporated: 27 April 2017
Net Worth Deficit: £149 *Total Assets:* £2
Registered Office: 170 Eachelhurst Road, Walmley, Sutton Coldfield, W Midlands, B76 1EL
Officers: John Sabharwal [1968] Director

Kintyre Holdings Limited
Incorporated: 17 December 1985
Net Worth: £56,207 *Total Assets:* £64,634
Registered Office: 45 Longrow, Campbeltown, Argyll, PA28 6ER
Parent: Carmichael Phillips Ltd
Officers: Michael Carmichael [1942] Director/Manager

KKR Wine Ltd
Incorporated: 24 October 2018
Registered Office: 100 Crawley Road, Horsham, W Sussex, RH12 4DT
Major Shareholder: Surinder Singh
Officers: Surinder Singh [1980] Director

KKS Fresh Fruits Ltd
Incorporated: 9 April 2018
Registered Office: 20-22 Wenlock Road, London, N1 7GU
Officers: Lawrence Henshaw [1985] Director

Klomar Ltd
Incorporated: 4 April 2018
Registered Office: 156a Burnt Oak Broadway, Edgware, Middlesex, HA8 0AX
Major Shareholder: Nikolaos Panagiotopoulos
Officers: Nikolaos Panagiotopoulos [1973] Director [Greek]

KML Home Limited
Incorporated: 1 March 2013
Net Worth: £199 *Total Assets:* £5,225
Registered Office: Unit 305 Vale Enterprise Centre, Hayes Road, Sully, Penarth, S Glamorgan, CF64 5SY
Major Shareholder: Jing Li
Officers: Yiding Guo [1969] Managing Director; Jing Li [1970] Finance Director

Knights Catering Impex Ltd
Incorporated: 6 October 2017
Registered Office: 41 Stoneleigh Avenue, Enfield, Middlesex, EN1 4HJ
Major Shareholder: Mesut Bayram
Officers: Mesut Bayram [1988] Director/Manager

Konon Limited
Incorporated: 2 February 2017
Net Worth: £11,877,676 *Total Assets:* £13,540,305
Registered Office: Unit 5 Lewis House, School Road, London, NW10 6TD
Parent: Aphea Fund Ltd-Mayfair Group Fund
Officers: Andreas Yanakopoulos [1963] Director [Greek]

KP Global Ltd
Incorporated: 15 December 2017
Registered Office: 32 Eton Avenue, Sudbury Town, Wembley, Middlesex, HA0 3AX
Major Shareholder: Kumar Patel
Officers: Kumar Patel [1961] Director/Manager

KPN Wholesale Ltd
Incorporated: 30 April 2018
Registered Office: 229 Central Park Road, London, E6 3AE
Major Shareholder: Mohanasegaram Kandasamy
Officers: Mohanasegaram Kandasamy [1971] Director [Swiss]

Kristals Trading Limited
Incorporated: 10 January 2019
Registered Office: 12 Singleton, Sutton Hill, Telford, Salop, TF7 4JQ
Officers: Sanija Irsina [1989] Director/Administrator [Latvian]

KSY Juice Blends UK Ltd
Incorporated: 1 November 2012
Net Worth: £728,565 *Total Assets:* £3,344,185
Registered Office: 8 Square Rigger Row, Plantation Wharf, York Road, Battersea, London, SW11 3TY
Shareholders: Orange Be Global Limited; FIF CompanyUK Limited; Orange Be Global Limited; FIF CompanyUK Ltd
Officers: Tim Peter Kaden [1965] Director [German]; Stavroula Makri [1982] Managing Director [Greek]

KT Wholesale Ltd
Incorporated: 18 May 2018
Registered Office: 40 Wardown Crescent, Luton, Beds, LU2 7JS
Major Shareholder: Koneswaran Thaneswaran
Officers: Koneswaran Thaneswaran [1976] Director [German]

KU Bargin Deals Ltd
Incorporated: 22 January 2019
Registered Office: 25 Wallington Grove, South Shields, Tyne & Wear, NE33 2RE
Major Shareholder: Khalid Uddin
Officers: Khalid Uddin [1994] Director

KU Supplies Ltd
Incorporated: 16 January 2019
Registered Office: 25 Wallington Grove, South Shields, Tyne & Wear, NE33 2RE
Major Shareholder: Khalid Uddin
Officers: Khalid Uddin [1994] Director

Kurd Scot Imports & Exports Ltd
Incorporated: 10 August 2011
Registered Office: 2/2, 266 Cumlodden Drive, Glasgow, G20 0JG
Officers: Anwar Muhammed Kadir [1975] Director

KVC Waffles Limited
Incorporated: 18 May 2006 *Employees:* 10
Net Worth Deficit: £287,260 *Total Assets:* £1,068,283
Registered Office: 68 Edinburgh House, 155 Maida Vale, London, W9 1QT
Major Shareholder: Sotirios Nikolopoulos
Officers: Sotirios Nikolopoulos [1979] Managing Director [Greek]

L & B Foods Ltd
Incorporated: 20 September 2012
Net Worth: £30,207 *Total Assets:* £46,268
Registered Office: 11 Milburn Avenue, Manchester, M23 0FB
Shareholder: Gurmail Singh
Officers: Gurmail Singh [1978] Director

L & D Services UK Limited
Incorporated: 26 June 2007
Net Worth: £330,127 *Total Assets:* £426,792
Registered Office: The Jubilee Centre, 10-12 Lombard Road, London, SW19 3TZ
Major Shareholder: Liviu Leuca
Officers: Liviu Leuca [1979] Director [Romanian]

L'Azur Ltd
Incorporated: 6 December 2017
Registered Office: 71-75 Shelton Street, Covent Garden, London, WC2H 9JQ
Shareholders: Stefania Roxana Lazurca; Mihaela Lazurca
Officers: Mihaela Lazurca [1973] Managing Director [Romanian]; Stefania Roxana Lazurca [1979] Managing Director [Romanian]

La Zgarici Ltd
Incorporated: 24 October 2017
Registered Office: 101 Prince Regent Lane, London, E13 8RW
Officers: Dan Ion [1983] Director [Romanian]

Ladeo Limited
Incorporated: 22 November 2016
Registered Office: 6D Peabody Square, London, N1 8RR
Shareholder: Adeola Adelakun
Officers: Halima Abiola [1981] Director/Owner; Adeola Adelakun [1979] Director/Owner [Nigerian]; Kabir Bakori Garba [1965] Director/Auditor [Nigerian]; Yasir Kabir [2000] Director/Student [Nigerian]

Lake Shore Distributors Ltd
Incorporated: 9 June 2011
Net Worth: £2 *Total Assets:* £2
Registered Office: 3 Rathfriland Street, Loughbrickland, Co Down, BT32 3NG
Officers: Fionnuala Gracey [1980] Director [Irish]

Lam Cash and Carry Limited
Incorporated: 19 October 1981
Registered Office: 24 Bedford Row, London, WC1R 4TQ
Shareholders: Amir Tayebali Kapadia; Sukhminder Amir Kapadia
Officers: Amir Tayebali Kapadia, Secretary; Sukhminder Amir Kapadia, Company Secretary; Amir Tayebali Kapadia [1953] Director; Rafique Amir Kapadia [1980] Director/Hotel Manager

Lana Nai UK Co. Ltd
Incorporated: 21 December 2016
Registered Office: c/o Blake & Co Accountants, Vicarage House, 58-60 Kensington Church Street, Kensington, London, W8 4DB
Major Shareholder: Najib Armanazi
Officers: Mohamed Najib Armanazi [1976] Director/Security Guard

Lanex Ltd
Incorporated: 8 February 2019
Registered Office: Apartment 23, 15 St Johns Gardens, Bury, Lancs, BL9 0QW
Major Shareholder: Ewelina Malgorzata Ahmad
Officers: Ewelina Malgorzata Ahmad [1987] Director

Lanza Foods Ltd
Incorporated: 23 January 2007 *Employees:* 6
Net Worth: £179,669 *Total Assets:* £351,409
Registered Office: 1 Kings Avenue, London, N21 3NA
Shareholders: Gaetano Salvatore Alfano; Antonio Alfano; Karin Jane Alfano
Officers: Gaetano Salvatore Alfano [1953] Director [Italian]

Laspremuta Limited
Incorporated: 8 March 2016
Net Worth Deficit: £16,261 *Total Assets:* £14,117
Registered Office: 11 Castle Hill, Maidenhead, Berks, SL6 4AA
Officers: Severina Stranieri [1984] Director [Italian]

Lawton Cross Limited
Incorporated: 19 May 2005
Registered Office: 1 Braemar Gardens, Hampton Park Road, Hereford, HR1 1SJ
Shareholders: Ian Robert Hudson; Marcus Frederick Loudon
Officers: Juliet Cordelia Loudon, Secretary; Ian Robert Hudson [1964] Director/Retailer; Marcus Frederick Loudon [1972] Director

Laz and Kol Ltd
Incorporated: 4 November 2014
Net Worth Deficit: £12,054 *Total Assets:* £3,416
Registered Office: Laz and Kol Ltd, WSS Storage, Oxford Street Industrial Park, Vulcan Road, Bilston, W Midlands, WV14 7LF
Major Shareholder: Laszlo Koles
Officers: Laszlo Koles [1975] Director/Driver [Hungarian]

LB Hussan Hussain Halal Meat Superstore Ltd
Incorporated: 25 July 2016 *Employees:* 3
Net Worth Deficit: £11,580 *Total Assets:* £5,420
Registered Office: 408 Farnham Road, Slough, Berks, SL2 1JA
Major Shareholder: Lateef Bibi
Officers: Zuhaib Hassan, Secretary; Javaid Hussain, Secretary; Lateef Bibi [1958] Director/Butchers Supermarket

LBSM Limited
Incorporated: 27 November 2018
Registered Office: Unit 7 Redborn Industrial Estate, Woodall Road, Enfield, Middlesex, EN3 4LQ
Officers: Suheyla Aygun, Secretary; Suheyla Aygun [1985] Director [Turkish]

Leathams Limited
Incorporated: 29 December 1982 *Employees:* 273
Net Worth: £29,785,000 *Total Assets:* £59,089,000
Registered Office: 227-255 Ilderton Road, Bermondsey, London, SE15 1NS
Parent: Leathams Holdings Ltd
Officers: Douglas Alexander Dunbar, Secretary; Terence Henry Faulkner [1958] Director; Mark Leatham [1955] Director; Oliver Nigel Leatham [1957] Director; Clive Wilson Moxham [1967] Director; Martin Sandler [1976] Director/Head of Operations; Christopher Edward Waters [1963] Director

Leoba Service Ltd
Incorporated: 31 December 2018
Registered Office: 1 Wilson Street, Hartlepool, Cleveland, TS26 8JX
Major Shareholder: Suvaissan Savarimuthu
Officers: Suvaissan Savarimuthu [1982] Director/Self Employed [Sri Lankan]

Lep Food & Wine Ltd
Incorporated: 24 September 2018
Registered Office: 437 Becontree Avenue, Dagenham, Essex, RM8 3UH
Officers: Kurosh Asemani [1981] Director/Businessman

Lifting Spirits Ltd
Incorporated: 18 September 2018
Registered Office: 9 Bellevue Road, Kirkintilloch, Glasgow, G66 1AL
Major Shareholder: Carianne Henriette Barteling-Doherty
Officers: Carianne Henriette Barteling-Doherty [1971] Director/Housewife [Dutch]

Like Like Ltd
Incorporated: 13 April 2017
Registered Office: 85 Great Portland Street, London, W1W 7LT
Officers: Dr Ali Lazem [1986] Director

Link International Ltd
Incorporated: 3 May 2018
Registered Office: 14 Florence Road, Smethwick, W Midlands, B66 4QT
Major Shareholder: Vimalakkannan Kanagalingam
Officers: Vimalakkannan Kanagalingam [1969] Director [Swiss]

Liquid Brand Exports Limited
Incorporated: 9 May 2018
Registered Office: 14 Merton Drive, Derby, DE22 4JJ
Major Shareholder: Kathryn Walker
Officers: Kathryn Walker, Secretary; Kathryn Walker [1983] Director

Liquidline Limited
Incorporated: 14 June 2010
Net Worth: £1,592,404 *Total Assets:* £4,840,311
Registered Office: 11 Holywells Close, Ipswich, Suffolk, IP3 0AW
Shareholders: Holywells Holdings Limited; Angus Frederick Pooley; Jodie Pooley; Janyce Pooley; Gavin William Pooley
Officers: Angus Frederick Pooley [1987] Director; Gavin William Pooley [1984] Director; Matthew James Pooley [1991] Director

Lithuanian Beer Limited
Incorporated: 27 March 2002 *Employees:* 7
Net Worth: £443,233 *Total Assets:* £1,208,640
Registered Office: 23a Thames Road, Barking, Essex, IG11 0HN
Shareholders: Aira Ruta Jakimaviciene; Egonas Jakimavicius
Officers: Aira Ruta Jakimaviciene, Secretary; Egonas Jakimavicius [1962] Director [Lithuanian]

Liverpool & Oriental Trading Company Limited
Incorporated: 30 September 2014
Net Worth Deficit: £3,232 *Total Assets:* £619
Registered Office: Muskers Building, 1 Stanley Street, Liverpool, L1 6AA
Shareholders: David Anastasiou; Eleftherios Eleftheriou
Officers: Timothy Molloy, Secretary; David Anastasiou [1962] Director; Eleftherios Eleftheriou [1959] Director

Log Cabin Fruits Ltd
Incorporated: 8 April 2015
Net Worth Deficit: £13,284 *Total Assets:* £2,119
Registered Office: 27 Nevis Walk, Thornaby on Tees, Cleveland, TS17 8FW
Major Shareholder: Darren Gosling
Officers: Darren Gosling [1971] Director

London Drinks Supplier Ltd
Incorporated: 29 December 2017
Registered Office: 20-22 Wenlock Road, London, N1 7GU
Major Shareholder: Ali Ulcay
Officers: Ali Ulcay [1992] Director/Mature Student

London Maya Sandwich Limited
Incorporated: 5 January 2017 *Employees:* 6
Net Worth: £379 *Total Assets:* £18,151
Registered Office: 114 Farringdon Road, London, EC1R 3AP
Major Shareholder: Erdogan Demir
Officers: Erdogan Demir [1977] Director

London UK Star Ltd
Incorporated: 3 April 2017
Net Worth: £2,015 *Total Assets:* £75,511
Registered Office: 61 Praed Street, London, W2 1NS
Shareholders: Jamal Merza Salih Salih; Mohammad Rasoul Yousif
Officers: Mohammad Rasoul Yousif [1974] Director

London Wholesale Ltd
Incorporated: 11 August 2011
Net Worth Deficit: £34,585 *Total Assets:* £234,661
Registered Office: G5 Hastingwood Trading Estate, 35 Harbet Road, Edmonton, London, N18 3HT
Major Shareholder: Shahbaz Ali Amjad Sheikh
Officers: Shahbaz Ali Amjad Sheikh [1949] Director

Longstar Trading Limited
Incorporated: 11 December 2013
Registered Office: Woodberry House, 2 Woodberry Grove, London, N12 0DR
Major Shareholder: Sean Patrick Murphy
Officers: Sean Patrick Murphy [1970] Director [Irish]

Lora Trading (Europe) Ltd
Incorporated: 13 October 2015
Net Worth: £10,726 *Total Assets:* £179,773
Registered Office: The Pinnacle, 170 Midsummer Boulevard, Milton Keynes, Bucks, MK9 1BP
Major Shareholder: Sonya Ramakrishnan
Officers: Sonya Ramakrishnan [1997] Director

Lord Eden Beverages Ltd
Incorporated: 5 January 2018
Registered Office: The Stables, Station Drive, Kirby Muxloe, Leicester, LE9 2ET
Major Shareholder: Simon Phillip Michaels
Officers: Simon Phillip Michaels [1972] Director/Businessman

Lore & Truth Ltd
Incorporated: 16 August 2018
Registered Office: 30 Spencer David Way, St Mellons, Cardiff, CF3 0QB
Major Shareholder: Julia Sarah Ann Gray
Officers: Julia Sarah Ann Gray [1981] Director/Teacher [German]

Loris Wholesale Ltd
Incorporated: 30 January 2019
Registered Office: 27 Rollason Road, Coventry, Warwicks, CV6 4AP
Major Shareholder: Arun Arulsothy
Officers: Arun Arulsothy [1991] Director/Sales Assistant [French]

Loughborough Student Services Limited
Incorporated: 29 March 1985
Net Worth: £166,056 *Total Assets:* £414,904
Registered Office: Union Building, Ashby Road, Loughborough, Leics, LE11 3TT
Shareholder: Paul Jonathan Barlow
Officers: Gary Chamberlain, Secretary; Fraser Barclay [1996] Director/Student; Paul Jonathan Barlow [1964] Director/Deputy General Manager; Sam Hanys [1996] Director/Union Executive Officer; Rahul Mathasing [1994] Director/Student; Trevor Andrew Page [1965] Union Director; Rory Pears [1996] Director/Student Executive Officer

Loyal Trader Ltd
Incorporated: 19 October 2018
Registered Office: 144 Dormers Wells Lane, Southall, Middlesex, UB1 3JB
Major Shareholder: Andrejs Smirnovs
Officers: Andrejs Smirnovs [1992] Director/Businessman

Luckova Ltd
Incorporated: 5 February 2019
Registered Office: 171 Barrington Street, Manchester, M11 4FB
Major Shareholder: Nikola Luckova
Officers: Nikola Luckova, Secretary; Nikola Luckova [1992] Director [Czech]

Luella Malmesbury Ltd
Incorporated: 23 March 2018
Registered Office: Pond House, Back Lane, Alderton, Glos, SN14 6NW
Major Shareholder: Stuart Townshend
Officers: Stuart Townshend [1948] Director/Consultant

Luso Shop Ltd
Incorporated: 3 July 2018
Registered Office: 116 Burton Road, Derby, DE1 1TG
Major Shareholder: Bruno Miguel Ribeiro E Silva Barros
Officers: Bruno Miguel Ribeiro E Silva Barros [1982] Director/Office Clerk [Portuguese]

Ly Hong Limited
Incorporated: 31 August 2007
Net Worth: £73,551 *Total Assets:* £292,856
Registered Office: 71-75 Shelton Street, Covent Garden, London, WC2H 9JQ
Major Shareholder: Andy Hai Ly
Officers: Lan Hoai Hong, Secretary; Andy Hai Ly [1979] Director

Lync Direct Limited
Incorporated: 1 August 2013
Registered Office: First Floor, Unit 3, 1161 Chester Road, Erdington, Birmingham, B24 0QY
Major Shareholder: Karan Singh Dhami
Officers: Aaron Rico Singh Dhami [1991] Director

M & M Emerald Ltd
Incorporated: 7 August 2017
Registered Office: Flat 16, Ealing Park Mansions, South Ealing Road, London, W5 4QD
Shareholders: Marta Iwaniak; Marcin Michal Wisniewski
Officers: Marta Iwaniak [1983] Director/Dental Care [Polish]; Marcin Michal Wisniewski [1974] Director/Builder [Polish]

M & M European Merchants Ltd
Incorporated: 18 December 2018
Registered Office: 77 Sandringham Road, Birmingham, B42 1PU
Major Shareholder: Marcus Rai
Officers: Marcus Rai [1968] Director

M & M Export Limited
Incorporated: 16 December 1997
Total Assets: £2,317
Registered Office: c/o Chatwani & Co, Kanta House, Victoria Road, South Ruislip, Middlesex, HA4 0JQ
Officers: Satish Jamnadas Chatwani, Secretary/Director; Jawahar Jamnadas Chatwani [1948] Director; Rashmi Jamnadas Chatwani [1954] Director; Satish Jamnadas Chatwani [1953] Director

M & S Trading (London) Limited
Incorporated: 4 January 2019
Registered Office: 2 Finance House, Maygrove Road, London, NW6 2EB
Major Shareholder: Muthulingam Sugirthan
Officers: Muthulingam Sugirthan [1978] Director/Business Consultant

M Trading Limited
Incorporated: 20 November 2015
Net Worth: £329,510 *Total Assets:* £734,681
Registered Office: 869 High Road, London, N12 8QA
Major Shareholder: Giuseppe Modiano
Officers: Laura Modiano [1986] Director [Italian]

M.R.S. Supplies Limited
Incorporated: 2 November 2010
Net Worth Deficit: £19,243 *Total Assets:* £26,347
Registered Office: 78 Ben Jonson Road, Stepney, London, E1 3NN
Major Shareholder: Rabia Rahman
Officers: Rabia Rahman [1973] Director

Macedo (UK) Limited
Incorporated: 18 February 1994 *Employees:* 1
Net Worth Deficit: £4,988 *Total Assets:* £114
Registered Office: Old Printers Yard, 156 South Street, Dorking, Surrey, RH4 2EU
Major Shareholder: Zvonko Grozdanov
Officers: Julijana Gjorgjievska, Secretary; Zvonko Grozdanov [1961] Director/Businessman [Macedonian]

Made in the States Limited
Incorporated: 20 July 2016
Net Worth Deficit: £4,294 *Total Assets:* £11,582
Registered Office: 34 Queen Street, Neath, W Glamorgan, SA11 1DL
Major Shareholder: Sean Reilly St John
Officers: Sean Reilly St John [1983] Director

Madina Drinks Ltd
Incorporated: 31 December 2018
Registered Office: 36 Shepherds Walk, London, NW2 7BS
Major Shareholder: Mohammed Amer Munir
Officers: Mohammed Amer Munir [1978] Director/Factory Worker

Magna Carta Drinks Limited
Incorporated: 11 February 2019
Registered Office: 38 Long Pastures, Glemsford, Sudbury, Suffolk, CO10 7SS
Shareholders: Gary Wilkinson; Melanie Mary Wilkinson
Officers: Gary Wilkinson [1962] Director; Melanie Mary Wilkinson [1962] Director

Magna Juice Ltd
Incorporated: 21 June 2018
Registered Office: 20-22 Wenlock Road, London, N1 7GU
Officers: Zavon Miller [1990] Director/Self Employed [Zimbabwean]; Tapiwa Tutisani [1992] Director/Marketing Executive

The Magnanimous Distribution T/A Pizzeria Hut Limited
Incorporated: 4 February 2014
Previous: The Magnanimous Distribution Limited
Net Worth: £6,730 *Total Assets:* £17,709
Registered Office: 149 Victoria Road, Barking, Essex, IG11 8PZ
Major Shareholder: Sheikh Shahid
Officers: Athar Shahzad [1982] Director/Production Line Worker [Pakistani]

Maira Trade Ltd
Incorporated: 18 May 2018
Registered Office: Unit 3 Westwood Business Centre, Featherstall Road South, Oldham, Lancs, OL9 6HN
Major Shareholder: Akhtar Mahmood
Officers: Akhtar Mahmood [1967] Director [Polish]

Majestic Foods Limited
Incorporated: 21 May 2015
Net Worth: £11,041 *Total Assets:* £207,258
Registered Office: 2a Sandy Lane, Business Park, Coventry, Warwicks, CV1 4DX
Major Shareholder: Muhammad Ikram Kayani
Officers: Muhammad Ikram Kayani [1968] Director/Wholesalers

Majestic Wholesale Ltd
Incorporated: 14 July 2014
Registered Office: 84 Bethel Road, Rotherham, S Yorks, S65 1QX
Major Shareholder: Wasim Ali Yunus
Officers: Waseem Ali Yunus [1985] Managing Director

Majit Drinks Ltd
Incorporated: 31 December 2018
Registered Office: 48 Pembroke Road, Ilford, Essex, IG3 8PH
Major Shareholder: Gurpreet Singh
Officers: Gurpreet Singh [1990] Director [Indian]

Major Foods Limited
Incorporated: 10 July 2013
Net Worth: £284,934 *Total Assets:* £824,094
Registered Office: Unit 2 Kingsbridge Road, Barking, Essex, IG11 0BP
Shareholders: Basharat Khan; Mohammed Siddique
Officers: Basharat Khan [1973] Director; Mohammed Siddique [1964] Director

Manchester Drinks Company Ltd
Incorporated: 8 June 2005 *Employees:* 4
Net Worth: £3,931,489 *Total Assets:* £6,903,282
Registered Office: Suite 412, Warth Road, Bury, Lancs, BL9 9TB
Shareholders: Brian Colin Levine; Ricard Benjamin
Officers: Brian Colin Levine, Secretary/Director; Richard Marc Benjamin [1970] Director; Brian Colin Levine [1968] Director

UK Wholesalers of Soft Drinks

Manchester Fruit and Vegetables Limited
Incorporated: 12 October 2017
Registered Office: 651 Prince of Wales Road, Sheffield, S9 4ES
Major Shareholder: Csaba Balogh
Officers: Csaba Balogh [1979] Director [Hungarian]

Mane and Rose Limited
Incorporated: 30 November 2018
Registered Office: 49a Elmore Street, London, N1 3AJ
Major Shareholder: Andre Lecointe-Gayle
Officers: Andre Lecointe-Gayle [1973] Managing Director

Mani Mathi Trading Ltd
Incorporated: 17 October 2018
Registered Office: 245B Northborough Road, London, SW16 4TR
Major Shareholder: Manivannan Mathiyalagan
Officers: Manivannan Mathiyalagan [1986] Director/Manager [Indian]

Manor Wholesale Ltd
Incorporated: 5 November 2018
Registered Office: 24 Woolston Manor, Abridge Road, Chigwell, Essex, IG7 6BX
Officers: Mohammed Khan [1985] Director

Manteo Trading Company Limited
Incorporated: 25 May 2018
Registered Office: 71-75 Shelton Street, London, WC2H 9JQ
Major Shareholder: Paul Woolnough
Officers: Paul Woolnough, Secretary; Paul Woolnough [1967] Director

Marathon Food Limited
Incorporated: 18 July 1986
Net Worth: £1,246,250 *Total Assets:* £1,501,561
Registered Office: Francis House, 2 Park Road, Barnet, Herts, EN5 5RN
Major Shareholder: Sotera Papanicolaou
Officers: Sotera Shimitra, Secretary; Sotera Shimitra [1959] Managing Director

Marcin & Son Ltd
Incorporated: 4 December 2018
Registered Office: 21 Travers Street, Salford, M7 3DN
Major Shareholder: Marcin Tadeusz Siudaj
Officers: Marcin Tadeusz Siudaj [1984] Sales Director [Polish]

Marco Polo Exotics Ltd
Incorporated: 22 March 2018
Registered Office: 50 Cullings Court, Waltham Abbey, Essex, EN9 3ED
Major Shareholder: Jordan Nicholas Humphrey
Officers: Jordan Nicholas Humphrey [1990] Director

MAS Trading Cast Ltd
Incorporated: 3 August 2017
Net Worth Deficit: £14,648 *Total Assets:* £2,934
Registered Office: 29 Bromwich Close, Thorpe Astley, Braunstone, Leicester, LE3 3RT
Major Shareholder: Andrzej Sacharzewski
Officers: Andrzej Sacharzewski [1973] Director/Manager [Polish]

Masca Holding Limited
Incorporated: 8 April 2014 *Employees:* 111
Net Worth: £10,888,703 *Total Assets:* £17,895,648
Registered Office: Unit A1-A3, Brantwood Industrial Estate, Brantwood Road, Tottenham, London, N17 0DX
Shareholders: Cetin Agcagul; Suleyman Cagin
Officers: Cetin Agcagul [1985] Director; Suleyman Cagin [1966] Director

Mashmoom International Limited
Incorporated: 13 March 2018
Registered Office: 77 Chaucer Way, Hitchin, Herts, SG4 0PE
Major Shareholder: Fakhar Ul Islam
Officers: Fakhar Ul Islam [1980] Director/Engineer [Pakistani]

Massafood Ltd
Incorporated: 29 January 2019
Registered Office: 15 Northumberland Gardens, Isleworth, Middlesex, TW7 5NT
Major Shareholder: Anas Dahdal
Officers: Anas Dahdal [1990] Director

Matlowone Limited
Incorporated: 9 March 2018
Registered Office: Office 57, 321-323 High Road, Romford, Essex, RM6 6AX
Major Shareholder: Muhammad Aamir Tufail
Officers: Muhammad Aamir Tufail [1986] Director

MB Drinks Ltd
Incorporated: 15 January 2019
Registered Office: 5 Evington Lane, Leicester, LE5 5PQ
Major Shareholder: Noreen Mahboob
Officers: Noreen Mahboob [1985] Director

MBS Ventures Limited
Incorporated: 27 April 2015 *Employees:* 1
Net Worth Deficit: £4,563 *Total Assets:* £5,026
Registered Office: 131 Great Junction Street, Edinburgh, EH6 5JB
Shareholders: Moses Boyenle Salako; Echezona Okwaje
Officers: Echezona Okwaje [1975] Director/Systems Analyst [Nigerian]; Moses Boyenle Salako [1962] Director [Nigerian]

MBW Traders Ltd
Incorporated: 5 February 2018
Registered Office: Flat 4, Door 44, Telegraph Mews, Goodmayes, Essex, IG3 8TF
Major Shareholder: Roy Clement
Officers: Roy Clement [1985] Director/Engineer

McBerries Ltd
Incorporated: 4 December 2018
Registered Office: Sterling House, 3 Wavell Drive, Rosehill Industrial Estate, Carlisle, Cumbria, CA1 2SA
Major Shareholder: Ryan James McPherson
Officers: Ryan James McPherson [1988] Director

MCIA Ltd
Incorporated: 11 December 2018
Registered Office: Unit 7, 9 Redburn Industrial Estate, Woodall Road, Enfield, Middlesex, EN3 4LQ
Officers: Guney Deniz [1982] Director

MD Investgroupp Ltd
Incorporated: 31 December 2018
Registered Office: 20-22 Wenlock Road, London, N1 7GU
Major Shareholder: Maria Covaliuc
Officers: Maria Covaliuc [1967] Director [Romanian]

MEA Health and Wellness Ltd
Incorporated: 23 November 2018
Registered Office: 2 Holdiford Road, Milford, Stafford, ST17 0UX
Major Shareholder: Thomas David Harley
Officers: Thomas David Harley [1980] Director

Meadow Harvest Ltd
Incorporated: 2 May 2018
Registered Office: 47 Gayton House, Chiltern Road, London, E3 4BX
Major Shareholder: Volodymyr Kozlovskyy
Officers: Volodymyr Kozlovskyy [1980] Director/Engineering

Adrian Mecklenburgh Limited
Incorporated: 25 February 1980 Employees: 27
Net Worth: £1,339,643 Total Assets: £2,129,189
Registered Office: Laurel House, Woodlands Park, Ashton Road, Newton-le-Willows, St Helens, Merseyside, WA12 0HH
Parent: Vimto (Out of Home) Limited
Officers: Timothy Croston, Secretary; Timothy John Croston [1963] Director; Nicholas Yates [1974] Sales & Operations Director

Medina Food World Ltd
Incorporated: 8 February 2018
Registered Office: 3 Medina Road, Coventry, Warwicks, CV6 5JB
Officers: Abdirazaq Salah Mohammed [1969] Director/Manager

Mediterranean International Ltd
Incorporated: 30 March 2015
Registered Office: 446 Roman Road, London, E3 5LU
Shareholder: Niez Maalej
Officers: Niez Maalej [1982] Director [Tunisian]; Petra Vaskova [1983] Director/Nurse [Slovak]

Meless Group Limited
Incorporated: 21 August 2002
Net Worth Deficit: £10,658 Total Assets: £780
Registered Office: 8 Eastmead Avenue, Greenford, Middlesex, UB6 9RA
Shareholders: Nathanael Lasme; Srikanthan Shanmugalingam

Menon Naturals Ltd
Incorporated: 23 October 2018
Registered Office: Kemp House, 160 City Road, London, EC1V 2NX
Officers: Resmi Menon [1980] Director

Mercado Da Saudade Ltd
Incorporated: 27 June 2018
Registered Office: Unit 2 Hereward Way Business Park, Harling Road, Norwich, NR16 2SR
Major Shareholder: Mara Felix
Officers: Mara Gisela Pestana Felix [1979] Director/Office Manager [Portuguese]

Merchantology Ireland Ltd
Incorporated: 1 February 2016
Net Worth: £90,170 Total Assets: £389,460
Registered Office: c/o Coddan CPM Ltd, Suite 140, 21 Botanic Avenue, Belfast, BT7 1JJ
Major Shareholder: Harvey David Poole
Officers: Harvey Poole, Secretary; Harvey David Poole [1974] Director/Sales Consultant

Merchantology Ltd
Incorporated: 15 May 2015 Employees: 2
Net Worth: £25,871 Total Assets: £53,475
Registered Office: 63 Old London Road, Benson, Wallingford, Oxon, OX10 6RR
Major Shareholder: Harvey David Poole
Officers: Harvey David Poole [1974] Director; Karen Poole [1977] Director

Mercury Wholesale Ltd
Incorporated: 15 February 2019
Registered Office: 50 Woodlands Road, Huyton, Merseyside, L36 4PH
Major Shareholder: Naveneethan Tavarajha
Officers: Naveneethan Tavarajha [1968] Director/Sales Assistant [Norwegian]

Merlin Distribution Limited
Incorporated: 21 August 2018
Registered Office: 82 Rochford Drive, Luton, Beds, LU2 8SR
Shareholder: Ovidiu Mocsi
Officers: Ovidiu Mocsi [1993] Director [Portuguese]; Sorin Stoica [1970] Director [Romanian]

Merlin's Beverages Limited
Incorporated: 26 October 2015
Registered Office: Autumn Lodge, Horns Drove, Rownhams, Southampton, SO16 8AJ
Officers: Maria Gutu [1984] Director/Wholesale [Romanian]

Merseyside Service Ltd
Incorporated: 11 April 2017
Net Worth: £48,567 Total Assets: £77,238
Registered Office: 109 Alderwood Avenue, Speke, Liverpool, L24 7RB
Major Shareholder: Gajan Selvan
Officers: Gajan Selvan [1983] Director/Customer Service Assistant

Mesh Facilities Limited
Incorporated: 27 February 2018
Registered Office: 86-90 Paul Street, London, EC2A 4NE
Major Shareholder: Abbie Stallabrass
Officers: Abbie Stallabrass [1995] Director

Mezin Distribution UK Limited
Incorporated: 4 July 2011 Employees: 5
Net Worth: £65,414 Total Assets: £153,543
Registered Office: 105 Upshire Road, Waltham Abbey, Essex, EN9 3PB
Major Shareholder: Ahmet Tilki
Officers: Leonidas Gedeou [1976] Director [Cypriot]

Middleton Wholesale Limited
Incorporated: 2 October 1984 Employees: 2
Net Worth: £749,754 Total Assets: £755,478
Registered Office: Unit 3 Stainburn Road, Manchester, M11 2DN
Parent: LWC Drinks Limited
Officers: Peter Sumner, Secretary; Robin MacEwan Gray [1951] Director; Ebrahim Kassam Mukadam [1957] Director

Mightybee Limited
Incorporated: 17 November 2014 Employees: 6
Net Worth Deficit: £555,770 Total Assets: £423,371
Registered Office: Studio 407, The Print Rooms, 164-180 Union Street, London, SE1 0LH
Major Shareholder: Xiao Min
Officers: Chi Tse, Secretary; Xiao Min [1989] Director [Chinese]; Chi Tse [1986] Director

Milky Milkshakes Ltd
Incorporated: 1 August 2018
Registered Office: 2 Rimmington Road, Liverpool, L17 0BD
Major Shareholder: Oliver Press
Officers: Oliver Press [1991] Director

Milton Sandford Wines Limited
Incorporated: 21 April 2006 Employees: 17
Net Worth: £2,496,290 Total Assets: £3,268,376
Registered Office: The Old Chalk Mine, Warren Row Road, Knowl Hill, Reading, Berks, RG10 8QS
Parent: Winchester Wines Group Limited
Officers: John Howard Winchester, Secretary; John Howard Winchester [1961] Director; Mary Rose Lyon Winchester [1968] Director

Mirpa Limited
Incorporated: 8 November 2012 Employees: 25
Net Worth: £1,959,086 Total Assets: £4,823,428
Registered Office: Stands 31-34, New Spitalfields Market, Sherrin Road, Leyton, London, E10 5SH
Parent: Masca Holding Limited
Officers: Cetin Agcagul [1985] Director; Suleyman Cagin [1966] Director

Mirza Trading Limited
Incorporated: 14 June 2018
Registered Office: 40 Kensington Gardens, Ilford, Essex, IG1 3EL
Major Shareholder: Iftikhar Ahmed
Officers: Iftikhar Ahmed [1949] Director

Henry Mitchell & Sons Limited
Incorporated: 22 February 1936 Employees: 7
Net Worth: £224,524 Total Assets: £302,124
Registered Office: South Lane, Holmfirth, W Yorks, HD9 1HN
Shareholders: Stephen Crossland; David Crossland
Officers: Lorna Crossland, Secretary; David Crossland [1967] Director/Manager; Stephen Crossland [1942] Director/Grocer

Mithun MM Limited
Incorporated: 29 March 2018
Registered Office: Bailiff Street Minimarket, 115 Bailiff Street, Northampton, NN1 3EA
Major Shareholder: Thankamylon Methunalan

Miwater Ltd
Incorporated: 25 July 2018
Registered Office: Broad House, The Broadway, Old Hatfield, Herts, AL9 5BG
Shareholders: Nina Fourie; Andries Benjamin Fourie; Juliana Fourie
Officers: Nina Fourie [1985] Director [South African]

MJ Trading (NW) Ltd
Incorporated: 17 October 2016
Net Worth: £54,900 Total Assets: £54,900
Registered Office: Europa House, Barcroft Street, Bury, Lancs, BL9 5BT
Major Shareholder: Imran Abbas
Officers: Imran Abbas, Secretary; Imran Abbas [1978] Director/Self Employed [Portuguese]

MK Bazaar Ltd
Incorporated: 26 November 2018
Registered Office: 147 Cranbrook Road, Ilford, Essex, IG1 4PU
Major Shareholder: Hasan Kadir Yakub
Officers: Hasan Kadir Yakub [1984] Director [Bulgarian]

MK Inter Ltd
Incorporated: 24 December 2018
Registered Office: 339 London Road, Camberley, Surrey, GU15 3HQ
Major Shareholder: Mikail Ozturk
Officers: Mikail Ozturk [1983] Director

MKM Group Trading & Investment Limited
Incorporated: 5 January 2018
Registered Office: 71-75 Shelton Street, Covent Garden, London, WC2H 9JQ
Major Shareholder: Mehmet Kemal Kosemusul
Officers: Mahmut Kosemusul [1968] Director [Turkish]

MLI Trading Limited
Incorporated: 17 January 2014
Net Worth Deficit: £196,288 Total Assets: £26,870
Registered Office: Hydes Farm, Epping Lane, Abridge, Essex, RM4 1TU
Major Shareholder: Michael Adrian Lait
Officers: Michael Lait, Secretary; Michael Adrian Lait [1992] Director/Businessman

MM Global Citrus Limited
Incorporated: 21 November 2006 Employees: 28
Net Worth: £2,230,000 Total Assets: £12,197,000
Registered Office: The Fresh Produce Centre, Transfesa Road, Paddock Wood, Kent, TN12 6UT
Parent: Fresca Group Limited
Officers: Veronica Warner, Secretary; Ian Alexander Craig [1957] Director; Christopher Peter Mack [1955] Director; Brett Geoffrey Sumner [1973] Finance Director; Nigel John Trood [1965] Director

Mock Drink Company Ltd
Incorporated: 21 February 2019
Registered Office: 21 Kingsley Place, Newcastle upon Tyne, NE6 5AN
Officers: Haidar Al Farisy [1995] Director/Student [Indonesian]; James Hayes [1994] Director/Student; Matthew Robert Hutchinson [1996] Director/Student; Joseph William Bolshaw Stephenson [1996] Director/Student

The Mocktail Company (2018) Ltd
Incorporated: 13 December 2018
Registered Office: 4th Floor, 7-10 Chandos Street, Cavendish Square, London, W1G 9DQ
Shareholders: Hasnain Karawalli; Zainab Karawalli
Officers: Hasnain Karawalli [1978] Director [Kenyan]; Zainab Karawalli [1981] Director

Modern Contradiction Limited
Incorporated: 23 August 2017
Registered Office: 1 Vincent Square, London, SW1P 2PN
Shareholders: Thomas Pugsley; Oliver Thomas Dixon
Officers: Oliver Thomas Dixon [1979] Director/Consultant; Andrew Mark Kanter [1969] Company Secretary/Director [American]; Thomas Pugsley [1980] Director/Consultant

Moju Ltd
Incorporated: 16 September 2014 Employees: 6
Net Worth Deficit: £11,383 Total Assets: £215,959
Registered Office: 7 Tanners Yard, 1-3 Treadway Street, London, E2 6QB
Shareholders: Charles Leet-Cook; Richard Goldsmith
Officers: Richard Goldsmith [1983] Director; Louis Jules Hydleman [1956] Non-Executive Director Chairman; Charles Leet-Cook [1986] Director

Monks Drinks Limited
Incorporated: 12 January 2012
Net Worth Deficit: £52,631 *Total Assets:* £3,333
Registered Office: 8-10 Station Road, Manor Park, London, E12 5BT
Major Shareholder: Amish Thakkar
Officers: Usha Thakkar [1952] Director

Monrone Health Ltd
Incorporated: 10 August 2018
Registered Office: Kemp House, 160 City Road, London, EC1V 2NX
Shareholders: Dilafruz Rakhmonova; Mohamed Saadeldin
Officers: Dilafruz Rakhmonova, Secretary; Dr Mohamed Saadeldin, Secretary; Dilafruz Rakhmonova [1985] Director/Businesswoman [Uzbek]

Montann Limited
Incorporated: 31 August 2016
Net Worth Deficit: £2,099 *Total Assets:* £26,774
Registered Office: 132-134 Great Ancoats Street, Manchester, M4 6DE
Shareholders: Jasmine Elaine Coleman; Helen Jane Crompton
Officers: Jasmine Elaine Coleman [1982] Director; Helen Jane Crompton [1971] Director

Moon Lynx Ltd
Incorporated: 15 July 2015
Net Worth: £500 *Total Assets:* £500
Registered Office: Kemp House, 152 City Road, London, EC1V 2NX
Major Shareholder: Jakub Mazurkiewicz
Officers: Jakub Mazurkiewicz [1977] Director [Polish]

More or Less Drinks Company Limited
Incorporated: 10 January 2013
Net Worth: £297,953 *Total Assets:* £595,876
Registered Office: 18 The Ropewalk, Nottingham, NG1 5DT
Major Shareholder: Stephen Hedley Norris
Officers: Christopher Arrigoni [1981] Director; Stephen Hedley Norris [1973] Director

Moreton Sweets (Wholesale) Ltd
Incorporated: 18 June 2018
Registered Office: 71-75 Shelton Street, Covent Garden, London, WC2H 9JQ
Major Shareholder: Robin Moreton
Officers: Robin Moreton, Secretary; Robin Moreton [1961] Director/Manager

Morinda UK Limited
Incorporated: 27 May 1999
Net Worth Deficit: £1,588,229 *Total Assets:* £218,248
Registered Office: 27-28 Eastcastle Street, London, W1W 8DH
Officers: Richard Carlos Rife, Secretary/General Counsel [American]; Richard Carlos Rife [1953] Director/General Counsel [American]; Randall N Smith [1954] Director/CFO and Treasurer [American]; Brent David Willis [1960] Director [American]

Moringa Superfoods UK Limited
Incorporated: 4 April 2018
Registered Office: Moringa House, 11 Alderlands Close, Crowland, Peterborough, PE6 0BS
Shareholders: Eirlys Sian Arulanantham; Amit Arulanantham
Officers: Amit Arulanantham [1980] Director [Indian]; Eirlys Sian Arulanantham [1972] Director

Mother Nature's Drinks Limited
Incorporated: 27 July 2017
Registered Office: 20-22 Wenlock Road, London, N1 7GU
Major Shareholder: Christiana Iliya
Officers: Christiana Iliya [1991] Director

Moudine Trade Ltd
Incorporated: 21 August 2018
Registered Office: 67 Wingate Square, London, SW4 0AF
Shareholders: Miguel Caiza; Jose Cueva
Officers: Miguel Caiza [1987] Director/Businessman [Ecuadorean]

MRU Wholesale Limited
Incorporated: 29 March 2016 *Employees:* 1
Net Worth: £2,393 *Total Assets:* £25,501
Registered Office: 232-234 Cannock Road, Wednesfield, Wolverhampton, W Midlands, WV10 8QD
Major Shareholder: Harwinder Kumar Chouhan
Officers: Harwinder Kumar Chouhan [1970] Director [Indian]; Kavita Kavita [1978] Director [Indian]

MS Rarytas Ltd
Incorporated: 6 June 2017 *Employees:* 1
Net Worth: £12,723 *Total Assets:* £25,128
Registered Office: 12 Sunnyside, Oxford, OX4 2NW
Shareholders: Maciej Blachut; Stanislaw Wolski
Officers: Maciej Blachut [1974] Director [Polish]; Stanislaw Wolski [1974] Director [Polish]

MSK Halal Ltd
Incorporated: 8 June 2018
Registered Office: 71-75 Shelton Street, Covent Garden, London, WC2H 9JQ
Major Shareholder: Afsana Azam
Officers: Afsana Azam [1978] Director/Housewife

MSM Foods Limited
Incorporated: 7 March 2008
Net Worth: £4,407 *Total Assets:* £141,893
Registered Office: Unit 5, M62 Trading Estate, New Potter Grange Road, Goole, E Yorks, DN14 6BZ
Shareholder: Sebastian Remigiusz Szczesny
Officers: Sebastian Remigiusz Szczesny, Secretary/Director [Polish]; Marek Lozowski [1962] Director [Polish]; Sebastian Remigiusz Szczesny [1979] Director, Secretary [Polish]

MTS Export Import Ltd
Incorporated: 11 June 2018
Registered Office: 30 St Phillips Drive, Royton, Oldham, Lancs, OL2 6AE
Major Shareholder: Tara Balda
Officers: Tara Balda [1969] Director/Self Employed

MU Distributors Ltd
Incorporated: 5 October 2018
Registered Office: 119 Randall Avenue, London, NW2 7SX
Major Shareholder: Arman Hussain
Officers: Shilpi Begum [1990] Director; Arman Hussain [1995] Director

J Mullens Ltd
Incorporated: 27 December 2018
Registered Office: 83 Sycamore Avenue, South Shields, Tyne & Wear, NE34 8BH
Major Shareholder: Jason Mullen
Officers: Jason Mullen [1972] Director

UK Wholesalers of Soft Drinks

Musielski Wholesale Ltd
Incorporated: 22 March 2018
Registered Office: 420 Brook Street, Fulwood, Preston, Lancs, PR2 3AH
Major Shareholder: Jakub Musielski
Officers: Jakub Musielski [1994] Director [Polish]

MX365 Energy Ltd
Incorporated: 29 August 2018
Registered Office: 1 Watson Avenue, St Andrews, Fife, KY16 8BY
Major Shareholder: Adrian John Allen Clatworthy
Officers: Adrian John Allen Clatworthy [1978] Director [South African/British]

My Smoothies Co Limited
Incorporated: 7 June 2018
Registered Office: 29 Champness Road, Barking, Essex, IG11 9PD
Officers: Literas Dragusin [1970] Director [Romanian]

N & B Foods Exeter Limited
Incorporated: 21 July 2015
Registered Office: Denmark House, Kestrel Way, Sowton Industrial Estate, Exeter, Devon, EX2 7LS
Shareholder: Anil Karavadra
Officers: Anil Karavadra [1985] Director; Nagajan Duda Karavadra [1956] Director

N & J Wholesale Foods Limited
Incorporated: 26 March 2002 *Employees:* 6
Net Worth Deficit: £59,967 *Total Assets:* £139,951
Registered Office: Unit 1 Chiltern Trading Estate, Earl Howe Road, Holmer Green, High Wycombe, Bucks, HP15 6QT
Major Shareholder: John Mark Goble
Officers: John Mark Goble [1956] Director

N'ife Limited
Incorporated: 16 February 2018
Registered Office: Flat 26, Mennie House, Royal Herbert Pavilions, Gilbert Close, London, SE18 4PR
Shareholders: Joy Temitayo Salaja; Olaitan Alabi
Officers: Olaitan Alabi [1985] Director/Co-owner; Joy Temitayo Salaja [1990] Co-Owner/Director [Irish]

Nacho Juice Limited
Incorporated: 13 October 2015
Net Worth: £4,160 *Total Assets:* £9,838
Registered Office: 80-83 Long Lane, London, EC1A 9ET
Officers: Nathaniel Frank [1982] Director/Finance [German]; Jochen Rudolf Gauger [1982] Director/Finance [German]

Nadban Limited
Incorporated: 26 September 2016
Registered Office: 31 Elmstead Crescent, Welling, Kent, DA16 1AU
Major Shareholder: Nadezhda Petrova
Officers: Nadezhda Petrova [1978] Director [German]

Najpol Ltd
Incorporated: 14 September 2017
Registered Office: Unit 5, M62 Trading Estate, New Potter Grange Road, Goole, E Yorks, DN14 6BZ
Shareholders: Sebastian Remigiusz Szczesny; Marek Lozowski
Officers: Marek Lozowski [1962] Director [Polish]; Sebastian Remigiusz Szczesny [1979] Director [Polish]

Nalla Sales Ltd
Incorporated: 22 March 2018
Registered Office: 82 Wheelwright Lane, Coventry, Warwicks, CV6 4HH
Major Shareholder: Arulan Nallathamby
Officers: Arulan Nallathamby [1964] Director/Sales Assistant [Norwegian]

Namar Limited
Incorporated: 29 December 2016 *Employees:* 1
Net Worth: £28,187 *Total Assets:* £294,986
Registered Office: 3 Pentland Close, London, N9 0XN
Major Shareholder: Namar Ghani
Officers: Nakash Ghani [1990] Director

Nar London Limited
Incorporated: 9 August 2017
Registered Office: 34 Navestock Crescent, Woodford Green, Essex, IG8 7AY
Major Shareholder: Tulin Nardali
Officers: Tulin Nardali [1975] Director/Businesswoman [Turkish]

Narayan Foods Limited
Incorporated: 21 June 2011 *Employees:* 4
Net Worth: £37,169 *Total Assets:* £538,079
Registered Office: The Gatehouse, 453 Cranbrook Road, Ilford, Essex, IG2 6EW
Officers: Jignaben Hitesh Patel [1979] Director [Indian]

Native Leaf Ltd
Incorporated: 11 November 2015
Net Worth Deficit: £8,137 *Total Assets:* £2,818
Registered Office: 48 Hangingstone Road, Berry Brow, Huddersfield, W Yorks, HD4 7QT
Major Shareholder: Jwan Khalaf
Officers: Jwan Khalaf [1986] Director/Software Developer

Natural Enzymes Limited
Incorporated: 4 February 2019
Registered Office: 40a Benthal Road, London, N16 7BX
Major Shareholder: Supradya Aursudkij
Officers: Supradya Aursudkij [1985] Director [Thai]

Natural Snacking Ltd
Incorporated: 7 March 2013 *Employees:* 2
Previous: Think Products Europe Ltd
Net Worth: £32,815 *Total Assets:* £197,705
Registered Office: Tower House, Parkstone Road, Poole, Dorset, BH15 2JH
Major Shareholder: Oliver Moorby
Officers: Oliver Moorby, Secretary; Oliver Moorby [1972] Director/IT Consultant

Natural Welsh Water Limited
Incorporated: 14 October 2005 *Employees:* 8
Net Worth: £136,281 *Total Assets:* £281,854
Registered Office: Conway House, Pattenden Lane, Marden, Tonbridge, Kent, TN12 9QJ
Parent: Water Wellbeing Limited
Officers: Simon Toby Pennington Edgar [1964] Director; Benjamin Raymond Stanley McGannan [1967] Director; Andrew Maurice Vickers [1964] Director

Naturally Fresh Drink Limited
Incorporated: 25 June 2018
Registered Office: 82 Balmoral Drive, Hayes, Middlesex, UB4 0BY
Major Shareholder: Selvananthan Navaratnam
Officers: Selvananthan Navaratnam [1984] Director/Driver [Sri Lankan]

Nature Fresh Limited
Incorporated: 12 December 2017
Registered Office: Flat 2, Sylvan Court, 41 Haling Park Road, South Croydon, Surrey, CR2 6NJ
Officers: Nalaka Weerasinghe, Secretary; Nalaka Weerasinghe [1981] Director

Nature on Tap Limited
Incorporated: 12 January 2015
Net Worth: £65,288 *Total Assets:* £171,543
Registered Office: 30 Portland Place, London, W1B 1LZ
Major Shareholder: Paul Lederer
Officers: Charles Hoare [1983] Director; Paul Lederer [1974] Director

Natures Vitality Limited
Incorporated: 8 May 2018
Registered Office: 24 Godolphin Close, London, N13 6LF
Parent: Optimal Living Group Limited
Officers: Gloria Amoah Osei, Secretary; Gloria Amoah Osei [1987] Director/Nutritionist

Naturshot Limited
Incorporated: 2 December 2016
Registered Office: Kemp House, 160 City Road, London, EC1V 2NX
Major Shareholder: Mina Prince
Officers: Mina Prince, Secretary; Mina Prince [1982] Director/Management Consultant

Navson Ltd
Incorporated: 16 May 2002 *Employees:* 14
Net Worth: £1,121,372 *Total Assets:* £3,567,701
Registered Office: Monarch House, Crabtree Office Village, Eversley Way, Egham, Surrey, TW20 8RY
Shareholders: Nevid Ahmed; Soner Kanal
Officers: Soner Kanal, Secretary; Nevid Ahmed [1976] Director; Soner Kanal [1975] Director

Nawab Traders Limited
Incorporated: 14 June 2018
Registered Office: 14 Woodfield Avenue, Batley, W Yorks, WF17 7EA
Officers: Mohammad Nazir Nawab [1965] Director/General Manager [Spanish]

Nazar Wholesale Limited
Incorporated: 12 March 2014
Net Worth: £71,691 *Total Assets:* £170,005
Registered Office: Unit 5 Status Business Park, Venture House, 1-2 Holbrook Lane, Coventry, Warwicks, CV6 4AF
Major Shareholder: Kenan Cigdem
Officers: Kenan Cigdem [1990] Managing Director

NBA Wholesale Ltd
Incorporated: 20 March 2018
Registered Office: 143 Essex Road, London, E12 6QR
Major Shareholder: Nicolae-Alexandru Baciu
Officers: Nicolae-Alexandru Baciu [1974] Director [Romanian]

NCE Trading KFT Ltd
Incorporated: 21 December 2017
Registered Office: 6 Neville Road, London, E7 9QX
Major Shareholder: Sandip Navnitbhai Patel
Officers: Sandip Navnitbhai Patel [1967] Director

Neelam Traders Ltd
Incorporated: 1 November 2017
Registered Office: 52 Henderson Road, London, E7 8EF
Major Shareholder: Sohail Tabassum
Officers: Sohail Tabassum [1968] Director

Nekta Food & Juice Bar Ltd
Incorporated: 25 February 2019
Registered Office: 61 Kelly Road, Hebburn, Tyne & Wear, NE31 2QN
Major Shareholder: Laura Finlay
Officers: Laura Finlay [1983] Director/Customer Service

Netmine Technologies Ltd
Incorporated: 8 April 2016
Registered Office: 86c Water Street, Birmingham, B3 1HL
Major Shareholder: Muhammad Akmal
Officers: Muhammad Akmal [1973] Director

Netto Stores Limited
Incorporated: 13 April 2017
Registered Office: 91 Albion Street, Hockley, Birmingham, B1 3AA
Officers: John Groce [1960] Director

Neubria Limited
Incorporated: 1 November 2017
Registered Office: Hamilton House, Church Street, Altrincham, Cheshire, WA14 4DR
Major Shareholder: Brian George Kennedy
Officers: Timothy John Halpin [1981] Finance Director; Adrian Christopher Kirk [1961] Finance Director

The New Drinking Ltd
Incorporated: 9 January 2019
Registered Office: 38 Fitzroy Street, London, W1T 4BP
Major Shareholder: Oscar Panizzon
Officers: Oscar Panizzon [1971] Director/Consultant [Italian]

New Global Ltd
Incorporated: 28 February 2019
Registered Office: 74 Breck Road, Anfield, Liverpool, L4 2RB
Major Shareholder: Maxime Bekhti
Officers: Maxime Bekhti [1958] Director/Manager [French]

New Kumasi Market 2 Ltd
Incorporated: 20 June 2018
Registered Office: 493 New Cross Road, London, SE14 6TQ
Major Shareholder: Gertrude Donkor
Officers: Gertrude Donkor [1982] Director/Trader

Newton Soft Drinks Wholesale Limited
Incorporated: 21 March 2018
Registered Office: Unit 6, 8 Eley Road, London, N18 3BB
Major Shareholder: Micheal Steven Newton
Officers: Micheal Steven Newton, Secretary; Micheal Steven Newton [1991] Director

Nexgen 2018 Ltd
Incorporated: 5 January 2018
Registered Office: 1 Pool Road, Chasetown, Burntwood, Staffs, WS7 3QW
Major Shareholder: Hardip Singh Talafair
Officers: Hardip Singh Talafair [1975] Director

Next Gen Drinks Limited
Incorporated: 4 December 2017
Registered Office: 85 Great Portland Street, London, W1W 7LT
Major Shareholder: Alastair James Manson
Officers: Alastair Manson, Secretary; Alastair James Manson [1974] Director/Chartered Accountant

Nextgen Distribution Limited
Incorporated: 3 May 2018
Registered Office: 15 Reynolds Road, New Malden, Surrey, KT3 5NG
Shareholders: Jamil Ahmad Qamar; Saad Agha
Officers: Saad Agha [1985] Director/Economist; Jamil Ahmad Qamar [1988] Director/Coordinator [German]

Nichols Dispense (S.W.) Limited
Incorporated: 7 November 2013
Net Worth Deficit: £24,812
Registered Office: Laurel House, Woodlands Park, Ashton Road, Newton-le-Willows, Merseyside, WA12 0HH
Parent: Nichols PLC
Officers: Andrew Stuart Johnson [1980] Director/Financial Controller

Nile Minar Enterprise Limited
Incorporated: 2 January 2018
Registered Office: Unit A, Anglian Industrial Estate, Atcost Road, Barking, Essex, IG11 0EQ
Major Shareholder: Khalid Sharks
Officers: Khalid Sharks [1985] Director

Nile Nutrients Ltd
Incorporated: 12 October 2018
Registered Office: 99 Wilton Way, London, E8 1BH
Major Shareholder: Edwin Kakaire
Officers: Edwin Kakaire [1980] Director/Self Employed

Nippon Trading Ltd
Incorporated: 25 February 2019
Registered Office: 439 High Street North, London, E12 6TJ
Major Shareholder: Sujeeban Yogaratnam
Officers: Sujeeban Yogaratnam [1991] Director [French]

Nirajen Ltd
Incorporated: 8 October 2018
Registered Office: 1a Carshalton Grove, Sutton, Surrey, SM1 4LY
Shareholders: Ajenth Sriganeshakuamr; Niroshankar Kandasamy
Officers: Niroshankar Kandasamy [1989] Director/Engineer [French]; Ajenth Sriganeshakuamr [1991] Director/Engineer

No Meat No Worries Limited
Incorporated: 25 July 2017
Registered Office: 48 Abbots Close, Walton-le-Dale, Preston, Lancs, PR5 4NU
Officers: Aaron Colin Jamieson [1974] Director/Consultant

Noah Brothers Ltd
Incorporated: 9 January 2019
Registered Office: 75 Gainsborough Green, Abingdon, Oxon, OX14 5JL
Major Shareholder: Gkor Tovmasian
Officers: Gkor Tovmasian [1991] Director [Greek]

Noble Naturals Ltd
Incorporated: 12 August 2014
Net Worth Deficit: £44,263   *Total Assets:* £95,645
Registered Office: Unit 5 Fen Place Farm, East Street, Turners Hill, Crawley, W Sussex, RH10 4QA
Major Shareholder: Abigail April Miller
Officers: Abigail April Miller [1975] Director/Retailer

The Noble Smokehouse Ltd
Incorporated: 26 February 2018
Registered Office: 47 Barnet Lane, Barnet, Herts, EN5 2DW
Major Shareholder: Slawomir Wlodarczyk
Officers: Slawomir Wlodarczyk [1962] Director/Fishmonger [Polish]

Nobu Distribution Ltd
Incorporated: 15 December 2017
Registered Office: Unit 7 Station Works, Station Road, Ecclesfield, Sheffield, S35 9YR
Major Shareholder: Craig Watson
Officers: Craig Watson [1974] Director

Nodus International Trade Ltd
Incorporated: 8 February 2017
Registered Office: 7 Maltby Square, Buckshaw Village, Chorley, Lancs, PR7 7GN
Officers: Jamel Khalifa, Secretary; Sihem Boussoufa-Khalifa [1967] Director/Manager

Nohew Trade Ltd
Incorporated: 1 December 2018
Registered Office: 63a Blakeland Street, Birmingham, B9 5XQ
Major Shareholder: Zaheer Ahmad
Officers: Zaheer Ahmad [1960] Director

Nootrilix Limited
Incorporated: 7 September 2018
Registered Office: Himley Rise, Pinewood Drive, Ashley Heath, Market Drayton, Salop, TF9 4PA
Shareholders: Rajveer Singh Athwal; Kuranveer Singh Jandu
Officers: Dr Rajveer Singh Athwal [1989] Director/Dentist; Kuranveer Singh Jandu [1988] Director/Regional Manager

Nor Oslo Service Ltd
Incorporated: 9 June 2017
Registered Office: 12 Evesham Green, Morden, Surrey, SM4 6PW
Officers: Arulanantham Sumramaniyam, Secretary; Arulanantham Sumramaniyam [1964] Director/Sales Manager [Norwegian]

Nordic Life Water UK Limited
Incorporated: 14 February 2019
Registered Office: Unit B, Network 331, Lysons Avenue, Ash Vale, Aldershot, Hants, GU12 5QF
Shareholders: George Arthur Dove; Duncan Norman Holloway
Officers: George Arthur Dove [1947] Managing Director; Duncan Norman Holloway [1963] Director/Consultant

Norfolk Punch (UK) Ltd
Incorporated: 5 November 2013
Registered Office: 2 New Terrace, Byfield, Daventry, Northants, NN11 6UY
Major Shareholder: Graham Trevitt
Officers: Graham Trevitt [1955] Director

Norfolk Punch Limited
Incorporated: 11 November 2009
Registered Office: Royal Bank Chambers, Newtown St Boswells, Melrose, Roxburghshire, TD6 0PN
Major Shareholder: William Ranald Boydell
Officers: William Ranald Boydell, Secretary; William Ranald Boydell [1965] Director/Businessman [Australian]

Northern Food Services Limited
Incorporated: 21 September 2018
Registered Office: 64 Longfield Road, Bolton, Lancs, BL3 3TB
Major Shareholder: Samira Yusuf
Officers: Samira Yusuf [1976] Director/Sales Manager [German]

Northern Lights Ltd.
Incorporated: 5 November 2018
Registered Office: 27 Old Gloucester Street, London, WC1N 3AX
Major Shareholder: John Michael Jorgensen
Officers: John Michael Jorgensen [1948] Director [Norwegian]

Val Norton Ltd
Incorporated: 30 November 2012
Net Worth: £46,493 *Total Assets:* £56,308
Registered Office: Pannanich Wells Hotel, South Deeside Road, Ballater, Aberdeenshire, AB35 5SJ
Major Shareholder: Valerie Christine Norton
Officers: Valerie Christine Norton [1943] Director

Nosh Detox Delivery Limited
Incorporated: 30 July 2009
Net Worth Deficit: £156,794 *Total Assets:* £102,970
Registered Office: Bank House, Southwick Square, Southwick, W Sussex, BN42 4FN
Major Shareholder: Sangeeta Kaur Sidhu-Robb
Officers: Sangeeta Sidhu-Robb [1967] Director/Lawyer

Not Another Beer Co Ltd
Incorporated: 3 August 2017
Registered Office: 14b High Street, Eccleshall, Stafford, ST21 6BZ
Major Shareholder: Luke Seymour Boase
Officers: Luke Seymour Boase [1981] Director/Executive

Notgin Ltd
Incorporated: 20 February 2018
Registered Office: P O Box 567, Torquay, Devon, TQ1 9HY
Shareholders: Geoffrey Karl Yates; Sarah Ellen Yates
Officers: Geoffrey Karl Yates [1956] Director/Business Executive; Sarah Ellen Yates [1962] Director/Businesswoman

Nova Wholesale Ltd
Incorporated: 9 August 2018
Registered Office: 82 Claremont Road, London, NW2 1AP
Major Shareholder: Sharron Constantine Palathis
Officers: Sharron Constantine Palathis [1994] Director/Sales Manager [French]

NQN Enterprises Limited
Incorporated: 11 January 2019
Registered Office: Kemp House, 160 City Road, London, EC1V 2NX
Officers: Azizul Ahmed [1979] Director/Self Employed

Nuli Life Ltd
Incorporated: 18 July 2017
Registered Office: 71-75 Shelton Street, Covent Garden, London, WC2H 9JQ
Major Shareholder: Ali Al-Aukati
Officers: Ali Al-Aukati, Secretary; Ali Al-Aukati [1986] Director

Numba UK Limited
Incorporated: 23 January 2019
Registered Office: 654 Warrington Road, Rainhill, Prescot, Merseyside, L35 0NS
Shareholders: Hiba El-Mohbi; Madelyn Gardner
Officers: Hiba El-Mohbi [1983] Director [Danish]; Madelyn Gardner [1994] Director

Number One Water Ltd
Incorporated: 13 November 2018
Registered Office: 515a Cambridge Heath Road, London, E2 9BU
Major Shareholder: Silvana Simeonova Ivanova
Officers: Silvana Simeonova Ivanova [1990] Director

Numidia Taste Ltd
Incorporated: 21 February 2018
Registered Office: 18 Osprey Close, Bicester, Oxon, OX26 6YH
Major Shareholder: Mohamed Ammani
Officers: Mohamed Ammani [1986] Director/Sales Advisor [Algerian]

NXSK UK Ltd
Incorporated: 16 March 2017
Registered Office: Kemp House, 160 City Road, London, EC1V 2NX
Officers: Naim Hamade, Secretary; Naim Hamade [1994] Director/CEO & Founder [Portuguese]

O & E Food Ltd
Incorporated: 17 September 2018
Registered Office: 99 Grays Inn Road, London, WC1X 8TY
Shareholders: Ozan Yadirgi; Erdal Karadag
Officers: Erdal Karadag [1975] Director; Ozan Yadirgi [1980] Director

Oasis Softdrinks Limited
Incorporated: 1 September 2010 *Employees:* 12
Net Worth: £253,800 *Total Assets:* £652,141
Registered Office: 17 Goldthorpe Industrial Estate, Commercial Road, Goldthorpe, Rotherham, S Yorks, S63 9BL
Major Shareholder: Benjamin Cartwright
Officers: Clair Cartwright, Secretary; Benjamin Cartwright [1977] Director

Oct Multi Services Limited
Incorporated: 19 December 2017
Registered Office: Flat 19, 305 Hornsey Road, London, N19 4HD
Major Shareholder: Oliver Cromwell Tohouri
Officers: Oliver Cromwell Tohouri [1968] Director

OK Brothers Ltd
Incorporated: 21 January 2013
Net Worth: £5,435 *Total Assets:* £75,242
Registered Office: 294 High Street North, London, E12 6SA
Major Shareholder: Yogalingam Kathiravelu
Officers: Yogalingam Kathiravelu [1969] Director [Argentinian]

Ola Acai Ltd
Incorporated: 21 September 2018
Registered Office: 16 Citrus House, Alverton Street, London, SE8 5NP
Major Shareholder: Michael de Campos Sell
Officers: Michael de Campos Sell [1990] Director/Analyst

UK Wholesalers of Soft Drinks dellam

Olsson Logistics Limited
Incorporated: 23 February 2016 *Employees:* 1
Net Worth: £750 *Total Assets:* £1,897
Registered Office: 99 Albert Carr Gardens, Streatham, London, SW16 3HE
Major Shareholder: Henry Okoye
Officers: Henry Okoye [1989] Director

Ombre Drinks Limited
Incorporated: 28 August 2018
Registered Office: 2 Goodwood Avenue, Enfield, Middlesex, EN3 5RP
Parent: Distinate Ltd
Officers: Danyal Adam Hussain [1995] Director; Rahul Patel [1997] Director

OMG Beverages Limited
Incorporated: 5 October 2005
Net Worth Deficit: £104,439 *Total Assets:* £13,984
Registered Office: Unit 6 Lakeside Business Park, Neptune Close, Medway City Estate, Rochester, Kent, ME2 4LT
Major Shareholder: Jaswinder Cheema
Officers: Jaswinder Cheema [1978] Director

One Grace LMT Ltd
Incorporated: 2 August 2018
Registered Office: Unit 1 Polmaise Park, Main Street, Fallin, Stirling, FK7 7JH
Major Shareholder: Malick Mamadi Sowe
Officers: Malick Mamadi Sowe [1980] Director/Retailer

One Stop Fruit & Veg Limited
Incorporated: 4 August 2017
Registered Office: 101 Oak Lane, Bradford, BD9 4QU
Major Shareholder: Suhail Khan
Officers: Sohail Khan [1992] Director

One Up Beverages Corporation (1 Up) Limited
Incorporated: 26 February 2018
Registered Office: Bridge House, 64-72 Mabgate, Leeds, LS9 7DZ
Major Shareholder: Diane Wilson
Officers: Diane Edith Wilson [1944] Director/Company Formation Agent Semi-Retired

Oneway Trading Ltd
Incorporated: 3 April 2018
Registered Office: 4 Tuppy Street, London, SE28 0GA
Major Shareholder: Sabir Mohamad
Officers: Sabir Mohamad [1967] Director/Sales Assistant [Portuguese]

Oneworlddistribution Ltd
Incorporated: 16 April 2018
Registered Office: Forde House, Nicholashayne, Wellington, Somerset, TA21 9QY
Major Shareholder: Ajit Singh Sangha
Officers: Ajit Sangha, Secretary; Ajit Singh Sangha [1965] Director

Onofrei Cash & Carry Ltd
Incorporated: 25 January 2019
Registered Office: 119 Beaumont Road, Middlesbrough, Cleveland, TS3 6NS
Major Shareholder: Maricica Onofrei
Officers: Maricica Onofrei [1981] Director [Romanian]

Ooberstock Limited
Incorporated: 2 July 2010
Net Worth: £113,427 *Total Assets:* £1,592,134
Registered Office: 9 Queens Square, Ascot Business Park, Ascot, Berks, SL5 9FE
Parent: Drinks21 Group Ltd
Officers: Nigel Kevin Morton, Secretary; Stephen Michael Brogan [1969] Director

Orange Be Global Ltd
Incorporated: 15 November 2012
Net Worth Deficit: £49,014 *Total Assets:* £276,202
Registered Office: 8 Square Rigger Row, London, SW11 3TZ
Major Shareholder: Christos Papadimitrakopoulos
Officers: Christos Papadimitrakopoulos [1970] Managing Director [Greek]

Orange Trading Ltd
Incorporated: 7 November 2017
Registered Office: 83 Ducie Street, Manchester, M1 2JQ
Major Shareholder: Rajah Ahmed Riaz Bhatti
Officers: Rajah Ahmed Riaz Bhatti [1970] Director

Oranka Fruit Juices Limited
Incorporated: 30 September 2002
Net Worth Deficit: £3,412,646 *Total Assets:* £2,069,942
Registered Office: Unit 9 Wornal Park, Menmarsh Road, Worminghall, Aylesbury, Bucks, HP18 9PH
Parent: MJJ Brandriet Holding BV
Officers: Bea Brandriet Lemmen, Secretary; Marco Johan Jakobus Brandriet [1973] Director [Dutch]; Troy Smith [1967] Managing Director

Orbit Food Ltd
Incorporated: 18 October 2016
Net Worth: £6,607 *Total Assets:* £107,411
Registered Office: Unit C5, Hilton Trading Estate, Hilton Road, Wolverhampton, W Midlands, WV4 6DW
Major Shareholder: Sarwat Fateh Jaf
Officers: Sarwat Fateh Jaf [1972] Director

Order2buy Ltd
Incorporated: 29 June 2016
Registered Office: 29a Shardlow Road, Alvaston, Derby, DE24 0JG
Major Shareholder: Sivatheeban Sivakrishnanathan
Officers: Sivatheeban Sivakrishnanathan [1977] Director/Sales Manager [German]

Organic Village Limited
Incorporated: 8 March 2007
Net Worth Deficit: £200,578 *Total Assets:* £58,914
Registered Office: 89a Teignmouth Road, London, NW2 4EA
Major Shareholder: Nerin Bilgin
Officers: Nerin Bilgin, Secretary; Nerin Bilgin [1960] Company Secretary/Director [Turkish]

Organica Vita Ltd
Incorporated: 12 February 2015
Net Worth Deficit: £44,256 *Total Assets:* £18,243
Registered Office: 16 Boileau Road, London, SW13 9BL
Officers: Tatjana Brkljac [1972] Director [Serbian]

Organix Ltd
Incorporated: 6 March 2018
Registered Office: 71-75 Shelton Street, London, WC2H 9JQ
Shareholders: Thomas Sellers; Paul Sellers
Officers: Paul Sellers [1968] Director/Producer; Thomas Sellers [1999] Director/Producer

Oriental Express London Limited
Incorporated: 11 February 2019
Registered Office: 78 St Leonard Street, Bromley by Bow, London, E3 3LR
Major Shareholder: Md Ahsan Habib
Officers: MD Ahsan Habib [1967] Director

Orpheus Tea Ltd
Incorporated: 9 February 2018
Registered Office: 63 Leonard Road, Chingford, London, E4 8NE
Officers: Kalin Todorov [1979] Director/Sales [Bulgarian]

Ozdil UK Limited
Incorporated: 5 November 1999 *Employees:* 11
Net Worth: £6,136,885 *Total Assets:* £7,846,391
Registered Office: Ozdil House, River Way, Harlow, Essex, CM20 2DR
Major Shareholder: Serhat Ozdil
Officers: Serhat Ozdil [1977] Director

Ozlem Limited
Incorporated: 31 March 1998 *Employees:* 20
Net Worth: £134,305 *Total Assets:* £649,019
Registered Office: Unit 2 Hotspur Industrial Estate, West Road, Tottenham, London, N17 0XJ
Major Shareholder: Mecit Cifci
Officers: Mecit Cifci [1962] Director

P & V Agents Ltd
Incorporated: 29 February 2012 *Employees:* 1
Net Worth: £19,437 *Total Assets:* £50,281
Registered Office: 8 Cavendish Court, Gordon Road, Chingford, London, E4 6DL
Shareholders: Petras Vilcinskas; Petras Vilcinskas
Officers: Petras Vilcinskas [1961] Director [Lithuanian]

P N New Ltd
Incorporated: 10 October 2018
Registered Office: 357 Abbeydale Road, Sheffield, S7 1FS
Major Shareholder: Arshad Mahmood Raja
Officers: Arshad Mahmood Raja [1960] Director/Shop Manager [Spanish]

Paddy and Scotts Launch Pad Ltd
Incorporated: 6 March 2018
Registered Office: The Bean Barn, Framlingham Road, Moat Park, Woodbridge, Suffolk, IP13 7SR
Parent: Paddy & Scotts Cafes Ltd
Officers: Scott Christian Russell [1971] Director

Paisley Drinks Co. Ltd
Incorporated: 4 June 2018
Registered Office: 1 MacDowall Street, Paisley, Renfrewshire, PA3 2NB
Major Shareholder: Brian O'Shea
Officers: Brian O'Shea [1981] Managing Director

Pallet Price Wholesale Ltd
Incorporated: 31 October 2017
Registered Office: 203 Western Road, Mickleover, Derby, DE3 9GU
Major Shareholder: Bhupinder Singh Sohal
Officers: Bhupinder Singh Sohal [1982] Director/Entrepreneur

Pamm Beverages Limited
Incorporated: 8 February 2017
Net Worth Deficit: £24,410 *Total Assets:* £12,021
Registered Office: 52 Appletree Avenue, Yiewsley, West Drayton, Middlesex, UB7 8BY
Major Shareholder: Priscilla Atalaye
Officers: Priscillia Atalaye [1974] Director/Businesswoman

Panda Rolls Ltd
Incorporated: 4 June 2018
Registered Office: 10 Cannon Gate, Slough, Berks, SL2 5NH
Officers: Raul Catalin Lutas [1992] Director/Self Employed [Romanian]

Panopoulos Forest Ltd
Incorporated: 1 June 2018
Registered Office: 5 Dallas Road, London, W5 3BW
Shareholders: Georgios Michanitzis; Georgios Panopoulos
Officers: Georgios Michanitzis [1966] Managing Director [Greek]; Georgios Panopoulos [1955] Director/Solicitor [Greek]

Panopoulos Waters Ltd
Incorporated: 18 July 2018
Registered Office: 6 Collingwood Court, 97 Hanger Lane, London, W5 3DA
Major Shareholder: Georgios Panopoulos
Officers: Georgios Michanitzis [1966] Director/General Manager [Greek]

Panton Ventures Limited
Incorporated: 16 August 2011
Net Worth Deficit: £1,664 *Total Assets:* £24,604
Registered Office: 32 Totternhoe Close, Kenton, Harrow, Middlesex, HA3 0HS
Major Shareholder: Feisal Mehmood Khan
Officers: Feisal Mehmood Khan [1981] Director

Panymoc Ltd
Incorporated: 23 November 2016
Registered Office: 68 George Street, Coventry, Warwicks, CV1 4HD
Officers: Antony Sayanthan Inpanathan, Secretary; Antony Sayanthan Inpanathan [1989] Director/Sales Manager [French]

Panymocc Limited
Incorporated: 7 June 2018
Registered Office: Wenta Business Centres Limited, Colne Way, Watford, Herts, WD24 7ND
Major Shareholder: Somalatha Ariyarathna Koongahawattage
Officers: Somalatha Ariyarathna Koongahawattage, Secretary; Somalatha Ariyarathna Koongahawattage [1951] Director [Sri Lankan]

Paradigm Red Limited
Incorporated: 23 April 2018
Registered Office: 66 Blagdon Road, New Malden, Surrey, KT3 4AE
Shareholders: Alexander James Wallbank; Xiangshou An
Officers: Guinan [1980] Director/Designer [Chinese]; Xiangshou [1983] Director/Senior IT Project Manager [Chinese]; Alexander James Wallbank [1984] Director/Head of Finance

Paramount Food and Drink (UK) Ltd.
Incorporated: 28 April 2017
Registered Office: 3rd Floor, 29 Market Street, Portadown, Craigavon, Co Armagh, BT62 3LD
Officers: Arin Necmi Cubuk [1992] Director; Yalcin Cubuk [1966] Director [Irish]

Parkway UK Wholesale Ltd
Incorporated: 6 July 2018
Registered Office: App 1 Dean Swift, Hamiltonbawn Road, Armagh, BT60 1DL
Major Shareholder: Stephen Patrick Hatzer
Officers: Stephen Patrick Hatzer, Secretary; Stephen Patrick Hatzer [1977] Director [Irish]

Passa Distribution Ltd
Incorporated: 23 March 2018
Registered Office: 420 Brook Street, Fulwood, Preston, Lancs, PR2 3AH
Major Shareholder: Mateusz Stanislaw Maciaszek
Officers: Mateusz Stanislaw Maciaszek [1992] Director [Polish]

Passa Wholesale Ltd
Incorporated: 22 March 2018
Registered Office: 54 Mellor Street, Rochdale, Lancs, OL12 6XD
Major Shareholder: Mateusz Stanislaw Maciaszek
Officers: Mateusz Stanislaw Maciaszek [1992] Commercial Director [Polish]

Patrik Trading Ltd
Incorporated: 30 May 2018
Registered Office: 71 Woodbridge Road, Leicester, LE4 7RJ
Major Shareholder: Patrik Horvath
Officers: Patrik Horvath [1998] Director [Hungarian]

Patson Foods Ltd
Incorporated: 19 September 2017
Registered Office: 56 Christchurch Avenue, Harrow, Middlesex, HA3 8NL
Shareholder: Praful Nanji Amipara
Officers: Praful Nanji Amipara [1965] Director; Surajbhai Dayalal Savaliya [1972] Director [Indian]; Chintankumar Chunilal Vaghasiya [1988] Director

Pavlinko Limited
Incorporated: 22 June 2017
Registered Office: 77 Pembroke Road, Erith, Kent, DA8 1BY
Major Shareholder: Pavandeep Guraya
Officers: Pavandeep Guraya, Secretary; Pavandeep Guraya [1992] Director/Bakery Operative

Paynesbb Limited
Incorporated: 2 November 2018
Registered Office: Lakeside Nursery, Paynes Lane, London, EN9 2EU
Officers: Baldassare Buoncuore [1955] Director [Italian]

Pem Trade Sales Ltd
Incorporated: 18 December 2018
Registered Office: 41 Bath Street, Southport, Merseyside, PR9 0DP
Major Shareholder: Pietro Enrico Marco Intonazzo
Officers: Pietro Enrico Marco Intonazzo [1972] Director/Manager

Peregrine Welsh Water Limited
Incorporated: 16 April 2018
Registered Office: Stone House, 17 High Street, Welshpool, Powys, SY21 7JP
Shareholders: James Patrick Blurton; Stephen John Evans
Officers: James Patrick Blurton [1957] Director; Stephen John Evans [1961] Director

Perfect Drinks Ltd
Incorporated: 14 November 2017
Registered Office: 29 Bailey Lane, Radcliffe on Trent, Notts, NG12 2EG
Major Shareholder: Jonathan Perfect
Officers: Jonathan Perfect [1980] Director

Phoenix Dispensed Drinks Limited
Incorporated: 23 May 2000 *Employees:* 19
Net Worth: £2,168,733 *Total Assets:* £3,287,415
Registered Office: Unit 1 Crescent Industrial Park, Pear Tree Lane, Dudley, W Midlands, DY2 0QQ
Parent: Phoenix Dispensed Drinks Holdings Limited
Officers: Adam Paul Turton [1983] Director; Adrian Scott Turton [1958] Director

Pick N Deliver Ltd
Incorporated: 29 June 2016
Registered Office: 5 The Lows, Oldham, Lancs, OL4 1AQ
Major Shareholder: Mohammed Junaid
Officers: Mohammed Junaid [1968] Director

Pick Pedal Pour Ltd
Incorporated: 26 February 2019
Registered Office: 6 High Street, Ilchester, Yeovil, Somerset, BA22 8NQ
Major Shareholder: Simon Alexander Rumbles
Officers: Simon Alexander Rumbles [1981] Director/Civil Servant

Pinnacle Drinks Limited
Incorporated: 4 April 2018
Registered Office: 40 Rodney Street, Liverpool, L1 9AA
Major Shareholder: John Devin
Officers: John Devin, Secretary; John Devin [1990] Director/Drinks Distributor

Pirm Trading Limited
Incorporated: 10 October 2018
Registered Office: Office 1, Izabella House, 24-26 Regent Place, Birmingham, B1 3NJ
Major Shareholder: Pirasaanthan Maheswaran
Officers: Pirasaanthan Maheswaran, Secretary; Pirasaanthan Maheswaran [1992] Director/Senior Manager [French]

Pixley Berries (Juice) Limited
Incorporated: 17 January 2007 *Employees:* 14
Net Worth: £735,004 *Total Assets:* £2,325,956
Registered Office: Poolend, Pixley, Ledbury, Herefords, HR8 2RB
Major Shareholder: Edward Ballard Thompson
Officers: Hannah Mary Parker, Secretary; Edward Ballard Thompson [1944] Director/Farmer

Platinum Group Midlands Ltd
Incorporated: 15 November 2017
Registered Office: 402 Ladypool Road, Birmingham, B12 8JZ
Officers: Usman Ali [1988] Sales Director

Platinum Packaging Ltd
Incorporated: 7 November 2018
Registered Office: 19 Ashley Road, Reading, Berks, RG1 6HT
Major Shareholder: Usman Aslam
Officers: Usman Aslam [1990] Director/Businessman

Platinum UK Drinks Ltd
Incorporated: 5 November 2018
Registered Office: Unit 3 Crondal Road, Exhall, Coventry, Warwicks, CV7 9NH
Major Shareholder: Zahoor Ahmed
Officers: Zahoor Ahmed [1973] Director

PMahesh Trading Limited
Incorporated: 10 October 2018
Registered Office: Kemp House, 160 City Road, London, EC1V 2NX
Major Shareholder: Pirasaanthan Maheswaran
Officers: Pirasaanthan Maheswaran, Secretary; Pirasaanthan Maheswaran [1992] Director/Senior Manager [French]

PMI Management Limited
Incorporated: 1 February 2018
Registered Office: PMI Management Limited, 272 Bath Street, Glasgow, G2 4JR
Major Shareholder: Mohammad Iqbal Patel
Officers: Mohammad Iqbal Patel [1962] Director

W.E.Pointon & Sons Limited
Incorporated: 26 January 1972
Net Worth: £16,920 Total Assets: £126,385
Registered Office: Unit 5 Greens Industrial Estate, Station Road, Hednesford, Staffs, WS12 0QS
Major Shareholder: John Lawrence Pointon
Officers: John Lawrence Pointon [1950] Director

Polat International Ltd
Incorporated: 21 October 2016
Previous: Safest D Limited
Net Worth: £12,222 Total Assets: £28,180
Registered Office: Broad Water Lodge, Higham Road, London, N17 6NN
Officers: Uzaifa Katende [1990] Director

Polski Wholesale Limited
Incorporated: 17 August 2018
Registered Office: 8 Harwell Road, Sheffield, S8 0ZN
Major Shareholder: Martin Maksymowicz
Officers: Martin Maksymowicz [1977] Managing Director [Polish]

Polwug Trading Ltd
Incorporated: 12 December 2017
Registered Office: 1 Badgers Copse, Camberley, Surrey, GU15 1HW
Officers: Syed Zulfaqar Haider [1978] Director/Managing Director

Potts of Goodness Limited
Incorporated: 15 September 2015
Net Worth Deficit: £13,044 Total Assets: £1,896
Registered Office: Orchard House, Kinton, nr Nesscliffe, Shrewsbury, Salop, SY4 1AZ
Shareholders: David Neil Potts; Michelle Dawn Potts
Officers: David Neil Potts [1951] Director; Michelle Dawn Potts [1966] Director

Pound Hill Ltd
Incorporated: 18 December 2018
Registered Office: 39 Crossfield Road, Birmingham, B33 9HS
Major Shareholder: Mohammed-Hasnain Jamaal Abdul
Officers: Mohammed-Hasnain Jamaal Abdul [1998] Director

PP Cash & Carry Ltd
Incorporated: 14 May 2018
Registered Office: 58 Muirhead Avenue, Liverpool, L11 1EL
Major Shareholder: Ponneswaran Ponnuthurai
Officers: Ponneswaran Ponnuthurai [1970] Director/Sales Assistant [Norwegian]

Premier Food & Beverage Limited
Incorporated: 20 July 2018
Registered Office: 71-75 Shelton Street, Covent Garden, London, WC2H 9JQ
Officers: Akeal Ahmed [1976] Director

Premier Marketing (NW) Ltd
Incorporated: 5 September 2011 Employees: 1
Net Worth Deficit: £75,624 Total Assets: £471
Registered Office: 72b New Court Way, Ormskirk, Lancs, L39 2YT
Shareholders: Iain Purslow; Gillian Dorothy Purslow
Officers: Iain Purslow [1962] Director

Premier Pubco Limited
Incorporated: 22 March 2001
Net Worth: £44,186 Total Assets: £209,606
Registered Office: 21 Navigation Way, Cannock, Staffs, WS11 7XU
Major Shareholder: James Barry Thomas
Officers: James Barry Thomas [1971] Operations Director; Susan Thomas [1960] Director

Premier Soft Drinks Ltd
Incorporated: 18 January 2018
Registered Office: Companies House, Default Address, Cardiff, CF14 8LH
Major Shareholder: Jake Avitable
Officers: Jake Avitable [1993] Director

Premium Drinks Distribution Ltd
Incorporated: 4 December 2018
Registered Office: 28 Goodhope Gardens, Bucksburn, Aberdeen, AB21 9NG
Shareholders: Amit Sharma; Ritika Khanna
Officers: Ritika Khanna [1987] Director [Indian]; Amit Sharma [1982] Director [Indian]

Premium Jacks Limited
Incorporated: 2 August 2018
Registered Office: 12 Westmorland Road, London, E17 8JA
Major Shareholder: Ibrahim Bulbulia
Officers: Ibrahim Bulbulia [1978] Director/Trader

Pres & Co. Limited
Incorporated: 7 December 2018
Registered Office: 115 Chamberlayne Road, London, NW10 3NS
Major Shareholder: Preslava Gyonkova
Officers: Preslava Gyonkova [1995] Executive Director [Bulgarian]

Prestwich Catering & Wholesale Ltd
Incorporated: 24 May 2018
Registered Office: 217 Bury Old Road, Prestwich, Manchester, M25 1JF
Major Shareholder: Ahmed Irfan Ghani
Officers: Ahmed Irfan Ghani [1981] Director

Primacena Ltd.
Incorporated: 19 October 2016
Registered Office: Mysliborice 13, 675 60 Mysliborice, Czech Republic
Parent: GCCB Group Ltd.
Officers: Ladislav Kruba [1975] Director [Czech]

UK Wholesalers of Soft Drinks

Primacy Trade Ltd
Incorporated: 2 May 2018
Registered Office: Suite 2a, Blackthorn House, St Pauls Square, Birmingham, B3 1RL
Major Shareholder: Narinder Mann
Officers: Narinder Mann [1987] Director/Customer Service

Printers Service Ltd
Incorporated: 30 June 2017
Net Worth: £100 *Total Assets:* £100
Registered Office: 6 Wake Street, Middlesbrough, Cleveland, TS3 6NU
Officers: Inpanathan Inparaji, Secretary; Inpanathan Inparaji [1983] Director/Sales Assistant [French]

Prir Group Limited
Incorporated: 11 December 2012
Previous: Enydro Limited
Net Worth Deficit: £32,087 *Total Assets:* £16,533
Registered Office: Oakhurst House, 57 Ashbourne Road, Derby, DE22 3FS
Shareholders: Danielle Phillips; Anthony Philip Royston Salway
Officers: Anthony Philip Royston Salway [1975] Director

Pro Nutrition Ltd
Incorporated: 22 March 2018
Registered Office: 4 St James Court, Friar Gate, Derby, DE1 1BT
Major Shareholder: Anil Narroya
Officers: Anil Narroya [1990] Director

Prod Act Ltd.
Incorporated: 6 February 2019
Registered Office: 9 Twickenham Gardens, Greenford, Middlesex, UB6 0LU
Major Shareholder: Epameinondas Stylopoulos
Officers: Cornel-Marius Plesca [1980] Director/Entrepreneur [Romanian]; Dionysios-Georgios Steriotis [1973] Director/Entrepreneur [Greek]; Epameinondas Stylopoulos [1981] Director/Lawyer [Greek]

PSB Trading Limited
Incorporated: 6 September 2011
Net Worth: £400 *Total Assets:* £7,994
Registered Office: 53 St Marys Road, Ilford, Essex, IG1 1QU
Major Shareholder: Parminder Singh Bassi
Officers: Parminder Singh Bassi [1988] Director

PTP Enterprise Limited
Incorporated: 6 September 2018
Registered Office: 15 Chelmsford Road, London, E11 1BT
Major Shareholder: Zahid Hussain
Officers: Zahid Hussain, Secretary; Zahid Hussain [1978] Director/Salesman

PU Trading Ltd
Incorporated: 25 January 2017
Registered Office: 58 Muirhead Avenue East, Liverpool, L11 1EL
Major Shareholder: Ponneswaran Ponnuthurai
Officers: Ponneswaran Ponnuthurai [1970] Director/General Manager [Norwegian]

Punchy Drinks Limited
Incorporated: 9 November 2017
Registered Office: 43 Adelaide Avenue, London, SE4 1LF
Major Shareholder: Paddy Charles Arthur Cavanagh-Butler
Officers: Daniel Bowers [1976] Director; Patrick Charles Arthur Cavanagh-Butler [1993] Director/Chief Executive; Charles Howard Hobhouse [1992] Director

Punjab Masala Ltd
Incorporated: 31 October 2018
Registered Office: 26 Morden Court Parade, London Road, Morden, Surrey, SM4 5HJ
Major Shareholder: Jahangir Tariq
Officers: Jahangir Tariq [1977] Director/Businessman [Swedish]

The Pure Juice Company Ltd
Incorporated: 19 March 2007
Net Worth Deficit: £69,220 *Total Assets:* £66,230
Registered Office: 9 Cheam Road, Epsom, Surrey, KT17 1SP
Major Shareholder: Rash Nagar
Officers: Nickolas Evangelopoulos [1956] Sales Director [Greek]; Rashik Nagar [1948] Director/Fruit Juice Distributors

Pure Organic Drinks Limited
Incorporated: 26 April 2018
Registered Office: Hamilton Office Park, 31 High View Close, Leicester, LE4 9LJ
Major Shareholder: The Arl Corporation Limited
Officers: Carmel Charmain Arthur [1975] Director; Thomas William Charles Lamb [1947] Director; Christopher Edward Ryan [1970] Director

Pure Pom Ltd
Incorporated: 15 December 2017
Registered Office: Liberty House, 30 Whitchurch Lane, Edgware, Middlesex, HA8 6LE
Shareholders: Nelo Durrani; Daoud Durrani
Officers: Daoud Durrani [1985] Director/Business Person; Nelo Durrani [1989] Director/Business Person

Pursuit of Excellence Group Ltd
Incorporated: 16 January 2014
Previous: Pursuit of Excellence Airline Training Limited
Net Worth: £716,789 *Total Assets:* £795,827
Registered Office: The Colmore Building, 20 Colmore Circus, Queensway, Birmingham, B4 6AT
Officers: Amarjit Singh [1970] Sales Director

PVS Trading Ltd
Incorporated: 5 July 2018
Registered Office: 24 Hockley Avenue, Eastham, London, E6 3AN
Major Shareholder: Amalathas Rajendram
Officers: Amalathas Rajendram [1989] Director [French]

PXL Drinks Ltd
Incorporated: 25 March 2016
Registered Office: Valley Lodge, Newlands Road, Riddings, Alfreton, Derbys, DE55 4ER
Shareholders: Adrian Robert Taylor; Gavin Braine
Officers: Joanne Elizabeth Taylor, Secretary; Gavin Braine [1982] Director; Adrian Robert Taylor [1969] Director

Qahhar Drinks Ltd
Incorporated: 15 December 2011
Net Worth: £19 *Total Assets:* £19
Registered Office: 86-90 Paul Street, London, EC2A 4NE
Shareholder: Nausheen Chaudhri
Officers: Niayyir Malik [1983] Director

Quando Drinks Limited
Incorporated: 13 May 2014 *Employees:* 11
Net Worth: £193,935 *Total Assets:* £687,103
Registered Office: The Big Red Shed, Cherry Tree Road, Doncaster, S Yorks, DN4 0BJ
Shareholders: Gary Kennedy; Daniel Rich; Iain Peter Screaton
Officers: Daniel Rich [1977] Director; Iain Peter Screaton [1983] Director

Quench Factory Limited
Incorporated: 18 May 2016
Registered Office: River House, 1 Maidstone Road, Sidcup, Kent, DA14 5RH
Officers: Thomas Edward Garrad [1991] Director

Quick Constuction Ltd
Incorporated: 11 December 2012
Registered Office: 134 Fore Street, London, N18 2XA
Major Shareholder: Harry Sivaramen Murday
Officers: Harry Sivaramen Murday [1976] Director/Salesman

Quick World Service Ltd
Incorporated: 29 May 2013
Registered Office: 83 High Street, Coningsby, Lincoln, LN4 4RB
Major Shareholder: Sooppaiya Pillayar
Officers: Sooppaiya Pillayar [1985] Director

Quicklemon UK Ltd
Incorporated: 30 September 2016
Net Worth Deficit: £377 *Total Assets:* £2,713
Registered Office: 20-22 Wenlock Road, London, N1 7GU
Parent: Derivados Citricos S.A.
Officers: Alejandro McIver Arranz [1983] Director/Head of Business Development [Spanish]

Quinton Trading Ltd
Incorporated: 7 June 2018
Registered Office: 26 The Drive, Feltham, Middlesex, TW14 0AJ
Major Shareholder: Nicholas Nunes
Officers: Nicholas Nunes [1980] Director/Manager [Portuguese]

R.A. Trading Limited
Incorporated: 27 April 2000 *Employees:* 19
Net Worth: £2,210,390 *Total Assets:* £5,374,917
Registered Office: 25 Mollison Avenue, Enfield, Middlesex, EN3 7NT
Shareholders: Zeynep Akgoz; Hasan Ertekin Kutlu; Niyazi Uludag
Officers: Niyazi Uludag, Secretary; Hasan Ertekin Kutlu [1961] Director; Niyazi Uludag [1967] Director

R.A.W. Goods Company Ltd
Incorporated: 7 June 2018
Registered Office: 20-22 Wenlock Road, London, N1 7GU
Officers: Andrew Richard Shaw [1964] Director/Self Employed

Rabia Food & Drinks Ltd
Incorporated: 2 July 2018
Registered Office: 2/1, 95 Coplaw Street, Glasgow, G42 7JG
Major Shareholder: Mirza Bilal Baig
Officers: Mirza Bilal Baig [1981] Director [Pakistani]

Racing Greens Nutraceuticals Limited
Incorporated: 17 December 2016
Net Worth Deficit: £29,147 *Total Assets:* £13,276
Registered Office: Keepers Nook, Holmes Chapel Road, Somerford, Cheshire, CW12 4SN
Officers: Paul Morgan [1965] Director; Roger Donald James Wood [1959] Director

Rahim Brothers Limited
Incorporated: 2 July 2009 *Employees:* 103
Net Worth: £1,203,137 *Total Assets:* £7,270,565
Registered Office: RAHIMS, Atlas Wharf, Berkshire Road, London, E9 5NB
Officers: Sharif Shuhel Hussain, Secretary; Mohammed Javed Hussain [1990] Director; Sharif Shuhel Hussain [1984] Director

Arif Rahim Ltd
Incorporated: 13 June 2018
Registered Office: 4a Bamville Road, Birmingham, B8 2TL
Major Shareholder: Mohammad Arif Abdulrahimzai
Officers: Mohammad Arif Abdulrahimzai [1965] Finance Director [Afghan]; Sayed Khan [1975] Director

Rahims Trading Ltd
Incorporated: 12 October 2018
Registered Office: Atlas Wharf, Berkshire Road, London, E9 5NB
Officers: Sharif Shuhel Hussain, Secretary; Mohammed Javed Hussain [1990] Director; Sharif Shuhel Hussain [1984] Director

MD Rahma Ltd
Incorporated: 8 February 2018
Registered Office: 286 The Hides, Harlow, Essex, CM20 3QX
Major Shareholder: Md Mizanur Rahman
Officers: MD Mizanur Rahman, Secretary; MD Mizanur Rahman [1982] Director [Bangladeshi]

Raji Service Ltd
Incorporated: 29 November 2017
Registered Office: 46 Alphonsus Street, Middlesbrough, Cleveland, TS3 6EA
Major Shareholder: Inpanathan Inparaji
Officers: Inpanathan Inparaji [1983] Director/Sales Assistant [French]

Rarewood (London) Limited
Incorporated: 12 January 2018
Registered Office: Studio 1, 305a Goldhawk Road, London, W12 8EU
Officers: Tessa Elizabeth Jayne John [1972] Director

Ravensbourne Wine Company Limited
Incorporated: 6 June 1986
Net Worth Deficit: £3,001 *Total Assets:* £94,410
Registered Office: 38 Penberth Road, London, SE6 1ES
Shareholder: Terence Reginald Short
Officers: Stephen John Williams, Secretary; Terence Reginald Short [1946] Director; Stephen John Williams [1949] Company Secretary and Director

Raw Is More Ltd.
Incorporated: 18 September 2015 *Employees:* 3
Net Worth Deficit: £32,448 *Total Assets:* £8,499
Registered Office: 3 Millwood Street, London, W10 6EH
Major Shareholder: Gabriel Bean
Officers: Victoria Bean, Secretary; Gabriel Bean [1993] Director/Founder; Brynmor Joe Ferris [1993] Director

Rayan Cash & Carry Ltd
Incorporated: 8 November 2018
Registered Office: Unit 30 Second Drove, Peterborough, Cambs, PE1 5XA
Major Shareholder: Jamal Ahmad
Officers: Jamal Ahmad [1979] Director [Iraqi]

Raylex Ltd
Incorporated: 1 July 2013
Net Worth: £272,016 *Total Assets:* £530,375
Registered Office: 9th Floor, 107 Cheapside, London, EC2V 6DN
Officers: Alex Kwun Hyn Lai [1989] Director/Beverages; Raymond Wai-Man Pang [1987] Director/Beverages; Chaitanya Rathi [1984] Director/Private Equity Professional [Indian]; Chun IP David Yeung [1976] Director [Chinese]

RB Beverages Ltd
Incorporated: 25 February 2019
Registered Office: 1782 Bristol Road South, Birmingham, B45 9PF
Major Shareholder: Russell Burden
Officers: Russell Burden, Secretary; Russell Burden [1981] Director/Self. Employed

RDM Polish Food Ltd
Incorporated: 24 September 2013
Net Worth: £33,543 *Total Assets:* £89,535
Registered Office: Block 3 Unit 3, Peffermill Industrial Estate, King's Haugh, Edinburgh, EH16 5UY
Major Shareholder: Damian Krzysztof Gasiorowski
Officers: Damian Krzysztof Gasiorowski [1975] Managing Director [Polish]

Real Natural UK Ltd
Incorporated: 16 October 2018
Registered Office: 61 Bridge Street, Kington, Herefords, HR5 3DJ
Major Shareholder: Graham Markham
Officers: Graham Markham [1984] Director [British/Canadian]

Realmix Beverage Ltd
Incorporated: 15 August 2018
Registered Office: Flat 5, 17 Riddfield Road, Birmingham, B36 8NX
Major Shareholder: Mohammad Arif Abdulrahimzai
Officers: Mohammad Arif Abdulrahimzai [1965] Finance Director [Afghan]; Sayed Khan [1975] Director/Self Employed

Red Baron Beverages Limited
Incorporated: 8 March 2018
Registered Office: Union International Drinks Corporation, Bridge House, 64-72 Mabgate, Regent Street, Leeds, LS9 7DZ
Major Shareholder: Diane Wilson
Officers: Diane Wilson [1944] Director/Company Formation Agent, Leeds

Red Bull Company Limited
Incorporated: 16 February 1993 *Employees:* 372
Net Worth: £26,002,000 *Total Assets:* £73,608,000
Registered Office: Seven Dials Warehouse, 42-56 Earlham Street, London, WC2H 9LA
Officers: Joao Paulo de Matos Tavares Esteves, Secretary; Peter Charles [1978] Managing Director; Joao Paulo de Matos Tavares Esteves [1972] Finance Director [Portuguese]; Dietrich Mateschitz [1944] Director [Austrian]; Chalerm Yoovidhya [1950] Director [Thai]

Redgate Imports Limited
Incorporated: 18 December 2017
Registered Office: 26 Wetherill Road, London, N10 2LT
Major Shareholder: Paul Healey
Officers: Paul Healey [1969] Director

Refribrit Ltd
Incorporated: 31 December 2018
Registered Office: Limetree, Station Road, St Pauls Cray, Orpington, Kent, BR5 3EH
Shareholders: Francisco Flaminio Dos Santos Junior; Nuno Miguel de Carvalho Ramalhoso; Igbinosa Dag Aghayere
Officers: Igbinosa Dag Aghayere [1975] Director/Lawyer; Francisco Flaminio Dos Santos Junior [1977] Director/Lawyer; Nuno Miguel de Carvalho Ramalhoso [1977] Director/Postman

Regal Trade Limited
Incorporated: 27 November 2018
Registered Office: 653 London Road, Wilmorton, Derby, DE24 8UQ
Major Shareholder: Hardeep Singh Matto
Officers: Hardeep Singh Matto [1976] Director/Business Manager

Regency Traders Ltd
Incorporated: 19 December 2018
Registered Office: 86c Water Street, Birmingham, B3 1HL
Major Shareholder: Mohammed Ashfaq
Officers: Mohammed Ashfaq [1967] Director

Reineta Limited
Incorporated: 26 May 2018
Registered Office: Flat 37, Goodchild Road, London, N4 2BA
Officers: Miguel Morales Moreno [1985] Director [Spanish]

Rejuveu Ltd
Incorporated: 29 May 2018
Registered Office: 4 Rustic Avenue, Tooting, London, SW16 6PD
Shareholders: Cynthia Patricia Young; Lourn Hugh Foster
Officers: Cynthia Patricia Young [1955] Director/Headmistress

Rex Drinks Limited
Incorporated: 12 May 2017
Net Worth Deficit: £93,661 *Total Assets:* £14,205
Registered Office: Chaddleworth, Streatley, Reading, Berks, RG8 9PR
Major Shareholder: Rex Morton Carter
Officers: Rex Morton Carter [1991] Director/Consultant

Rexcel Trading Ltd
Incorporated: 31 May 2017
Registered Office: 71-75 Shelton Street, Covent Garden, London, WC2H 9JQ
Major Shareholder: Md Saiful Alam Bhuiyan
Officers: MD Saiful Alam Bhuiyan [1987] Director [Bangladeshi]

RHM Trading UK Limited
Incorporated: 29 October 2018
Registered Office: 20-22 Wenlock Road, London, N1 7GU
Officers: Rizwaan Hussain [1995] Director

Rich Energy Limited
Incorporated: 23 September 2015 *Employees:* 3
Net Worth: £868,868 *Total Assets:* £2,711,662
Registered Office: Hyde Park House, 5 Manfred Road, London, SW15 2RS
Major Shareholder: William John Storey
Officers: William John Storey [1978] Director/Computer Consultant; Zoran Terzic [1976] Director/Keep Fit Instructor [Croatian]

Rick's Wine Ltd
Incorporated: 28 June 2004
Net Worth Deficit: £12,367 *Total Assets:* £10,000
Registered Office: 75 Kenton Street, London, WC1N 1NN
Major Shareholder: Rick Raymond Wells
Officers: Cynthia Polemis, Secretary; Richard Raymond Collingwood Wells [1956] Director

Riddles Bros Limited
Incorporated: 30 March 2004 *Employees:* 22
Net Worth: £215,126 *Total Assets:* £3,361,628
Registered Office: 34 Lupin Avenue, Dunamanagh, Strabane, Co Tyrone, BT82 0PG
Shareholders: Robert Riddles; David Riddles
Officers: Robert Riddles, Secretary; David Riddles [1951] Director/Builder - Sand & Gravel Quarry; Robert Riddles [1960] Director/Sand and Gravel Contractor

Rimpex-UK Limited
Incorporated: 29 January 2019
Registered Office: Rookery Nook, Church Street, Reepham, Norfolk, NR10 4JW
Shareholder: Alan Arthur Buckwell
Officers: Alan Arthur Buckwell [1950] Director/Proprietor

Rio Mata Atlantica Limited
Incorporated: 24 April 2018
Registered Office: 41 Great Portland Street, London, W1W 7LA
Shareholders: Justin James; Michael Jospeh Smith
Officers: Justin James [1976] Director; Michael Joseph Smith [1971] Director

Risco Service Ltd
Incorporated: 6 December 2018
Registered Office: Kiosk 7, Terrace Food Court, West Orchards, Smithford Way, Coventry, Warwicks, CV1 1QX
Major Shareholder: Antony Sayanthan Inpanathan
Officers: Antony Sayanthan Inpanathan [1989] Director/Sales Manager [French]

Rivella (U.K.) Limited
Incorporated: 21 December 1998
Registered Office: 55 Baker Street, London, W1U 7EU
Shareholders: Rudolf Alexander Hans Barth; Christine Barth
Officers: Christian Mom, Secretary; Rudolf Alexander Hans Barth [1952] Director [Swiss]

Riverroll Limited
Incorporated: 9 July 2018
Registered Office: Kemp House, 160 City Road, London, EC1V 2NX
Officers: Adebanke Oluborode, Secretary; Adebanke Oluborode [1971] Director/Entrepreneur [Irish]; Joshua Oluborode [1967] Director/Accountancy [Irish]

RJ Traders Ltd
Incorporated: 3 September 2018
Registered Office: 26 Morden Court Parade, London Road, Morden, Surrey, SM4 5HJ
Major Shareholder: Jahangir Tariq
Officers: Jahangir Tariq [1977] Director/Businessman [Swedish]

RMGL Ltd
Incorporated: 8 September 2016
Net Worth: £3,404 *Total Assets:* £9,230
Registered Office: 4 Cover Drive, Rochdale, Lancs, OL11 3DB
Major Shareholder: Richard Michael Clark
Officers: Richard Michael Clark [1961] Director

RMGL Trading Limited
Incorporated: 13 October 2017
Registered Office: 5 Brooklands Place, Brooklands Road, Sale, Cheshire, M33 3SD
Major Shareholder: Richard Michael Clark
Officers: Ian Leonard Bearpark [1952] Director; Richard Michael Clark [1961] Director; John Thornton [1956] Director

Robinson Alimentation Ltd
Incorporated: 3 March 2017
Registered Office: 136 Muirhead Avenue East, Liverpool, L11 1EW
Officers: Rameskumar Sivapatham, Secretary; Rameskumar Sivapatham [1975] Director/Manager [Norwegian]

Rocktails Drinks Limited
Incorporated: 12 February 2013 *Employees:* 3
Previous: Frozen Rocktails Limited
Net Worth Deficit: £499,636 *Total Assets:* £76,040
Registered Office: Netley House, Harrowbarrow, Callington, Cornwall, PL17 8BG
Major Shareholder: Christopher George Yandell
Officers: Christopher George Yandell [1981] Director

Roeser Limited
Incorporated: 1 February 2016
Registered Office: 5 Mason Gardens, West Row, Bury St Edmunds, Suffolk, IP28 8PH
Officers: Charlotte Roeser [1993] Director/Student [German]; Richard Roeser [1993] Director/Student [German]

Rolan Excel Limited
Incorporated: 21 December 2018
Registered Office: Basepoint Business Centre, The Old Rectory, Springhead Road, Northfleet, Kent, DA11 8HN
Major Shareholder: Vellautham Sivaloganathan
Officers: Vellautham Sivaloganathan [1958] Director/Manager

Rook Trading Ltd
Incorporated: 24 October 2018
Registered Office: 337 Old Liverpool Road, Warrington, Cheshire, WA5 1EB
Major Shareholder: Inpanathan Inparaji
Officers: Inpanathan Inparaji [1983] Director/Sales Manager [French]

Route 33 Limited
Incorporated: 11 October 2017
Registered Office: 37 Warren Street, London, W1T 6AD
Shareholders: Warren Douglas Pole; Erica Emily Eva Pole
Officers: Daniel Jeffery Lameire [1969] Director/Consultant [Canadian]; Erica Emily Eva Pole [1970] Director; Warren Douglas Pole [1973] Director

Row & Smith Ltd
Incorporated: 4 May 2016 *Employees:* 1
Net Worth: £3,218 *Total Assets:* £31,391
Registered Office: Onega House, 112 Main Road, Sidcup, Kent, DA14 6NE
Officers: Tristan Smith [1998] Director/Consultant

Roxane UK Limited
Incorporated: 24 May 1993 *Employees:* 95
Net Worth: £38,935,076 *Total Assets:* £80,282,240
Registered Office: Hangars 3, 4 & 5, Wood End Lane, Fradley Park, Lichfield, Staffs, WS13 8EL
Officers: Pascal Jankowski [1960] Director [French]; Donald Michael Wightman [1954] Director

Rozana Foods Limited
Incorporated: 4 February 2019
Registered Office: Suite 6, 3rd Floor, Justin Plaza 2, 341 London Road, Mitcham, Surrey, CR4 4BE
Shareholders: Deepak Singh Hakimzada; Muhammad Ramzan
Officers: Mirza Shahid Anwer Baig [1966] Director/Businessman [Pakistani]; Deepak Singh Hakimzada [1978] Director/Businessman; Muhammad Ramzan [1971] Director/Businessman [Pakistani]

UK Wholesalers of Soft Drinks

RSS Fast Food Suppliers Ltd
Incorporated: 5 December 2014
Net Worth: £155,843 *Total Assets:* £361,639
Registered Office: 9A-B, Twin Bridges Estate, Selsdon Road, South Croydon, Surrey, CR2 6PL
Shareholders: Ajaz Ahmad Hussain; Iyanarlingam Mariyan
Officers: Ajaz Ahmad Hussain [1973] Director/Entrepreneur [Dutch]; Selvarajah Jithenthrakumar [1973] Director/Entrepreneur; Iyanarlingam Mariyan [1978] Director; Sockalingam Nantheeswaran [1972] Director/Entrepreneur; Prasanna Sivanathan [1977] Director/Entrepreneur

RTH Healthcare PLC
Incorporated: 7 March 2018
Registered Office: 3rd Floor, 207 Regent Street, London, W1B 3HH
Major Shareholder: Julian John Howard Walford
Officers: Julian Walford, Secretary; Harry Drnec [1946] Director [American]; Julian John Howard Walford [1957] Director

Rush Energy Drinks Ltd
Incorporated: 24 October 2012 *Employees:* 2
Net Worth: £106,769 *Total Assets:* £237,061
Registered Office: Unit 3 Waterside Business Park, New Lane, Burscough, Lancs, L40 8JX
Shareholder: Lee Routledge
Officers: Lee Routledge, Secretary; Katie Routledge [1980] Director; Lee Routledge [1976] Director

S & B Wholesale Limited
Incorporated: 14 December 2018
Registered Office: 62 Fairlop Road, Ilford, Essex, IG2 2EN
Major Shareholder: Aliza Khan
Officers: Aliza Khan [1974] Director

S & B's Mart Ltd.
Incorporated: 15 August 2016
Net Worth: £7,329 *Total Assets:* £8,194
Registered Office: Unit A, Longmeadow Industrial Estate, Ringwood Road, Three Legged Cross, Dorset, BH21 6RD
Shareholders: Nicholas Sellar; Jack Anthony Mark Patrick Browne
Officers: Jack Anthony Mark Patrick Browne [1992] Director; Nicholas Sellar [1992] Director

S & F Distribution Ltd
Incorporated: 23 September 2011
Net Worth Deficit: £6,292 *Total Assets:* £13,024
Registered Office: 29 Charford Road, London, E16 1QQ
Major Shareholder: Sabia Khatun
Officers: Sabia Khatun [1973] Director

S & M (Wholesale Supplies) Limited
Incorporated: 31 March 1998
Net Worth: £289,335 *Total Assets:* £900,039
Registered Office: 23c Pensbury Place, London, SW8 4TP
Major Shareholder: Mohamed Gouhar
Officers: Sharon Gouhar, Secretary; Mohamed Gouhar [1964] Director/Catering Consultant

S K Enteprises Ltd
Incorporated: 19 December 2018
Registered Office: 86c Water Street, Birmingham, B3 1HL
Major Shareholder: Mohammed Ashfaq
Officers: Mohammed Ashfaq [1967] Director

Saapos Ltd
Incorporated: 14 December 2011
Registered Office: 32 Spinnells Road, Harrow, Middlesex, HA2 9RA
Officers: Collin Carr [1972] Director [Jamaican]

Sabroso Food UK Ltd
Incorporated: 19 September 2017
Registered Office: 14 Adrienne Avenue, Southall, Middlesex, UB1 2QW
Major Shareholder: Ali Nisar
Officers: Ali Nisar [1986] Director [Pakistani]

Sabziwala Limited
Incorporated: 25 May 2016
Registered Office: 237 Southcroft Road, London, SW16 6QT
Major Shareholder: Syed Haider Reza Zaidi
Officers: Syed Haider Reza Zaidi [1954] Director

Saga Trading Ltd
Incorporated: 14 August 2018
Registered Office: 13 Opal Close, London, E16 3TT
Major Shareholder: Mailvaganam Genkatharan
Officers: Mailvaganam Genkatharan [1977] Director [French]

Sahej UK Limited
Incorporated: 31 May 2002
Net Worth Deficit: £56,558 *Total Assets:* £50,982
Registered Office: Room No 614, 6th Floor, Hyde Park Hayes 3, Millington Road, Hayes, Middlesex, UB3 4AZ
Major Shareholder: Sahej Kaur Lamba
Officers: Sahej Kaur Lamba [1979] Director/Business Executive [Afghan]

Samco Global Foods Ltd
Incorporated: 17 May 2011
Net Worth: £1,181 *Total Assets:* £5,420
Registered Office: Unit 6 Tulketh Industrial Estate, Manchester, M40 9LY
Shareholder: Kenechukwu Chukwuemeka Orazu
Officers: Kenechukwu Chukwuemeka Orazu [1983] Director/Manager; Virginia Uju Orazu [1960] Director/Trading [Nigerian]

Sams Fast Foods Limited
Incorporated: 21 February 2005 *Employees:* 38
Previous: Sams Fast Food Limited
Net Worth: £658,446 *Total Assets:* £2,499,371
Registered Office: c/o Murugesu & Associates, 77 Milson Road, West Kensington, London, W14 0LH
Major Shareholder: Bogahawatte Kumararatne Chandrasinghe
Officers: Bogahawatte Kumararatne Chandrasinghe [1947] Director; Dharshanie Nirupa Casinar Chandrasinghe [1956] Director/Administrator; Nicole Shinika Chandrasinghe [1985] Director/Sales Manager; Sheehan Arjuna Chandrasinghe [1983] Director/Purchasing Manager

Sannel Foods Limited
Incorporated: 1 April 1998 *Employees:* 45
Net Worth: £249,464 *Total Assets:* £629,458
Registered Office: Unit B, Horizon Business Centre, 84 Goodwin Road, London, N9 0BJ
Major Shareholder: Ali Sancak
Officers: Ebru Sancak, Secretary; Ali Sancak [1958] Director; Erhan Sancak [1990] Director

The Santa Monica Company Ltd
Incorporated: 2 June 2017
Net Worth Deficit: £28,782 *Total Assets:* £9,218
Registered Office: Millshaw, Ring Road, Leeds, LS11 8EG
Major Shareholder: Oliver William Roderick Evans
Officers: Oliver William Roderick Evans [1996] Director/Chairman

Sanus Foods Ltd
Incorporated: 3 December 2018
Registered Office: NFC1, Western International Market, Hayes Road, Southall, Middlesex, UB2 5XJ
Shareholders: Stephane Siha; Marcus Isaacs
Officers: Stephane Siha [1992] Director/Marketing Manager

Saravanan Traders (UK) Ltd
Incorporated: 7 January 2019
Registered Office: 3 Popplewell Close, Belton, Doncaster, S Yorks, DN9 1TF
Major Shareholder: Saravanan Elangovan
Officers: Saravanan Elangovan, Secretary; Saravanan Elangovan [1996] Director/Businessman [Indian]

Sarl Import Export Mondial Ltd
Incorporated: 4 September 2015
Registered Office: 82 Wheelwright Lane, Coventry, Warwicks, CV6 4HH
Major Shareholder: Arulan Nallathamy
Officers: Arulan Nallathamby [1964] Director/Sales Assistant [Norwegian]

Sasa Super Foods Ltd
Incorporated: 27 September 2018
Registered Office: 12 Smithy Street, London, E1 3HP
Major Shareholder: Mohamed Azeem Abdul Basheer
Officers: Mohamed Azeem Abdul Basheer [1978] Director

Sativatech Ltd
Incorporated: 18 October 2018
Registered Office: Armadillo MUMB#81355, 8 Parkway Avenue, Sheffield, S9 4WA
Major Shareholder: Jordan Gors
Officers: Jordan Gors, Secretary; Jordan Gors [1994] Director [Australian]

Savers Stop Wholesalers Ltd
Incorporated: 6 April 2016
Net Worth Deficit: £3,640 *Total Assets:* £21,190
Registered Office: 33 The Market, Wrythe Lane, Carshalton, Surrey, SM5 1AG
Major Shareholder: Prasad Kumar Hegde
Officers: Prasad Kumar Hegde [1970] Director/Trader

D.E. Scorer Limited
Incorporated: 19 September 1979 *Employees:* 16
Net Worth: £37,368 *Total Assets:* £259,382
Registered Office: 115 Chester Road, Sunderland, Tyne & Wear, SR4 7HG
Shareholders: Gary Sayers; David Edward Scorer
Officers: Robert Adamson Lye, Secretary; Gary Sayers [1962] Managing Director; David Edward Scorer [1949] Director; Susan Scorer [1950] Managing Director

Seafire Brewing Co. Ltd
Incorporated: 22 February 2019
Registered Office: 10 Seafire Place, Dalgety Bay, Dunfermline, Fife, KY11 9GY
Major Shareholder: Kiera Browne
Officers: Kiera Browne [1982] Director/Chief Executive

Seagull Energy Drinks Ltd
Incorporated: 1 March 2016
Net Worth Deficit: £38,867 *Total Assets:* £16,860
Registered Office: 81 Southfield, London, NW4 4NA
Major Shareholder: Abdul Jelil Shinwari
Officers: Abdul Jelil Shinwari [1976] Director

Season Harvest (NI) Limited
Incorporated: 25 June 1999
Net Worth: £291,584 *Total Assets:* £784,811
Registered Office: 34 Market Street, Strabane, Co Tyrone, BT82 8BH
Major Shareholder: Gabrielle McLaughlin
Officers: Kienan McLaughlin, Secretary; Diarmaid McLaughlin [1982] Director/Manager; Gabrielle McLaughlin [1956] Director [Irish]; Kienan McLaughlin [1978] Director/Manager

Seasons East Ltd
Incorporated: 5 September 2013 *Employees:* 1
Net Worth Deficit: £24,789 *Total Assets:* £16,613
Registered Office: 85 Main Street, Seamer, Scarborough, N Yorks, YO12 4RF
Major Shareholder: Mark Andrew Richards
Officers: Mark Andrew Richards [1961] Director/Engineer

Secspirits Ltd
Incorporated: 18 July 2018
Registered Office: Kemp House, 160 City Road, London, EC1V 2NX
Officers: Christopher Hughes, Secretary; Christopher Hughes [1986] Director/Consultant

Anna Seed 83 Limited
Incorporated: 16 November 2017
Registered Office: 71-75 Shelton Street, Covent Garden, London, WC2H 9JQ
Major Shareholder: Benjamin John Branson
Officers: Benjamin John Branson [1983] Director

Seedlip Ltd
Incorporated: 6 May 2014
Net Worth: £1,656,372 *Total Assets:* £1,870,877
Registered Office: 71-75 Shelton Street, London, WC2H 9JQ
Parent: Diageo DV Limited
Officers: Benjamin Branson [1983] Director; Tanya Maria Clarke [1974] Director [Irish]; Benet Dunstan Slay [1961] Director

Seiyas Watercoolers Ltd
Incorporated: 1 December 2017
Registered Office: 21 Gough Road, Leicester, LE5 4AL
Major Shareholder: Adam Yusuf Esat
Officers: Adam Yusuf Esat, Secretary; Adam Yusuf Esat [1993] Director/Self Employed

Sepandero Venturi UK Limited
Incorporated: 4 April 2018
Registered Office: 6 Queens Walk, Chingford, London, E4 7EP
Major Shareholder: Nikolas Kakoulli
Officers: Nikolas Kakoulli [1967] Director/Self Employed [Cypriot]

Seven Bros Cookware Ltd
Incorporated: 6 August 2014
Net Worth: £56,767 *Total Assets:* £138,107
Registered Office: 37 Cromwell Road, Luton, Beds, LU3 1DP
Major Shareholder: Musaib Ahmed Siddiqy
Officers: Musaib Ahmed Siddiqy [1980] Director/Businessman

Shac International Limited
Incorporated: 17 September 2018
Registered Office: Apt 9, 115 Woolwich Road, London, SE10 0RF
Major Shareholder: Fei Huang
Officers: Fei Huang [1983] Director [Chinese]

UK Wholesalers of Soft Drinks   dellam

Shack Drinks Limited
Incorporated: 16 March 2017
Registered Office: Brickhouse Farm, Edwyn Ralph, Bromyard, Herefords, HR7 4LU
Shareholders: James David Manning; Richard Manning
Officers: James David Manning [1987] Director; Richard Manning [1990] Director

Shake It Up! The Protein Smoothie Company Ltd
Incorporated: 10 November 2017
Registered Office: 166 Birches Head Road, Stoke on Trent, Staffs, ST1 6LN
Major Shareholder: Mohammad Havaei-Ahary
Officers: Mohammad Havaei-Ahary [1993] Director/Chef

Shane's Consortium Limited
Incorporated: 20 October 2016
Registered Office: 5 Albany Road, Coventry, Warwicks, CV5 6JQ
Officers: Shane Tamana [1995] Director

Shapla Cash & Carry Ltd
Incorporated: 5 February 1997
Net Worth: £73,951 *Total Assets:* £1,211,535
Registered Office: 115-117 Golden Hillock Road, Small Heath, Birmingham, B10 0DP
Officers: Nanu Kazi Mohammed Miah, Secretary; Mohammed Abdul Ahad [1956] Director/Restaurant Owner; Rokib Ali [1958] Director/Catering/Restaurateur; Mohammed Azad [1968] Director/Catering/Restaurateur; Jahanara Begum [1955] Director; Kazi Mohammed Angur Miah [1958] Director/Restaurant Owner; Nanu Kazi Mohammed Miah [1964] Director; Wali Muktha [1957] Director/Businessman

Sharewater Ltd
Incorporated: 14 November 2014
Net Worth Deficit: £5,220
Registered Office: Flat 15, 272 Cambridge Heath Road, London, E2 9DA
Major Shareholder: Ahmed Amarouch
Officers: Ahmed Amarouch [1988] Director [German]

Shark Trading Ltd
Incorporated: 15 February 2019
Registered Office: 50 Woodlands, Huyton, Merseyside, L36 4PH
Major Shareholder: Vimalan Kanagaratnam
Officers: Vimalan Kanagaratnam [1982] Director/Manager [Swedish]

Sheikh Super Store Ltd
Incorporated: 21 September 2018
Registered Office: 94 Market Place, Romford, Essex, RM1 3ER
Major Shareholder: Muhammad Usman Nisar
Officers: Muhammad Usman Nisar [1983] Director/Entrepreneur [Pakistani]

Shelby Co Vending Limited
Incorporated: 28 February 2019
Registered Office: 245 Coe Street, Bolton, Lancs, BL3 6BU
Shareholders: Callum Jordan Jackson; Curtis Roy David Jackson; Samuel Oliver Royle
Officers: Curtis Roy David Jackson [1999] Director/Manager

Shibui Beverage Co Ltd
Incorporated: 23 August 2017
Registered Office: 6 Park View, London, N21 1QX
Major Shareholder: Sharif Alam Ansar
Officers: Sharif Alam Ansar [1977] Director; Steven Lawrence Ruhle [1971] Director/Management Consultant [New Zealander]

Shimroon Limited
Incorporated: 4 April 2002 *Employees:* 6
Net Worth: £15,293 *Total Assets:* £162,529
Registered Office: Cavendish Suite, The Saxon Centre, 11 Bargates, Christchurch, Dorset, BH23 1PZ
Major Shareholder: Ghollam Reza Aghajanzadeh
Officers: Reza Aghajanzadeh [1958] Director/Retailer [Iranian]

Shokers Wines & Spirits Limited
Incorporated: 13 March 2003 *Employees:* 3
Net Worth: £11,033 *Total Assets:* £14,210
Registered Office: 82 Holyhead Road, Wednesbury, W Midlands, WS10 7PA
Shareholders: Bahader Singh; Jora Singh
Officers: Bahader Singh, Secretary; Bahader Singh [1955] Director/Retailer; Jora Singh [1953] Director/Retailer

Shopocus Ltd
Incorporated: 1 December 2018
Registered Office: 63A Blakeland Street, Birmingham, B9 5XQ
Major Shareholder: Zaheeer Ahmad
Officers: Zaheeer Ahmad [1960] Director

Shree Sai Trading Ltd
Incorporated: 16 February 2011
Net Worth: £621,444 *Total Assets:* £1,426,703
Registered Office: Unit 21 Clipper Park Industrial Estate, Thurrock Park Way, Tilbury, Essex, RM18 7HG
Major Shareholder: Surag Narpatsinh Sayania
Officers: Surag Narpatsinh Sayania [1984] Director

Shruthinaya Ltd
Incorporated: 7 February 2019
Registered Office: Kemp House, 160 City Road, London, EC1V 2NX
Major Shareholder: Suresh Senthil Nathan Joseph
Officers: Suresh Senthil Nathan Joseph, Secretary; Suresh Senthil Nathan Joseph [1972] Director

Shu Enterprise Ltd
Incorporated: 15 February 2017
Net Worth: £824 *Total Assets:* £14,378
Registered Office: 86c Water Street, Birmingham, B3 1HL
Shareholders: Salma Nasreen; Salma Nasreen
Officers: Mohammed Ashfaq [1967] Director; Salma Nasreen [1969] Director

Silvercall Limited
Incorporated: 25 September 2013
Registered Office: 2nd Floor, Broadway Market, Fencepiece Road, Ilford, Essex, IG6 2JT
Shareholder: Lavan Arulchelvananthan
Officers: Lavan Arulchelvananthan [1981] Director/Self Employed

Simex International Ltd
Incorporated: 12 April 2016
Net Worth: £3,674 *Total Assets:* £26,494
Registered Office: 294 Merton Road, London, SW18 5JW
Major Shareholder: Hadj Said Boulerouah
Officers: Hadj Said Boulerouah [1962] Director

Simorgh Limited
Incorporated: 4 December 2013
Net Worth: £33,756 *Total Assets:* £55,803
Registered Office: 137-139 Brent Street, Hendon, London, NW4 4DJ
Major Shareholder: Mohammad Reza Hassan Zadeh K A Sorkhabi
Officers: Mohammad Reza Hassan Zadeh K a Sorkhabi [1975] Director

Simple Brands Ltd
Incorporated: 13 February 2019
Registered Office: 192 Queens Road, Watford, Herts, WD17 2NT
Officers: Muhammad Asim Butt [1982] Managing Director; Muhammad Arif Khan Tareen [1978] Managing Director

Simple Nature Limited
Incorporated: 10 February 2016
Net Worth: £700 *Total Assets:* £700
Registered Office: 1 Billesley, Alcester, Warwicks, B49 6NE
Major Shareholder: Oak Aaron Kerby-Steele
Officers: Oak Kerby-Steele, Secretary; Oak Kerby-Steele [1995] Director

Simply Spirits Limited
Incorporated: 3 February 2011
Registered Office: 48-52 Penny Lane, Liverpool, L18 1DG
Major Shareholder: Rakesh Ishwar Daryanani
Officers: Rakesh Ishwar Daryanani [1982] Director/Publican

Sips MCR Ltd
Incorporated: 12 February 2019
Registered Office: Flat 7, Elite Close, Manchester, M8 9FL
Major Shareholder: Yissochor Dov Merlin
Officers: Yissochor Dov Merlin [1995] Director/General Manager

JJ Sis Limited
Incorporated: 16 May 2018
Registered Office: 27 Selan Gardens, Hayes, Middlesex, UB4 0EA
Shareholders: Yalini Inbaruban; Visagaperumal Inbaruban
Officers: Visagaperumal Inbaruban [1978] Director [Sri Lankan]; Yalini Inbaruban [1981] Director

Skyfall Enterprise Ltd
Incorporated: 22 August 2017
Registered Office: 41 Runnymede Road, Birmingham, B11 3BN
Shareholders: Muhammad Akmal; Muhammad Akmal
Officers: Muhammad Akmal [1973] Director

SLB Wholesale Ltd
Incorporated: 16 June 2016
Previous: Laks Developments Ltd
Registered Office: 187 Albany Park Avenue, Enfield, Middlesex, EN3 5NY
Major Shareholder: Suthahar Chandramohan
Officers: Suthahar Chandramohan, Secretary; Suthahar Chandramohan [1981] Director/Manager

Slimsters Sports Drinks Limited
Incorporated: 6 March 2018
Registered Office: Union International Drinks Corp, Bridge House, 64-72 Mabgate, Leeds, LS9 7DZ
Major Shareholder: Robert (Elias) Wilson
Officers: Robert Wilson [1941] Director (CEO)

Sloane Avenue Group Ltd
Incorporated: 9 February 2015
Net Worth: £865,999 *Total Assets:* £867,512
Registered Office: 53 Harwood Road, London, SW6 4QL
Shareholder: Yaroslav Khromyak
Officers: Ivan Kavchak [1988] Director [American]; Yaroslav Khromyak [1986] Director; Mark Stephens [1949] Director/Consultant [American]

Slurps Ice Ltd
Incorporated: 10 August 2017
Registered Office: 54 Bannerman Road, Leicester, LE5 5LA
Major Shareholder: Yamin Achhodi
Officers: Yamin Achhodi [1987] Director/Engineer

SM Supplies Ltd
Incorporated: 18 December 2017
Registered Office: 40 Broad Avenue, Leicester, LE5 4PR
Major Shareholder: Manjinder Singh
Officers: Manjinder Singh [1986] Director [Indian]

Smart Buyer Wholesale Limited
Incorporated: 3 October 2013
Net Worth: £27,373 *Total Assets:* £97,401
Registered Office: Unit 9, 52 Alexandra Road, Enfield, Middlesex, EN3 7EH
Major Shareholder: Osman Deral
Officers: Osman Deral [1990] Director/Buyer

Smith & Munden Ltd
Incorporated: 12 May 2018
Registered Office: 124c Green Lane, Northwood, Middlesex, HA6 1AW
Officers: Senathirajah Muruganandan [1960] Director [German]

Smoothie Fresh (International) Ltd
Incorporated: 11 December 2014
Registered Office: Unit 22 Plumpton House, Plumpton Road, Hoddesdon, Herts, EN11 0LB
Major Shareholder: Angela Savva
Officers: Angela Savva [1980] Director

Smoothie Fresh Ltd
Incorporated: 6 June 2013
Net Worth: £35,688 *Total Assets:* £58,729
Registered Office: Unit 6 Plumpton House, Plumpton Road, Hoddesdon, Herts, EN11 0LB
Officers: Paul Syrichas [1982] Director

SmsZee Limited
Incorporated: 7 August 2018
Registered Office: 57 Cornwall Street, Grangetown, Cardiff, CF11 6PP
Officers: Waheeda Tasleem Sattar, Secretary; Abdul Sattar [1970] Director; Sahar Sattar [1988] Director; Sana Sattar [1996] Director; Waheeda Tasleem Sattar [1974] Director

Snackpax Distribution Limited
Incorporated: 20 May 2015 *Employees:* 3
Net Worth: £29,122 *Total Assets:* £304,809
Registered Office: Beacon House, White House Road, Ipswich, Suffolk, IP1 5PB
Parent: Vertas Group Limited
Officers: Keith Paul Buet [1960] Director; Jo Lardent [1969] Group Commercial Director; Ian Surtees [1971] Director; Marcus Stanley Yarham [1974] Director/Chartered Accountant

Snacks Dist Limited
Incorporated: 5 February 2019
Registered Office: 58 Racecourse Avenue, Shrewsbury, Salop, SY2 5BS
Major Shareholder: Gurpreet Singh
Officers: Gurpreet Singh [1985] Director [Indian]

UK Wholesalers of Soft Drinks

The Social Drinking Company Limited
Incorporated: 19 November 2018
Registered Office: 151 Church Road, Teddington, Middlesex, TW11 8QH
Shareholders: Susannah Clare Day; Fiona Jane Lawlor
Officers: Susannah Clare Day [1967] Director/Brand Consultant, Social Entrepreneur; Fiona Jane Lawlor [1963] Director/Lawyer

Soft Drink UK Limited
Incorporated: 22 April 2003 *Employees:* 5
Net Worth: £27,970 *Total Assets:* £239,591
Registered Office: Sher House, 46 Houghton Place, Bradford, W Yorks, BD1 3RG
Major Shareholder: Syed Intizar Haider Rizvi
Officers: Syed Intizar Haider Rizvi [1946] Director

Solerco Products Limited
Incorporated: 2 April 1976
Net Worth: £279,299 *Total Assets:* £326,680
Registered Office: Unit 6 Bramhall Moor Technology Park, Pepper Road, Hazel Grove, Stockport, Cheshire, SK7 5BW
Officers: Jean Winifred Capaldi [1952] Director

SOS Hydration Limited
Incorporated: 13 November 2013 *Employees:* 2
Net Worth Deficit: £403,644 *Total Assets:* £27,207
Registered Office: 10 John Street, London, WC1N 2EB
Major Shareholder: James Robert Mayo
Officers: James Robert Mayo [1974] Director

Sotomayor Imports Limited
Incorporated: 26 May 2017
Registered Office: Unit 8 Holles House, Overton Road, London, SW9 7AP
Officers: Maria Cristina Garcia Soto [1981] Director/Manager [Colombian]

Source 360 Ltd
Incorporated: 16 May 2018
Registered Office: 55 Tring Road, Wilstone, Tring, Herts, HP23 4PE
Shareholders: James Francis McKenzie Brown; Nicholas John Benson
Officers: Nicholas John Benson [1965] Commercial Director; James Francis McKenzie Brown [1967] Managing Director

Sow Limited
Incorporated: 14 February 2019
Registered Office: The Shippon, St Mellion, Saltash, Cornwall, PL12 6PY
Shareholders: Victoria Louise Mavin; Daniel Arthur John Mavin
Officers: Daniel Arthur John Mavin [1987] Director/Therapist; Victoria Louise Mavin [1988] Director/Therapist

Springwater Direct Ltd.
Incorporated: 15 October 1996 *Employees:* 1
Net Worth Deficit: £1,244 *Total Assets:* £35,302
Registered Office: 28 Townsend Place, Kirkcaldy, Fife, KY1 1HB
Major Shareholder: Gordon David Laing Ross
Officers: James Campbell Ross, Secretary; Gordon David Laing Ross [1961] Director

Squishy Drinks Limited
Incorporated: 19 June 2015
Net Worth: £4,222 *Total Assets:* £7,573
Registered Office: NBV Enterprise Centre, David Lane, Basford, Nottingham, NG6 0JU
Shareholder: John Wachira Kamau
Officers: Dr Elizabeth Wachira, Secretary; John Kamau [1986] Director; Elizabeth Muthoni Wachira [1987] Director

Sris International Ltd
Incorporated: 23 April 2018
Registered Office: 17 Kingsley Mews, Ley Street, Ilford, Essex, IG1 4BT
Officers: Soma Kumari [1982] Director [Indian]

SS Midland Ltd
Incorporated: 20 July 2018
Registered Office: 29a Shardlow Road, Alvaston, Derby, DE24 0JG
Major Shareholder: Sivatheeban Sivakrishnanathan
Officers: Sivatheeban Sivakrishnanathan [1977] Director/Sales Manager [German]

Stack United Limited
Incorporated: 13 April 2017
Net Worth: £2 *Total Assets:* £2
Registered Office: 44 Queens Court Ride, Cobham, Surrey, KT11 1BB
Major Shareholder: Kemasiri Wickramage
Officers: Kemasiri Wickramage, Secretary; Kemasiri Wickramage [1975] Director [Sri Lankan]

Stalker U.K Limited
Incorporated: 5 December 2017
Registered Office: H5 Ash Tree Court, Nottingham Business Park, Nottingham, NG8 6PY
Major Shareholder: Alper Aksu
Officers: Julia Gothardson, Secretary; Alper Aksu [1979] Director/Owner [Belgian]

Star Direct Hospitality Limited
Incorporated: 21 November 2017
Registered Office: 254 Staines Road, Twickenham, Middlesex, TW2 5AR
Major Shareholder: Kapil Mahendra Thakrar
Officers: Kapil Mahendra Thakrar [1967] Director

Star International Ltd
Incorporated: 20 December 2018
Registered Office: Unit 13 & 13a, Ashley House, Ashley Road, London, N17 9LZ
Major Shareholder: Ildaz Fukova
Officers: Ildaz Fukova [1983] Director [Bulgarian]

Starburst Hub Ltd
Incorporated: 4 June 2018
Registered Office: 55 Collingwood Avenue, Surbiton, Surrey, KT5 9PU
Major Shareholder: Riadh Arfaoui
Officers: Hatem Arfaoui [1974] Managing Director

The Start-Up Drinks Lab Limited
Incorporated: 13 June 2017
Net Worth: £121,474 *Total Assets:* £206,699
Registered Office: Unit 4 Building D, Kelburn Business Park, Port Glasgow, Inverclyde, PA14 6BL
Shareholders: Craig Robert Strachan; Hannah Magdaline Fisher
Officers: John Ross Brodie [1964] Director; Hannah Magdaline Fisher [1983] Marketing Director; Craig Robert Strachan [1988] Finance Director

Stirling Castle Water Ltd
Incorporated: 15 September 2016
Registered Office: 6 Fairyburn Road, Alloa, Clackmannanshire, FK10 2LE
Major Shareholder: Andrew Baxter McGhie
Officers: Ronald Patrick Hunter Blair [1944] Director; Andrew Baxter McGhie [1955] Director

Stockwell Beverages Ltd
Incorporated: 21 September 2017
Registered Office: 71-75 Shelton Street, London, WC2H 9JQ
Officers: Nicu Bogdan Bascau [1983] Director/Manager [Romanian]; Sonya Dholliwar [1978] Director

Stockwell Wholesalers Limited
Incorporated: 7 March 2018
Registered Office: 71-75 Shelton Street, London, WC2H 9JQ
Major Shareholder: Anuvinder Kaur
Officers: Anuvinder Kaur, Secretary; Anuvinder Kaur [1986] Director/Doctor

Stonefruit Ltd
Incorporated: 30 August 2017
Registered Office: 71-75 Shelton Street, Covent Garden, London, WC2H 9JQ
Officers: Dea Emini [1994] Director/Accountant

Storesrealm Limited
Incorporated: 6 October 1978 *Employees:* 10
Net Worth: £238,126 *Total Assets:* £404,033
Registered Office: 39 Deacons Hill Road, Elstree, Borehamwood, Herts, WD6 3HZ
Shareholder: John Daniel Donavan
Officers: John Daniel Donovan, Secretary; David Donovan [1961] Director/Warehouse Manager; John Daniel Donovan [1953] Director

Street Food Solutions UK Ltd
Incorporated: 10 June 2015
Previous: National Soft Drinks Distribution Limited
Net Worth: £55,829 *Total Assets:* £279,733
Registered Office: 21 Clos Nant Y Cwm, Pontprennau, Cardiff, CF23 8LG
Major Shareholder: Lee Raymond Davies
Officers: Lee Davies, Secretary; Lee Raymond Davies [1982] Director

Strong Pound Ltd
Incorporated: 27 December 2018
Registered Office: 18 Malvern Street, South Shields, Tyne & Wear, NE33 5LE
Major Shareholder: Vishnu Baboolal
Officers: Vishnu Baboolal [1961] Director [Trinidadian]

Sub Enterprises Ltd
Incorporated: 9 July 2014
Net Worth: £77,972 *Total Assets:* £124,655
Registered Office: Flat 954A, Manchester Road, Linthwaite, Huddersfield, W Yorks, HD7 5QS
Officers: Shashi Sahota [1968] Director

Sublime Corporation Limited
Incorporated: 17 August 2018
Registered Office: 34 Ellen Wilkinson House, Usk Street, London, E2 0QH
Major Shareholder: Zied Ferchichi
Officers: Zied Ferchichi [1986] Director/General Manager

Sublime Distributors Limited
Incorporated: 10 March 2010
Net Worth: £650 *Total Assets:* £15,063
Registered Office: 18(S) Beehive Lane, Ilford, Essex, IG1 3RD
Major Shareholder: Zubair Zubair
Officers: Zubair Ahmad [1968] Director

Suha World Ltd
Incorporated: 3 July 2017
Registered Office: 4 Murchison Road, London, E10 6NB
Major Shareholder: Krisztian Suha
Officers: Krisztian Suha, Secretary; Krisztian Suha [1986] Director [Hungarian]

Sun Exotic Wholesale Ltd
Incorporated: 17 December 2013
Net Worth: £27,648 *Total Assets:* £86,360
Registered Office: Unit 6 Mayfields Farms, Sheering Road, Harlow, Essex, CM17 0JP
Major Shareholder: Nihat Ender
Officers: Nihat Ender [1981] Director

Suncrops UK Limited
Incorporated: 3 October 2015 *Employees:* 1
Net Worth: £113,984 *Total Assets:* £165,851
Registered Office: 11 Old Jewry, London, EC2R 8DU
Officers: Vincent Jacques Jean Marie Noguera [1961] Director/Businessman [French]; Thomas Xavier Germain Ribes [1989] Director [French]

Sunspice UK Limited
Incorporated: 1 February 2018
Registered Office: 6a Mitcham Park, Mitcham, Surrey, CR4 4EG
Officers: Kebera Baptiste, Secretary; Kebera Brenda Patricia Baptiste [1962] Director/Customer Service Agent; Colin Lee-Own [1956] Director/Project Manager

Suntrack Ltd
Incorporated: 23 January 2019
Registered Office: 6 Plaistow Park Road, London, E13 0SD
Major Shareholder: Moshiur Karim Mesu
Officers: Moshiur Karim Mesu [1990] Director/Manager [Bangladeshi]

Sunugal Trading Limited
Incorporated: 11 September 2018
Registered Office: Kemp House, 152-169 City Road, London, EC1V 2NX
Major Shareholder: Mamadou Laye Diop
Officers: Mamadou Laye Diop [1983] Director [Senegalese]

Super Food Base Ltd
Incorporated: 10 September 2018
Registered Office: 3 & 4 Park Place, Newdigate Road, Harefield, Uxbridge, Middlesex, UB9 6EJ
Major Shareholder: Olavo Lobo de Rezende Neto
Officers: Olavo Lobo de Rezende Neto [1974] Managing Director [Brazilian]

The Super Smoo-V Company Ltd
Incorporated: 22 November 2017
Registered Office: 45 Hill Road, Pinner, Middlesex, HA5 1LB
Major Shareholder: Romile Sheikh
Officers: Romile Sheikh [1979] Director

Super Tidy Drinks Limited
Incorporated: 13 May 2015
Registered Office: 4b Village Way, Tongwynlais, Cardiff, CF15 7NE
Parent: H.Fox & Co Limited
Officers: Duncan Miles Newport-Black [1977] Director

UK Wholesalers of Soft Drinks　　　　　　　　　　　　　　　　　　　　　　　　　　　　dellam

Supermalt UK Limited
Incorporated: 8 July 1991 *Employees:* 9
Net Worth: £1,465,655 *Total Assets:* £2,572,578
Registered Office: P1-004, Old Truman Brewery, 91 Brick Lane, London, E1 6QL
Parent: Royal Unibrew A/S
Officers: Patrick Topsoe-Jensen Plucnar, Secretary; Stephen David Gray [1972] Managing Director; Lars Jensen [1973] Director [Danish]; Johannes Fredericus Christiaan Maria Savonije [1956] Director [Dutch]

Superyacht Supplies Limited
Incorporated: 20 January 2003 *Employees:* 9
Net Worth: £236,849 *Total Assets:* £439,175
Registered Office: Parva Dene, Little Hatfield, E Yorks, HU11 4UZ
Shareholder: Ian Frank Jarvis
Officers: Carla Jarvis, Secretary; Carla Jarvis [1946] Director [Italian]; Ian Jarvis [1950] Director

Supreme Links Limited
Incorporated: 10 August 2018
Registered Office: 15 Scott Street, London, E1 5DH
Major Shareholder: Arju Miah
Officers: Arju Miah [1987] Director/Administrator

Surprisingly Treaty Ltd
Incorporated: 26 June 2018
Registered Office: Brookland Villa, Shripney Road, Bognor Regis, W Sussex, PO22 9LN
Shareholders: Lewis Daniel Austin; Briony Mae Carter
Officers: Lewis Daniel Austin [1995] Director

Sutaka UK Limited
Incorporated: 10 November 2010 *Employees:* 13
Net Worth: £847,775 *Total Assets:* £2,245,673
Registered Office: Northside House, Mount Pleasant, Barnet, Herts, EN4 9EE
Shareholders: Anis Suterwalla; Jehangir Suterwalla
Officers: Anis Suterwalla [1974] Director; Jehangir Suterwalla [1970] Director

SVM Trading Ltd
Incorporated: 21 December 2018
Registered Office: 27 Sovereign Road, Barking, Essex, IG11 0XQ
Major Shareholder: Vimalakkannan Kanagalingam
Officers: Vimalakkannan Kanagalingam [1969] Director [Swiss]

Swallow Dispensed Drinks Solutions Limited
Incorporated: 2 October 2015 *Employees:* 2
Net Worth Deficit: £141,695 *Total Assets:* £453,365
Registered Office: Stonehouse Lane, Bartley Green, Birmingham, B32 3AH
Parent: Swallow Soft Drinks (Beer and Cider Wholesalers) Limited
Officers: Stephen Thomas Land [1956] Director

Swallow Holdings Limited
Incorporated: 14 October 1994 *Employees:* 267
Net Worth: £8,757,254 *Total Assets:* £13,913,017
Registered Office: Creamline Dairies, Mellors Road, Trafford Park, Manchester, M17 1PB
Shareholders: Christopher David Swallow; Robert Kenneth Berry Purvis
Officers: Christopher David Swallow, Secretary/Management Executive; Robert Kenneth Berry Purvis [1969] Director/Management Executive; Anthony David Swallow [1940] Director/Executive; Christopher David Swallow [1970] Director/Management Executive; Helga Hildegard Gertrud Swallow [1935] Director/Housewife [German]

Sweet Caroline Ltd
Incorporated: 12 September 2018
Registered Office: 99 Abbeyfields Close, London, NW10 7EG
Major Shareholder: Corina Liana Stan
Officers: Corina Liana Stan [1984] Director [Romanian]

Sweet Sally Limited
Incorporated: 12 September 2013
Net Worth Deficit: £45,396 *Total Assets:* £26
Registered Office: 4 Capricorn Centre, Cranes Farm Road, Basildon, Essex, SS14 3JJ
Major Shareholder: Gwendolyn Nicole Vaughan
Officers: Gwendolyn Nicole Vaughan [1980] Director [American]

Sweetprod Ltd
Incorporated: 28 August 2015
Registered Office: c/o JSA Partners, 41 Skylines, Limeharbour, London, E14 9TS
Major Shareholder: Miklos Pasztor
Officers: Miklos Pasztor [1966] Director [Hungarian]

Syed Drinks Limited
Incorporated: 7 August 2018
Registered Office: Kemp House, 160 City Road, London, EC1V 2NX
Officers: Syed Za [1987] Director/Manager [Pakistani]

Sylvy Glosry Limited
Incorporated: 21 February 2019
Registered Office: Forsyth House, Cromac Square, Belfast, BT2 8LA
Major Shareholder: Vellautham Sivaloganathan
Officers: Vellautham Sivaloganathan [1958] Director/Manager

Symphony Fine Foods Ltd
Incorporated: 14 October 2018
Registered Office: 71-75 Shelton Street, London, WC2H 9JQ
Major Shareholder: Sharifa Lewis
Officers: Sharifa Lewis [1961] Director

Syntex Trading Ltd
Incorporated: 16 August 2017
Registered Office: 22 Ellison Close, Leicester, LE18 4QH
Major Shareholder: Gurpal Singh Sidhu
Officers: Gurpal Singh Sidhu [1987] Director/Engineer [Indian]

Syon Distributors Ltd
Incorporated: 11 March 2018
Registered Office: 2nd Floor, 142 High Road, Wood Green, London, N22 6EB
Major Shareholder: Premananthini Nanthan
Officers: Premananthini Nanthan [1978] Director

Syphony Water Limited
Incorporated: 8 June 2018
Registered Office: 95 King Street, Lancaster, LA1 1RH
Shareholders: Tomasz Barczynski; Elzbieta Makowska
Officers: Tomasz Barczynski [1975] Director [Polish]; Elzbieta Makowska [1982] Director [Polish]

T & A Import and Export Trading Ltd
Incorporated: 6 October 2017
Registered Office: Unit 38 Eurolink Business Centre, 49 Effra Road, London, SW2 1BZ
Major Shareholder: Tahir Ali Tahir
Officers: Tahir Ali Tahir [1964] Director/Manager

T & K Wholesale Ltd
Incorporated: 22 June 2015
Net Worth: £49,290 Total Assets: £65,621
Registered Office: 12 Evesham Green, Morden, Surrey, SM4 6PW
Major Shareholder: Thakshila Rathnayake Mudiyanselage
Officers: Thakshila Rathnayake Mudiyanselage [1979] Director/Sales Assistant [Sri Lankan]

T's Dazzling Delicious Sweets Ltd
Incorporated: 16 July 2018
Registered Office: 20-22 Wenlock Road, London, N1 7GU
Officers: Muhammed Ajolaoluwa Daniel Disu [2002] Director; Oluwatosin Abdulrahman Disu [1977] Director; Titilola Aduni Olowa [1978] Director

Taj Restaurant Supplies Ltd
Incorporated: 3 February 2014
Previous: Taj Restuarant Limited
Net Worth: £217,381 Total Assets: £613,107
Registered Office: 20 North Audley Street, London, W1K 6HX
Officers: Jack Parsler [1991] Director/Manager

Talbot & Barr Limited
Incorporated: 15 May 2015 Employees: 2
Net Worth Deficit: £34,045 Total Assets: £28,966
Registered Office: Suite 1, 3rd Floor, 11-12 St James's Square, London, SW1Y 4LB
Major Shareholder: Hugh Francis Froggatt
Officers: Hugh Francis Froggatt [1947] Director/Retired; Craig Martin William Van Der Venter [1963] Managing Director [South African]

Tas Services UK Limited
Incorporated: 17 July 2002
Net Worth: £2,606 Total Assets: £3,056
Registered Office: Woodlea, Four Elms, Edenbridge, Kent, TN8 6NE
Major Shareholder: Paul Jeremy Cole
Officers: Paul Jeremy Cole [1965] Director/Retailer; Tone Louise Stuart Cole [1965] Director/Administrator

Tasman Bay Foods Europe Ltd
Incorporated: 24 June 2015
Net Worth Deficit: £41,652 Total Assets: £15,692
Registered Office: Dominion House, 69 Lion Lane, Haslemere, Surrey, GU27 1JL
Parent: Both Hemispheres Holdings Ltd
Officers: Daman Singh, Secretary; Andrew David Coulson [1963] Director; Daniel Frank Shaw [1959] Director; Daman Raj Singh [1948] Director/Retired

Tasnim Recruiting & Consultancy Services Ltd
Incorporated: 3 September 2012
Previous: Tasnim Agro Trade International Ltd.
Net Worth Deficit: £22,573 Total Assets: £8,721
Registered Office: 40 Sandy Lane, Walton on Thames, Surrey, KT12 2EQ
Officers: Liluba Begum [1970] Director/Nurse

Taste Merchants Ltd
Incorporated: 16 February 2015 Employees: 10
Previous: Taste Traders Limited
Net Worth: £961,251 Total Assets: £1,234,247
Registered Office: 41 Mochdre Enterprise Park, Newtown, Powys, SY16 4LE
Officers: Craig Andrew Hawgood [1980] Director; Dale Peter Hawgood [1987] Director; Duncan James Hawgood [1973] Director; Geoffrey Frank Hawgood [1945] Director; Neville John Hawgood [1969] Director; Rosemary Ann Hawgood [1946] Director

Taste of Crete Ltd
Incorporated: 16 May 2017
Net Worth Deficit: £12,017 Total Assets: £4,760
Registered Office: 10 Blair Road, Manchester, M16 8NS
Major Shareholder: Gerasimos Pefanis
Officers: Gerasimos Pefanis [1982] Director/Manager [Greek]

Tastebuds Trading Ltd
Incorporated: 5 July 2018
Registered Office: 8 St Anns Close, Dewsbury, W Yorks, WF12 0BA
Major Shareholder: Abdul Yusuf Valli
Officers: Abdul Yusuf Valli [1967] Director

Tata Trade Ltd
Incorporated: 18 September 2017
Registered Office: 39 Hazel Drive, Leicester, LE3 2JE
Major Shareholder: Ayshdeep Singh
Officers: Ayshdeep Singh [1968] Director/Driver

Tate-Smith Limited
Incorporated: 21 March 1960 Employees: 45
Net Worth: £2,500,703 Total Assets: £3,811,111
Registered Office: Sundella House, Castlegate, Malton, N Yorks, YO17 7EE
Officers: Catherine Louise Tate-Smith, Secretary/Company Accountant; Catherine Louise Tate-Smith [1963] Director/Company Secretary; Constance Maria Tate-Smith [1932] Director [Dutch]; Paul Thomas Tate-Smith [1962] Managing Director

Tatry Trade Ltd
Incorporated: 12 February 2018
Registered Office: Unit 9 Bewsey Road, Warrington, Cheshire, WA5 0JU
Major Shareholder: Rastislav Charitun
Officers: Rastislav Charitun [1975] Director [Slovak]

Taza Food Limited
Incorporated: 11 February 2016
Net Worth Deficit: £4,039 Total Assets: £10,123
Registered Office: 99 Malmesbury Road, Small Heath, Birmingham, B10 0JG
Major Shareholder: Salahudin Al Shamim
Officers: Salahudin Al Shamim [1982] Director/Manager

Tazah Ltd
Incorporated: 22 December 2014
Net Worth: £10,200 Total Assets: £32,510
Registered Office: 12 Queens Parade, Hanger Lane, London, W5 3HU
Major Shareholder: Othman Nooraldin Abdul Kareem
Officers: Othman Nooraldin Abdul Kareem [1998] Director [Iraqi]

Temperance Drinks Limited
Incorporated: 26 January 2017
Registered Office: Sitwell Barn, The Square, Long Itchington, Southam, Warwicks, CV47 9PE
Officers: Richard Jonathan Phillips [1980] Director

Temple Wines (Cash & Carry) Limited
Incorporated: 27 September 1991 Employees: 19
Net Worth: £7,947,957 Total Assets: £9,808,691
Registered Office: 472 Church Lane, Kingsbury, London, NW9 8UA
Officers: Nalin Kataria, Secretary; Rajni Kataria [1947] Director/Manager

UK Wholesalers of Soft Drinks

TFC Wholesale Ltd
Incorporated: 7 December 2005
Net Worth: £401,775 Total Assets: £479,969
Registered Office: 108a Lobley Hill Road, Gateshead, Tyne & Wear, NE8 4YG
Shareholders: Trentino Carpinelli; Denise Carpinelli; Francesco Carpinelli
Officers: Denise Carpinelli, Secretary; Denise Carpinelli [1956] Director/Wholesaler; Francesco Carpinelli [1980] Director/Wholesaler; Trentino Carpinelli [1955] Director/Wholesaler

Thailand 11234501 International Trade Co., Ltd
Incorporated: 5 March 2018
Registered Office: 8 Standard Road, London, NW10 6EU
Major Shareholder: Xiumei Sun
Officers: Xiumei Sun [1965] Director [Chinese]

Thamby Trading Ltd
Incorporated: 13 November 2017
Registered Office: 82 Wheelwright Lane, Coventry, Warwicks, CV6 4HH
Major Shareholder: Arulan Nallathamby
Officers: Arulan Nallathamby [1964] Director/Sales Assistant [Norwegian]

Thames Wholesale Ltd
Incorporated: 17 January 2019
Registered Office: Flat 77, Longland Court, Rolls Road, London, SE1 5HB
Major Shareholder: David Santos Jimenez
Officers: David Santos Jimenez [1958] Director [Spanish]

Thass Ltd
Incorporated: 19 November 2018
Registered Office: Kemp House, 160 City Road, London, EC1V 2NX
Major Shareholder: Pasupathypillai Jeevathasan
Officers: Pasupathypillai Jeevathasan, Secretary; Pasupathypillai Jeevathasan [1982] Director [German]

Theodore Global Limited
Incorporated: 20 February 2018
Registered Office: The Incuba, 1 Brewers Hill Road, Dunstable, Beds, LU6 1AA
Shareholders: Janet Theodore; Nicola Roberts
Officers: Nicola Roberts [1987] Director; Bethany Theodore [1995] Director; Janet Ann Theodore [1962] Director/Family Practitioner

Think Power Limited
Incorporated: 28 June 2011
Net Worth Deficit: £27,954 Total Assets: £2,279
Registered Office: Piccadilly House, 49 Piccadilly, Manchester, M1 2AP
Major Shareholder: Bency Silvester
Officers: Bency Silvester [1990] Managing Director

Third Eye Nutrition Ltd
Incorporated: 23 August 2018
Registered Office: 20-22 Wenlock Road, London, N1 7GU
Major Shareholder: Stephen Francis Cotter
Officers: Stephen Francis Cotter [1986] Director

Thirst Call Ltd
Incorporated: 31 December 2018
Registered Office: 18 Malvern Street, South Shields, Tyne & Wear, NE33 5LE
Major Shareholder: Vishnu Baboolal
Officers: Vishnu Baboolal [1964] Director [Trinidadian]

Thirst Quenchers (UK) Limited
Incorporated: 16 April 2009
Net Worth: £282,132 Total Assets: £853,525
Registered Office: 334-336 Goswell Road, London, EC1V 7RP
Shareholder: Chandrakant Jivanbhai Chohan
Officers: Ashok Jivanbhai Chohan, Secretary; Chandrakant Jivanbhai Chohan [1958] Director

Thirstee Business Limited
Incorporated: 17 July 2000 Employees: 3
Net Worth: £50,866 Total Assets: £116,767
Registered Office: 15 High Street, Brackley, Northants, NN13 7DH
Major Shareholder: Anthony Timothy Wynter
Officers: Anthony Timothy Wynter, Secretary/Director; Anthony Timothy Wynter [1961] Director/Machine Dispenser

Thirsty Work Limited
Incorporated: 14 January 2010 Employees: 45
Net Worth: £904,048 Total Assets: £8,144,996
Registered Office: c/o Francis Clark LLP, North Quay House, Sutton Harbour, Plymouth, PL4 0RA
Shareholders: William John Haviland Hiley; Andrew Brian Vickery
Officers: Matthew Stimpson [1981] Director; Andrew Brian Vickery [1964] Managing Director

Thistle Foods Limited
Incorporated: 31 October 2013
Net Worth: £31,741 Total Assets: £202,172
Registered Office: 1007 Argyle Street, Glasgow, G3 8LZ
Officers: Mohamed Haniba Haja [1978] Director

Thremhall Limited
Incorporated: 17 November 1995
Net Worth: £331,410 Total Assets: £407,541
Registered Office: 10-12 Mulberry Green, Old Harlow, Essex, CM17 0ET
Major Shareholder: David Michael Thomas
Officers: James Robert Furze [1954] Commercial Director

Thriftys Wholesale Limited
Incorporated: 10 January 2013
Net Worth: £5,117 Total Assets: £44,912
Registered Office: 135 Higher Parr Street, St Helens, Merseyside, WA9 1DA
Officers: Navin Soni [1979] Director

Thusi Wholesale Ltd
Incorporated: 25 February 2019
Registered Office: 102 Wheatlands, Hounslow, Middlesex, TW5 0SB
Major Shareholder: Thusi Maju
Officers: Thusi Maju [1984] Director

Tiqle Global Limited
Incorporated: 19 November 2018
Registered Office: 71-75 Shelton Street, London, WC2H 9JQ
Major Shareholder: Theo Thiebaut
Officers: Theo Thiebaut [1999] Director/Chief Executive [French]

TN Global Service Ltd
Incorporated: 29 November 2017
Registered Office: 50 Woodlands Road, Huyton, Merseyside, L36 4PH
Major Shareholder: Naveneethan Tavarajha
Officers: Naveneethan Tavarajha [1968] Director/Sales Assistant [Norwegian]

TN Sales Ltd
Incorporated: 14 July 2017
Registered Office: 50 Woodlands Road, Huyton, Merseyside, L36 4PH
Officers: Naveneethan Tavarajha, Secretary; Naveneethan Tavarajha [1968] Director/Customer Assistant [Norwegian]

Toffoc Ltd
Incorporated: 15 April 2004 *Employees:* 2
Net Worth Deficit: £115,661 *Total Assets:* £79,655
Registered Office: Bryn Mair, Llanbedrgoch, Sir Ynys Mon, LL76 8TZ
Shareholders: Padrig Huws; Dewi Roberts
Officers: Diana Ellen Roberts, Secretary; Padrig Huws [1961] Director; Dewi Roberts [1958] Director

Tolmid International Ltd
Incorporated: 5 March 2018
Registered Office: 5 Dent Close, South Ockendon, Essex, RM15 5DS
Shareholders: Olufemi Tolulope Elemide; Olaide Olubunmi Jinadu; Oluwaseyi Grace Elemide-Emis
Officers: Oluwaseyi Grace Elemide-Emis, Secretary; Olufemi Tolulope Elemide [1967] Director/Engineer [Nigerian]; Olaide Olubunmi Jinadu [1970] Director/Manager [Irish]

Tomatelios UK Ltd
Incorporated: 10 September 2018
Registered Office: Mallard House, Boundary Lane, Saltney, Chester, CH4 8RD
Major Shareholder: Athanasios Kourtoglou
Officers: Athanasios Kourtoglou [1979] Director [Greek]; Ana Marita Cruz Monroy [1974] Director

Tomato Tantrum Ltd
Incorporated: 15 October 2018
Registered Office: 1 Shelvers Way, Tadworth, Surrey, KT20 5QJ
Major Shareholder: Viraj Kaku Sunil Acharya
Officers: Viraj Kaku Sunil Acharya [1997] Director

Tongue in Peat Limited
Incorporated: 16 November 2016
Net Worth: £1,199 *Total Assets:* £1,199
Registered Office: Unit 5 Block D, Kelburn Business Park, Port Glasgow, Inverclyde, PA14 6TD
Major Shareholder: Hannah Fraser
Officers: Hannah Magdaline Fisher [1983] Director

Top Pops Wholesaler of Soft Drinks Limited
Incorporated: 10 January 2005 *Employees:* 17
Net Worth: £9,111 *Total Assets:* £553,643
Registered Office: Unit 1 Ynyscedwyn Industrial Estate, Ystradgynlais, Swansea, SA9 1DT
Major Shareholder: Huw Morgan
Officers: Michelle Morgan, Secretary; Huw Morgan [1946] Director

Top Selection Limited
Incorporated: 7 June 2000 *Employees:* 8
Net Worth: £181,581 *Total Assets:* £1,316,558
Registered Office: 19-20 Bourne Court, Southend Road, Woodford Green, Essex, IG8 8HD
Shareholders: Akos Forczek; Michelle Carin Speckhardt Forczek
Officers: Michelle Carin Speckhardt Forczek, Secretary/Consultant; Akos Forczek [1967] Director; Michelle Carin Speckhardt Forczek [1965] Director/Management Consultant

Topmost Foods Distribution Ltd.
Incorporated: 18 June 2018
Registered Office: 65 Samuel Street, London, SE18 5LF
Parent: Topmost Foods Limited
Officers: Adekunle Akanji Ademola [1955] Director

Topstop Wholesalers Limited
Incorporated: 13 November 2018
Registered Office: 71-75 Shelton Street, London, WC2H 9JQ
Major Shareholder: Anthony Duffy
Officers: Anthony Duffy, Secretary; Anthony Duffy [1990] Director

Toschi UK Limited
Incorporated: 17 August 2016 *Employees:* 1
Net Worth Deficit: £42,724 *Total Assets:* £208,573
Registered Office: Rivermead House, 7 Lewis Court, Grove Park, Leicester, LE19 1SD
Officers: John Philip Rundlett [1964] Director

Total Cellar Supplies Limited
Incorporated: 10 February 2016 *Employees:* 6
Net Worth Deficit: £4,095 *Total Assets:* £295,655
Registered Office: 6 Houndiscombe Road, Plymouth, PL4 6HH
Shareholders: Iain Samuel Woodhead; Elisa Susan Jane Woodhead
Officers: Elisa Susan Jane Woodhead [1970] Director; Iain Samuel Woodhead [1963] Director/Sales Manager

Total Fast Food Supplies Limited
Incorporated: 13 February 2017
Registered Office: Unit 11 Llandough Trading Estate, Penarth Road, Cardiff, CF11 8RR
Officers: Nazrul Islam [1987] Managing Director; Maqbool Sadiq [1971] Commercial Director; Tehmoor Ahmed Tariq [1988] Finance Director

Total Refreshment Solutions Limited
Incorporated: 29 September 1997 *Employees:* 9
Net Worth Deficit: £675,251 *Total Assets:* £362,559
Registered Office: 98/7 Eastfield Drive, Eastfield Industrial Estate, Penicuik, Midlothian, EH26 8HJ
Major Shareholder: Benjamin James McCosh
Officers: Benjamin James McCosh, Secretary; Benjamin James McCosh [1979] Managing Director

Trade HQ Ltd
Incorporated: 6 March 2018
Registered Office: 121 Evington Drive, Leicester, LE5 5PH
Shareholders: Iqramulhaq Saburi; Mohmed Adil Saburi
Officers: Iqramulhaq Saburi [1995] Director; Mohmed Adil Saburi [2000] Director

Tradinguk55 Limited
Incorporated: 4 January 2018
Registered Office: 61 Queens Road, Blackburn, BB1 1QF
Major Shareholder: Abdul-Qadeer Hayat
Officers: Dr Abdul-Qadeer Hayat [1956] Director/Consultant [Norwegian]

Transgh Limited
Incorporated: 6 April 2016
Registered Office: 18 Roneo Corner, Romford, Essex, RM12 4TN
Major Shareholder: Eugenia Mensah Panford
Officers: Eugenia Mensah Panford [1977] Director/Registered Nurse

Tri Star Wholesale Limited
Incorporated: 12 January 2009
Registered Office: 71 Cobham Close, Edgware, Middlesex, HA8 5QG
Major Shareholder: Samuel Nathaniel Yoganathan
Officers: Samuel Nathaniel Yoganathan [1984] Managing Director

Tricape UK Ltd
Incorporated: 25 October 2017
Registered Office: 27 Old Gloucester Street, London, WC1N 3AX
Shareholders: Olukolajo Lawanson; Patrick Adim Okafor
Officers: Olukolajo Lawanson [1983] Commercial Director [Nigerian]; Patrick Adim Okafor [1982] Commercial Director [Nigerian]

Triple R Industries Limited
Incorporated: 13 October 2014
Net Worth Deficit: £2,112 Total Assets: £172,712
Registered Office: Bede House, Pauls Hill, Penn, High Wycombe, Bucks, HP10 8NZ
Officers: Raina Catherine Carvey [1962] Director/Manager; Trevor Godfrey Carvey [1962] Director/Manager

Triumph Foodservice Limited
Incorporated: 13 August 2014
Net Worth: £19,131 Total Assets: £76,650
Registered Office: 165b Ravensbourne Avenue, Shortlands, Bromley, Kent, BR2 0AY
Shareholder: Jijan Uddin
Officers: Sarah Chaudhry [1980] Director; Jijan Uddin [1980] Director/Owner

Tronika Traders Limited
Incorporated: 10 January 2018
Registered Office: 14 Wintergreen Close, London, E6 5UQ
Officers: Mahmudur Rahman [1994] Director/Sales Manager

Tropical Ice (England) Ltd
Incorporated: 1 June 2016
Registered Office: Tropical Ice, Karing International House, Bridgeman Street, Walsall, W Midlands, WS2 9PG
Major Shareholder: Asif Mukhtar
Officers: Asif Mukhtar [1971] Director/Manager

Tropical Produce Limited
Incorporated: 30 March 2015
Net Worth Deficit: £24,633 Total Assets: £4,090
Registered Office: The Stable Yard, Vicarage Road, Stony Stratford, Milton Keynes, Bucks, MK11 1BN
Shareholder: David Hugh Duff
Officers: Ekroop Kular [1954] Director/Retired; Joginder Singh Kular [1945] Director [Indian]

Trust in Global Food Ltd
Incorporated: 24 September 2013
Net Worth Deficit: £13,049 Total Assets: £9,260
Registered Office: 116 Stechford Road, Birmingham, B34 6BJ
Major Shareholder: Vikram Verma
Officers: Vikram Verma [1976] Director [Indian]

TSK Trade Limited
Incorporated: 5 February 2018
Registered Office: 40 Wand Street, Leicester, LE4 5BS
Shareholder: Rohitkumar Narendra Radia
Officers: Sheetal Rohit Radia, Secretary; Rohitkumar Narendra Radia [1981] Director; Sheetal Radia [1982] Director

TTS Private Ltd
Incorporated: 25 June 2018
Registered Office: 24 Hockley Avenue, Eastham, London, E6 3AN
Major Shareholder: Kimbulu-Ernest Lumumba
Officers: Kimbulu-Ernest Lumumba [1979] Director [Romanian]

Turkish Kitchinn Wholesale Ltd
Incorporated: 7 June 2017
Registered Office: 449 West Green Road, London, N15 3PL
Major Shareholder: Emre Kars
Officers: Emre Kars [1983] Managing Director

Turner Hardy & Co Limited
Incorporated: 1 September 2016
Net Worth: £11,104 Total Assets: £46,551
Registered Office: Old Salisbury Lane, Awbridge, Romsey, Hants, SO51 0GD
Shareholders: Hugo Charles Hardman; Edward James Turner
Officers: Graham Christopher Ralph, Secretary; Hugo Charles Hardman [1966] Director; Edward James Turner [1967] Director

TVS Private Ltd
Incorporated: 2 July 2018
Registered Office: 229 Central Park Road, London, E6 3AE
Major Shareholder: Jesan Nagarajah
Officers: Jesan Nagarajah [1995] Director [German]

Tydene Limited
Incorporated: 1 July 2003
Net Worth: £1,923,598 Total Assets: £4,867,077
Registered Office: 239-241 Kennington Lane, London, SE11 5QU
Major Shareholder: Erkan Tarim
Officers: Erkan Tarim [1970] Director/Sales Person

U.D.C. Wholesale Ltd
Incorporated: 14 September 2018
Registered Office: Suite 203, Empire House, Empire Way, Wembley, Middlesex, HA9 0EW
Major Shareholder: Pando Kerimiyan
Officers: Pando Kerimiyan [1979] Director [Bulgarian]

The Ubuntu Trading Company Limited
Incorporated: 8 December 2006
Registered Office: 6b Palmer Street, Frome, Somerset, BA11 1DS
Officers: Leonard Waling Van Geest [1950] Director

Uddin Discount Ltd
Incorporated: 22 January 2019
Registered Office: 25 Wallington Grove, South Shields, Tyne & Wear, NE33 2RE
Major Shareholder: Khalid Uddin
Officers: Khalid Uddin [1994] Director

Ufton Limited
Incorporated: 10 August 2017
Registered Office: Kemp House, 160 City Road, London, EC1V 2NX
Major Shareholder: George Asfour
Officers: George Asfour, Secretary; George Asfour [1986] Director [Irish]

UK Beer & Soft Drinks Ltd
Incorporated: 9 June 2015
Net Worth Deficit: £959 *Total Assets:* £1
Registered Office: 6th Floor, Amp House, Dingwall Road, Croydon, Surrey, CR0 2LX
Major Shareholder: Yostinappu Philip Thavarajah
Officers: Yostinappu Philip Thavarajah [1970] Director/Delivery Manager

UK Brighton Food & Nutrition Research Centre Ltd
Incorporated: 13 August 2018
Registered Office: Unit G25, Waterfront Studios, 1 Dock Road, London, E16 1AH
Major Shareholder: Xingzhong Deng
Officers: Xingzhong Deng [1986] Director [Chinese]

UK Cloud Business PLC
Incorporated: 16 June 2017
Registered Office: Fourth Floor, 3 Gower Street, London, WC1E 6HA
Major Shareholder: Guo Cheng
Officers: Guo Cheng [1983] Director [Chinese]; Haitao Zhang [1984] Director [Chinese]

UK Star Services Limited
Incorporated: 24 May 2016
Registered Office: 6 Muirfield Close, Wrexham, Clwyd, LL13 9FX
Major Shareholder: Ashok Kumar
Officers: Ashok Kumar [1960] Director [German]

UK Traders (Leics) Ltd
Incorporated: 7 September 2017
Registered Office: 1 Camden Street, Leicester, LE1 2AP
Major Shareholder: Aamir Haroon
Officers: Aamir Haroon [1974] Director

UK Wings Limited
Incorporated: 4 April 2018
Registered Office: 71-75 Shelton Street, London, WC2H 9JQ
Major Shareholder: Sohail Ahmed Malik
Officers: Sohail Ahmed Malik [1954] Director/Accountant

UKFast Service Ltd
Incorporated: 17 October 2013
Registered Office: 41 Carlyle Avenue, Southall, Middlesex, UB1 2LN
Major Shareholder: Vijayaraghavan Subramaniyan Thangavel
Officers: Vijayaraghavan Subramaniyan Thangavel [1989] Director/Sale Assistant [Indian]

Ultimum Drinks Limited
Incorporated: 30 May 2018
Registered Office: 1 Eastdale Road, Liverpool, L15 4HN
Major Shareholder: James Billington
Officers: James Billington, Secretary; James Billington [1987] Director/Drinks Distributor

Under The Sun Europe Ltd
Incorporated: 10 April 2018
Registered Office: Kemp House, 160 City Road, London, EC1V 2NX
Officers: Michael Samuels, Secretary; Samuel Jones [1957] Director

Unicorn Foodline Ltd
Incorporated: 30 August 2018
Registered Office: Unit 6 Trafalger Mill, Trafalger Street, Burnley, Lancs, BB11 1TQ
Major Shareholder: Florin Marian Dumitru
Officers: Daniel Demeter [1998] Director [Hungarian]

Unione Trading Europe Ltd
Incorporated: 15 March 2017
Net Worth Deficit: £4,468 *Total Assets:* £195,160
Registered Office: 46-50 Coombe Road, New Malden, Surrey, KT3 4QF
Shareholder: Jongdae Kim
Officers: Jongdae Kim [1976] Director/Manager [South Korean]

Unique Lines Ltd
Incorporated: 30 June 2017
Registered Office: 13 Regina Road, Southall, Middlesex, UB2 5PL
Shareholders: Abdullahi Mohamed Sheikh Ali; Yussuf Mohamed Haji
Officers: Abdullahi Mohamed Sheikh Ali [1979] Director; Yussuf Mohamed Haji [1982] Director

Unite Foods Trading Limited
Incorporated: 26 November 2012 *Employees:* 1
Net Worth: £38,137 *Total Assets:* £214,745
Registered Office: 55 Station Road, Beaconsfield, Bucks, HP9 1QL
Major Shareholder: Tareq Ashraf Fouad Ghali
Officers: Tareq Ashraf Fouad Ghali [1989] Director/Food Industry

Urban Distribution Ltd
Incorporated: 7 September 2016
Net Worth: £1,174,234 *Total Assets:* £1,248,184
Registered Office: 148-151 Bromsgrove Street, Birmingham, B5 6RG
Officers: Amanjit Singh [1988] Director/General Manager

Usedsoft Ltd
Incorporated: 30 October 2012
Registered Office: 3rd Floor, 207 Regent Street, London, W1B 3HH
Shareholders: Klaus-Peter Kraatz; Gerard Donat
Officers: Gerard Donat [1954] Director/Contractor [French]; Klaus-Peter Kraatz [1956] Director/Contractor [German]

Usmoothie Ltd
Incorporated: 17 May 2010
Net Worth: £4,806 *Total Assets:* £6,282
Registered Office: Frampton Cottage, Pankridge Street, Crondall, Hants, GU10 5QU
Shareholders: Neil Kelvin Dockar; Jaquelene Simone Venn
Officers: Neil Kelvin Dockar [1957] Director; Jaquelene Simone Venn [1965] Director

Usqueeze Limited
Incorporated: 14 November 2005
Registered Office: Frampton Cottage, Pankridge Street, Crondall, Farnham, Surrey, GU10 5QU
Major Shareholder: Neil Kelvin Dockar
Officers: Neil Kelvin Dockar [1957] Director; Jaquelene Simone Venn [1965] Director

Utku Emre Ltd
Incorporated: 23 March 2015
Net Worth Deficit: £112,819 *Total Assets:* £34,798
Registered Office: 53-55 Lothair Road, Leicester, LE2 7QE
Major Shareholder: Hasan Karaoglan
Officers: Hasan Karaoglan [1972] Director

UK Wholesalers of Soft Drinks

V Wholesalers Ltd
Incorporated: 29 September 2016
Net Worth Deficit: £18,647 *Total Assets:* £14,341
Registered Office: 33 Hamilton Road, Ilford, Essex, IG1 2EU
Major Shareholder: Jolly Shah
Officers: Jolly Shah [1981] Director [Indian]

Valley Water Limited
Incorporated: 8 August 2016
Net Worth: £2,269 *Total Assets:* £5,126
Registered Office: 3 Nursery Road, Leicester, LE5 2HP
Major Shareholder: Irfan Vali Patel
Officers: Irfan Vali Patel [1983] Director

Vangoo Enterprise Holding Limited
Incorporated: 22 January 2019
Registered Office: Flat 8, Fairlands Court, Hunting Place, Hounslow, Middlesex, TW5 0NN
Officers: Fanao Jin [1981] Director [Chinese]

Variety Food Fair Limited
Incorporated: 13 January 2017
Net Worth: £1,089 *Total Assets:* £36,116
Registered Office: 1 Parsloes Avenue, Dagenham, Essex, RM9 5PA
Major Shareholder: Gulshan Nisa
Officers: Gulshan Nisa [1977] Director

Veg & City Drinks Limited
Incorporated: 14 September 2011 *Employees:* 25
Net Worth Deficit: £5,156,539 *Total Assets:* £1,452,763
Registered Office: 2nd Floor, Waverley House, 7-12 Noel Street, London, W1F 8GQ
Shareholders: Guka Tavberidze; AGC Equity Partners Special Opportunities Fund I LP
Officers: Lenka Ellmann, Secretary; Lenka Ellmann [1975] Director/Accountant [Czech]; James Yates [1990] Director/Investment Associate

Vendit (Harrow) Limited
Incorporated: 13 January 1967 *Employees:* 10
Net Worth: £395,086 *Total Assets:* £485,051
Registered Office: 1364 London Road, Norbury, London, SW16 4DE
Major Shareholder: Anthony Oliver Adlington
Officers: Nigel Adlington, Secretary; Anthony Oliver Adlington [1938] Director Sales; Nigel Adlington [1969] Director/Manager

Venkat Ltd
Incorporated: 29 August 2018
Registered Office: 142 Colegrave Road, Leyton, London, E15 1EA
Officers: Venkat Varma Subash Chandra Bose [1992] Director [Indian]

Verdict International Ltd
Incorporated: 24 June 2013
Previous: Eco and Green Deal Limited
Net Worth: £50,000 *Total Assets:* £50,000
Registered Office: 317b Old Wakefield Road, Huddersfield, W Yorks, HD5 8AA
Major Shareholder: Azara Ayub
Officers: Azara Ayub [1984] Director

Vezlon Limited
Incorporated: 27 August 2016
Registered Office: Apartment 1804, 1 St Gabriel Walk, London, SE1 6FB
Officers: Mohsin Zahir [1992] Director

Vidi Vici Trading Ltd
Incorporated: 15 December 2016
Registered Office: Brulimar House, Jubilee Road, Middleton, Manchester, M24 2LX
Major Shareholder: Pinchas Grosskopf
Officers: Pinchas Grosskopf [1990] Director/Sales

Vild Water Limited
Incorporated: 8 June 2018
Registered Office: Kemp House, 160 City Road, London, EC1V 2NX
Major Shareholder: Robert Watkins
Officers: Robert Watkins [1992] Director/Professional Services

Village Quality Products Limited
Incorporated: 24 January 2013 *Employees:* 36
Net Worth: £1,582,735 *Total Assets:* £3,473,561
Registered Office: Unit A3, Circular Point, Hickman Avenue, London, E4 9JG
Parent: Masca Holding Limited
Officers: Cetin Agcagul [1985] Director; Suleyman Cagin [1966] Director

Vimto (Out of Home) Limited
Incorporated: 29 November 2013 *Employees:* 45
Previous: Nichols Dispense Limited
Net Worth: £28,617,000 *Total Assets:* £64,299,000
Registered Office: Laurel House, Woodlands Park, Ashton Road, Newton-le-Willows, Merseyside, WA12 0HH
Parent: Nichols PLC
Officers: Timothy John Croston [1963] Finance Director; Nicholas Yates [1974] Director

Vinroe Distribution Ltd
Incorporated: 13 February 2018
Registered Office: Kemp House, 160 City Road, London, EC1V 2NX
Officers: Kelvin Monroe [1951] Director

Vinz Ltd
Incorporated: 14 December 2018
Registered Office: 64 Gledwood Avenue, Hayes, Middlesex, UB4 0AW
Shareholders: Kansiah Satheeshumar; Imran Afzal
Officers: Kansiah Satheeshumar [1970] Director/Businessman

Viserra Limited
Incorporated: 9 March 2011 *Employees:* 14
Net Worth: £174,613 *Total Assets:* £594,758
Registered Office: Unit 1, 112A Warner Road, London, SE5 9HQ
Major Shareholder: Vera Isabel Ramos
Officers: Vera Isabel Rodrigues Ramos [1982] Director/Administrator [Portuguese]

Vision Global Enterprise Ltd
Incorporated: 13 July 2018
Registered Office: 203 Bearstead Court, 28 Underwood Road, London, E1 5AW
Major Shareholder: Rahima Akter Shemu
Officers: Rahima Akter Shemu [1997] Director/Businesswoman [Bangladeshi]

Vitamin Well Limited
Incorporated: 15 June 2017 Employees: 2
Net Worth: £6,257 Total Assets: £137,997
Registered Office: c/o WeWork, 2 Eastbourne Terrace, London, W2 6LG
Shareholders: Bridgepoint Advisers II Limited; BDC III GP LLP
Officers: Matthew Stuart Hollier [1974] Director; Ted Arthur Kristensson [1982] Director/Head of International Expansion [Swedish]; Samir Jonas Pettersson [1974] Director/CEO of Vitamin Well AB [Swedish]

Vitamor Limited
Incorporated: 13 February 2018
Registered Office: Ground Floor, 2 Child's Street, London, SW5 9RY
Major Shareholder: Erica Valeiras Bernad
Officers: Erica Valeiras Bernad [1989] Director/Self Employed [Spanish]

Vitte Nutrition Ltd
Incorporated: 21 September 2018
Registered Office: Unit A, Gainsborough Studios East, 1 Poole Street, London, N1 5ED
Shareholders: Oliver James Thirlwell-Pearce; Phoebe Thirlwell-Pearce
Officers: Oliver James Thirlwell-Pearce [1989] Director; Phoebe Thirlwell-Pearce [1989] Director

Vittorio Ottavio Ltd
Incorporated: 21 February 2013
Net Worth Deficit: £2,657 Total Assets: £902
Registered Office: 35 District Road, Wembley, Middlesex, HA0 2LE
Major Shareholder: Krzysztof Szaradowski
Officers: Krzysztof Szaradowski [1973] Director [Polish]

Viva Avo Ltd
Incorporated: 10 August 2017
Registered Office: 318 Norbury Avenue, London, SW16 3RL
Major Shareholder: Hamza Zaveri
Officers: Hamza Zaveri [1990] Director/Sales

Vivid Vitality Ltd
Incorporated: 26 January 2011
Net Worth: £293,483 Total Assets: £533,909
Registered Office: Exchange House, 12-14 The Crescent, Taunton, Somerset, TA1 4EB
Shareholder: James Robert Shillcock
Officers: Robert Shillcock, Secretary; Matthew James O'Kane [1977] Director/Corporate Finance; Michael John Rusbridge [1955] Director; Tanzil Ismail Sayed [1981] Director [Indian]; James Robert Shillcock [1987] Director; Robert Leslie Shillcock [1956] Director/Accountant; Patrick Nnamdi Spiropoulos [1978] Director/Accounts Manager

Vivo Viva Beverages Limited
Incorporated: 6 March 2018
Registered Office: Union International Drinks Corporation, Bridge House, 64-72 Mabgate, Leeds, LS9 7DZ
Major Shareholder: Robert (Elias) Wilson
Officers: Diane Wilson [1944] Director/Company Formation Agent Semi-Retired; Robert Wilson [1941] Director (CEO)

W D L Wholesale Limited
Incorporated: 13 October 2017
Registered Office: WD Estates, Office 11, Green Industrial Estate, The Roe, St Asaph, Denbighshire, LL17 0LT
Officers: Joshua Lewis, Secretary; Gary Durkin [1954] Director; Ryan Lewis [1975] Director

Wades & Ellie Ltd
Incorporated: 16 September 2009
Net Worth: £92,620 Total Assets: £193,227
Registered Office: 155 Martha Street, London, E1 2PG
Major Shareholder: Debbie Kadir
Officers: Debbie Kadir [1969] Director/Service

Walbrokers Limited
Incorporated: 15 July 1996 Employees: 2
Net Worth: £11,353 Total Assets: £41,314
Registered Office: 28 Highbank, Brighton, BN1 5GB
Shareholders: Mark John Wall; David Lee Wall
Officers: David John Wall [1937] Director/Sales; Mark John Wall [1960] Director/Salesman

C. J. Walls Trading UK Limited
Incorporated: 9 September 2013
Net Worth Deficit: £9,371 Total Assets: £21,667
Registered Office: 30 Bedford Road, East Finchley, London, N2 9DA
Major Shareholder: Chinedu Jude Ekeocha
Officers: Chinedu Jude Ekeocha [1975] Director

Waltrix Publishing Ireland Ltd
Incorporated: 16 May 2018
Registered Office: 1 Dalton Road, Armagh, BT60 4AE
Major Shareholder: Anthony Duffy
Officers: Anthony Duffy, Secretary; Anthony Duffy [1990] Director

Warren Farm Shop Ltd
Incorporated: 30 July 2018
Registered Office: 193 Collier Row Lane, Romford, Essex, RM5 3JA
Major Shareholder: Mark Phillip Kay
Officers: Mark Phillip Kay [1961] Director

J Water Disabled Children Limited
Incorporated: 9 July 2018
Registered Office: 13 Patience Avenue, Seaton Burn, Newcastle upon Tyne, NE13 6HF
Major Shareholder: James Man
Officers: James Manager [1965] Director

Water Wellbeing Limited
Incorporated: 25 August 1977 Employees: 149
Previous: Water for Work and Home Limited
Net Worth: £1,332,104 Total Assets: £4,044,968
Registered Office: Conway House, Pattenden Lane, Marden, Tonbridge, Kent, TN12 9QJ
Shareholders: Benjamin Raymond Stanley McGannan; Nigel Geoffrey Ackerman
Officers: Benjamin Raymond McGannan, Secretary; Nigel Geoffrey Ackerman [1951] Director/Retired; Simon Toby Pennington Edgar [1964] Director; Stephen Gary Hill [1955] Director/Retired; Benjamin Raymond Stanley McGannan [1967] Director; Andrew Maurice Vickers [1964] Finance Director

Watercoolers Southern Limited
Incorporated: 14 January 2003
Net Worth: £653,807 Total Assets: £762,803
Registered Office: Conway House, Pattenden Lane, Marden, Tonbridge, Kent, TN12 9QJ
Parent: Water Wellbeing Limited
Officers: Andrew Maurice Vickers, Secretary; Simon Toby Pennington Edgar [1964] Director; Benjamin Raymond Stanley McGannan [1967] Director; Andrew Maurice Vickers [1964] Director

Waterline (UK) Ltd
Incorporated: 14 December 1998
Net Worth: £9,699 *Total Assets:* £9,699
Registered Office: Unit 4 Brandon Business Centre, Putney Close, Brandon, Suffolk, IP27 0PA
Parent: Water Wellbeing Limited
Officers: Stephen Gary Hill, Secretary; Stephen Gary Hill [1955] Director/Chartered Accountant; Benjamin Raymond Stanley McGannan [1967] Director

Watt Energy Drink (UK) Ltd
Incorporated: 31 January 2014
Net Worth Deficit: £67,960 *Total Assets:* £1,734
Registered Office: The Howarth Armsby Suite, New Broad Street House, 35 New Broad Street, London, EC2M 1NH
Major Shareholder: Ramadan Bessim
Officers: Ramadan Bessim [1966] Director; Tamas Konecsnyi [1978] Director [Hungarian]

Welat & Othman Limited
Incorporated: 5 January 2017 *Employees:* 4
Net Worth: £3,365 *Total Assets:* £30,577
Registered Office: 359-361 Dudley Road, Edgbaston, Birmingham, B18 4HB
Major Shareholder: Omran Hassan
Officers: Omran Hassan [1987] Director [Syrian]

Welldrinks Ltd
Incorporated: 21 August 2018
Registered Office: Flat 1, 54 Westbourne Terrace, London, W2 3UJ
Major Shareholder: Alex Nikolov
Officers: Alex Nikolov [1970] Director [Bulgarian]

Wenlock Spring Water Limited
Incorporated: 16 March 2001 *Employees:* 46
Net Worth: £1,313,523 *Total Assets:* £4,027,848
Registered Office: Bungalows, Wolverton, Church Stretton, Salop, SY6 6RR
Major Shareholder: Robert Sidney Orme
Officers: Susan Margaret Orme, Secretary/Director; Bruce Robert Orme [1970] Director/Retail Sales Manager; Matthew John Orme [1973] Director/Contract Sales Manager; Robert Sidney Orme [1945] Director; Susan Margaret Orme [1947] Director

West Green Supply Ltd
Incorporated: 11 August 2014
Net Worth: £13,553 *Total Assets:* £20,167
Registered Office: 46c St Marks Road, London, W10 6NR
Major Shareholder: Hassan Rohani Jahanpour
Officers: Hassan Rohani Jahanpour [1963] Director/Manager

WGTSS Ltd
Incorporated: 13 March 2018
Registered Office: 71-75 Shelton Street, London, WC2H 9JQ
Major Shareholder: Abderrahmane Ifsasse
Officers: Abderrahmane Ifsasse [1966] Director

The Whiskey and Bourbon Club Ltd
Incorporated: 14 December 2018
Registered Office: 41 Acacia Avenue, Verwood, Dorset, BH31 6XF
Major Shareholder: Oliver Lewis Irwin
Officers: Oliver Lewis Irwin [1996] Director

White World Service Ltd
Incorporated: 27 November 2018
Registered Office: 80 Ince Avenue, Anfield, Liverpool, L4 7UY
Major Shareholder: Parunanthu Ustinnerio
Officers: Parunanthu Ustinnerio [1964] Director/Sales Assistant [French]

V.A. Whitley & Co. Limited
Incorporated: 27 October 1949 *Employees:* 84
Net Worth: £9,218,757 *Total Assets:* £11,013,765
Registered Office: Milward House, Fir Street, Heywood, Lancs, OL10 1NW
Officers: Christopher Mark Rogers, Secretary; Stephen James Duxbury [1972] Director/Certified Accountant; Anthony Milward Rogers [1937] Director; Catherine Helen Rogers [1967] Director; Christopher Mark Rogers [1964] Director; Elizabeth Margaret Rogers [1938] Director; Michael Robert Wallace [1957] Director

Wholesale Your Way Ltd
Incorporated: 31 December 2018
Registered Office: 18 Malvern Street, South Shields, Tyne & Wear, NE33 5LE
Major Shareholder: Vishnu Baboolal
Officers: Vishnu Baboolal [1961] Director [Trinidadian]

Wild Cat Distribution UK Limited
Incorporated: 5 May 2016
Net Worth: £2 *Total Assets:* £2
Registered Office: 24 High View Close, Leicester, LE4 9LJ
Shareholders: Kassam Barkatali Rajani; Hasnein Dhirani
Officers: Hasnein Dhirani [1975] Director; Kassam Barkatali Rajani [1974] Director

Wild Cat Energy Drink Ltd
Incorporated: 24 October 2011
Net Worth Deficit: £130,582 *Total Assets:* £31,069
Registered Office: 24 High View Close, Vantage Park, Leicester, LE4 9LJ
Shareholders: Kassam Barkatali Rajani; Hasnein Dhirani
Officers: Gurminder Singh Basra [1970] International Sales Director; Shantilal Chauhan [1946] Director/Microbiologist; Hasnein Dhirani [1975] Director; Kassam Barkatali Rajani [1974] Director; Shubnit Singh Rehal [1993] Operations Director

Wildcat International Limited
Incorporated: 13 October 2015
Registered Office: 24 High View Close, Leicester, LE4 9LJ
Major Shareholder: Kassam Barkatali Rajani
Officers: Kassam Barkatali Rajani [1974] Director

Willow World Ltd
Incorporated: 8 January 2019
Registered Office: 82 Claremont Road, London, NW2 1AP
Major Shareholder: Sharron Constantine Palathis
Officers: Sharron Constantine Palathis [1994] Director/Sales Assistant [French]

Windfall Logistics Limited
Incorporated: 20 March 2007 *Employees:* 7
Net Worth: £163,940 *Total Assets:* £877,970
Registered Office: Windfall House, D1, The Courtyard, Alban Park, St Albans, Herts, AL4 0LA
Major Shareholder: Angelos Panayiotou
Officers: Angelos Panayiotou, Secretary; Angelos Panayiotou [1975] Director/Accountant; Michael Sears [1956] Director

Wine City Limited
Incorporated: 4 April 2018
Registered Office: c/o The Store Room, P O Box 7, Unit 7 Foxholes Road, Leicester, LE3 1TH
Shareholders: Basil Enok; Wilson Enwerem
Officers: Basil Enok [1975] Director; Wilson Enwerem [1975] Director

Winewise Ltd
Incorporated: 14 May 2015
Net Worth: £1,000 *Total Assets:* £1,000
Registered Office: 9a High Street, West Drayton, Middlesex, UB7 7QG
Officers: Mohammed Farooq Khan [1956] Director

Winnack and Hart Industries Ltd
Incorporated: 19 December 2018
Registered Office: 155a Queens Road, Leicester, LE2 3FN
Shareholders: Jack Andrei Geoffrey Winnack; Samuel Lewis Hart
Officers: Samuel Lewis Hart [1993] Director/Consultant; Jack Andrei Geoffrey Winnack [1990] Director/Management Accountant

Winz International UK Ltd
Incorporated: 30 March 2017
Registered Office: 3rd Floor, 207 Regent Street, London, W1B 3HH
Officers: Huarong Zhang [1955] Director [Chinese]

Wisdom of Nature Limited
Incorporated: 24 November 2003
Registered Office: Unit E, Foster Road, Ashford Business Park, Sevington, Ashford, Kent, TN24 0SH
Parent: Natural Distribution (Holdings) Limited
Officers: Marcos David Pozo Caballero [1973] Business Development Director [Spanish]

Wishing Tree Limited
Incorporated: 8 April 2017
Registered Office: 26 Kingscourt Road, West Derby, Liverpool, L12 8RD
Major Shareholder: James Aaron Sweetin
Officers: Edward Samuel Francis Byrne [1995] Director/Software Engineer; James Aaron Sweetin [1979] Managing Director

WLH Food Ltd
Incorporated: 8 May 2018
Registered Office: 9a Silver Street, Durham, DH1 3RB
Shareholders: Jun Wang; Guang Han He
Officers: Jun Wang [1984] Director

WLL Wholesale Ltd
Incorporated: 26 April 2018
Registered Office: c/o Trustax Services Limited, Unit V15 Howitt Building, Lenton Boulevard, Nottingham, NG7 2BY
Shareholders: Kapil Lathia; Zepeng Wen
Officers: Kapil Lathia [1982] Director; Zepeng Wen [1988] Director [Chinese]

Wobblegate Limited
Incorporated: 8 April 2015
Net Worth: £423 *Total Assets:* £165,042
Registered Office: East View Cottage, Old Mill House Farm, Cowfold Road, Bolney, Haywards Heath, W Sussex, RH17 5SE
Officers: Peter William Hazell [1984] Director; Thomas Stephens [1984] Director

Wolf Wholesale Limited
Incorporated: 6 February 2018
Registered Office: Flat 6, 74 Worksop Road, Sheffield, S9 3TN
Major Shareholder: Csaba Farkas
Officers: Csaba Farkas, Secretary; Csaba Farkas [1979] Director [Hungarian]

Woodchester International Ltd
Incorporated: 11 July 2017
Net Worth: £77 *Total Assets:* £75,911
Registered Office: Manderson House, Unit 5230 Valiant Court, Delta Way, Gloucester Business Park, Brockworth, Gloucester, GL3 4FE
Parent: Woodchester Enterprises Limited
Officers: Elaine Birchall [1966] Director [Irish]; Arthur William Richmond [1966] Director

Woodstar Limited
Incorporated: 9 March 2017
Registered Office: 54 Hillbury Avenue, Harrow, Middlesex, HA3 8EW
Major Shareholder: Andrew Stanley Baker
Officers: Andrew Stanley Baker [1959] Director

World Trade Values Limited
Incorporated: 2 December 2008
Net Worth Deficit: £33,996 *Total Assets:* £14,787
Registered Office: 15 Evington Close, Leicester, LE5 5PJ
Major Shareholder: Atef Fathi Mohamed Abd El Ghani
Officers: Atef Fathi Mohamed Abd El Ghani [1957] Director

Worldwide Essentials Limited
Incorporated: 23 August 2017
Registered Office: 71-75 Shelton Street, Covent Garden, London, WC2H 9JQ
Major Shareholder: Stuart Andrew Yates
Officers: Stuart Andrew Yates [1957] Director/Salesman

G & Y Wynne Limited
Incorporated: 10 June 2004 *Employees:* 52
Net Worth: £297,745 *Total Assets:* £690,024
Registered Office: Broncoed House, Broncoed Business Park, Wrexham Road, Mold, Flintshire, CH7 1HP
Shareholders: David Gareth Wynne; Yvonne Rosemary Wynne
Officers: David Gareth Wynne, Secretary/Retailer; David Gareth Wynne [1961] Director/Retailer; Yvonne Rosemary Wynne [1962] Director/Retailer

Xorta Global Management Limited
Incorporated: 4 May 2016
Net Worth: £1,101 *Total Assets:* £2,801
Registered Office: c/o Lohur & Co, 35 New England Road, Brighton, BN1 4GG
Major Shareholder: Amanda Denise Miranda
Officers: Amanda Denise Miranda, Secretary; Amanda Denise Miranda [1967] Director

Y Acay Berry Ltd
Incorporated: 14 December 2018
Registered Office: Suite 5, Charan House, 18 Union Road, London, SW4 6JP
Major Shareholder: Emmanuelle Trogu
Officers: Emmanuelle Trogu [1981] Director [Italian]

Yachinelyaoui Limited
Incorporated: 15 October 2018
Registered Office: Flat 5, 51 Kenninghall Road, London, E5 8BS
Major Shareholder: Yachine Lyaoui
Officers: Yachine Lyaoui [1995] Director [French]

UK Wholesalers of Soft Drinks

Yardely Ltd
Incorporated: 1 December 2010
Net Worth: £718 *Total Assets:* £3,637
Registered Office: 144 Chatham Street, Stockport, Cheshire, SK3 9LN
Major Shareholder: Abolfazl Sedighigilani
Officers: Abolfazl Sedighigilani [1967] Director

Yashrab Ltd
Incorporated: 7 October 2018
Registered Office: 16 Albemarle Street, London, W1S 4HW
Major Shareholder: Mohammed Zaheer Mughal
Officers: Mohammed Zaheer Mughal [1981] Director/Consultant

Yorkshire Enterprise Ltd
Incorporated: 17 August 2016
Registered Office: c/o Yorkshire Accountancy Limited, First Floor Offices, County House, Dunswell Road, Cottingham, E Yorks, HU16 4JT
Major Shareholder: Gabriel Atsu Sikanku
Officers: Gabriel Atsu Sikanku, Secretary; Gabriel Atsu Sikanku [1982] Director/Businessman

Yorkshire Exports Limited
Incorporated: 14 March 2018
Registered Office: 12 Tenby Terrace, Halifax, W Yorks, HX1 4PU
Officers: Tibor Nagy [1991] Director [Hungarian]

Youngs Vintage Management Ltd
Incorporated: 10 October 2018
Registered Office: 14 Fairlawns, 159 Kingsway, Hove, E Sussex, BN3 4FZ
Major Shareholder: William Young
Officers: William Young [1961] Director/Manager

Your Water Ltd
Incorporated: 16 May 2018
Registered Office: 7 Church Avenue, Easton, Bristol, BS5 6DY
Major Shareholder: Nathan Christopher Stokes
Officers: Nathan Christopher Stokes [1989] Director

Yourchoice Wholesale Ltd
Incorporated: 18 December 2018
Registered Office: 15 Approach Road, Margate, Kent, CT9 2AN
Major Shareholder: Ryan-Paul Nolan
Officers: Ryan-Paul Nolan [1999] Director

YummyColombia Ltd
Incorporated: 8 May 2018
Registered Office: 21 Wordsworth Avenue, London, E12 6SU
Major Shareholder: Richard Caroprese
Officers: Richard Caroprese [1995] Director/Student [Italian]; Ashfaqur Rahman [1978] Director/IT Manager

Z & Z Global Ltd
Incorporated: 19 December 2018
Registered Office: 86c Water Street, Birmingham, B3 1HL
Major Shareholder: Mohammed Ashfaq
Officers: Mohammed Ashfaq [1967] Director

Zacely Limited
Incorporated: 8 November 2010 *Employees:* 2
Net Worth: £4,604 *Total Assets:* £122,271
Registered Office: 10 High Street, Poole, Dorset, BH15 1BP
Shareholders: Paul Wallace; Diana Novoa
Officers: Diana Novoa [1982] Director [Canadian]; Paul Wallace [1979] Director

Zaid & Besher Ltd
Incorporated: 15 May 2018
Registered Office: 310-312 Charminster Road, Bournemouth, BH8 9RT
Shareholders: Zaid Daghstani; Besher Abo Gadda Sabbagh
Officers: Besher Abo Ghada Sabbagh [1995] Director [Syrian]; Zaid Daghstani [1994] Director/Warehouse Manager [Syrian]

Zanzi Products Limited
Incorporated: 14 November 2011 *Employees:* 2
Previous: Zanzi Frozen Foods Ltd
Net Worth Deficit: £54,179 *Total Assets:* £390,370
Registered Office: Rubicon House, Unit 5 Second Way, Wembley, Middlesex, HA9 0YJ
Shareholders: Nareshchandra Gordhandas Nagrecha; Veena Nagrecha
Officers: Radha Nagrecha Gagneja [1982] Director/Accountant; Davendra Parbat Khimani [1972] Director; Neel Nagrecha [1980] Director

Zauq Services Ltd
Incorporated: 6 November 2018
Registered Office: 91 Medlicott Road, Birmingham, B11 1UB
Major Shareholder: Farrukh Nazir
Officers: Farrukh Nazir, Secretary; Farrukh Nazir [1969] Director [Pakistani]

Zayyan Foods Distribution Ltd
Incorporated: 13 February 2017
Registered Office: 431a High Street, North Manor Park, London, E12 6TJ
Major Shareholder: Muhammad Rizwan Arshad
Officers: Muhammad Rizwan Arshad [1982] Director

Zentio Limited
Incorporated: 9 August 2013
Net Worth: £1,149 *Total Assets:* £14,740
Registered Office: Unit 5 Martinbridge Trading Estate, 240-242 Lincoln Road, Enfield, Middlesex, EN1 1SP
Major Shareholder: Kathirkaman Pillai Rajendran
Officers: Arthihasan Chandramohan [1987] Director/Manager

Zero Options Ltd
Incorporated: 22 February 2018
Registered Office: c/o Mary Mackle & Co, CIDO Innovation Centre, 73 Charlestown Road, Portadown, Craigavon, Co Armagh, BT63 5PP
Shareholders: Stuart Decodt; Tom Maguire
Officers: Stuart Decodt, Secretary; Stuart Decodt [1960] Director/Wholesale Distributor [French]; Tom Maguire [1960] Director/Wholesale Distributor

Zeroholic Ltd
Incorporated: 5 November 2018
Registered Office: 12 Chestnut Court, Parc Menai, Bangor, Gwynedd, LL57 4FH
Shareholders: Bethan Morris de Souza; Huw Dafydd Parry
Officers: Bethan Morris de Souza [1965] Director; Huw Dafydd Parry [1987] Director

Zeyroj Soft Drinks Ltd
Incorporated: 11 July 2018
Registered Office: Unit 5 Centenary Industrial Estate, Jefferys Road, Enfield, Middlesex, EN3 7UF
Major Shareholder: Ali Canbolat
Officers: Ali Canbolat [1990] Director/Businessman

Ziro Ltd
Incorporated: 4 November 2013 *Employees:* 1
Net Worth Deficit: £331,792 *Total Assets:* £20,047
Registered Office: 79 College Road, Harrow, Middlesex, HA1 1BD
Shareholders: Lily Rogath; Meryl Zises
Officers: Lily Rogath [1988] Director/Entrepreneur [German]; Meryl Zises [1988] Director/Entrepreneur [American]

Zolex Global Limited
Incorporated: 19 December 2017
Registered Office: Flat 1, Wren Court, 29 Bounds Green Road, Wood Green, London, N22 8SD
Shareholders: Alexandra Georgopoulou; Zoltan Feher
Officers: Zoltan Feher [1985] Director [Hungarian]

Zoop Up Energy Ltd
Incorporated: 13 February 2018
Registered Office: 20-22 Wenlock Road, London, N1 7GU
Shareholders: Ross Gerald Wilkins; Darius Campbell
Officers: Darius Campbell [1985] Director; Ross Generald Wilkins [1990] Director/Civil Engineer

ZSlush Ltd
Incorporated: 24 January 2018
Registered Office: Suite 3-04 Peel House, London Road, Morden, Surrey, SM4 5BT
Major Shareholder: Zeeshan Ahmed
Officers: Zeeshan Ahmed [1989] Director

ZSM Traders Ltd
Incorporated: 25 April 2018
Registered Office: 3rd Floor, 113 Cranbrook Road, Ferguson House, Ilford, Essex, IG1 4PU
Major Shareholder: Zahid Akhtar
Officers: Zahid Akhtar [1972] Director/Businessman [Belgian]

Zumi Natural Limited
Incorporated: 4 December 2012 *Employees:* 2
Net Worth Deficit: £63,980 *Total Assets:* £37,515
Registered Office: 4th Floor, Park Gate, 161-163 Preston Road, Brighton, BN1 6AF
Major Shareholder: Millan Mahendra Gudka
Officers: Millan Mahendra Gudka [1979] Director/Accountant

Zummo Central Limited
Incorporated: 7 September 2005 *Employees:* 4
Net Worth: £33,677 *Total Assets:* £96,186
Registered Office: Crowsmoor Farm, Aston on Clun, Craven Arms, Salop, SY7 8EF
Major Shareholder: Christopher Leonard Gaunt Wesson
Officers: Christopher Leonard Gaunt Wesson [1955] Director

Index of Directorships

Abbas, Imran
MJ Trading (NW) Ltd

Abd El Ghani, Atef Fathi Mohamed
World Trade Values Limited

Abdel Rahman, Osama
Arab World Ltd

Abdollahei, Erfan
Colbury Limited

Abdul Basheer, Mohamed Azeem
Sasa Super Foods Ltd

Abdul, Mohammed-Hasnain Jamaal
Pound Hill Ltd

Abdulrahimzai, Mohammad Arif
Arif Rahim Ltd
Realmix Beverage Ltd

Abiola, Halima
Ladeo Limited

Abioye, Oluyemisi Tolani
Elias Trading Limited

Abo Ghada Sabbagh, Besher
Zaid & Besher Ltd

Abratkiewicz, Andrzej Pawel
Eurodrinks Ltd

Abukor, Edil Abdi
Abukor Ltd

Acharya, Viraj Kaku Sunil
Tomato Tantrum Ltd

Achhodi, Yamin
Slurps Ice Ltd

Ackerman, Nigel Geoffrey
Water Wellbeing Limited

Adam, Jhasen
Alicia's Coffee House Limited

Adams, Oumie
Jamarec UK Limited

Adegbite, Moses Adedoyin
Bellwether Impex (UK) Limited

Adelakun, Adeola
Ladeo Limited

Adelowo, Adesola
Abijah Global Limited

Ademola, Adekunle Akanji
Topmost Foods Distribution Ltd.

Adepegba, Margaret Olubunmi
Funbella Ltd

Adlington, Anthony Oliver
Vendit (Harrow) Limited

Adlington, Nigel
Vendit (Harrow) Limited

Adnan, Faisal
F & T Enterprise Ltd.

Afruz, Mahbubul Hoque
A to Z Veg Ltd

Agcagul, Cetin
Artos Foods Limited
Cyprofood Limited
Masca Holding Limited
Mirpa Limited
Village Quality Products Ltd

Agha, Saad
Nextgen Distribution Limited

Aghajanzadeh, Reza
Shimroon Limited

Aghayere, Igbinosa Dag
Refribrit Ltd

Agrawal, Nileshkumar
Gemini Wholesalers Limited

Ahad, Mohammed Abdul
Shapla Cash & Carry Ltd

Ahluwalia, Prabhsharan Singh
Asia Direct Limited

Ahmad, Awais
Elham Elliethy Ltd

Ahmad, Ewelina Malgorzata
Lanex Ltd

Ahmad, Jamal
Rayan Cash & Carry Ltd

Ahmad, Zaheeer
Shopocus Ltd

Ahmad, Zaheer
Fexty Ltd
Hillcrest WM Ltd
Nohew Trade Ltd

Ahmad, Zubair
Sublime Distributors Limited

Ahmed, Akeal
Premier Food & Beverage Ltd

Ahmed, Azizul
NQN Enterprises Limited

Ahmed, Iftikhar
Mirza Trading Limited

Ahmed, Ishtiaq
Darkhorse Universal Limited

Ahmed, Jamil
Emperor Trades Limited

Ahmed, Khudeza Begum
K.A Top Traders Limited

Ahmed, Nevid
Navson Ltd

Ahmed, Rzgar
Caspian Foods Cash & Carry Ltd

Ahmed, Saika Tehzim
A H K Wholesaler Ltd

Ahmed, Waqas
Evoca UK Distribution Limited

Ahmed, Zahoor
Platinum UK Drinks Ltd

Ahmed, Zeeshan
ZSlush Ltd

Aidoo, Omari
Juicydee Ltd

Akgun, Ramazan
Akgun Food Ltd

Akhtar, Zahid
ZSM Traders Ltd

Akin, Hakan
FMCG Enterprises Limited

Akkaya, Fatma
Eagle Beer Ltd

Akmal, Muhammad
Benson International Ltd
Netmine Technologies Ltd
Skyfall Enterprise Ltd

Aksakal, Serkan
Choise Group Ltd

Aksu, Alper
Stalker U.K Limited

Aktar, Nasima
Capital Drinks London Limited

Al-Aukati, Ali
Nuli Life Ltd

Al-Kawamleh, Hanan
Falafel Factory Ltd

Al-Saeed, Ammar Mohammad
Dreams Food 1 Limited

Alabede, Ola
Discount on Drinks Ltd

Alabi, Kolawole Hakeem
Hesana Ltd

Alabi, Olaitan
N'ife Limited

Alam Bhuiyan, MD Saiful
Rexcel Trading Ltd

Alaywan, Talal Abdul Rahim
Aqua Distribution Limited

Alexander, Joan Campbell
Fresh Produce Deliveries Ltd

Alfano, Gaetano Salvatore
Lanza Foods Ltd

Alhagri, Abubaker Abood
A & H Trading Ltd

Ali, Abdulkadir Mohamed
Glinter UK Ltd

Ali, Abdullahi Mohamed Sheikh
Unique Lines Ltd

Ali, Arshad
Arsi Soft Drinks Limited

Ali, Rokib
Shapla Cash & Carry Ltd

Ali, Shumon
Atlantis Spring Water Limited

Ali, Usman
Platinum Group Midlands Ltd

Allen, Andrea Mary
J.C. Dudley & Co. Ltd

Almiron Martinez, Antonio Jose
Importonics Limited

Alti, Musamettin
Alti's Catering Limited

Aly, Ahmed
Eltrados Ltd

Aly, Katarzyna
Eltrados Ltd

Alyouseff, Abdulhadi
Dreams Food 1 Limited

Amarouch, Ahmed
Sharewater Ltd

Ambekar, Prakash
ABNN Fresh UK Ltd

Amici, Andrea
Bibere Ltd.

Amipara, Praful Nanji
Patson Foods Ltd

Amirramathan, Arkad
Global Food Wholesalers Ltd

Ammani, Mohamed
Numidia Taste Ltd

Amurtherajan, Cowthom
Drinx Division Ltd

An, Guinan
Paradigm Red Limited

An, Xiangshou
Paradigm Red Limited

Anam, Hayel Nabil Hayel Saeed
Dining Capital Limited

Anam, Mohamed Nabil Hayel Saeed
Dining Capital Limited

Anastasi, Andriani
Dolphin Trading Limited

Anastasiou, David
Liverpool & Oriental Trading Co Ltd

Anderson, Caitlin Sian
Anderson Beverages Ltd

Anderson, Chloe Dawn
Anderson Beverages Ltd

Andrews, Michael John
Artisan Drinks Co Ltd

Anjum, Mian Salahuddin
Avigail Dairies Limited
Avigail Limited

Anolue, Ogonna Solomon
Jascera UK Ltd

Ansar, Sharif Alam
Shibui Beverage Co Ltd

Arfaoui, Hatem
Starburst Hub Ltd

Arlauskaite, Eksandra
Kardelen Water Limited

Armanazi, Mohamed Najib
Lana Nai UK Co. Ltd

Armstrong Carey, Patrick Guy
All English Distribution Ltd.

Armstrong, Curtis
All Vending Services Limited

Aroleeb, Shazia
Desi Trading Ltd

Arora, Sonam
AFZ Trade Ltd

Arrigoni, Christopher
More or Less Drinks Co Ltd

Arshad, Muhammad Rizwan
Zayyan Foods Distribution Ltd

Arthur, Carmel Charmain
Pure Organic Drinks Limited

Arthurs, Richard
Jaden Wholesale Limited

Arulanantham, Amit
Moringa Superfoods UK Limited

Arulanantham, Eirlys Sian
Moringa Superfoods UK Limited

Arulchelvananthan, Lavan
Silvercall Limited

Arulsothy, Arun
Eagle Drinks Ltd
Loris Wholesale Ltd

Ascani, Maurizia
Giovanni Food & Wine Limited

Asemani, Kurosh
Lep Food & Wine Ltd

Asfour, George
Ufton Limited

Ashfaq, Mohammed
Regency Traders Ltd
S K Enteprises Ltd
Shu Enterprise Ltd
Z & Z Global Ltd

Ashley, George, Dr
Active Root 2 Ltd

Ashman, Stuart John
Afterall Ltd

Asif, Muhammad
7 Star Trading Ltd

Aslam, Usman
Platinum Packaging Ltd

Asmatpoor, Ehsanullah
Amou Limited

Atalaye, Priscillia
Pamm Beverages Limited

Athwal, Rajveer Singh, Dr
Nootrilix Limited

Atkin, Andrew
ADA Beverages Ltd

Atkins, Julian
Franklin 1886 Limited

Attieh, Nidal
Abevco Limited

Aursudkij, Supradya
Natural Enzymes Limited

Austin, David
DWR Cerist Cyf

Austin, Lewis Daniel
Surprisingly Treaty Ltd

Avery, Mary Louise
Better Tasting Drinks Co. Ltd

Avitable, Jake
Premier Soft Drinks Ltd

Awada, Houssein
AWA Nature Ltd

Awan, Shoaib
H2O Supplies Ltd

Aygun, Suheyla
LBSM Limited

Ayub, Azara
Verdict International Ltd

Ayub, Zishan Saad
I S Traders Limited

Azad, Mohammed
Shapla Cash & Carry Ltd

Azam, Afsana
MSK Halal Ltd

Azam, Javed
Janama Trading Co Ltd

Azam, Sohail
Direct Source Distribution Ltd

Azim, Abdul
Gulzar Traders Ltd

Aziz, Khalid
Bri Trade Solutions Limited

Aziz, Mudassar
Ch@i Drinks Ltd

Azouri, Ilan
Flow 33 UK Limited

Baboolal, Vishnu
Strong Pound Ltd
Wholesale Your Way Ltd

Baboolal, Vishnu
Thirst Call Ltd

Baciu, Nicolae-Alexandru
NBA Wholesale Ltd

Bacon, Shaun
Franklin 1886 Limited

Baig, Mirza Bilal
Rabia Food & Drinks Ltd

Baig, Mirza Saeed Ahmed
Jonsen International Ltd

Baig, Mirza Shahid Anwer
Rozana Foods Limited

Bailey, Ashley
The Cafe Collective UK Trading Co Ltd

Bailey, James
3BW Ltd

Bailey, Matthew William
Future Generation Foods U.K. Ltd

Baker, Andrew Stanley
Woodstar Limited

Bakir, Mehmet
Kaplan Int Limited

Bal, Surinder Kaur
Drayton Limited

Balaam, Khalid
Fast Food Traders Ltd

Balan, Catalina
Fresh Pal Ltd

Balda, Tara
MTS Export Import Ltd

Balog, Lajos
Agrotrade International Trading Ltd
Bioactive Live Ltd

Balogh, Csaba
Manchester Fruit and Vegetables Ltd

Bamber, Simon Peter
Botanic Lab Ltd

Baptiste, Kebera Brenda Patricia
Sunspice UK Limited

Barclay, Fraser
Loughborough Student Services Ltd

Barclay, Jenna Zoe
Clear Drinks Limited

Barczynski, Tomasz
Syphony Water Limited

Bari, Hawa
ERE Igga Ltd

Barlow, Michael John
DWR Cerist Cyf

Barlow, Paul Jonathan
Loughborough Student Services Ltd

Barlow, Philip Roger
Gerrard Seel Limited

Barozzi, Franco James
Giovanni Food & Wine Limited

Barran, Patrick Robin
Clarion Wines Limited

Barrett, Damian Paul
Cellar Twelve Limited

Barrett, John Andrew
Bristol Spirits Limited

Barteling-Doherty, Carianne Henriette
Lifting Spirits Ltd

Barth, Rudolf Alexander Hans
Rivella (U.K.) Limited

Bascau, Nicu Bogdan
Stockwell Beverages Ltd

Basra, Gurminder Singh
Wild Cat Energy Drink Ltd

Bassi, Parminder Singh
PSB Trading Limited

Bates, Adam Richard
Easy CBD Limited

Bath, Jaipreet Singh
Harsimran K Ltd

Batista, Roeiner Santos
Healthy Hit Ltd

Battersbee, Ronald Peter John
Fruit Slush 'n' Shake Ltd

Bayram, Mesut
Knights Catering Impex Ltd

Bean, Gabriel
Raw Is More Ltd.

Bearpark, Ian Leonard
RMGL Trading Limited

Beart, Nicholas Anthony
Cawston Press Limited

Beckford-Miller, Laurenzay
Firewater Merchants Ltd

Beever, Graham William
GWB Associates Limited

Begum, Jahanara
Shapla Cash & Carry Ltd

Begum, Liluba
Tasnim Recruiting & Consultancy Services

Begum, Shilpi
MU Distributors Ltd

Bekhti, Maxime
New Global Ltd

Belal, Lutfur Rahman
Azka Impex (London) Limited
Azka Impex Limited

Bello, Gbola Daud
Gabby & Bello Enterprises Ltd

Benjamin, Richard Marc
Manchester Drinks Co Ltd

Bennett, Caroline Mary
Golden Eagle Foods Edinburgh Ltd
Golden Eagle Trade Edinburgh Ltd

Benson, Nicholas John
Source 360 Ltd

Beriwal, Anil Ram Kumar
Direct Source 2 Limited

Beriwal, Meena Anil
Direct Source 2 Limited

Beriwal, Pushpak Anil
Direct Source 2 Limited

Berkley Matthews, Richard John
Clarion Wines Limited

Berry, Paul Andrew
Paul Berry Limited

Bessim, Ramadan
Watt Energy Drink (UK) Ltd

Bhatti, Rajah Ahmed Riaz
Orange Trading Ltd

Bibi, Lateef
LB Hussan Hussain Halal Meat Superstore

Bickerton, Andrew Philip
A & A Wines Limited

Bilbas, Farhad Khalnd
Global Food Wholesalers Ltd

Bilgin, Nerin
Organic Village Limited

Billington, James
Ultimum Drinks Limited

Bilsland, David
Fresh Produce Deliveries Ltd

Birch, Patrick, Dr
Birch Boost Ltd

Birchall, Elaine
Woodchester International Ltd

Blachut, Maciej
MS Rarytas Ltd

Blewitt, Neil
Aspire Brands Int Ltd.

Blewitt, Neil David
Aspire Drinks Limited

Blurton, James Patrick
Peregrine Welsh Water Limited

Boase, Luke Seymour
Not Another Beer Co Ltd

Bogdan, Marian
AVM UK Private Limited

Bolliger Villalobos, Sebastian
Geminiz Ltd

Bonders, Martins
Elham Elliethy Ltd

Bortacki, Tomasz
Bor-Tom Ltd

Boukhebelt, Said
Said Boukhebelt Ltd

Boulerouah, Hadj Said
Simex International Ltd

Boussoufa-Khalifa, Sihem
Nodus International Trade Ltd

Bowden, Oliver
3BW Ltd

Bowers, Daniel
Punchy Drinks Limited

Boydell, William Ranald
Norfolk Punch Limited

Brady, Siobhan Cathrina Maria
GB Heritage Ltd

Braine, Gavin
PXL Drinks Ltd

Bramhall, Leane
Kineta Drinks Limited

Branchflower, Andrew
Fevertree Europe Limited
Fevertree Row Limited
Fevertree UK Limited
Fevertree US Limited

Brandriet, Marco Johan Jakobus
Oranka Fruit Juices Limited

Branson, Benjamin
Seedlip Ltd

Branson, Benjamin John
Anna Seed 83 Limited

Brazza, Michele
D D S Food Imports Ltd

Brett, Daphne
Asta Barista Baby Ltd

Bridgeman, Stephen Dennis
Alivini (North) Limited
Alivini Co Ltd

Brkljac, Tatjana
Organica Vita Ltd

Brodie, John Ross
The Start-Up Drinks Lab Ltd

Brogan, Stephen Michael
Ooberstock Limited

Brookes, Nicholas Anthony
AQ Branding Ltd

Brookes, Ruth Elizabeth
AQ Branding Ltd

Browett, Ben David Hulton
Browett & Fair Ltd

Brown, Cecil
BG Drinks Ltd

Brown, James Francis McKenzie
Source 360 Ltd

Brown, Michael Nathan
Juice on the Go Ltd

Browne, Jack Anthony Mark Patrick
S & B's Mart Ltd.

Browne, Kiera
Seafire Brewing Co. Ltd

Bucceri, Natalie Antonina
Caleno Drinks Ltd

Buckwell, Alan Arthur
Rimpex-UK Limited

Buet, Keith Paul
Snackpax Distribution Limited

Bukhari, Syed Muhammed Ali
Bukhari and Tanweer Limited

Bulbulia, Ibrahim
Premium Jacks Limited

Buoncuore, Baldassare
Paynesbb Limited

Burden, Russell
RB Beverages Ltd

Burris, Joseph
Bennu Rising Ltd.

Busby, Mark Anthony
Buzbees Beverages Limited

Busuioc, Alin Grigoras
All in One Household Ltd

Butt, Muhammad Asim
Simple Brands Ltd

Butt, Zahid Sharif
Haltrade UK Ltd

Butt, Zulfiqar
Jaguar Power Energy Drinks Ltd.

Buttimore, Tim
3BW Ltd

Buza, Nicolae
Astra Import Ltd.

Byrne, Edward Samuel Francis
Wishing Tree Limited

Cagin, Suleyman
Artos Foods Limited
Cyprofood Limited
Masca Holding Limited
Mirpa Limited
Village Quality Products Ltd

Caiza, Miguel
Moudine Trade Ltd

Caktu, Ali Hidir
Dimark Limited

Calka, Daniel
KD-Pol Ltd

Calka, Katarzyna
KD-Pol Ltd

Cameron, Dorothy Anne
Bristol Spirits Limited

Cameron, Nicholas Mark
Cameron Soft Drinks Limited

Camille, Janine
Camii Punch Ltd

Campbell, Darius
Zoop Up Energy Ltd

Canbolat, Ali
Zeyroj Soft Drinks Ltd

Canham, Christopher James
C J Canham Drinks Limited

Canham, Gina Frances
C J Canham Drinks Limited

Capaldi, Jean Winifred
Solerco Products Limited

Carcu, Corneliu Alin
Aura Gold Water Ltd

Carless, John Bradley
Global Sports Trade Ltd

Carlton, Alexander Jonathan
Elegantly Spirited Limited

Carmichael, Michael
Kintyre Holdings Limited

Caroprese, Richard
YummyColombia Ltd

Carpenter, Tripty Gurung
Flux Investment Ltd

Carpinelli, Denise
TFC Wholesale Ltd

Carpinelli, Francesco
TFC Wholesale Ltd

Carpinelli, Trentino
TFC Wholesale Ltd

Carr, Collin
Saapos Ltd

Carrick, Anh Dao
AZ Health Food Center Ltd

Carter, Rex Morton
Rex Drinks Limited

Carter, Steven
Frobishers Juices Limited

Cartwright, Benjamin
Oasis Softdrinks Limited

Carvey, Raina Catherine
Triple R Industries Limited

Carvey, Trevor Godfrey
Triple R Industries Limited

Cavanagh-Butler, Patrick Charles Arthur
Punchy Drinks Limited

Cazabet, Remy
Remy Cazabet Ltd

Chahal, Devinder Singh
Dark Invest Ltd

Chahal, Kamaldeep Kaur
Dark Invest Ltd

Chahal, Narender Singh
BS and Sons London Limited

Challinor, Lewis Dan
Bright Smoothies Ltd

Chamberlain, Robert Hugo
Hurly Burly Foods Limited

Chamberlain, Stephen Paul
Collette International Limited

Chandramohan, Ambika
DN World Ltd

Chandramohan, Arthihasan
Zentio Limited

Chandramohan, Suthahar
SLB Wholesale Ltd

Chandrasinghe, Bogahawatte Kumararatne
Sams Fast Foods Limited

Chandrasinghe, Dharshanie Nirupa Casinar
Sams Fast Foods Limited

Chandrasinghe, Nicole Shinika
Sams Fast Foods Limited

Chandrasinghe, Sheehan Arjuna
Sams Fast Foods Limited

Chansiri, Dejphon
Elev8 Energy Drink Limited

Charitun, Rastislav
Tatry Trade Ltd

Charles, Peter
Red Bull Co Ltd

Chatwani, Jawahar Jamnadas
M & M Export Limited

Chatwani, Rashmi Jamnadas
M & M Export Limited

Chatwani, Satish Jamnadas
M & M Export Limited

Chaudhry, Sarah
Triumph Foodservice Limited

Chaudhry, Shamila
Iwater Inc Ltd

Chauhan, Arun Kumar, Dr
Anya Global Limited

Chauhan, Shantilal
Wild Cat Energy Drink Ltd

Chawla, Omair Mateen
Ch@i Drinks Ltd

Cheema, Jaswinder
OMG Beverages Limited

Cheng, Guo
UK Cloud Business PLC

Chetiyawardana, Ryan
Cheti & Co Holdings Limited
Cheti & Co Limited

Cheyne, Desmond Victor James
Deveron Direct Limited

Chikhi, Hassan
Amsterdam Taste Ltd

Chillingworth, Paul
Cubico Limited

Chimuchere, Gideon William Chataika
Fresh Produce International Ltd

China, Laxmibai
Jalkhushi Fresh & Frozen Fish Ltd

Chohan, Chandrakant Jivanbhai
Thirst Quenchers (UK) Limited

Choi, Yuk Lam
Choi's Trading & Co Ltd

Chondrorizos, Georgios
Creative Properties and Investments Ltd
Evogue Limited

Chosen, Arthur
Chosen Enterprises Limited

Choudry, Shazad Hussain
GT Traders Ltd.

Chouhan, Harwinder Kumar
MRU Wholesale Limited

Christofi, Christopher
D D C Foods Limited

Christophi, Polly
D D C Foods Limited

Christy, Sophie Louise
Ipro Sport Corporation Limited
Ipro Sport Distribution Ltd
Ipro Sport International Ltd
Ipro Sport Medical Limited

Cianti, Gianfranco
Forward Moving Limited

Cifci, Mecit
Ozlem Limited

Cigdem, Kenan
Nazar Wholesale Limited

Cimenlik, Ilker
First Food Ltd

Clark, Andrew
Frobishers Juices Limited

Clark, Philip
Beverage Brothers Limited

Clark, Richard Michael
RMGL Ltd
RMGL Trading Limited

Clark, Sean
Grillburger Holdings Limited

Clarke, Lesley Jane
Acquisto Limited

Clarke, Tanya Maria
Seedlip Ltd

Clatworthy, Adrian John Allen
MX365 Energy Ltd

Clavijo, Eduardo Jose
CCM Enterprises Limited

Clement, Roy
MBW Traders Ltd

Clydesdale, Mark James
First Fruits Drinks Ltd

Cole, Paul Jeremy
Tas Services UK Limited

Cole, Tone Louise Stuart
Tas Services UK Limited

Coleman, David John
Colemans ABC Ltd

Coleman, Jasmine Elaine
Montann Limited

Coleman, Teresa Ann
Colemans ABC Ltd

Colman, Catherine
Active Protein Limited

Colman, Max
Active Protein Limited

Connor, Andrew Paul
A & A Wines Limited

Constantine Palathis, Sharron
Jasmine Blue Ltd
Nova Wholesale Ltd
Willow World Ltd

Cooper, Steven William
Artisan Drinks Co Ltd

Cordwell, Mark
Fitness Prostar Ltd

Correia, Belisa Enide de Oliveira
Afromax Ltd

Correia, Telmo Monteiro
Afromax Ltd

Cotter, Stephen Francis
Third Eye Nutrition Ltd

Coulson, Andrew David
Tasman Bay Foods Europe Ltd

Covaliuc, Maria
MD Investgroupp Ltd

Craig, Ian Alexander
MM Global Citrus Limited

Crawley, Charles Murray
Anytime Drinks Limited

Crecan, Elena
Ana Express Ltd

Crompton, Helen Jane
Montann Limited

Crossland, David
Henry Mitchell & Sons Limited

Crossland, Stephen
Henry Mitchell & Sons Limited

Croston, Timothy John
Cabana Soft Drinks Limited
DJ Drink Solutions Limited
Adrian Mecklenburgh Limited
Vimto (Out of Home) Limited

Cubuk, Arin Necmi
Paramount Food and Drink (UK) Ltd.

Cubuk, Yalcin
Paramount Food and Drink (UK) Ltd.

Cudalb, Vladislav
Albert Altima Trade House Ltd

Cullinane, Michael Dennis
Crop's Foods Ltd.

Cummiskey, James
Failte Wholesale Limited

Cummiskey, Margaret
Failte Wholesale Limited

Curtis, Michael James
Drink Warehouse UK Limited

Cutrale F, Rosana
Burlingtown UK Limited

Cutrale Junior, Jose Luis
Burlingtown UK Limited

Cutrale, Graziela
Burlingtown UK Limited

Cutrale, Jose Henrique
Burlingtown UK Limited

Cutrale, Jose Luis
Burlingtown UK Limited

Czar, Cristian
Czar & Co (UK) Limited

D'auria, Alberto
D'Auria Brothers Ice Cream and Catering

D'auria, Alfonso
D'Auria Brothers Ice Cream and Catering

Dadial, Inderjit Singh
Cali Juices Limited

Daghstani, Zaid
Zaid & Besher Ltd

Dagnell, Stephen Howard
Baldwin's Sarsaparilla Limited

Dahdal, Anas
Massafood Ltd

Dallas, Edward John Henry
Anytime Drinks Limited

Dallas, Matilda Charlotte
Freestar Drinks Ltd

Dalton, Jonathan Charles
Bloomsbury Drinks Ltd

Daniel, Brian
Active Protein Limited

Danin, Max
Brighton Brew Co Ltd

Daryanani, Rakesh Ishwar
Drinks R Us Limited
Drinkslynx Limited
Simply Spirits Limited

Davenport, Christopher Mark
Great British Beverages Ltd

Davey, Emma Caroline
Ideal Lincs Limited

Davey, Paul MacKenzie
Ideal Lincs Limited

Davey, Richard MacKenzie
Ideal Lincs Limited

Davidson, Mark
Artisan Drinks Co Ltd

Davies, Billie Georgina
Drink Fitness Ltd

Davies, Lee Raymond
Street Food Solutions UK Ltd

Davies, Malcolm
J.C.Davies & Hall Limited

Davies, Richard Glyn
House Water Limited

Davison, Angus James
Aduna Limited

Dawson, Peter Maxwell
Dawsons (Wales) Limited

Day, Susannah Clare
The Social Drinking Co Ltd

De Alwis, Buddhika
Buddthi Ltd

De Barros, Anabella
Aquabella London Ltd

De Ruosi, Domenico
Hoversy Technologies Ltd

De Santana Pereira Couto, Alexandre Alan
Couto & Machado Ltd

Decodt, Stuart
Zero Options Ltd

Dede, Mahmut
Juice Junkie London Limited

Delbaere, Michel
Crop's Foods Ltd.

Delbaere, Pieter Anthony
Crop's Foods Ltd.

Demeter, Daniel
Unicorn Foodline Ltd

Demir, Erdogan
London Maya Sandwich Limited

Demirarslan, Kazim
Aroma Soft Drinks & Water Ltd

Demirkaya, Mehmet
Golden Fastfood Limited

Deng, Xingzhong
UK Brighton Food & Nutrition Research Centre

Deniz, Guney
MCIA Ltd

Dennis, Michel
Coot Service Ltd

Deral, Osman
Smart Buyer Wholesale Limited

Derbas, Wajih
Al-Shahba Ltd

Desai, Purushottam Pandurang
Drea Ltd

Devi, Jesvinder
Go Fresh Ltd

Devin, John
Pinnacle Drinks Limited

Dhami, Aaron Rico Singh
Lync Direct Limited

Dhami, Jagdeep Singh
F.R.D Wholesale Limited

Dhanji, Mahesh Devshi
Best Trading One Limited

Dhingra, Dev
DNG Group Ltd

Dhingra, Priya
DNG Trading Ltd

Dhirani, Hasnein
Wild Cat Distribution UK Ltd
Wild Cat Energy Drink Ltd

Dholakia, Kirit
Kadey Limited

Dholliwar, Sonya
Stockwell Beverages Ltd

Di Costanzo, Davide
Hubit General Trading Ltd

Dimitrov, Antoan Lyubomirov
5of5 Juices Ltd

Dincer, Victoria
Eda Quality Foods North UK Ltd

Diop, Mamadou Laye
Sunugal Trading Limited

Dirie, Mohamud Somalia
Al Kass General Trading Ltd

Disu, Muhammed Ajolaoluwa Daniel
T's Dazzling Delicious Sweets Ltd

Disu, Oluwatosin Abdulrahman
T's Dazzling Delicious Sweets Ltd

Dixon, Callum Robert William
Evo Fit Ltd

Dixon, Oliver Thomas
Modern Contradiction Limited

Dobrik, Claudiu
Aur'a Natural Gold Water Ltd

Dockar, Neil Kelvin
Usmoothie Ltd
Usqueeze Limited

Dodhia, Tushar
Eldoflora Limited

Doherty, Desmond
Football Special Ltd

Donat, Gerard
Usedsoft Ltd

Donkor, Gertrude
New Kumasi Market 2 Ltd

Donmez, Yildiray
Anatolian Foods Ltd
Anatolian Limited

Donnelly, Heath
Freshwater Direct Limited

Donovan, David
Storesrealm Limited

Donovan, John Daniel
Storesrealm Limited

Dore, Christopher
Fernhill Wholesale Ltd

Dos Santos, Custudio Jose
Alivini (North) Limited
Alivini Co Ltd

Dove, George Arthur
Nordic Life Water UK Limited

Downer, Ornel Emanuel
Inside Out Life Drinks Ltd

Dragusin, Literas
My Smoothies Co Limited

Draisey, Stephen Michael
Active Protein Limited

Drnec, Harry
RTH Healthcare PLC

Duan, Rui Ming
Dragon Rise Limited

Dudley, Mark Jonathon Cheyney
J.C. Dudley & Co. Ltd

Dudley, Michael Richard Cheyney
J.C. Dudley & Co. Ltd

Duffy, Anthony
Topstop Wholesalers Limited
Waltrix Publishing Ireland Ltd

Durkin, Gary
W D L Wholesale Limited

Durrani, Daoud
Pure Pom Ltd

Durrani, Nelo
Pure Pom Ltd

Dussek, Steven Charles
Dan International (UK) Limited

Duxbury, Stephen James
V.A. Whitley & Co. Limited

Dyttwach, Artur
Ammart Ltd

Edgar, Simon Toby Pennington
Natural Welsh Water Limited
Water Wellbeing Limited
Watercoolers Southern Limited

Edwards, Howard Ian
Energy Drinks Ltd

Ekeocha, Chinedu Jude
C. J. Walls Trading UK Limited

El Basyouni, Omar
Farida Import Export Ltd

El-Hamdoon, Ibrahim
Emara Soft Drinks Ltd

El-Mohbi, Hiba
Numba UK Limited

El-Yafi, Khaled
The Berry Juice Co Ltd

Elangovan, Saravanan
Saravanan Traders (UK) Ltd

Eleftheriou, Eleftherios
Liverpool & Oriental Trading Co Ltd

Elemide, Olufemi Tolulope
Tolmid International Ltd

Ellingham, Joy
Fresh Produce Imports UK Ltd

Ellmann, Lenka
Veg & City Drinks Limited

Elwerfalli, Amin
Evrywater Ltd

Elyafi, Ghias
The Berry Juice Co Ltd

Emini, Dea
Stonefruit Ltd

Enchev, Lyubomir
Big Horn UK Ltd

Encheva, Gergana
Big Horn UK Ltd

Ender, Nihat
Sun Exotic Wholesale Ltd

Enok, Basil
Wine City Limited

Enwerem, Wilson
Wine City Limited

Eren, Erkan
Blue Trading International Ltd

Esat, Adam Yusuf
Seiyas Watercoolers Ltd

Escorcio Machado, Lino
Couto & Machado Ltd

Esteves, Joao Paulo de Matos Tavares
Red Bull Co Ltd

Evangelopoulos, Nickolas
The Pure Juice Co Ltd

Evans, Oliver William Roderick
The Santa Monica Co Ltd

Evans, Stephen John
Peregrine Welsh Water Limited

Fair, Nicholas William
Browett & Fair Ltd

Falconetti, Salvatore
Falcos Food Ltd

Faqir Zada, Ameed
Faqir Billionaire Ltd

Farisy, Haidar Al
Mock Drink Co Ltd

Farkas, Csaba
Wolf Wholesale Limited

Farley, Leanne
Drink Warehouse UK Limited

Faulkner, Terence Henry
Leathams Limited

Faure Rolland, Andrea
Bedrock Trade Ltd

Fayyaz, Asmat
AFZ Trade Ltd

Fearis, Amy Louise
Fearis Beverages Ltd

Feher, Zoltan
Zolex Global Limited

Feildorf, Mette Marie
CPH Games UK Limited

Felix, Mara Gisela Pestana
Mercado Da Saudade Ltd

Ferchichi, Zied
Sublime Corporation Limited

Fernando, Joseph Reginold
Patrick Fernando & Sons UK Ltd

Fernando, Krishco
Choice Asia Ltd
Freedom Sale Ltd

Ferreira Falcao Chantre, Malik Mauro
DMK Wholesale Ltd

Ferris, Brynmor Joe
Raw Is More Ltd.

Ficsor, Laszlo
Budaquelle Beverages International Ltd

Fine, David Elias
Golden Pride Export Limited

Finlay, Laura
Nekta Food & Juice Bar Ltd

Fiordilino, Brigidino
H Two Eau International Ltd

Fishburn, Andrew
78 Degrees Limited

Fisher, Hannah Magdaline
The Start-Up Drinks Lab Ltd
Tongue in Peat Limited

Fleming, Kristian Richard
Condimental Ltd

Fletcher, Gillian
Fletcher's Fruit & Veg Ltd

Fletcher, Joseph James
Fletcher's Fruit & Veg Ltd

Fletcher, Madeline
Fletcher's Fruit & Veg Ltd

Folkes, Patrick John Surtees
CBD Globe Distributors Ltd

Folkman, David Thomas
Elderbrook Drinks Limited

Fomychov, Andrew
Acqua Nordica Ltd

Forczek, Akos
Top Selection Limited

Ford, Hayley Louise
The Good Gut Guys Ltd

Fotheringham, George Andrew
Hydra Cubed Limited

Fourie, Nina
Miwater Ltd

Fox, Andrew Marcus
Bot Trading Co Ltd

Fox, Vincent James
Green Ambition Limited

Frank, Nathaniel
Nacho Juice Limited

Frank, Osbourne Victor
Caribbean Trade Ltd

Franke, Teresa Elizabeth
Ferment Revolution Limited

Frarenganadaayer, Visvanadane
Abel Service Ltd

Fremel, David Paul
Aquaid Franchising Limited

Freud, George
Emmunity Limited

Friedman, Menachem Michael
C & M Wholesale Limited

Friedman, Yoel Elimelech
C & M Wholesale (UK) Limited

Froggatt, Hugh Francis
Talbot & Barr Limited

Fugard, William
Gusto Organic Ltd

Fukova, Ildaz
Star International Ltd

Fuller, Alan John
Eatwell Catering Contractors (Norwich)

Furze, James Robert
Furze Young Limited
Thremhall Limited

Gafsi, Ali
AG Fresh Produce Limited

Gagneja, Radha Nagrecha
Ahara Ventures Ltd
Zanzi Products Limited

Ganan Burgoa, Veronica
The Cafe Collective UK Trading Co Ltd

Ganatra, Mahek
Ace Incorporation Ltd

Garba, Kabir Bakori
Ladeo Limited

Garcia Perez, Sebastian
Franklin 1886 Limited

Garcia Soto, Maria Cristina
Sotomayor Imports Limited

Gardner, Madelyn
Numba UK Limited

Garner, Reece
JustGeneralTradingServices Ltd

Garrad, Thomas Edward
Healthy Hydration Limited
Ipro Sport Distribution Ltd
Quench Factory Limited

Gasiorowski, Damian Krzysztof
RDM Polish Food Ltd

Gauger, Jochen Rudolf
Nacho Juice Limited

Gec, Murat
Anatolian Foods Ltd
Anatolian Limited

Gedeou, Leonidas
Mezin Distribution UK Limited

Genkatharan, Mailvaganam
Saga Trading Ltd

Georgiades, Anastassis Christos
Adamson's Drinks Ltd.

Geraghty, Aidan Anthony
Aquaid Franchising Limited

Gerrard, Clare Susannah
Ferment Revolution Limited

Ghali, Tareq Ashraf Fouad
Unite Foods Trading Limited

Ghani, Ahmed Irfan
Prestwich Catering & Wholesale Ltd

Ghani, Nakash
Brand Distributors Limited
Namar Limited

Ghuman Begum, Azrar Ahmed
A A Suppliers Ltd

Giles, Martin
Ion Distribution Ltd

Gill, Avtar
AKKG Enterprise Limited

Gill, Salinder Kaur
Jeet (UK) Limited

Goble, John Mark
N & J Wholesale Foods Limited

Godinet, Rachael
The Juice Warrior Ltd

Godley-Maynard, Sally
Alfresco Drinks Limited

Gogar, Amrit
Ariana International Ltd

Goggins, Peter
Castle Warehouse Management Ltd

Gohir, Amandeep
Gohir Soft Drinks Ltd
A Gohir Soft Drinks UK Limited

Goldney, Darren Paul
Acquisto Limited

Goldsmith, Richard
Moju Ltd

Gollu, Dursun
Classic Catering (UK) Ltd

Gonera, Seweryn Stefan
Going Ahead Ltd

Gordon, Christopher John
Condimental Ltd

Gordon, Hamish Christian
The Driver's Drinks Co Ltd

Gorog, Ferenc
Gorog Trading Limited

Gors, Jordan
Sativatech Ltd

Gosling, Darren
Log Cabin Fruits Ltd

Gottschalk, Jane Elizabeth
Jax Coco UK Ltd.

Gouhar, Mohamed
S & M (Wholesale Supplies) Ltd

Gourlay, Ross McLean
Acquisto Limited

Gowland, Ricci Francesca
Essential Juices Ltd

Gracey, Fionnuala
Lake Shore Distributors Ltd

Gracey, Patrick
BG Drinks Ltd

Grant, Cary
Bravocservices Ltd

Gray, Julia Sarah Ann
Lore & Truth Ltd

Gray, Matthew
Cambridge Juice Co. Limited

Gray, Robin MacEwan
Middleton Wholesale Limited

Gray, Stephen David
Supermalt UK Limited

Green, Kevin
Jays Trading Ltd

Griffiths, Gareth Rhys
Crux Energy Drinks Ltd

Groce, John
Netto Stores Limited

Grosch, Tomas
Hell Beverages UK Ltd

Grosskopf, Pinchas
Vidi Vici Trading Ltd

Grozdanov, Zvonko
Macedo (UK) Limited

Gudka, Millan Mahendra
Zumi Natural Limited

Guglielmi, Giosue
HDL Trading Limited

Guimba, Rose Anne
Fusecutter Ltd

Gul, Mian
GM Catering Supplies Ltd

Gulliver, Martin William
GH Brands Ltd

Guo, Yiding
KML Home Limited

Guraya, Pavandeep
Pavlinko Limited

Gutierrez Gomez, Jhampoll
The Cafe Collective UK Trading Co Ltd

Gutu, Maria
Merlin's Beverages Limited

Gyonkova, Preslava
Pres & Co. Limited

Habib, MD Ahsan
Oriental Express London Ltd

Habiboglu, Murad
Eurozone Limited

Haider, Syed Zulfaqar
Polwug Trading Ltd

Haja, Mohamed Haniba
Thistle Foods Limited

Haji, Suleyman
HF Food International Ltd

Haji, Yussuf Mohamed
Unique Lines Ltd

Hakimzada, Deepak Singh
Rozana Foods Limited

Hales, Richard Louis
Gerrard Seel Limited

Hall, James
J.C.Davies & Hall Limited

Hall, Rebekah Marie
Botanic Lab Ltd

Halm, Henry Michael
HMH Wholesale Ltd

Halpin, Timothy John
Neubria Limited

Hamade, Naim
NXSK UK Ltd

Hannaway, Christopher John
Infinite Session Ltd

Hannaway, Thomas Eamon
Infinite Session Ltd

Hansen, Uffe Fodgaard
Aquaid Franchising Limited

Hanys, Sam
Loughborough Student Services Ltd

Harb, Semaan
East2west Traders Ltd

Hardman, Hugo Charles
Turner Hardy & Co Limited

Harley, Thomas David
MEA Health and Wellness Ltd

Haroon, Aamir
UK Traders (Leics) Ltd

Haroon, Humza
Continent Foods Limited

Harrison, Antony Richard
In2rehab Brands Limited

Harrison, Antony Thomas, Lord
Fresh Food Concepts Ltd

Hart, Samuel Lewis
Winnack and Hart Industries Ltd

Hasin, Syeda Amrana
Azka Impex Limited

Hassall, Daniel Michael
J M & D Limited

Hassan Zadeh K a Sorkhabi, Mohammad Reza
Simorgh Limited

Hassan, Omran
Welat & Othman Limited

Hastings, Max
Arthur's Juice Co Ltd

Hatsek, Gusztav Jozsef
Alpha Aliment Ltd

Hatzer, Stephen Patrick
Parkway UK Wholesale Ltd

Havaei-Ahary, Mohammad
Shake It Up! The Protein Smoothie Co Ltd

Hawgood, Craig Andrew
Taste Merchants Ltd

Hawgood, Dale Peter
Taste Merchants Ltd

Hawgood, Duncan James
Taste Merchants Ltd

Hawgood, Geoffrey Frank
Taste Merchants Ltd

Hawgood, Neville John
Taste Merchants Ltd

Hawgood, Rosemary Ann
Taste Merchants Ltd

Hayat, Abdul-Qadeer, Dr
Tradinguk55 Limited

Hayes, James
Mock Drink Co Ltd

Haystead, Gavin Michael
Codex Limited

UK Wholesalers of Soft Drinks

Hazelhurst, Jack Desmond
Alpine Water Coolers Ltd

Hazell, Peter William
Wobblegate Limited

Healey, Paul
Redgate Imports Limited

Hegde, Prasad Kumar
Savers Stop Wholesalers Ltd

Helvacioglu, Firat
Feel Group Limited

Henderson, George
Arollo Trade Ltd

Hendrickx-Butt, Maximiliana Theresia Henrica
Haltrade UK Ltd

Henshaw, Lawrence
KKS Fresh Fruits Ltd

Herbert, Mark Andrew
GH Brands Ltd

Heydon, Joardar
Buffalo Refreshments Ltd

Heydon, Stephen Lesley
Buffalo Refreshments Ltd

Heynen, Charlotte
The Cafe Collective UK Trading Co Ltd

Hicklin, Justin
Elderbrook Drinks Limited

Hill, Matthew
Ceci-Hill Limited

Hill, Stephen Gary
Water Wellbeing Limited
Waterline (UK) Ltd

Hitchins, Nicholas Charles Vedat
Caspian Black Limited

Hoare, Charles
Nature on Tap Limited

Hobhouse, Charles Howard
Punchy Drinks Limited

Hodgson, John
Drink Natural Limited

Hofstedt, John Ivar Peter
Drink Your Fruit Limited

Holland, Graham Paget
Frobishers Juices Limited

Hollier, Matthew Stuart
Vitamin Well Limited

Holloway, Duncan Norman
Nordic Life Water UK Limited

Holmes, James Harry
JFC Trading Limited

Holtham, Gregory Keith
Bevanda Solutions Limited

Holtham, Margaret Elizabeth
Bevanda Solutions Limited

Hordell, Joshua
Abantu Moringa Ltd

Horscroft, Dunneese
Easy Squeeze Limited

Horscroft, William James
Easy Squeeze Limited

Horvath, Janos Richard
Janos Horvath Ltd

Horvath, Laszlo
Endetrox Ltd.

Horvath, Patrik
Patrik Trading Ltd

Hounsell, Ronald Mark
Highland Cow Motor Home Ltd

Howard, Catherine Elizabeth
Aberystwyth Soft Drinks Ltd

Howard, Christopher Frank
Aberystwyth Soft Drinks Ltd

Hreniuc, Irina-Maria
IMH Traders Limited

Hrisca, Costica
Bucovina Cash & Carry Ltd

Huang, Fei
Shac International Limited

Huang, Po Hsin
Enzyme's Secret Limited

Hudson, Ian Robert
Lawton Cross Limited

Hughes, Christopher
Secspirits Ltd

Hugill, Jared Alexander
Cameron Soft Drinks Limited

Hull, Richard John
Export and Import Trading Ltd

Humphrey, Jordan Nicholas
Marco Polo Exotics Ltd

Hunt, Andrew David
Aduna Limited

Hunter Blair, Ronald Patrick
Stirling Castle Water Ltd

Hurst, Richard George
GSKB Ltd

Hussain, Abid
AB Catering (Blackburn) Ltd

Hussain, Ajaz Ahmad
RSS Fast Food Suppliers Ltd

Hussain, Arman
MU Distributors Ltd

Hussain, Asif
Dark Night Beverages Ltd

Hussain, Danyal Adam
Ombre Drinks Limited

Hussain, Ibrar
AB Catering (Blackburn) Ltd

Hussain, Mohammed Javed
Rahim Brothers Limited
Rahims Trading Ltd

Hussain, Naghman
Dessert Makers Limited

Hussain, Nazar
Big Brand Distributors UK Ltd

Hussain, Qadeer
Global Food (Nelson) Ltd

Hussain, Riaz
I Star Wholesale Limited

Hussain, Rizwaan
RHM Trading UK Limited

Hussain, Shaban
Global Food (Ashton) Ltd

Hussain, Shahid
901WD Ltd

Hussain, Sharif Shuhel
Rahim Brothers Limited
Rahims Trading Ltd

Hussain, Zahid
PTP Enterprise Limited

Hussein, Abdul-Fattah Ghassan Mustafa
Alicia's Coffee House Limited

Hutchinson, Matthew Robert
Mock Drink Co Ltd

Huws, Padrig
Toffoc Ltd

Hydleman, Louis Jules
Moju Ltd

Hymanson, Gary David
GDH Distribution Limited

I'anson, Toby William Crowther
Clarion Wines Limited

Ibba, Mauro Battista
Flavours of Sardinia Limited

Ibis, Mete
Jasmine Direct Limited

Ifsasse, Abderrahmane
WGTSS Ltd

Ilie, Petrut Vili
Ilie Cash & Carry Ltd

Iliesiu, Petrica
Dora Distribution Ltd

Iliya, Christiana
Mother Nature's Drinks Limited

Inbaruban, Visagaperumal
JJ Sis Limited

Inbaruban, Yalini
JJ Sis Limited

Inpanathan, Antony Sayanthan
Asi Wholesale & Retail Ltd
Panymoc Ltd
Risco Service Ltd

Inparaji, Inpanathan
Basil World Ltd
IR Global Service Ltd
Printers Service Ltd
Raji Service Ltd
Rook Trading Ltd

Intonazzo, Pietro Enrico Marco
Pem Trade Sales Ltd

Ion, Dan
La Zgarici Ltd

Iqbal, Nadeem Guffoor
Direct Traders Ltd

Irsina, Sanija
Kristals Trading Limited

Irwin, Oliver Lewis
The Whiskey and Bourbon Club Ltd

Islam, Fakhar Ul
Mashmoom International Limited

Islam, Nazrul
Total Fast Food Supplies Ltd

Ismat, Ahmad Jawid
Amou Limited

Ismat, Ghaith Imad
Haggard.Grb Ltd

Ivanova, Daniela Yordanova
GI Food Group Limited

Ivanova, Silvana Simeonova
Number One Water Ltd

Iwaniak, Marta
M & M Emerald Ltd

Jabbar, Adil
Feeders Foods Wholesale Ltd

Jackson, Curtis Roy David
Shelby Co Vending Limited

Jackson, John Haydon
JA & MD Limited

Jackson, Jonathan Charles
Cheti & Co Holdings Limited
Cheti & Co Limited

Jackson, Shelley
Jacksons Milk Deliveries Ltd

Jaf, Sarwat Fateh
Orbit Food Ltd

Jagtenberg, Karel Albert
Just Aqua Ltd.

Jagtenberg-Bakker, Maria Rika Christiana
Just Aqua Ltd.

Jahan, Sitwat
Arsi Soft Drinks Limited

Jahanpour, Hassan Rohani
West Green Supply Ltd

Jakimavicius, Egonas
Lithuanian Beer Limited

Jalil, Kamal
Kepenek Food Ltd

Jameel, Mohammad
Avigail Dairies Limited
Avigail Limited

James, Justin
Rio Mata Atlantica Limited

James, Mark Peter
Franklin 1886 Limited

Jameson-Card, Louis
Jameson's Trading Ltd

Jamieson, Aaron Colin
No Meat No Worries Limited

Jandu, Kuranveer Singh
Nootrilix Limited

Janere, Benedicta
Janere UK Limited

Jankowski, Pascal
Roxane UK Limited

Jarvis, Carla
Superyacht Supplies Limited

Jarvis, Ian
Superyacht Supplies Limited

Jasinskaite, Jurate
JJ Import/Export Ltd

Javed, Mohammed Omair
GT Traders Ltd.

Javed, Salman
Five Star Cash & Carry Ltd

Jayasekera, Thilanka Isuru
Colbury Limited

Jeevathasan, Pasupathypillai
Thass Ltd

Jensen, Lars
Supermalt UK Limited

Jeyaseelan, Antony Suthagaran
Hatton Wholesale Ltd

Jichev, Bojidar
Bia Trade Ltd

Jimenez, David Santos
Thames Wholesale Ltd

Jin, Fanao
Vangoo Enterprise Holding Ltd

Jinadu, Olaide Olubunmi
Tolmid International Ltd

Jithenthrakumar, Selvarajah
RSS Fast Food Suppliers Ltd

Johansson, Bjorn Filip Botvid
Eliya Europe Ltd

John, Tessa Elizabeth Jayne
Rarewood (London) Limited

Johnson, Adebowale
413 Limited

Johnson, Andrew Stuart
Nichols Dispense (S.W.) Ltd

Johnson, Jacqueline Karen
Fruitex Limited

Johnson, Simon Harcourt
Czar & Co (UK) Limited

Jolly, Roger Melville
Gold Star Soft Drinks Westcountry Ltd

Jones, Catherine Susan Marian
Jones Bros. 1877 Ltd

Jones, Craig Ian
Elderbrook Drinks Limited

Jones, Gillian
Clean-Coco Ltd

Jones, Henry David
Jones Bros. 1877 Ltd

Jones, Henry Llewellyn Michael
Jones Bros. 1877 Ltd

Jones, Nicholas Keith Arthur
House Kitchen Limited

Jones, Samuel
Under The Sun Europe Ltd

Jorgensen, John Michael
Northern Lights Ltd.

Joseph, Suresh Senthil Nathan
Shruthinaya Ltd

Josephs, Joanne Elizabeth
Domore Imports Ltd

Judd, Susan Anne
C1 Trading Ltd

Junaid, Mohammed
Pick N Deliver Ltd

Junior, Francisco Flaminio Dos Santos
Refribrit Ltd

Juozapaityte, Juste
Alitasa Ltd

Kabir, Yasir
Ladeo Limited

Kaden, Tim Peter
KSY Juice Blends UK Ltd

UK Wholesalers of Soft Drinks

Kadir, Anwar Muhammed
Kurd Scot Imports & Exports Ltd

Kadir, Debbie
Wades & Ellie Ltd

Kaggwa, Jane Nakalanzi
Aquavita II UK Limited

Kahraman, Ferdi
Hero Catering Supplies Limited

Kakaire, Edwin
Nile Nutrients Ltd

Kakkar, Harmit Singh
Kakkar Enterprises Ltd

Kakoulli, Nikolas
Sepandero Venturi UK Limited

Kalaiyarasan, Gajendran
KG Wholesale Ltd

Kalavady, Thirudan
EWF Wine Force Ltd

Kamau, John
Squishy Drinks Limited

Kanadia, Bhavna Sanchez
Jeeva Natural UK Ltd

Kanagalingam, Vimalakkannan
Link International Ltd
SVM Trading Ltd

Kanagaratnam, Vimalan
Shark Trading Ltd

Kanal, Soner
Navson Ltd

Kanamia, Faruk
Afrimalt UK Ltd

Kanamia, Hanif
Afrimalt UK Ltd

Kanamia, Ibrahim
Afrimalt UK Ltd

Kandasamy, Mohanasegaram
Indigo Private Ltd
KPN Wholesale Ltd

Kandasamy, Niroshankar
Nirajen Ltd

Kanter, Andrew Mark
Modern Contradiction Limited

Kapadia, Amir Tayebali
Lam Cash and Carry Limited

Kapadia, Rafique Amir
Lam Cash and Carry Limited

Kaplan, Olcay
A2Z Fruit & Veg Ltd

Karadag, Erdal
O & E Food Ltd

Karakilcik, Mutlu
Adanali Limited

Karaoglan, Hasan
Utku Emre Ltd

Karatay, Tahsin
Anadolu Catering Limited

Karavadra, Anil
N & B Foods Exeter Limited

Karavadra, Nagajan Duda
N & B Foods Exeter Limited

Karawalli, Hasnain
The Mocktail Company (2018) Ltd

Karawalli, Zainab
The Mocktail Company (2018) Ltd

Kareem, Othman Nooraldin Abdul
Tazah Ltd

Kars, Emre
Turkish Kitchinn Wholesale Ltd

Karsli, Giray
GCA Foods Edinburgh Ltd

Karunakara Arachchige, Kasun Tharindu Madushanka
Kasgo Limited

Karunarajah, Balasomasuntharam
GVK Wholesale Ltd

Karuppiah, Sakthivel
Apollo Fruit & Veg UK Ltd

Kataria, Rajni
Temple Wines (Cash & Carry) Ltd

Katende, Uzaifa
Estelon Holdings Limited

Katende, Uzaifa
Polat International Ltd

Kathiravelu, Yogalingam
OK Brothers Ltd

Kathiresan, Rajamohan
Connect Waze Private Limited

Kaur, Anuvinder
Stockwell Wholesalers Limited

Kaur, Ravinder
Globe Imex Ltd

Kavchak, Ivan
Sloane Avenue Group Ltd

Kavita, Kavita
MRU Wholesale Limited

Kay, Mark Phillip
Warren Farm Shop Ltd

Kayani, Muhammad Ikram
Majestic Foods Limited

Kazilionis, Mindaugas
Kaz Enterprise Limited

Kearns, Stephen
Cawston Press Limited

Keijsers, Andreas Ruben
Jax Coco UK Ltd.

Keith, Kieron
Boomshakes Ltd

Kendall, William Bruce
Better Tasting Drinks Co. Ltd
Cawston Press Limited

Kent, Helen Susan
Bristol Spirits Limited

Kerby-Steele, Oak
Simple Nature Limited

Kerimiyan, Pando
U.D.C. Wholesale Ltd

Khalaf, Jwan
Native Leaf Ltd

Khalid, Fukhera
Stefan Frank Ltd

Khalid, Hassan
Fresh N Green Ltd

Khalid, Javed
JK Manchester Ltd

Khalid, Rahim
Drinks Europe Ltd
Exel Distribution Ltd

Khan, Ahmed
Cityfresh Limited

Khan, Aliza
S & B Wholesale Limited

Khan, Basharat
Major Foods Limited

Khan, Feisal Mehmood
Panton Ventures Limited

Khan, Habib Ur Rehman
Eurostar HRK Ltd

Khan, Mohammed
Manor Wholesale Ltd

Khan, Mohammed Farooq
Winewise Ltd

Khan, Muhammad Saad
Biofresh Cosmos Ltd

Khan, Samaera
Freshfield Exotics Ltd

Khan, Sayed
Arif Rahim Ltd
Realmix Beverage Ltd

Khan, Sohail
One Stop Fruit & Veg Limited

Khan, Zafar
Daneisa Ltd

Khanna, Ritika
Premium Drinks Distribution Ltd

Khatun, Sabia
S & F Distribution Ltd

Khemdoudi, Mohamed Saber
Fruitfullest Ltd.

Khimani, Davendra Parbat
Ahara Ventures Ltd
Zanzi Products Limited

Khirani, Sid Ahmed
Assala Limited

Khromyak, Yaroslav
Sloane Avenue Group Ltd

Kilic, Huseyin
International Catering & Foods Ltd

Kim, Jongdae
Unione Trading Europe Ltd

King, Andrew Saulez
Elegantly Spirited Limited

King, Julian
Cooray King Holdings Limited

King, Justin Francis St Clair
Cooray King Holdings Limited

Kinsey-Quick, Kenneth
Gentian Global Ltd

Kirk, Adrian Christopher
Neubria Limited

Kisakye, Rose
Chosen Enterprises Limited

Kochan, Mustafa
Bornova Import Export Limited

Kodoud, Weaam
Caju Drinks Ltd

Kokorashvili, Zura
Georgian Wine Co Ltd

Koles, Laszlo
Laz and Kol Ltd

Konecsnyi, Tamas
Watt Energy Drink (UK) Ltd

Kooner, Gurchetan Singh
Belgard Trading Ltd

Koongahawattage, Somalatha Ariyarathna
Panymocc Limited

Korakkottil, Mohamed
Green Warehouse Hodge Hill Ltd
Green Warehouse Washwood Ltd

Kosemusul, Mahmut
MKM Group Trading & Investment Ltd

Koszegi, Zsolt
Crescent Moon World Project Ltd.

Kourtoglou, Athanasios
Tomatelios UK Ltd

Kozlovskyy, Volodymyr
Meadow Harvest Ltd

Kraatz, Klaus-Peter
Usedsoft Ltd

Kristensson, Ted Arthur
Vitamin Well Limited

Kruba, Ladislav
Primacena Ltd.

Kuhn-Zowada, Anna
Europol Trade Ltd.

Kular, Ekroop
Tropical Produce Limited

Kular, Joginder Singh
Tropical Produce Limited

Kumar, Ashok
UK Star Services Limited

Kumar, Gaurav Kukar
Key Traders Ltd

Kumar, Mukesh
BS and Sons London Limited

Kumari, Soma
Sris International Ltd

Kunicka-Michalak, Walentyna Oliwia
K.M Food & Drinks Ltd

Kutlu, Hasan Ertekin
R.A. Trading Limited

Kuzu, Metin
Bogazici Ltd

Kyofa Matovu, Dantwo
Fruits & Vegetables Ltd.

Lacerda Santana, Weuber
Acai Express Ltd

Ladhar, Rosh
Budget Logistics Ltd

Laginaf, Mohsin
B4Sport Ltd.

Lai, Alex Kwun Hyn
Raylex Ltd

Lait, Michael Adrian
MLI Trading Limited

Lakman, Harjit Singh
Frutex Limited

Lamb, Thomas William Charles
Pure Organic Drinks Limited

Lamba, Sahej Kaur
Sahej UK Limited

Lameire, Daniel Jeffery
Route 33 Limited

Land, Stephen Thomas
Swallow Dispensed Drinks Solutions

Langella, Carmine
Carmine Ciao & Co Ltd

Langlais, Tyrell Neil
Earths Greatest Ltd

Lardent, Jo
Snackpax Distribution Limited

Lascaris, Reginald
Gentian Global Ltd

Lasme, Nathanael
GO4 Beverages Limited

Lathia, Kapil
WLL Wholesale Ltd

Laughland, Andrew Iain Stewart
Drink Free Ltd

Lavender, David
Collette International Limited

Lavender, Kathryn Mary
Collette International Limited

Lawanson, Olukolajo
Tricape UK Ltd

Lawlor, Fiona Jane
The Social Drinking Co Ltd

Lax Banon, Enrique
House Kitchen Limited

Lazem, Ali, Dr
Like Like Ltd

Lazurca, Mihaela
L'Azur Ltd

Lazurca, Stefania Roxana
L'Azur Ltd

Le Morellec, Alexis
Boukashka Ltd

Leatham, Mark
Leathams Limited

Leatham, Oliver Nigel
Leathams Limited

Lecointe-Gayle, Andre
Mane and Rose Limited

Lederer, Paul
Nature on Tap Limited

Lee, Lisa
Inspire Drinks Ltd

Lee-Own, Colin
Sunspice UK Limited

Leech, Eliyohu Simchoh
ESL Trading Ltd

Leet-Cook, Charles
Moju Ltd

Leonard, Anthony Alfred John
Aster Service Ltd

Leuca, Liviu
L & D Services UK Limited

Lever, Thomas
Arollo Trade Ltd

Lever, Thomas Oliver Ellwood
Artis Trade Ltd

UK Wholesalers of Soft Drinks

Levin, Brett
Golden Pride Export Limited

Levine, Brian Colin
Manchester Drinks Co Ltd

Lewis, Ryan
W D L Wholesale Limited

Lewis, Sharifa
Symphony Fine Foods Ltd

Li, Jing
KML Home Limited

Li, Rong
Hua Lin Trade Import Limited

Lim, Qiuji
Gloucester Wholesale Ltd

Lindfield, Naomi Nicholette
Bevtec Services Limited

Lindfield, Paul
Bevtec Services Limited

Linnell, Darren Keith
Aspire Brands Int Ltd.
Aspire Drinks Limited

Lipman, Michael
Huskiblu Ltd

Liu, Kai Manager
Alchemy Biotics Limited

Lobo de Rezende Neto, Olavo
Super Food Base Ltd

Lockwood, David Jonathan
Bella Refreshments Ltd.

Loftsson, Birgir
Acqua Nordica Ltd

Loudon, Marcus Frederick
Lawton Cross Limited

Lozowski, Marek
MSM Foods Limited
Najpol Ltd

Luckova, Nikola
Luckova Ltd

Lumumba, Kimbulu-Ernest
TTS Private Ltd

Luscombe, Timothy Lawrence
Club Consultants Ltd

Lutas, Raul Catalin
Panda Rolls Ltd

Ly, Andy Hai
Ly Hong Limited

Lyaoui, Yachine
Yachinelyaoui Limited

Lykidis, Evangelos
Hellenic Grocery Limited

M'bow, Birahim
Hesana Ltd

M'bow, Lamine
Hesana Ltd

Maalej, Niez
Mediterranean International Ltd

MacDonald, David Graeme
Cellar Twelve Limited

MacLennan, Alistair
Grillburger Holdings Limited

Maciaszek, Mateusz Stanislaw
Passa Distribution Ltd
Passa Wholesale Ltd

Mack, Christopher Peter
MM Global Citrus Limited

Maggiora, Luca Giorgio
Carnaby and Kingly Limited

Maggs, Kathryn Jane
First Fruits Drinks Ltd

Maguire, Tom
Zero Options Ltd

Mahboob, Noreen
MB Drinks Ltd

Maheswaran, Pirasaanthan
PMahesh Trading Limited
Pirm Trading Limited

Mahinc, Bernadette
Angel Global Export Ltd

Mahmood Raja, Arshad
P N New Ltd

Mahmood, Akhtar
Maira Trade Ltd

Mahmood, Faisal
FIBM Wholesale Ltd

Mahmood, Sheikh Sabir
Evershine Trading Limited
Ideal Trading Limited

Mahmood, Talat
Exoshell UK Ltd

Mahmoud, Mohammed Ali
Babylon Foods Limited

Main, Steven James
ABZ Food Ltd

Maina, Samwel
Intercontinental Trade Solutions Ltd

Maiwish, Zunaira
AB (Cheshire) Group Ltd

Majithia, Sarjool
Grouptype Limited

Majithia, Sonia
Grouptype Limited

Maju, Thusi
Thusi Wholesale Ltd

Makowska, Elzbieta
Syphony Water Limited

Makri, Stavroula
KSY Juice Blends UK Ltd

Maksymowicz, Martin
Polski Wholesale Limited

Malhi, Jaswant
FMCG Express Limited

Malik, Niayyir
Qahhar Drinks Ltd

Malik, Sohail Ahmed
UK Wings Limited

Malinowska, Malgorzata
Kasgo Limited

Maljee, Abdul Hak
Fast Car Sales Services Ltd

Maljee, Muhammad
Fast Car Sales Services Ltd

Mammadov, Anar
Global Vitality Ltd.

Man, James
J Water Disabled Children Ltd

Manak, Gurdip Singh
Drinks2u Ltd

Mandy, Francois
Ets Mandy SPRL Ltd.

Mangrio, Nehal
China Cambrian Limited

Mann, Narinder
Primacy Trade Ltd

Manning, James David
Shack Drinks Limited

Manning, Richard
Shack Drinks Limited

Manson, Alastair James
Next Gen Drinks Limited

Maragh, Patrick
Castleton International Ltd

Maraslioglu, Ali
Fruit & Veg 2 U Ltd

Marcelin, Jason
Ice Guys Ltd

Mariyan, Iyanarlingam
RSS Fast Food Suppliers Ltd

Markham, Graham
Real Natural UK Ltd

Maroof, Shazia
HT Sweets (UK) Limited

Marshall, Chris
Bella Refreshments Ltd.

Martin, Charles Edward
Burrows & Sturgess Ltd

Martin, Emma Elizabeth
Burrows & Sturgess Ltd

Martinelli, Adryan
51 Plus Ltd

Martinelli, Chantal Lara Francesca
51 Plus Ltd

Martocsan, Attila
Attila Martocsan Ltd

Massamba, Ntsimba Monica Elvire
Cybel Ltd

Massamba, Nzouzi Julia Trecy
Cybel Ltd

Mateschitz, Dietrich
Red Bull Co Ltd

Mathasing, Rahul
Loughborough Student Services Ltd

Mathiyalagan, Manivannan
Mani Mathi Trading Ltd

Matto, Hardeep Singh
Boisson Limited
Regal Trade Limited

Mattu, Parmjit
Bambu Drinks Limited

Maude-Roxby, Richard Gay
Alfresco Drinks Limited

Mavin, Daniel Arthur John
Sow Limited

Mavin, Victoria Louise
Sow Limited

Mayo, James Robert
SOS Hydration Limited

Mazurkiewicz, Jakub
Moon Lynx Ltd

Mboob, Ebrima
Jamarec UK Limited

McCosh, Benjamin James
Total Refreshment Solutions Ltd

McCusker, Hilary
Highland Cow Motor Home Ltd

McDaid, Edward
Football Special Ltd

McDaid, Seamus
Football Special Ltd

McDonagh, Mark
The Juicery Ltd

McGannan, Benjamin Raymond Stanley
Natural Welsh Water Limited
Water Wellbeing Limited
Watercoolers Southern Limited
Waterline (UK) Ltd

McGhie, Andrew Baxter
Stirling Castle Water Ltd

McIver Arranz, Alejandro
Quicklemon UK Ltd

McKay, Brian Francis
Ital World Ltd

McLaughlin, Diarmaid
Season Harvest (NI) Limited

McLaughlin, Gabrielle
Season Harvest (NI) Limited

McLaughlin, Kienan
Season Harvest (NI) Limited

McNelly, Melanie Joanne
The Chiltern Mix Limited

McPhee, Peter Jonathan
House Kitchen Limited

McPherson, Ryan James
McBerries Ltd

Mechell, Alex Frederick
AB Trade Direct Ltd

Meehan, Kevin Andrew
CCM Enterprises Limited

Mehmood, Shaukat
Bedford Halal Meat & Grocceries Ltd

Melrose, Adam Roy
Bare Drinks Limited

Mendes Da Silva, David Wilson Barros
Aquabella London Ltd

Mendes Da Silva, Edson Luis Barros
Aquabella London Ltd

Menon, Resmi
Menon Naturals Ltd

Merlin, Yissochor Dov
Sips MCR Ltd

Mesu, Moshiur Karim
Suntrack Ltd

Miah, Arju
Supreme Links Limited

Miah, Kazi Mohammed Angur
Shapla Cash & Carry Ltd

Miah, Nanu Kazi Mohammed
Shapla Cash & Carry Ltd

Michaels, Simon Phillip
Lord Eden Beverages Ltd

Michanitzis, Georgios
Panopoulos Forest Ltd
Panopoulos Waters Ltd

Miller, Abigail April
Noble Naturals Ltd

Miller, Zavon
After Eight Alcohol Concierge Ltd
Magna Juice Ltd

Min, Xiao
Mightybee Limited

Miranda, Amanda Denise
Xorta Global Management Ltd

Mirza, Asif Mahmood
Hayat Supermarket Ltd

Mirza, Atif Arslan
Hayat Supermarket Ltd

Mirza, Yousaf Islam
Hayat Supermarket Ltd

Mirzo, Ali
Al-Shahba Ltd

Mishra, Harshit
The BV Group UK Limited
BVG Distributors Limited

Mocsi, Ovidiu
Merlin Distribution Limited

Modiano, Laura
M Trading Limited

Mohamad, Sabir
Oneway Trading Ltd

Mohamed Haleeldeen, Mohamed Hasme
A & H Trading Ltd

Mohammadi, Saeed
Jaguar Beverage Ltd

Mohammed, Abdirazaq Salah
Medina Food World Ltd

Mohammed, Saeed
Apollo Distribution Limited

Mohammed, Shabir
Epson Trading Limited

Mohanaraj, Paramagurusamy
Aquamarine Limited

Moidu, Musthafa Thiruvoth Peedikayil
Brilliant Beverage Co Ltd

Molla, Mohammad Kaykous
Azka Impex (London) Limited

Monroe, Kelvin
Vinroe Distribution Ltd

Monroy, Ana Marita Cruz
Tomatelios UK Ltd

Moorby, Oliver
Natural Snacking Ltd

Moosa, Ahtesham Nazir
Doorstep Desserts Distribution Ltd

Moosa, Oubed Nazir
Doorstep Desserts Distribution Ltd

Morales Moreno, Miguel
Reineta Limited

Moreton, Robin
Moreton Sweets (Wholesale) Ltd

Morgan, Huw
Top Pops Wholesaler of Soft Drinks

Morgan, Ivan Percival
Juice de Vine Limited

Morgan, Jack David
D D C Foods Limited

Morgan, Paul
Racing Greens Nutraceuticals Ltd

Morgan, Stephen John
D D C Foods Limited

Morley, Steven Adam
Elev8 Life Limited

Morris de Souza, Bethan
Zeroholic Ltd

Mortimer, Jason
Asta Barista Baby Ltd

Moxham, Clive Wilson
Leathams Limited

Mozil, Sami
Global Fresh Ltd

Mubiru, Derrick
Agrofresh Ltd

Mubiru, Fiona
Agrofresh Ltd

Mughal, Abdul Rauf
Big Star Trader Ltd
Blackbird Trader Ltd

Mughal, Mohammed Zaheer
Yashrab Ltd

Mukadam, Ebrahim Kassam
Middleton Wholesale Limited

Mukhtar, Asif
Tropical Ice (England) Ltd

Muktha, Wali
Shapla Cash & Carry Ltd

Mullen, Jason
J Mullens Ltd

Munir, Mohammed Amer
Madina Drinks Ltd

Munusamy, Raguraman, Dr
Emaya Foods Limited

Murday, Harry Sivaramen
Quick Constuction Ltd

Murphy, Sean Patrick
Longstar Trading Limited

Muruganandan, Senathirajah
Smith & Munden Ltd

Musani, Hasanali Pyaralli
HM Wholesale Supplies Limited

Musielski, Jakub
Musielski Wholesale Ltd

Muwanguzi, Isac
Chosen Enterprises Limited

Mylvaganam, Asokkumar
AMG Wholesale Ltd

Nabil, Eddib
Kheira Ltd

Nagar, Rashik
The Pure Juice Co Ltd

Nagarajah, Jesan
TVS Private Ltd

Nagrecha, Neel
Zanzi Products Limited

Nagrecha, Neel Naresh
Ahara Ventures Ltd

Nagy, David
CC Trade Ltd

Nagy, Tibor
Yorkshire Exports Limited

Nallathamby, Arulan
Nalla Sales Ltd
Sarl Import Export Mondial Ltd
Thamby Trading Ltd

Nandwani, Laxman
Inc. Trading Limited

Nanthan, Premananthini
Syon Distributors Ltd

Nantheeswaran, Sockalingam
RSS Fast Food Suppliers Ltd

Naqvi, Syed Haider Ali
Cooper & Partner Ltd

Nardali, Tulin
Nar London Limited

Narroya, Anil
Pro Nutrition Ltd

Nasreen, Salma
Shu Enterprise Ltd

Natenadze, Ioseb
Georgian Food and Beverages Ltd

Nathan Sankaran, Venkatesh
Debbie and Venky Ltd

Navarasalingam, Thushyanthan
Delta Tip Limited

Navaratnam, Selvananthan
Naturally Fresh Drink Limited

Nazir Nawab, Mohammad
Nawab Traders Limited

Nazir, Farrukh
Zauq Services Ltd

Negru, Robert Ovidiu
Carpatica International Ltd

Neill, Fraser David
Evo Fit Ltd

Nemeth, Arpad
Artesian Springs Limited

Neufelt, Panayiotis
Artathlon Beverages Limited
Artathlon Water Limited

Newport-Black, Duncan Miles
Super Tidy Drinks Limited

Newton, Micheal Steven
Newton Soft Drinks Wholesale Ltd

Nikolopoulos, Sotirios
KVC Waffles Limited

Nikolov, Alex
Welldrinks Ltd

Nisa, Gulshan
Variety Food Fair Limited

Nisar, Ali
Sabroso Food UK Ltd

Nisar, Muhammad Usman
Sheikh Super Store Ltd

Noguera, Vincent Jacques Jean Marie
Suncrops UK Limited

Nolan, Ryan-Paul
Yourchoice Wholesale Ltd

Noman, Ashar
Bedford Halal Meat & Grocceries Ltd

Norris, Stephen Hedley
More or Less Drinks Co Ltd

Norton, Valerie Christine
Val Norton Ltd

Norwood Hill, Alexander Gregor
Cordus Ltd

Novoa, Diana
Zacely Limited

Nowak, Wojciech Marek
The Beverages Group Limited

Nti-Appiah, Paulina
Global Sunshine Distribution Ltd

Nunes, Nicholas
Quinton Trading Ltd

Nur, Abdiaziz Omar
Glinter UK Ltd

Nuzhath, Hawwa
Fresh N Green Ltd

Nwokoro, Jude
J & H Global UK Ltd

O'Donoghue, Michael
Aquaid Franchising Limited

O'Kane, Matthew James
Vivid Vitality Ltd

O'Neill, Francis Austin
H & F Export Limited

O'Niel, Beau Christopher
Claddagh Food and Drink Ltd

O'Rourke, Lucy Catherine
Jones Bros. 1877 Ltd

O'Rourke, Stephen Terence
Jones Bros. 1877 Ltd

O'Shea, Brian
Paisley Drinks Co. Ltd

Obrien, Dennis Michael
Eurotrade Supply Limited

Ogden, Richard Neville
Albanblue Elementals Limited

Ogunniyi, Victoria Ibidun
The Drinks Bay Limited

Okafor, Patrick Adim
Tricape UK Ltd

Okoye, Henry
Olsson Logistics Limited

Okwaje, Echezona
MBS Ventures Limited

Olaniyan, Kofo
Firewater Merchants Ltd

Oliva, Guiseppe John
Bespoke Contracts (UK) Ltd

Olowa, Titilola Aduni
T's Dazzling Delicious Sweets Ltd

Olszewska, Alicja
Alicja Food Ltd

Oluborode, Adebanke
Riverroll Limited

Oluborode, Joshua
Riverroll Limited

Onofrei, Maricica
Onofrei Cash & Carry Ltd

Orazu, Kenechukwu Chukwuemeka
Samco Global Foods Ltd

Orazu, Virginia Uju
Samco Global Foods Ltd

Orme, Bruce Robert
Wenlock Spring Water Limited

Orme, Matthew John
Wenlock Spring Water Limited

Orme, Robert Sidney
Wenlock Spring Water Limited

Orme, Susan Margaret
Wenlock Spring Water Limited

Osei, Gloria Amoah
Natures Vitality Limited

Oteng, Samuel
Global Sunshine Distribution Ltd

Ozdil, Serhat
Ozdil UK Limited

Ozgur, Ahmet
Eren Catering Ltd

Ozturk, Mikail
MK Inter Ltd

Ozturk, Ramazan
Hayat Supermarket Ltd

Pabbi, Mohit
Britannia International Wholesalers Ltd

Padgett, Cassandra Lianne
Becsco Limited

Padgett, Scott
Becsco Limited
Bella Refreshments Ltd.

Page, Dianne Lesley
C S Drinks Ltd

Page, Stephen Bernard
C S Drinks Ltd

Page, Trevor Andrew
Loughborough Student Services Ltd

Palanivel, Saravanan
Drinksparadies Ltd

Palmer, Mark Richard
Better Tasting Drinks Co. Ltd
Cawston Press Limited

Palushi, Endrit
Frutex UK PVT Limited

Panagiotopoulos, Nikolaos
Klomar Ltd

Panayiotou, Angelos
Ch@i Drinks Ltd
Windfall Logistics Limited

Pandele, Constantin
Bio Icecream Ltd

Panessar, Kulwant Singh
Euro Globe Distributors Ltd

Panford, Eugenia Mensah
Transgh Limited

Pang, Raymond
420 Beverages Ltd

Pang, Raymond Wai-Man
Raylex Ltd

Panizzon, Oscar
The New Drinking Ltd

Panopoulos, Georgios
Panopoulos Forest Ltd

Papadimitrakopoulos, Christos
Biofresh Cosmos Ltd
Orange Be Global Ltd

Parillon, Connie Petronella
Exoteeque Limited

Parmar, Suresh
AJ Fruit & Vegetable Enterprises Ltd

Parry, Huw Dafydd
Zeroholic Ltd

Parsler, Jack
Taj Restaurant Supplies Ltd

Pasztor, Miklos
Sweetprod Ltd

Patel, Aadil, Dr
East Lancs Suppliers Ltd

Patel, Aaishah, Dr
East Lancs Suppliers Ltd

Patel, Aneesa
Budgie Juices Ltd

Patel, Arju Atul
Camelot Chilled Foods Ltd

Patel, Arjun
Atlas Halal Ltd

Patel, Atul Kantibhai
Camelot Chilled Foods Ltd

Patel, Irfan Vali
Valley Water Limited

Patel, Jignaben Hitesh
Narayan Foods Limited

Patel, Kumar
KP Global Ltd

Patel, Maulikkumar Ashokbhai
Deeti Wholesale Limited

Patel, Mohammad Iqbal
PMI Management Limited

Patel, Praful
Joo Soft Drinks Limited

Patel, Rahul
Ombre Drinks Limited

Patel, Sandip Navnitbhai
NCE Trading KFT Ltd

Patel, Shahina
East Lancs Suppliers Ltd

Patel, Shoaib
Butterfly Foods and Packaging Ltd

Patel, Zabir Mohammed
East Lancs Suppliers Ltd

Pathak, Heman
Hello Coco Limited

Pathak, Poonam
Debbie and Venky Ltd

Pearce, David Michael
Frobishers Juices Limited

Pears, Rory
Loughborough Student Services Ltd

UK Wholesalers of Soft Drinks

Pechta, Mariusz
Amedame International Ltd

Pefanis, Gerasimos
Taste of Crete Ltd

Perez Lopez, Cristian
Avic Trading Limited

Perez, Steven James Garcia
Franklin 1886 Limited

Perfect, Jonathan
Perfect Drinks Ltd

Petrova, Nadezhda
Nadban Limited

Pettersson, Samir Jonas
Vitamin Well Limited

Pezzack, Stephen Robert
GFT Retail UK Limited

Phillips, Richard Jonathan
Temperance Drinks Limited

Piagno, Silmara
Direct2door Food & Beverage Ltd.

Pillai, Sunil Soman
Delamore Trading UK Ltd

Pillayar, Sooppaiya
Buy & Sales Trading Ltd
Frosty Service Ltd
Quick World Service Ltd

Pirapatharan, Sharmala
Afro Lanka Ltd

Pires, Jose de Nobrega
Alivini (North) Limited
Alivini Co Ltd

Pirozzi, Antonio
Alivini (North) Limited
Alivini Co Ltd

Plesca, Cornel-Marius
Prod Act Ltd.

Pointon, John Lawrence
W.E.Pointon & Sons Limited

Polat, Mustafa
A2Z Fruit & Veg Ltd

Pole, Erica Emily Eva
Route 33 Limited

Pole, Warren Douglas
Route 33 Limited

Poleon, Stefan
Stefan Frank Ltd

Polyzos, Paschalis
Amphipolis Limited

Ponnuthurai, Ponneswaran
Birch Sales Ltd
PP Cash & Carry Ltd
PU Trading Ltd

Poole, Harvey David
Merchantology Ireland Ltd
Merchantology Ltd

Poole, Karen
Merchantology Ltd

Pooley, Angus Frederick
Liquidline Limited

Pooley, Gavin William
Liquidline Limited

Pooley, Matthew James
Liquidline Limited

Potts, David Neil
Potts of Goodness Limited

Potts, Michelle Dawn
Potts of Goodness Limited

Pozo Caballero, Marcos David
Wisdom of Nature Limited

Press, Oliver
Milky Milkshakes Ltd

Prince, Mina
Naturshot Limited

Pugsley, Thomas
Modern Contradiction Limited

Purslow, Iain
Premier Marketing (NW) Ltd

Purvis, Robert Kenneth Berry
Creamline Dairies Limited
Swallow Holdings Limited

Qamar, Jamil Ahmad
Nextgen Distribution Limited

Rac, Jozef
Jojo Best Coffee Ltd

Rachidi, Mohamed
E & R Fruits Limited

Radia, Rohitkumar Narendra
TSK Trade Limited

Radia, Sheetal
TSK Trade Limited

Radman, Mohammed Abdulgalil Radman
A & H Trading Ltd

Rafiq, Mohammed
ATR Catering Supplies Limited

Rafique, Mohammad Sohail
Africa Global Village. Com Ltd

Rahman, Ashfa
Alisha Fish Bazar Ltd

Rahman, Ashfaqur
YummyColombia Ltd

Rahman, Atikur
Alisha Fish Bazar Ltd

Rahman, MD Mizanur
MD Rahma Ltd

Rahman, Mahmudur
Tronika Traders Limited

Rahman, Rabia
M.R.S. Supplies Limited

Rai, Marcus
M & M European Merchants Ltd

Rainey, Simon
Canafizz Ltd

Raja, Shameem
Bargain Food and Wine Ltd

Rajani, Kassam Barkatali
Wild Cat Distribution UK Ltd
Wild Cat Energy Drink Ltd
Wildcat International Limited

Rajaratnam, Anthony Manoj
Kaluwa Ltd

Rajaratnam, Jeyakumar
BudgetForU Limited
JR Quality Service Ltd

Rajendram, Amalathas
PVS Trading Ltd

Rakhmonova, Dilafruz
Monrone Health Ltd

Ramakrishnan, Sonya
Lora Trading (Europe) Ltd

Ramalhoso, Nuno Miguel de Carvalho
Refribrit Ltd

Ramgharya, Anilbai
Eastway Cash & Carry Limited

Ramsay, Dawn Patricia
Herbs 4 Healthy Living Ltd

Ramzan, Muhammad
Rozana Foods Limited

Rana, Abdul Rahim
Gone Fresh Limited

Rasul, Amir
All Fresh Bradford Ltd

Rasul, Shazia
Ariana International Ltd

Rathi, Chaitanya
Raylex Ltd

Rathnayake Mudiyanselage, Thakshila
T & K Wholesale Ltd

Ratra, Rohit
Hermes Chariot Ltd

Rattu, Sunil
Hermes Chariot Ltd

Rehal, Shubnit Singh
Wild Cat Energy Drink Ltd

Rehman, Azhar
Kaspas Distribution Ltd

Rehman, Mazhar
Kaspas Distribution Ltd

Rehman, Qasim Ali
Kaspas Distribution Ltd

Rezazadeh Helmi, Faraz
Fanal Ltd

Ribeiro E Silva Barros, Bruno Miguel
Luso Shop Ltd

Ribes, Thomas Xavier Germain
Suncrops UK Limited

Rich, Daniel
Quando Drinks Limited

Richards, Mark Andrew
Seasons East Ltd

Richmond, Arthur William
Woodchester International Ltd

Riddles, David
Riddles Bros Limited

Riddles, Robert
Riddles Bros Limited

Ridgway, Keith Robert
GI Food Group Limited

Rife, Richard Carlos
Morinda UK Limited

Rijnders, Rob
Basecamp Brews Ltd

Rimkus, Darius
Fruit & Veg Imports Ltd

Rizvi, Rahat
Al Taj Al Malaki General Trading UK Ltd

Rizvi, Syed Intizar Haider
Soft Drink UK Limited

Roberts, Aled
R. & I. Jones Limited

Roberts, Dewi
Toffoc Ltd

Roberts, Dorothy
R. & I. Jones Limited

Roberts, Meirion
R. & I. Jones Limited

Roberts, Nicola
Theodore Global Limited

Rocca, Jordan
Carnaby and Kingly Limited

Rocha de Andrade, Jose Pedro
Indigo Traders Ltd

Rodrigues Ramos, Vera Isabel
Viserra Limited

Roeser, Charlotte
Roeser Limited

Roeser, Richard
Roeser Limited

Rogath, Lily
Ziro Ltd

Rogers, Anthony Milward
V.A. Whitley & Co. Limited

Rogers, Catherine Helen
V.A. Whitley & Co. Limited

Rogers, Christopher Mark
V.A. Whitley & Co. Limited

Rogers, Elizabeth Margaret
V.A. Whitley & Co. Limited

Rooprah, Harphjan Singh
Jeeva Natural UK Ltd

Ross, Gordon David Laing
Springwater Direct Ltd.

Rossi, Paul
Ayr Brewing Co Ltd

Roth, Robert Marius
Good Prices Ltd

Routledge, Katie
Rush Energy Drinks Ltd

Routledge, Lee
Rush Energy Drinks Ltd

Roya, Faisal
Dutch Delight UK Limited

Rozidar, Tengku
Haltrade UK Ltd

Ruhle, Steven Lawrence
Shibui Beverage Co Ltd

Rumbles, Simon Alexander
Pick Pedal Pour Ltd

Rundlett, John Philip
Toschi UK Limited

Rusbridge, Michael John
Vivid Vitality Ltd

Rushmere, Grant Keen
Chum Bites Limited

Rushton, Frederick Johnthomas
Hamer & Perks Limited

Russell, Nicholas
Cobell Ltd

Russell, Scott Christian
Paddy and Scotts Launch Pad Ltd

Rusu, Octavian
Green Cash & Carry Ltd

Ryan, Christopher Edward
Pure Organic Drinks Limited

Sabharwal, John
Kingsbury Wholesale Ltd

Saburi, Iqramulhaq
Trade HQ Ltd

Saburi, Mohmed Adil
Trade HQ Ltd

Sacharzewski, Andrzej
MAS Trading Cast Ltd

Sadedine, Malika
Ewid Ltd

Sadiq, Maqbool
Total Fast Food Supplies Ltd

Sahota, Gurpreet
GSTWholesale Limited

Sahota, Shashi
Sub Enterprises Ltd

Saiyed, Mustakim Azharbhai
Beverages Stars Ltd

Sajikumar, Velupillai
5S Import Ltd

Salaja, Joy Temitayo
N'ife Limited

Salako, Moses Boyenle
MBS Ventures Limited

Salem, Omer Babakar
Best Brand Food & Drinks (BBFD) Ltd

Salih, Abdelhamid
Eqoob Limited

Salter, Nicholas Kyffin
Aduna Limited

Salway, Anthony Philip Royston
Hydra Cubed Limited
Prir Group Limited

Samarasena, Ishara Buddika
Aiden Service Ltd

Sams, Craig Lynn
Gusto Organic Ltd

Sancak, Ali
Sannel Foods Limited

Sancak, Erhan
Sannel Foods Limited

Sandler, Martin
Leathams Limited

Sangha, Ajit Singh
Oneworlddistribution Ltd

Santos-Pires, Maria Vitoria
Alivini (North) Limited
Alivini Co Ltd

Sassooni, Parham
Innerji Ltd

Satayaprakorb, Arnon
Alpha Energy Drink Limited

Satheeshumar, Kansiah
Vinz Ltd

Sattar, Abdul
SmsZee Limited

Sattar, Sahar
SmsZee Limited

Sattar, Sana
SmsZee Limited

Sattar, Waheeda Tasleem
SmsZee Limited

Savaliya, Surajbhai Dayalal
Patson Foods Ltd

Savarimuthu, Suvaissan
Bossco Headland Ltd
Leoba Service Ltd

Savonije, Johannes Fredericus Christiaan Maria
Supermalt UK Limited

Savva, Angela
Smoothie Fresh (International) Ltd

Sayania, Surag Narpatsinh
Shree Sai Trading Ltd

Sayed, Tanzil Ismail
Vivid Vitality Ltd

Sayers, Gary
D.E. Scorer Limited

Scarborough, Ian
Humble Bumble Ltd

Schaper, Heinrich Friedrich Ludwig
Cobell Ltd

Schofield, John
Acquisto Limited

Schubert-Nicolas, Nicole
Ferment Revolution Limited

Scorer, David Edward
D.E. Scorer Limited

Scorer, Susan
D.E. Scorer Limited

Screaton, Iain Peter
Quando Drinks Limited

Sealey, Adam Edward
Gladiator Nutrition Supplements Ltd

Searle, Kirsten Ronsholt
Aquaid Franchising Limited

Searle, Paul Melville
Aquaid Franchising Limited

Sears, Michael
Windfall Logistics Limited

Sedighigilani, Abolfazl
Yardely Ltd

Seenivasan, Gnanapriya
Priya Even Limited

Segatta, Gianni
Alivini (North) Limited
Alivini Co Ltd

Sell, Michael de Campos
Ola Acai Ltd

Sellar, Nicholas
S & B's Mart Ltd.

Sellers, Paul
Organix Ltd

Sellers, Thomas
Organix Ltd

Selvan, Gajan
Glitter Service Ltd
Merseyside Service Ltd

Sethi, Hamza
Acquire Consultancy Limited

Sethi, Nadia
Acquire Consultancy Limited

Sghir, El Houssain
Bakhta Moroccan Mint Iced Tea Ltd

Shaffiq, Mohammed
ATR Catering Supplies Limited

Shah, Amer
Apollo Distribution Limited

Shah, Bhavesa Popatlal
Brandin Marketing Limited

Shah, Bimalkumar
Brandin Marketing Limited

Shah, Binny
City Beer Limited

Shah, Jolly
V Wholesalers Ltd

Shah, Kavit
City Beer Limited

Shah, Ketan
City Beer Limited

Shahzad, Athar
The Magnanimous Distribution T/A Pizzeria Hut

Shaikh, Faysal
FS Wholesale Distributors (UK) Ltd

Shamim, Salahudin Al
Taza Food Limited

Shanmugasundaram, Elenchezhiyan
Elan Import and Export Limited

Sharks, Khalid
Nile Minar Enterprise Limited

Sharma, Amit
Premium Drinks Distribution Ltd

Sharpe, Anita
Fruity Cards Ltd

Shaw, Andrew Richard
R.A.W. Goods Co Ltd

Shaw, Daniel Frank
Tasman Bay Foods Europe Ltd

Sheekh Aly, Mohamad Anas
Ifood Trading Ltd

Sheikh, Mahmood Qadir
K2 (Northwest) Limited

Sheikh, Mohammed Ali
Alancia Fruit & Vegetable Ltd

Sheikh, Romile
The Super Smoo-V Co Ltd

Sheikh, Shahbaz Ali Amjad
London Wholesale Ltd

Shemu, Rahima Akter
Vision Global Enterprise Ltd

Sheppard, Robin Michael Philpot
Alfresco Drinks Limited

Sherwani, Rabia
Food Brands Ltd

Shillcock, James Robert
Vivid Vitality Ltd

Shillcock, Robert Leslie
Vivid Vitality Ltd

Shimitra, Sotera
Marathon Food Limited

Shinde, Sandeep
Flavour Foods & Drinks Ltd

Shinwari, Abdul Jelil
Seagull Energy Drinks Ltd

Shirley-Beavan, John Michael
Ecopure Waters International Ltd

Shirley-Beavan, Sophia Elinor
Ecopure Waters International Ltd

Shojaee, Seyed Ali
Healthy Food and Drink Online Ltd

Short, Terence Reginald
Ravensbourne Wine Co Ltd

Siddique, Mohammed
Major Foods Limited

Siddiqy, Musaib Ahmed
Seven Bros Cookware Ltd

Sidhu, Gurpal Singh
Syntex Trading Ltd

Sidhu-Robb, Sangeeta
Nosh Detox Delivery Limited

Sigdyal, Basant
Allure International Ltd

Siha, Stephane
Sanus Foods Ltd

Sikanku, Gabriel Atsu
Yorkshire Enterprise Ltd

Sikka, Sankalp Rajen
Iturn Global Ltd

Silvester, Bency
Think Power Limited

Simpson, Javan
JSJuices Ltd

Simsek, Ahmet Turgay
C.N.A. Catering Logistics Ltd

Singh, Amanjit
Urban Distribution Ltd

Singh, Amarjit
Pursuit of Excellence Group Ltd

Singh, Ayshdeep
Tata Trade Ltd

Singh, Bahader
Shokers Wines & Spirits Ltd

Singh, Brijmohan
2 Brothers Birmingham Ltd

Singh, Chelsea Alexa
815 Distributors (UK) Ltd

Singh, Courtney Montrose
815 Distributors (UK) Ltd

Singh, Daman Raj
Tasman Bay Foods Europe Ltd

Singh, Gurmail
L & B Foods Ltd

Singh, Gurpreet [1985]
Snacks Dist Limited

Singh, Gurpreet [1990]
Ammy Trading Ltd
Majit Drinks Ltd

Singh, Hardeep
AI Pixel Points Limited

Singh, Harminder
Britlines Limited

Singh, Jora
Shokers Wines & Spirits Ltd

Singh, Kamaljit
Jessica Worldwide Ltd

Singh, Manjinder
SM Supplies Ltd

Singh, Narrinder
Globe Imex Ltd

Singh, Rajinder
Hi Fresh Limited

Singh, Rajinder Pal
Kanpes G Ltd

Singh, Ranjeev
Kaleboard Limited

Singh, Ranjit
FMCG Express Limited

Singh, Sanjeev
S Jee Enterprises Ltd

Singh, Shamsher
Agencia Ltd

Singh, Surinder [1980]
KKR Wine Ltd

Singh, Surinder [1974]
East and West Foods Cash and Carry

Singh, Suzanne Oliviene
815 Distributors (UK) Ltd

Siudaj, Marcin Tadeusz
Marcin & Son Ltd

Sivakrishnanathan, Sivatheeban
Order2buy Ltd
SS Midland Ltd

Sivalingam, Jansan
Geema Service Ltd

Sivaloganathan, Vellautham
Alpha Neno Limited
Eslan Lookray Ltd
Rolan Excel Limited
Sylvy Glosry Limited

Sivanathan, Prasanna
RSS Fast Food Suppliers Ltd

Sivapatham, Rameskumar
Altra Service Ltd
Bongo Sale Ltd
Robinson Alimentation Ltd

Slater, Simon Anthony
Broadwater Supply and Distribution Ltd

Slay, Benet Dunstan
Seedlip Ltd

Smalley, Roger
Bevtec Services Limited

Smirnovs, Andrejs
Loyal Trader Ltd

Smith, James Carl William
Broadwater Supply and Distribution Ltd

Smith, Michael Joseph
Rio Mata Atlantica Limited

Smith, Randall N
Morinda UK Limited

Smith, Rowan
Gentian Global Ltd

Smith, Tristan
Row & Smith Ltd

Smith, Troy
Oranka Fruit Juices Limited

Smuczynski, Maciej
AWA Water Ltd

Snyman, Johanna Elizabeth
Greenme Ltd

Sodha, Vishal
DRGN Global Ltd.

Sohal, Bhupinder Singh
Pallet Price Wholesale Ltd

Sohal, Kulwant
Apex Sourcing International Ltd

Soiledis, Panagiotis
Hellenic Agora Limited

Soni, Navin
Thriftys Wholesale Limited

Soto Mercado, Miguel Angel
Geminiz Ltd

Sowe, Malick Mamadi
One Grace LMT Ltd

Speckhardt Forczek, Michelle Carin
Top Selection Limited

Spice, William Edward
Green Ambition Limited

Spiropoulos, Patrick Nnamdi
Vivid Vitality Ltd

Sprague, Nicholas Simon
Frobishers Juices Limited

Sqarou, Naouar
Juicer Ltd

Sriganeshakuamr, Ajenth
Nirajen Ltd

Sriskantharajah, Luxan
J & D Wholesalers Ltd

St John, Sean Reilly
Made in the States Limited

Stacey, Andrew Clive
Herbarium Limited

Stael Thykier, Svend Christoffer
House Kitchen Limited

Stallabrass, Abbie
Mesh Facilities Limited

Stan, Corina Liana
Sweet Caroline Ltd

Starr, Adam
21st Century Nutrition Limited

Stephens, Mark
Sloane Avenue Group Ltd

Stephens, Thomas
Wobblegate Limited

Stephenson, Joseph William Bolshaw
Mock Drink Co Ltd

Steriotis, Dionysios-Georgios
Prod Act Ltd.

Stevens, Timothy Reginald
A1 Best Traders Ltd

Stimpson, Matthew
Thirsty Work Limited

UK Wholesalers of Soft Drinks — dellam

Stockwell, Matthew Colin
Coconutty Ltd

Stoica, Sorin
Merlin Distribution Limited

Stokes, Nathan Christopher
Your Water Ltd

Storey, William John
Rich Energy Limited

Strachan, Craig Robert
Foal Limited
The Start-Up Drinks Lab Ltd

Strafford, Nicola Ruth
Getfreshjuiceco Limited

Stranack de Ballestas, Ruth Mary
Fruto del Espiritu C.I.C.

Stranieri, Severina
Laspremuta Limited

Stylopoulos, Epameinondas
Prod Act Ltd.

Subash Chandra Bose, Venkat Varma
Venkat Ltd

Subramaniyan Thangavel, Vijayaraghavan
UKFast Service Ltd

Sugar, Alan Michael, Lord
Buzbees Beverages Limited

Sugirthan, Muthulingam
M & S Trading (London) Limited

Suha, Krisztian
Suha World Ltd

Suleman, Saqib
Glow Penny Ltd

Sumner, Brett Geoffrey
MM Global Citrus Limited

Sumra, Ana Magdalena
Brewed 4 U Ltd

Sumramaniyam, Arulanantham
Nor Oslo Service Ltd

Sun, Xiumei
Thailand 11234501 International Trade Co.,

Sun, Yao
Hua Lin Trade Import Limited

Sundbom, Andreas
Ibiza Recharge Limited

Surtees, Ian
Snackpax Distribution Limited

Suterwalla, Anis
Sutaka UK Limited

Suterwalla, Jehangir
Sutaka UK Limited

Suvaissan, Sinthupiriya
Bossco Headland Ltd

Swallow, Anthony David
Creamline Dairies Limited
Swallow Holdings Limited

Swallow, Christopher David
Creamline Dairies Limited
Swallow Holdings Limited

Swallow, Helga Hildegard Gertrud
Creamline Dairies Limited
Swallow Holdings Limited

Swayamprakasam, Kirubanandam
Aquamarine Limited

Sweetin, James Aaron
Wishing Tree Limited

Symeou, Andrew
AKM Trading Services Ltd

Symeou, Constantine
AKM Trading Services Ltd

Syrichas, Paul
Smoothie Fresh Ltd

Szachniewicz, Adrian Damian
DSA Frozen Foods Ltd

Szaradowski, Krzysztof
Vittorio Ottavio Ltd

Szatkowski, Mariusz Wojciech
Fresh Fruit Direct Limited

Szczesny, Sebastian Remigiusz
MSM Foods Limited
Najpol Ltd

Szilagyi, Laszlo
Interseel Ltd

Tabassum, Sohail
Neelam Traders Ltd

Tahir, Tahir Ali
T & A Import and Export Trading Ltd

Tajer, Younes
Global Market Solutions Ltd

Talafair, Hardip Singh
Nexgen 2018 Ltd

Talukder, Mohammed Imran Abdal
Imran Brothers Limited

Tamana, Shane
Shane's Consortium Limited

Tareen, Muhammad Arif Khan
Simple Brands Ltd

Targas Marcilla, Joan
Importonics Limited

Tarim, Erkan
Tydene Limited

Tariq, Jahangir
Punjab Masala Ltd
RJ Traders Ltd

Tariq, Tehmoor Ahmed
Total Fast Food Supplies Ltd

Tate-Smith, Catherine Louise
Tate-Smith Limited

Tate-Smith, Constance Maria
Tate-Smith Limited

Tate-Smith, Paul Thomas
Tate-Smith Limited

Taton, Marcin
Hannah & Ted Ltd

Taukoor, Baboo Oomeshwarsingh
Dodotraders UK Limited

Tavarajha, Naveneethan
Mercury Wholesale Ltd
TN Global Service Ltd
TN Sales Ltd

Taylor, Adrian Robert
PXL Drinks Ltd

Taylor, Ian Charles
Frobishers Juices Limited

Tayyab, Muhammad
F & T Enterprise Ltd.
FS Wholesale Distributors (UK) Ltd

Televantidis, Anastasis
Dolphin Trading Limited

Terzic, Zoran
Rich Energy Limited

Thakkar, Usha
Monks Drinks Limited

Thakorlal, Praneal Jitendra
E-Natural Limited

Thakorlal, Rakhee
E-Natural Limited

Thakrar, Kapil Mahendra
Star Direct Hospitality Ltd

Thaneswaran, Koneswaran
KT Wholesale Ltd

Thavarajah, Yostinappu Philip
UK Beer & Soft Drinks Ltd

Thawethe, Kondwa
Abantu Moringa Ltd

Theodore, Bethany
Theodore Global Limited

Theodore, Janet Ann
Theodore Global Limited

Thiebaut, Theo
Tiqle Global Limited

Thirlwell-Pearce, Oliver James
Vitte Nutrition Ltd

Thirlwell-Pearce, Phoebe
Vitte Nutrition Ltd

Thomas, James Barry
Premier Pubco Limited

Thomas, Susan
Premier Pubco Limited

Thompson, Edward Ballard
Pixley Berries (Juice) Limited

Thompson, Jermaine
Juice Junkiez Limited

Thornton, John
RMGL Trading Limited

Thuvaraganathan, Navaradnam
Great Wins Ltd

Tiber, Melinda
Crescent Moon World Project Ltd.

Todorov, Kalin
Orpheus Tea Ltd

Tohouri, Oliver Cromwell
Oct Multi Services Limited

Tokarev, Igor Krisztian
Bluetech Marketing Ltd

Toussaint, Yolanda
Imperial House of 3 Kings Ltd

Tovmasian, Gkor
Bassen Ltd
Noah Brothers Ltd

Townsend, William
Active Root 2 Ltd

Townshend, Stuart
Luella Malmesbury Ltd

Traboulssi Barake, Abdelrahman
Herbaleva Ltd

Trevitt, Graham
Norfolk Punch (UK) Ltd

Trogu, Emmanuelle
Y Acay Berry Ltd

Trood, Nigel John
MM Global Citrus Limited

Tse, Chi
Mightybee Limited

Tsvetkov, Nikolay Penkov
5of5 Juices Ltd

Tucker, Danny Lee
DT Fruits Ltd

Tufail, Muhammad Aamir
Matlowone Limited

Tuffour-Kensah, Dennis Paul
Bubra Drinks Ltd

Turano, Clare
Cibo (London) Limited

Turano, Franco
Cibo (London) Limited

Turcan, Irina
Erbology Ltd

Turcan, Ludmila
Erbology Ltd

Turcan, Victor
Erbology Ltd

Turk, Ebru
Dalina Limited

Turner, Edward James
Turner Hardy & Co Limited

Turness, Peter Laurence
House Water Limited

Turton, Adam Paul
Phoenix Dispensed Drinks Ltd

Turton, Adrian Scott
Phoenix Dispensed Drinks Ltd

Tutisani, Tapiwa
Magna Juice Ltd

Tyler, Steven John
D D C Foods Limited

Ucar, Dogan
DLG Wholesale Ltd

Ucur, Ercan
Eda Quality Foods Limited
Eda Quality Foods North UK Ltd
Fresh Star Fruit & Veg Limited

Ucur, Huseyin
Eda Quality Foods Limited

Ucur, Sercihan Yusuf
Ever-Tree Wholesale & Retail Ltd

Uddin, Jijan
Triumph Foodservice Limited

Uddin, Khalid
KU Bargin Deals Ltd
KU Supplies Ltd
Uddin Discount Ltd

Uddin, Sheikh Mohammed Goyas
Green Foods International Ltd

Ulcay, Ali
London Drinks Supplier Ltd

Ullah, Maroof
HT Sweets (UK) Limited

Uludag, Niyazi
R.A. Trading Limited

Umoru, Lawrence
Govmalt & H.U.M.M.E.R. Beverages Global Co

Umoru, Victoria
Govmalt & H.U.M.M.E.R. Beverages Global Co

Unwin, Stephen Edward
Cawston Press Limited

Uppal, Sukhvinder Singh
Drinks International Birmingham Ltd

Ustinnerio, Parunanthu
White World Service Ltd

Uygun, Simge
Huma Gida UK Limited

Vaghasiya, Chintankumar Chunilal
Patson Foods Ltd

Vajigaran, Thurairajan
Beeston General Store & Off Licences Ltd

Vajja, Harsha Vardhan Babu
H N D Trading Limited

Vajja, Srinivasa Rao
H N D Trading Limited

Valeiras Bernad, Erica
Vitamor Limited

Valenti, Anthony
Ayr Brewing Co Ltd

Valli, Abdul Yusuf
Tastebuds Trading Ltd

Valvis, Jean
Aqua Carpatica UK Ltd

Van Bockel, Huib
Basecamp Brews Ltd

Van Der Venter, Craig Martin William
Talbot & Barr Limited

Van Geest, Leonard Waling
The Ubuntu Trading Co Ltd

Van Groeningen, Petrus Wilhelmus
Basecamp Brews Ltd

Van Lambaart, Thomas Fokko
Chum Bites Limited

Varga, Janos
Aquacoll UK Ltd

Vasilache, Gabriela
Bucovina Cash & Carry Ltd

Vaskova, Petra
Mediterranean International Ltd

Vaughan, Gwendolyn Nicole
Sweet Sally Limited

Veerakathipillai, Thevachandran
Crab Trading Ltd

Venn, Jaquelene Simone
Usmoothie Ltd
Usqueeze Limited

Ventriglia Senior, Nicola
Fourseasons Fruiterers Ltd

Ventriglia, Franco
Fourseasons Fruiterers Ltd

Verma, Vikram
Trust in Global Food Ltd

Veselaj, Sokol
Drinkable Ltd

UK Wholesalers of Soft Drinks — dellam

Vickers, Andrew Maurice
Natural Welsh Water Limited
Water Wellbeing Limited
Watercoolers Southern Limited

Vickery, Andrew Brian
Thirsty Work Limited

Videloup, Fabian
All for You Beverages Limited

Vilcinskas, Petras
P & V Agents Ltd

Volf, Michael Joseph
The Gibraltar Gin Co Ltd

Von Hurter, Felix Ferdinand
Anytime Drinks Limited

Vora, Parag Vinodbhai
Delamore Trading UK Ltd

Vu, Dac Huu
DH Exotic Produce Ltd

Wachira, Elizabeth Muthoni
Squishy Drinks Limited

Wahbi, Hicham
HF Food International Ltd

Wahid, Muhammad
AFC Food (UK) Limited

Walford, Julian John Howard
RTH Healthcare PLC

Walker, Kathryn
Liquid Brand Exports Limited

Wall, David John
Walbrokers Limited

Wall, Mark John
Walbrokers Limited

Wallace, Michael Robert
V.A. Whitley & Co. Limited

Wallace, Paul
Zacely Limited

Wallbank, Alexander James
Paradigm Red Limited

Walsh, Alan
Artisan Drinks Co Ltd

Walton, Mark Corin
Bloomsbury Drinks Ltd

Wang, Dakun
Good News International Trading Ltd

Wang, Jun
WLH Food Ltd

Ward, Gary Jonathan
Astral Nutrition Limited

Ward, Jonathan Edward Hedderly
Ecopure Waters International Ltd

Warner, Jennifer Patricia
Domore Imports Ltd

Warrillow, Timothy Daniel Gray
Fevertree Europe Limited
Fevertree Row Limited
Fevertree UK Limited
Fevertree US Limited

Warrington, Dennis John
Bill Bean Limited

Warrington, Sally Ann
Bill Bean Limited

Waters, Christopher Edward
Leathams Limited

Watkins, Robert
Vild Water Limited

Watson, Craig
Nobu Distribution Ltd

Weatherby, Paul Andrew
Crop's Foods Ltd.

Webb, Eleanor Roxanne
Caleno Drinks Ltd

Weerasinghe, Nalaka
Nature Fresh Limited

Wei, Xiangyu
H & F Export Limited

Wells, Richard Raymond Collingwood
Rick's Wine Ltd

Wen, Zepeng
WLL Wholesale Ltd

Wesson, Christopher Leonard Gaunt
Zummo Central Limited

West, Kenneth Milne
Deveron Direct Limited

West, Russell Paul
Club Consultants Ltd

Whitchurch, Adam
Hydra Cubed Limited

Wickramage, Kemasiri
Stack United Limited

Wightman, Donald Michael
Roxane UK Limited

Wilkins, Ross Generald
Zoop Up Energy Ltd

Wilkinson, Alan
The Farm Shop at Ombersley Ltd

Wilkinson, Andrew
Discount Brands (London) UK Ltd

Wilkinson, Gary
Magna Carta Drinks Limited

Wilkinson, Jonathan Peter
3BW Ltd

Wilkinson, Melanie Mary
Magna Carta Drinks Limited

Williams, Stephen John
Ravensbourne Wine Co Ltd

Willis, Brent David
Morinda UK Limited

Wilson, Dawn
The Cane Press Ltd

Wilson, Diane
Dollshouse Childrens Drinks Ltd
Red Baron Beverages Limited
Vivo Viva Beverages Limited

Wilson, Diane Edith
One Up Beverages Corporation (1 Up)

Wilson, Robert
Harp & Crown Cider Co Ltd
Slimsters Sports Drinks Ltd
Vivo Viva Beverages Limited

Winchester, John Howard
Milton Sandford Wines Limited

Winchester, Mary Rose Lyon
Milton Sandford Wines Limited

Winnack, Jack Andrei Geoffrey
Winnack and Hart Industries Ltd

Wisniewski, Marcin Michal
M & M Emerald Ltd

Wlodarczyk, Slawomir
The Noble Smokehouse Ltd

Wolski, Stanislaw
MS Rarytas Ltd

Wood, Roger Donald James
Racing Greens Nutraceuticals Ltd

Woodhead, Elisa Susan Jane
Total Cellar Supplies Limited

Woodhead, Iain Samuel
Total Cellar Supplies Limited

Woodley, Julian
JCW Foods Ltd

Woodward, Lynn Catherine
Elderbrook Drinks Limited

Woolnough, Paul
Manteo Trading Co Ltd

Wright, Samuel James
Bare Drinks Limited

Wylie, Andrew Gregor
Adamson's Drinks Ltd.

Wynne, David Gareth
G & Y Wynne Limited

Wynne, Richard Patrick
Cape Crown Global Goods Ltd

Wynne, Yvonne Rosemary
G & Y Wynne Limited

Wynter, Anthony Timothy
Thirstee Business Limited

Yadav, Yashpal Singh
Anya Global Limited

Yadirgi, Ozan
O & E Food Ltd

Yakub, Hasan Kadir
MK Bazaar Ltd

Yanakopoulos, Andreas
Creative Properties and Investments Ltd
Konon Limited

Yandell, Christopher George
Rocktails Drinks Limited

Yang, Fei
Kang Med Limited

Yang, Yanyan
China Cambrian Limited

Yarham, Marcus Stanley
Snackpax Distribution Limited

Yates, Geoffrey Karl
Notgin Ltd

Yates, James
Veg & City Drinks Limited

Yates, Nicholas
Adrian Mecklenburgh Limited
Vimto (Out of Home) Limited

Yates, Sarah Ellen
Notgin Ltd

Yates, Stuart Andrew
Worldwide Essentials Limited

Yeung, Chun IP David
Raylex Ltd

Yoganathan, Samuel Nathaniel
Tri Star Wholesale Limited

Yogaratnam, Sujeeban
Nippon Trading Ltd

Yoovidhya, Chalerm
Red Bull Co Ltd

Younes, Tahir Mehmood
Brands Nexus Ltd

Young, Cynthia Patricia
Rejuveu Ltd

Young, William
Youngs Vintage Management Ltd

Yousif, Mohammad Rasoul
London UK Star Ltd

Yun, Justin
HP Juicery Ltd

Yunus, Waseem Ali
Majestic Wholesale Ltd

Yusuf, Samira
Northern Food Services Limited

Za, Syed
Syed Drinks Limited

Zahid, Zayd
The Berry Juice Co Ltd

Zahir, Mohsin
Vezlon Limited

Zaidi, Syed Haider Reza
Sabziwala Limited

Zaidova, Gunel
Bazaar Store Ltd

Zalewski, Krzysztof
K & E Wholesale Ltd

Zaveri, Hamza
Viva Avo Ltd

Zeloof, Jason
Ely & Sidney Limited

Zerpa Torres, Edgar Alexander
Aliss UK Limited

Zhang, Haitao
UK Cloud Business PLC

Zhang, Huarong
Winz International UK Ltd

Zhang, Xin
Hua Lin Trade Import Limited

Zhang, Yi
Bi Fa Limited

Zises, Meryl
Ziro Ltd

Ziyagham, Sabah
Alamirat Limited

Standard Industrial Classification
excluding
Wholesale of fruit and vegetable juices, mineral water and soft drinks

01130 Growing of vegetables and melons, roots and tubers
Go Fresh Ltd
Rozana Foods Limited

01160 Growing of fibre crops
Organix Ltd

02100 Silviculture and other forestry activities
Primacena Ltd.

08110 Quarrying of ornamental and building stone, limestone, gypsum, chalk and slate
China Cambrian Limited

08120 Operation of gravel and sand pits; mining of clays and kaolin
Riddles Bros Limited

10200 Processing and preserving of fish, crustaceans and molluscs
Noble Smokehouse Ltd
Sunugal Trading Limited

10320 Manufacture of fruit and vegetable juice [16]
AWA Nature Ltd
Bennu Rising Ltd.
Bright Smoothies Ltd
CCM Enterprises Limited
Cane Press Ltd
J.C.Davies & Hall Limited
Fruitfullest Ltd.
Go Fresh Ltd
Gold Star Soft Drinks Westcountry Ltd
Juice Junkie London Limited
Juice Junkiez Limited
Juice Warrior Ltd
McBerries Ltd
Pixley Berries (Juice) Limited
Rejuveu Ltd
Route 33 Limited

10390 Other processing and preserving of fruit and vegetables
Eda Quality Foods Limited
Emaya Foods Limited
Herbs 4 Healthy Living Ltd
KKS Fresh Fruits Ltd
Pixley Berries (Juice) Limited
Riverroll Limited

10410 Manufacture of oils and fats
Easy CBD Limited

10511 Liquid milk and cream production
Creamline Dairies Limited
Swallow Holdings Limited

10520 Manufacture of ice cream
Bio Icecream Ltd
Ice Guys Ltd
Juicydee Ltd
Panda Rolls Ltd

10710 Manufacture of bread; manufacture of fresh pastry goods and cakes
Healthy Hit Ltd
House Kitchen Limited

10720 Manufacture of rusks and biscuits; manufacture of preserved pastry goods and cakes
UK Brighton Food & Nutrition Research Centre

10831 Tea processing
Ion Distribution Ltd
Lore & Truth Ltd
Orpheus Tea Ltd

10832 Production of coffee and coffee substitutes
Alicia's Coffee House Limited
House Kitchen Limited
UK Brighton Food & Nutrition Research Centre

10840 Manufacture of condiments and seasonings
Condimental Ltd

10850 Manufacture of prepared meals and dishes
Birch Boost Ltd
House Kitchen Limited

10860 Manufacture of homogenized food preparations and dietetic food
Birch Boost Ltd
Tiqle Global Limited

10890 Manufacture of other food products n.e.c.
Canafizz Ltd
Good Gut Guys Ltd
Green Foods International Ltd
Mane and Rose Limited
Natures Vitality Limited
Organica Vita Ltd

11010 Distilling, rectifying and blending of spirits
Gibraltar Gin Co Ltd
Start-Up Drinks Lab Limited

11030 Manufacture of cider and other fruit wines
Woodstar Limited

11040 Manufacture of other non-distilled fermented beverages
Elegantly Spirited Limited

11050 Manufacture of beer
Infinite Session Ltd
Seafire Brewing Co. Ltd

11070 Manufacture of soft drinks; production of mineral waters and other bottled waters [58]
413 Limited
Acqua Nordica Ltd
Alitasa Ltd
Alpha Energy Drink Limited
Artathlon Beverages Limited
Artathlon Water Limited
Artisan Drinks Co Ltd
B4Sport Ltd.
Bennu Rising Ltd.
Biofresh Cosmos Ltd
Birch Boost Ltd
Bright Smoothies Ltd
Budaquelle Beverages International Ltd
Club Consultants Ltd
Creative Properties and Investments Ltd
DRGN Global Ltd.
Driver's Drinks Co Ltd
Eliya Europe Ltd
Evogue Limited
Exoteeque Limited
Ferment Revolution Limited
Flow 33 UK Limited
Foal Limited
GB Heritage Ltd
GO4 Beverages Limited
Gibraltar Gin Co Ltd
Green Foods International Ltd
H Two Eau International Ltd
Hello Coco Limited
Humble Bumble Ltd
Infinite Session Ltd
JSJuices Ltd
Konon Limited
Lord Eden Beverages Ltd
MB Drinks Ltd
Moringa Superfoods UK Limited
Mother Nature's Drinks Limited
N'ife Limited
Paisley Drinks Co. Ltd
Raw Is More Ltd.
Real Natural UK Ltd
Rocktails Drinks Limited
Saapos Ltd
Santa Monica Co Ltd
Seafire Brewing Co. Ltd
Sharewater Ltd
Simple Nature Limited
Sips MCR Ltd
Start-Up Drinks Lab Limited
Sweet Sally Limited
Temperance Drinks Limited
Theodore Global Limited
UK Brighton Food & Nutrition Research Centre
Vitte Nutrition Ltd
Vivo Viva Beverages Limited
J Water Disabled Children Ltd
Wild Cat Energy Drink Ltd
Your Water Ltd

13200 Weaving of textiles
UK Cloud Business PLC

16290 Manufacture of other products of wood; manufacture of articles of cork, straw and plaiting materials
MK Inter Ltd

22220 Manufacture of plastic packing goods
MK Inter Ltd

36000 Water collection, treatment and supply
Artathlon Water Limited
UK Cloud Business PLC
Waterline (UK) Ltd

41100 Development of building projects
BV Group UK Limited
Creative Properties and Investments Ltd
Cubico Limited
Konon Limited
MKM Group Trading & Investment Ltd

43341 Painting
Interseel Ltd

43999 Other specialised construction activities n.e.c.
Riddles Bros Limited

45112 Sale of used cars and light motor vehicles
Bia Trade Ltd
Cooper & Partner Ltd
Eltrados Ltd
Fast Car Sales Services Ltd
Hermes Chariot Ltd
Panton Ventures Limited
Zolex Global Limited

45190 Sale of other motor vehicles
Fast Car Sales Services Ltd
Sepandero Venturi UK Limited

45310 Wholesale trade of motor vehicle parts and accessories
Global Market Solutions Ltd
KP Global Ltd

45320 Retail trade of motor vehicle parts and accessories
Bedrock Trade Ltd
Cooper & Partner Ltd

45400 Sale, maintenance and repair of motorcycles and related parts and accessories
Kheira Ltd

46110 Agents selling agricultural raw materials, livestock, textile raw materials and semi-finished goods
Prod Act Ltd.

46120 Agents involved in the sale of fuels, ores, metals and industrial chemicals
AKM Trading Services Ltd
Albert Altima Trade House Ltd
Bespoke Contracts (UK) Ltd
Tricape UK Ltd

46130 Agents involved in the sale of timber and building materials
Agencia Ltd
China Cambrian Limited

46140 Agents involved in the sale of machinery, industrial equipment, ships and aircraft
Medina Food World Ltd

46150 Agents involved in the sale of furniture, household goods, hardware and ironmongery
Allure International Ltd
ESL Trading Ltd
Intercontinental Trade Solutions Ltd
MKM Group Trading & Investment Ltd
Seven Bros Cookware Ltd

46160 Agents involved in the sale of textiles, clothing, fur, footwear and leather goods
Allure International Ltd
Avigail Limited
ESL Trading Ltd
Maira Trade Ltd
NQN Enterprises Limited

46170 Agents involved in the sale of food, beverages and tobacco [45]
815 Distributors (UK) Ltd
901WD Ltd
AKKG Enterprise Limited
AWA Water Ltd
Alfresco Drinks Limited
Amedame International Ltd
Asta Barista Baby Ltd
BVG Distributors Limited
Cafe Collective UK Trading Co Ltd
Cheti & Co Holdings Limited
Cheti & Co Limited
Dining Capital Limited
Drinks Europe Ltd
J.C. Dudley & Co. Ltd
Easy CBD Limited
F & T Enterprise Ltd.
Fanal Ltd
Stefan Frank Ltd
Funbella Ltd
Gentian Global Ltd
Going Ahead Ltd
Good News International Trading Ltd
Hubit General Trading Ltd
JustGeneralTradingServices Ltd
KKR Wine Ltd
KP Global Ltd
Liquid Brand Exports Limited
MKM Group Trading & Investment Ltd
Menon Naturals Ltd
Nacho Juice Limited
Numba UK Limited
Ooberstock Limited
Organix Ltd
Polwug Trading Ltd
Pres & Co. Limited
Sativatech Ltd
Slimsters Sports Drinks Ltd
Sunspice UK Limited
Sweetprod Ltd
Tasman Bay Foods Europe Ltd
Tomatelios UK Ltd
Toschi UK Limited
Tricape UK Ltd
Ufton Limited
Zeroholic Ltd

46180 Agents specialised in the sale of other particular products
901WD Ltd
Allure International Ltd
CBD Globe Distributors Ltd
Dan International (UK) Limited
Europol Trade Ltd.
Kheira Ltd
Monrone Health Ltd
Quinton Trading Ltd

46190 Agents involved in the sale of a variety of goods [21]
815 Distributors (UK) Ltd
Albert Altima Trade House Ltd
Fanal Ltd
Stefan Frank Ltd
Grouptype Limited
Hellenic Agora Limited
Hubit General Trading Ltd
Intercontinental Trade Solutions Ltd
J & H Global UK Ltd
JustGeneralTradingServices Ltd
Kristals Trading Limited
Ladeo Limited
Menon Naturals Ltd
Moon Lynx Ltd
New Kumasi Market 2 Ltd
RJ Traders Ltd
Springwater Direct Ltd.
Tasnim Recruiting & Consultancy Services
Tricape UK Ltd
Wildcat International Limited
Worldwide Essentials Limited

46210 Wholesale of grain, unmanufactured tobacco, seeds and animal feeds
Astra Import Ltd.
ESL Trading Ltd
Natures Vitality Limited
YummyColombia Ltd

46220 Wholesale of flowers and plants
Amedame International Ltd
Attila Martocsan Ltd
Bespoke Contracts (UK) Ltd
Fresh Produce Deliveries Ltd
Fresh Produce Imports UK Ltd
Gorog Trading Limited
Marco Polo Exotics Ltd

46230 Wholesale of live animals
Fruits & Vegetables Ltd.

46310 Wholesale of fruit and vegetables [121]

A2Z Fruit & Veg Ltd
AB (Cheshire) Group Ltd
AB Catering (Blackburn) Ltd
ABNN Fresh UK Ltd
AKKG Enterprise Limited
Acquire Consultancy Limited
Afro Lanka Ltd
Agrofresh Ltd
Aliss UK Limited
Alti's Catering Limited
Ammart Ltd
Anadolu Catering Limited
Apollo Fruit & Veg UK Ltd
Aquamarine Limited
Assala Limited
Avigail Dairies Limited
Azka Impex (London) Limited
Azka Impex Limited
Bedford Halal Meat & Grocceries Ltd
Bill Bean Limited
Blue Trading International Ltd
Bravocservices Ltd
Britannia International Wholesalers Ltd
Bukhari and Tanweer Limited
Caribbean Trade Ltd
Chosen Enterprises Limited
Cityfresh Limited
Crop's Foods Ltd.
DSA Frozen Foods Ltd
Dragon Rise Limited
Drea Ltd
J.C. Dudley & Co. Ltd
Eldoflora Limited
Emaya Foods Limited
Estelon Holdings Limited
Ever-Tree Wholesale & Retail Ltd
Evershine Trading Limited
FMCG Enterprises Limited
Farida Import Export Ltd
Feeders Foods Wholesale Ltd
First Food Ltd
Fresh N Green Ltd
Fresh Produce Deliveries Ltd
Fresh Produce Imports UK Ltd
Fresh Produce International Ltd
Fruit & Veg 2 U Ltd
Fruit & Veg Imports Ltd
Fruitfullest Ltd.
Fruits & Vegetables Ltd.
Fruto del Espiritu C.I.C.
Future Generation Foods U.K. Ltd
GI Food Group Limited
GT Traders Ltd.
Geminiz Ltd
Gloucester Wholesale Ltd
Golden Fastfood Limited
Good News International Trading Ltd
Hayat Supermarket Ltd
Hellenic Grocery Limited
Hero Catering Supplies Limited
Hi Fresh Limited
I Star Wholesale Limited
Ideal Trading Limited
Inc. Trading Limited
Iturn Global Ltd
J & H Global UK Ltd
Jameson's Trading Ltd
Jasmine Blue Ltd
Jones Bros. 1877 Ltd
JustGeneralTradingServices Ltd
K.M Food & Drinks Ltd
KKS Fresh Fruits Ltd
La Zgarici Ltd
Log Cabin Fruits Ltd
Loris Wholesale Ltd
MSK Halal Ltd
MTS Export Import Ltd
Majestic Foods Limited
Manchester Fruit and Vegetables Ltd
Manteo Trading Co Ltd
Marco Polo Exotics Ltd
Meadow Harvest Ltd
Mightybee Limited
NCE Trading KFT Ltd
Nadban Limited
Nar London Limited
Nazar Wholesale Limited
Nodus International Trade Ltd
O & E Food Ltd
Ola Acai Ltd
Orange Trading Ltd
Organica Vita Ltd
Ozlem Limited
Polat International Ltd
Pres & Co. Limited
Quick Constuction Ltd
Rahims Trading Ltd
Reineta Limited
Risco Service Ltd
Rozana Foods Limited
Sabziwala Limited
Samco Global Foods Ltd
Sannel Foods Limited
Simex International Ltd
Sub Enterprises Ltd
Symphony Fine Foods Ltd
Taj Restaurant Supplies Ltd
Taza Food Limited
Thistle Foods Limited
Tomatelios UK Ltd
Trade HQ Ltd
Under The Sun Europe Ltd
Unique Lines Ltd
Usedsoft Ltd
Vangoo Enterprise Holding Ltd
Venkat Ltd
WGTSS Ltd
WLH Food Ltd
White World Service Ltd
Winz International UK Ltd
Yourchoice Wholesale Ltd

46320 Wholesale of meat and meat products [92]

AB Catering (Blackburn) Ltd
ABZ Food Ltd
AFC Food (UK) Limited
Alicja Food Ltd
Alivini (North) Limited
Alivini Co Ltd
Alti's Catering Limited
Ammart Ltd
Amsterdam Taste Ltd
Anadolu Catering Limited
Angel Global Export Ltd
Apollo Distribution Limited
Assala Limited
Atlas Halal Ltd
Bazaar Store Ltd
Bedford Halal Meat & Grocceries Ltd
Bi Fa Limited
Bot Trading Co Ltd
Brands Nexus Ltd
Bri Trade Solutions Limited
Butterfly Foods and Packaging Ltd
Camelot Chilled Foods Ltd
Choise Group Ltd
Creative Properties and Investments Ltd
Dimark Limited
Dragon Rise Limited
Dutch Delight UK Limited
East and West Foods Cash and Carry
Eda Quality Foods Limited
Eda Quality Foods North UK Ltd
Eltrados Ltd
Evogue Limited
FS Wholesale Distributors (UK) Ltd
Feeders Foods Wholesale Ltd
Fresh N Green Ltd
Fresh Produce International Ltd
GCA Foods Edinburgh Ltd
GI Food Group Limited
GM Catering Supplies Ltd
GT Traders Ltd.
Gloucester Wholesale Ltd
Golden Eagle Foods Edinburgh Ltd
Golden Eagle Trade Edinburgh Ltd
Golden Fastfood Limited
Good News International Trading Ltd
Good Prices Ltd
Hayat Supermarket Ltd
Hellenic Grocery Limited
Hero Catering Supplies Limited
Ideal Lincs Limited
Imran Brothers Limited
Jays Trading Ltd
Kaleboard Limited
Konon Limited
La Zgarici Ltd
Leathams Limited
Longstar Trading Limited
MBS Ventures Limited
MBW Traders Ltd
MD Investgroupp Ltd
MS Rarytas Ltd
MSK Halal Ltd
MSM Foods Limited
Magnanimous Distribution T/A Pizzeria Hut
Majestic Foods Limited
Major Foods Limited
Mesh Facilities Limited
N & J Wholesale Foods Limited
Najpol Ltd
Nazar Wholesale Limited
Netto Stores Limited
Northern Food Services Limited
O & E Food Ltd
Ozlem Limited
Pursuit of Excellence Group Ltd
RSS Fast Food Suppliers Ltd
Rahim Brothers Limited
Rahims Trading Ltd
Sabroso Food UK Ltd
Sams Fast Foods Limited
Superyacht Supplies Limited
Syon Distributors Ltd
Thistle Foods Limited
Triumph Foodservice Limited
Usedsoft Ltd
Vangoo Enterprise Holding Ltd
Venkat Ltd
W D L Wholesale Limited
WLH Food Ltd
Whiskey and Bourbon Club Ltd

UK Wholesalers of Soft Drinks

V.A. Whitley & Co. Limited
Zayyan Foods Distribution Ltd

46330 Wholesale of dairy products, eggs and edible oils and fats [90]

7 Star Trading Ltd
AB Catering (Blackburn) Ltd
ABZ Food Ltd
AFC Food (UK) Limited
Ace Incorporation Ltd
Alicja Food Ltd
Aliss UK Limited
Alivini Co Ltd
All Fresh Bradford Ltd
Anadolu Catering Limited
Apollo Distribution Limited
Aquamarine Limited
Assala Limited
Avigail Dairies Limited
Avigail Limited
Paul Berry Limited
Bia Trade Ltd
Bill Bean Limited
Bor-Tom Ltd
Britannia International Wholesalers Ltd
Butterfly Foods and Packaging Ltd
Camelot Chilled Foods Ltd
Cibo (London) Limited
Creamline Dairies Limited
D'Auria Brothers Ice Cream and Catering
Doorstep Desserts Distribution Ltd
E-Natural Limited
Easy CBD Limited
Eda Quality Foods Limited
Eda Quality Foods North UK Ltd
Epson Trading Limited
FS Wholesale Distributors (UK) Ltd
Feel Group Limited
Fresh N Green Ltd
Fruit & Veg 2 U Ltd
GCA Foods Edinburgh Ltd
GI Food Group Limited
GM Catering Supplies Ltd
Globe Imex Ltd
Golden Eagle Foods Edinburgh Ltd
Golden Eagle Trade Edinburgh Ltd
Golden Fastfood Limited
Good Prices Ltd
Gulzar Traders Ltd
Hatton Wholesale Ltd
Hayat Supermarket Ltd
Hellenic Grocery Limited
Herbaleva Ltd
Hero Catering Supplies Limited
Ideal Lincs Limited
Ifood Trading Ltd
Jacksons Milk Deliveries Ltd
Jones Bros. 1877 Ltd
LB Hussan Hussain Halal Meat Superstore
La Zgarici Ltd
Leathams Limited
Majestic Foods Limited
Marco Polo Exotics Ltd
Mercado Da Saudade Ltd
N & J Wholesale Foods Limited
Nazar Wholesale Limited
Nodus International Trade Ltd
Orange Trading Ltd
Ozlem Limited
Premier Food & Beverage Ltd
Primacena Ltd.
RDM Polish Food Ltd

RSS Fast Food Suppliers Ltd
Rabia Food & Drinks Ltd
Rahim Brothers Limited
Rahims Trading Ltd
Sabroso Food UK Ltd
Sams Fast Foods Limited
Shapla Cash & Carry Ltd
Sheikh Super Store Ltd
Sunspice UK Limited
Superyacht Supplies Limited
Swallow Holdings Limited
Symphony Fine Foods Ltd
Syon Distributors Ltd
Tatry Trade Ltd
Topmost Foods Distribution Ltd.
Under The Sun Europe Ltd
Vangoo Enterprise Holding Ltd
Viserra Limited
W D L Wholesale Limited
Wades & Ellie Ltd
V.A. Whitley & Co. Limited
Yourchoice Wholesale Ltd
Zauq Services Ltd

46342 Wholesale of wine, beer, spirits and other alcoholic beverages [164]

A A Suppliers Ltd
AKM Trading Services Ltd
Ace Incorporation Ltd
After Eight Alcohol Concierge Ltd
Agencia Ltd
Albert Altima Trade House Ltd
Alivini (North) Limited
Alivini Co Ltd
All English Distribution Ltd.
Ana Express Ltd
Anderson Beverages Ltd
Anya Global Limited
Apna Distribution Ltd
Asta Barista Baby Ltd
Ayr Brewing Co Ltd
BV Group UK Limited
Bassen Ltd
Bazaar Store Ltd
Bellwether Impex (UK) Limited
Beverage Brothers Limited
Bibere Ltd.
Bloomsbury Drinks Ltd
Brewed 4 U Ltd
Brighton Brew Co Ltd
Browett & Fair Ltd
Bubra Drinks Ltd
Camii Punch Ltd
Caribbean Trade Ltd
Caspian Black Limited
Cellar Twelve Limited
Cheti & Co Holdings Limited
Cheti & Co Limited
Choise Group Ltd
City Beer Limited
Colemans ABC Ltd
D D S Food Imports Ltd
DLG Wholesale Ltd
DNG Group Ltd
DNG Trading Ltd
Deeti Wholesale Limited
Direct2door Food & Beverage Ltd.
Dodotraders UK Limited
Drink Free Ltd
Drinkable Ltd
Drinks Bay Limited
Drinks R Us Limited

Drinks2u Ltd
Drinkslynx Limited
ERE Igga Ltd
East and West Foods Cash and Carry
Eda Quality Foods North UK Ltd
Ely & Sidney Limited
Estelon Holdings Limited
Eurotrade Supply Limited
Ever-Tree Wholesale & Retail Ltd
Export and Import Trading Ltd
Firewater Merchants Ltd
Five Star Cash & Carry Ltd
Flavour Foods & Drinks Ltd
Forward Moving Limited
GM Catering Supplies Ltd
GWB Associates Limited
Gabby & Bello Enterprises Ltd
Georgian Wine Co Ltd
Gibraltar Gin Co Ltd
Giovanni Food & Wine Limited
Green Cash & Carry Ltd
H & F Export Limited
Hamer & Perks Limited
Harp & Crown Cider Co Ltd
Hatton Wholesale Ltd
Hellenic Agora Limited
Hoversy Technologies Ltd
Infinite Session Ltd
Intercontinental Trade Solutions Ltd
Interseel Ltd
Iturn Global Ltd
J & D Wholesalers Ltd
J M & D Limited
Jaguar Beverage Ltd
Jascera UK Ltd
Jays Trading Ltd
Kaleboard Limited
Kasgo Limited
Knights Catering Impex Ltd
Liquid Brand Exports Limited
Lithuanian Beer Limited
London Drinks Supplier Ltd
London Wholesale Ltd
Lora Trading (Europe) Ltd
Loughborough Student Services Ltd
MBW Traders Ltd
MSM Foods Limited
Magna Juice Ltd
Manchester Drinks Co Ltd
Manor Wholesale Ltd
Manteo Trading Co Ltd
Marathon Food Limited
Marcin & Son Ltd
Adrian Mecklenburgh Limited
Meless Group Limited
Henry Mitchell & Sons Limited
Montann Limited
More or Less Drinks Co Ltd
NCE Trading KFT Ltd
Najpol Ltd
Noah Brothers Ltd
O & E Food Ltd
Ooberstock Limited
PSB Trading Limited
Pallet Price Wholesale Ltd
Panton Ventures Limited
Paradigm Red Limited
Pick N Deliver Ltd
Polat International Ltd
Premier Pubco Limited
Punchy Drinks Limited
Pure Organic Drinks Limited

Rarewood (London) Limited
Ravensbourne Wine Co Ltd
Rimpex-UK Limited
Samco Global Foods Ltd
Saravanan Traders (UK) Ltd
Sativatech Ltd
Seafire Brewing Co. Ltd
Shack Drinks Limited
Sheikh Super Store Ltd
Shree Sai Trading Ltd
Simply Spirits Limited
SmsZee Limited
Source 360 Ltd
Stack United Limited
Star Direct Hospitality Ltd
Stockwell Beverages Ltd
Stockwell Wholesalers Limited
Storesrealm Limited
Suntrack Ltd
Supermalt UK Limited
Superyacht Supplies Limited
Swallow Dispensed Drinks Solutions
TFC Wholesale Ltd
Talbot & Barr Limited
Taste Merchants Ltd
Tate-Smith Limited
Temple Wines (Cash & Carry) Ltd
Thames Wholesale Ltd
Thirstee Business Limited
Tolmid International Ltd
Topmost Foods Distribution Ltd.
Triumph Foodservice Limited
Trust in Global Food Ltd
Turkish Kitchinn Wholesale Ltd
UK Beer & Soft Drinks Ltd
Usedsoft Ltd
Utku Emre Ltd
Viserra Limited
W D L Wholesale Limited
WLL Wholesale Ltd
Whiskey and Bourbon Club Ltd
Windfall Logistics Limited
Wine City Limited
Winnack and Hart Industries Ltd
Winz International UK Ltd
Xorta Global Management Ltd

46350 Wholesale of tobacco products [13]

Ace Incorporation Ltd
Dawsons (Wales) Limited
Faqir Billionaire Ltd
Gemini Wholesalers Limited
J & D Wholesalers Ltd
R. & I. Jones Limited
Henry Mitchell & Sons Limited
Saravanan Traders (UK) Ltd
Sheikh Super Store Ltd
Thames Wholesale Ltd
Trade HQ Ltd
Vendit (Harrow) Limited
Venkat Ltd

46360 Wholesale of sugar and chocolate and sugar confectionery [74]

A A Suppliers Ltd
AB (Cheshire) Group Ltd
Acquisto Limited
Alicja Food Ltd
Apna Distribution Ltd
Avic Trading Limited
Bedford Halal Meat & Grocceries Ltd

Bellwether Impex (UK) Limited
Bia Trade Ltd
Bibere Ltd.
Bor-Tom Ltd
Bravocservices Ltd
Britannia International Wholesalers Ltd
CBD Globe Distributors Ltd
Cafe Collective UK Trading Co Ltd
Codex Limited
Crescent Moon World Project Ltd.
Dimark Limited
Doorstep Desserts Distribution Ltd
E-Natural Limited
East2west Traders Ltd
Epson Trading Limited
Evershine Trading Limited
FMCG Enterprises Limited
FMCG Express Limited
Farida Import Export Ltd
GSKB Ltd
GT Traders Ltd.
Gemini Wholesalers Limited
Good Prices Ltd
Grouptype Limited
Huma Gida UK Limited
Ifood Trading Ltd
JFC Trading Limited
Jameson's Trading Ltd
R. & I. Jones Limited
Kasgo Limited
Kepenek Food Ltd
Klomar Ltd
Knights Catering Impex Ltd
Ladeo Limited
Merlin Distribution Limited
Merseyside Service Ltd
More or Less Drinks Co Ltd
Moreton Sweets (Wholesale) Ltd
NXSK UK Ltd
Northern Lights Ltd.
Ooberstock Limited
Organic Village Limited
Paradigm Red Limited
Parkway UK Wholesale Ltd
W.E.Pointon & Sons Limited
Premier Food & Beverage Ltd
Primacy Trade Ltd
Rabia Food & Drinks Ltd
Rexcel Trading Ltd
S & B's Mart Ltd.
Savers Stop Wholesalers Ltd
Seven Bros Cookware Ltd
SmsZee Limited
Sris International Ltd
Surprisingly Treaty Ltd
Sweetprod Ltd
Taste Merchants Ltd
Tatry Trade Ltd
Topmost Foods Distribution Ltd.
Toschi UK Limited
Trade HQ Ltd
Ufton Limited
Unite Foods Trading Limited
Viserra Limited
Walbrokers Limited
Zaid & Besher Ltd
Zauq Services Ltd

46370 Wholesale of coffee, tea, cocoa and spices [79]

815 Distributors (UK) Ltd
A & H Trading Ltd

A2Z Fruit & Veg Ltd
AB (Cheshire) Group Ltd
AZ Health Food Center Ltd
Abevco Limited
Al Taj Al Malaki General Trading UK Ltd
Al-Shahba Ltd
Alicia's Coffee House Limited
Ana Express Ltd
Anya Global Limited
Apna Distribution Ltd
Astra Import Ltd.
Avigail Dairies Limited
Bassen Ltd
Bedrock Trade Ltd
Buddthi Ltd
Buy & Sales Trading Ltd
CBD Globe Distributors Ltd
Cafe Collective UK Trading Co Ltd
DJ Drink Solutions Limited
Dimark Limited
Direct2door Food & Beverage Ltd.
Drea Ltd
E-Natural Limited
Europol Trade Ltd.
Falcos Food Ltd
Faqir Billionaire Ltd
Feeders Foods Wholesale Ltd
Fresh Produce Imports UK Ltd
Globe Imex Ltd
Gulzar Traders Ltd
Haltrade UK Ltd
Hannah & Ted Ltd
Healthy Hit Ltd
Hoversy Technologies Ltd
Huma Gida UK Limited
Ifood Trading Ltd
Ion Distribution Ltd
Jaguar Beverage Ltd
Kaluwa Ltd
Kepenek Food Ltd
Liquidline Limited
Luso Shop Ltd
M.R.S. Supplies Limited
MAS Trading Cast Ltd
MEA Health and Wellness Ltd
Adrian Mecklenburgh Limited
Mercado Da Saudade Ltd
Merlin Distribution Limited
NQN Enterprises Limited
NXSK UK Ltd
Orpheus Tea Ltd
Panymocc Limited
Premier Food & Beverage Ltd
Punjab Masala Ltd
RDM Polish Food Ltd
Rabia Food & Drinks Ltd
Rahim Brothers Limited
Reineta Limited
S & B's Mart Ltd.
Shapla Cash & Carry Ltd
Shruthinaya Ltd
Smart Buyer Wholesale Limited
Stack United Limited
Sunspice UK Limited
Super Food Base Ltd
TSK Trade Limited
Taste Merchants Ltd
Tatry Trade Ltd
Thass Ltd
Toschi UK Limited
Total Refreshment Solutions Ltd
U.D.C. Wholesale Ltd

UK Wholesalers of Soft Drinks

Under The Sun Europe Ltd
Unite Foods Trading Limited
Winz International UK Ltd
Yorkshire Enterprise Ltd
YummyColombia Ltd

46380 Wholesale of other food, including fish, crustaceans and molluscs [49]

7 Star Trading Ltd
Agrofresh Ltd
Al-Shahba Ltd
Alisha Fish Bazar Ltd
Aliss UK Limited
Alivini (North) Limited
Ammart Ltd
Anatolian Limited
Aquamarine Limited
Bibere Ltd.
Bot Trading Co Ltd
Buddthi Ltd
Caspian Foods Cash & Carry Ltd
Crop's Foods Ltd.
D'Auria Brothers Ice Cream and Catering
Direct Traders Ltd
ERE Igga Ltd
Eltrados Ltd
Emmunity Limited
Global Food Wholesalers Ltd
Gloucester Wholesale Ltd
Green Foods International Ltd
Jalkhushi Fresh & Frozen Fish Ltd
Jeet (UK) Limited
KVC Waffles Limited
Knights Catering Impex Ltd
London Wholesale Ltd
M & M Emerald Ltd
MK Inter Ltd
MSM Foods Limited
MTS Export Import Ltd
Marathon Food Limited
Medina Food World Ltd
N & J Wholesale Foods Limited
Najpol Ltd
Noble Smokehouse Ltd
Oct Multi Services Limited
Panymocc Limited
Punjab Masala Ltd
Rozana Foods Limited
Shruthinaya Ltd
Sunugal Trading Limited
Tasnim Recruiting & Consultancy Services
Thass Ltd
Triumph Foodservice Limited
Unite Foods Trading Limited
Urban Distribution Ltd
WLH Food Ltd
V.A. Whitley & Co. Limited

46390 Non-specialised wholesale of food, beverages and tobacco [102]

7 Star Trading Ltd
901WD Ltd
ABZ Food Ltd
Acquisto Limited
Amedame International Ltd
Anatolian Foods Ltd
Apollo Distribution Limited
Aster Service Ltd
Basil World Ltd
Bassen Ltd
Bazaar Store Ltd
Beeston General Store & Off Licences Ltd
Berry Juice Co Ltd
Birch Sales Ltd
Bogazici Ltd
Bongo Sale Ltd
BudgetForU Limited
CC Trade Ltd
Carpatica International Ltd
Castle Warehouse Management Ltd
Choise Group Ltd
DNG Trading Ltd
Deeti Wholesale Limited
Dining Capital Limited
Direct2door Food & Beverage Ltd.
Dollshouse Childrens Drinks Ltd
Drinks Europe Ltd
ERE Igga Ltd
Eastway Cash & Carry Limited
Eatwell Catering Contractors (Norwich)
Elham Elliethy Ltd
Elias Trading Limited
Epson Trading Limited
Erbology Ltd
Export and Import Trading Ltd
F & T Enterprise Ltd.
Fanal Ltd
Farida Import Export Ltd
Funbella Ltd
Geminiz Ltd
Gentian Global Ltd
Glitter Service Ltd
Globe Imex Ltd
Green Cash & Carry Ltd
Hatton Wholesale Ltd
J & D Wholesalers Ltd
Kaluwa Ltd
Kanpes G Ltd
Kasgo Limited
Lam Cash and Carry Limited
Lanza Foods Ltd
Loris Wholesale Ltd
Macedo (UK) Limited
Mashmoom International Limited
Adrian Mecklenburgh Limited
Mercado Da Saudade Ltd
Mercury Wholesale Ltd
Moudine Trade Ltd
Nexgen 2018 Ltd
Northern Food Services Limited
Nova Wholesale Ltd
Numba UK Limited
Orbit Food Ltd
Order2buy Ltd
PP Cash & Carry Ltd
Pallet Price Wholesale Ltd
Passa Distribution Ltd
Pick Pedal Pour Ltd
Risco Service Ltd
Rook Trading Ltd
S & B's Mart Ltd.
S & F Distribution Ltd
SLB Wholesale Ltd
SS Midland Ltd
Sannel Foods Limited
Savers Stop Wholesalers Ltd
Sepandero Venturi UK Limited
Shark Trading Ltd
Shimroon Limited
Shree Sai Trading Ltd
SmsZee Limited
Snacks Dist Limited
Stack United Limited
Star International Ltd
Stockwell Beverages Ltd
Stockwell Wholesalers Limited
TSK Trade Limited
Tasman Bay Foods Europe Ltd
Temperance Drinks Limited
Thass Ltd
Tomatelios UK Ltd
Topstop Wholesalers Limited
U.D.C. Wholesale Ltd
Unicorn Foodline Ltd
Urban Distribution Ltd
Vinz Ltd
Willow World Ltd
Wisdom of Nature Limited
Xorta Global Management Ltd
Yourchoice Wholesale Ltd
Zaid & Besher Ltd
Zumi Natural Limited

46410 Wholesale of textiles

Avic Trading Limited
Codex Limited
Connect Waze Private Limited
Evershine Trading Limited
Ewid Ltd
Cooray King Holdings Limited
M & M Emerald Ltd
Thames Wholesale Ltd
WGTSS Ltd

46420 Wholesale of clothing and footwear [13]

Anya Global Limited
Avic Trading Limited
Evo Fit Ltd
Ewid Ltd
FMCG Enterprises Limited
Gladiator Nutrition Supplements Ltd
Cooray King Holdings Limited
M & M Emerald Ltd
MJ Trading (NW) Ltd
Manteo Trading Co Ltd
Mirza Trading Limited
Moudine Trade Ltd
Vittorio Ottavio Ltd

46439 Wholesale of radio, television goods & electrical household appliances (other than records, tapes, CDs)

Bluetech Marketing Ltd

46440 Wholesale of china and glassware and cleaning materials

Cheti & Co Holdings Limited
Cheti & Co Limited
Ely & Sidney Limited

46450 Wholesale of perfume and cosmetics [12]

Bedrock Trade Ltd
Endetrox Ltd.
Haltrade UK Ltd
Herbaleva Ltd
MEA Health and Wellness Ltd
MS Rarytas Ltd
Monrone Health Ltd
NXSK UK Ltd
Rexcel Trading Ltd
Tradinguk55 Limited
WGTSS Ltd
Wisdom of Nature Limited

46460 Wholesale of pharmaceutical goods
Bri Trade Solutions Limited
Herbaleva Ltd
Lam Cash and Carry Limited
Neubria Limited
Rexcel Trading Ltd
Zolex Global Limited

46470 Wholesale of furniture, carpets and lighting equipment
Gorog Trading Limited

46499 Wholesale of household goods (other than musical instruments) n.e.c
Delamore Trading UK Ltd
Grouptype Limited
KML Home Limited
London Wholesale Ltd
Shac International Limited
Tasnim Recruiting & Consultancy Services
Urban Distribution Ltd

46520 Wholesale of electronic and telecommunications equipment and parts
Brands Nexus Ltd
Jeet (UK) Limited

46610 Wholesale of agricultural machinery, equipment and supplies
Fresh Pal Ltd
Patrik Trading Ltd

46650 Wholesale of office furniture
Monrone Health Ltd

46690 Wholesale of other machinery and equipment
BG Drinks Ltd
Zummo Central Limited

46720 Wholesale of metals and metal ores
Meless Group Limited

46730 Wholesale of wood, construction materials and sanitary equipment
Castle Warehouse Management Ltd

46740 Wholesale of hardware, plumbing and heating equipment and supplies
Castle Warehouse Management Ltd

46900 Non-specialised wholesale trade [49]
AZ Health Food Center Ltd
Agencia Ltd
Astra Import Ltd.
Bellwether Impex (UK) Limited
Bespoke Contracts (UK) Ltd
Blue Trading International Ltd
Butterfly Foods and Packaging Ltd
Caspian Foods Cash & Carry Ltd
Chosen Enterprises Limited
Eldoflora Limited
Elham Elliethy Ltd
Eqoob Limited
Eurotrade Supply Limited
Exoshell UK Ltd
Export and Import Trading Ltd
Faqir Billionaire Ltd
GCA Foods Edinburgh Ltd
Golden Eagle Foods Edinburgh Ltd
Golden Eagle Trade Edinburgh Ltd
Haltrade UK Ltd
Huma Gida UK Limited
JFC Trading Limited
JJ Import/Export Ltd
Jays Trading Ltd
KP Global Ltd
Kaleboard Limited
Kaspas Distribution Ltd
Ladeo Limited
Leathams Limited
MS Rarytas Ltd
Maira Trade Ltd
Moudine Trade Ltd
NQN Enterprises Limited
Nar London Limited
Northern Lights Ltd.
Orange Trading Ltd
Patson Foods Ltd
Platinum Group Midlands Ltd
Primacena Ltd.
Pursuit of Excellence Group Ltd
Quando Drinks Limited
MD Rahma Ltd
S & F Distribution Ltd
Shac International Limited
Smart Buyer Wholesale Limited
Verdict International Ltd
World Trade Values Limited
Zentio Limited
Zolex Global Limited

47110 Retail sale in non-specialised stores with food, beverages or tobacco predominating [20]
Aster Service Ltd
Bargain Food and Wine Ltd
Bi Fa Limited
Bongo Sale Ltd
Budgie Juices Ltd
CC Trade Ltd
Chosen Enterprises Limited
Crop's Foods Ltd.
Dining Capital Limited
Elev8 Energy Drink Limited
Falcos Food Ltd
Fletcher's Fruit & Veg Ltd
Neubria Limited
Nexgen 2018 Ltd
One Up Beverages Corporation (1 Up)
Orpheus Tea Ltd

Sativatech Ltd
Vild Water Limited
Wine City Limited
Zentio Limited

47190 Other retail sale in non-specialised stores [10]
A & H Trading Ltd
Bi Fa Limited
Eldoflora Limited
GO4 Beverages Limited
Interseel Ltd
London Drinks Supplier Ltd
PTP Enterprise Limited
Premier Marketing (NW) Ltd
Super Smoo-V Co Ltd
Wine City Limited

47210 Retail sale of fruit and vegetables in specialised stores [14]
Abantu Moringa Ltd
Blue Trading International Ltd
Bravocservices Ltd
Emaya Foods Limited
Fruit & Veg Imports Ltd
Fruitfullest Ltd.
Iturn Global Ltd
Jalkhushi Fresh & Frozen Fish Ltd
LB Hussan Hussain Halal Meat Superstore
London Drinks Supplier Ltd
MBS Ventures Limited
Nadban Limited
Ola Acai Ltd
PTP Enterprise Limited

47220 Retail sale of meat and meat products in specialised stores
A & H Trading Ltd
LB Hussan Hussain Halal Meat Superstore

47230 Retail sale of fish, crustaceans and molluscs in specialised stores
Afromax Ltd
Fresh Produce International Ltd
Fruits & Vegetables Ltd.
Jalkhushi Fresh & Frozen Fish Ltd
Noble Smokehouse Ltd
Oct Multi Services Limited

47240 Retail sale of bread, cakes, flour confectionery and sugar confectionery in specialised stores
Global Sunshine Distribution Ltd
Hannah & Ted Ltd
J & H Global UK Ltd
No Meat No Worries Limited
T's Dazzling Delicious Sweets Ltd

47250 Retail sale of beverages in specialised stores [21]
ADA Beverages Ltd
Arsi Soft Drinks Limited
Artathlon Beverages Limited
Asi Wholesale & Retail Ltd
Budgie Juices Ltd
CC Trade Ltd
Cybel Ltd
Elev8 Energy Drink Limited
Energy Drinks Ltd

UK Wholesalers of Soft Drinks

Lord Eden Beverages Ltd
Luso Shop Ltd
Nuli Life Ltd
One Up Beverages Corporation (1 Up)
Red Baron Beverages Limited
Shokers Wines & Spirits Ltd
Slimsters Sports Drinks Ltd
Toffoc Ltd
Vild Water Limited
Vivo Viva Beverages Limited
Wenlock Spring Water Limited
Zeroholic Ltd

47290 Other retail sale of food in specialised stores [13]
Afromax Ltd
Cybel Ltd
Luso Shop Ltd
Mane and Rose Limited
Medina Food World Ltd
Samco Global Foods Ltd
Sris International Ltd
Sweet Caroline Ltd
T's Dazzling Delicious Sweets Ltd
Worldwide Essentials Limited
Y Acay Berry Ltd
ZSM Traders Ltd
Zauq Services Ltd

47410 Retail sale of computers, peripheral units and software in specialised stores
Angel Global Export Ltd
Pursuit of Excellence Group Ltd

47421 Retail sale of mobile telephones
Angel Global Export Ltd
SM Supplies Ltd

47429 Retail sale of telecommunications equipment other than mobile telephones
Matlowone Limited

47510 Retail sale of textiles in specialised stores
New Kumasi Market 2 Ltd
OK Brothers Ltd
ZSM Traders Ltd

47610 Retail sale of books in specialised stores
Hannah & Ted Ltd
MBS Ventures Limited

47640 Retail sale of sports goods, fishing gear, camping goods, boats and bicycles
Global Sports Trade Ltd

47710 Retail sale of clothing in specialised stores
Luella Malmesbury Ltd
Vittorio Ottavio Ltd

47760 Retail sale of flowers, plants, seeds, fertilizers, pet animals and pet food in specialised stores
Ion Distribution Ltd

47789 Other retail sale of new goods in specialised stores (not commercial art galleries and opticians)
Ital World Ltd

47810 Retail sale via stalls and markets of food, beverages and tobacco products
Artathlon Beverages Limited
Bright Smoothies Ltd
Fruto del Espiritu C.I.C.
Geminiz Ltd
Go Fresh Ltd
Herbs 4 Healthy Living Ltd
Lord Eden Beverages Ltd
Numba UK Limited

47820 Retail sale via stalls and markets of textiles, clothing and footwear
Maira Trade Ltd

47890 Retail sale via stalls and markets of other goods
51 Plus Ltd
Vild Water Limited

47910 Retail sale via mail order houses or via Internet [19]
51 Plus Ltd
AZ Health Food Center Ltd
Artis Trade Ltd
Condimental Ltd
Discount on Drinks Ltd
Elham Elliethy Ltd
Falcos Food Ltd
Fruto del Espiritu C.I.C.
JJ Import/Export Ltd
L'Azur Ltd
Natures Vitality Limited
Neubria Limited
Norfolk Punch Limited
Nosh Detox Delivery Limited
Rocktails Drinks Limited
Simple Nature Limited
Tomato Tantrum Ltd
Y Acay Berry Ltd
Zeroholic Ltd

47990 Other retail sale not in stores, stalls or markets
Al Taj Al Malaki General Trading UK Ltd
Creamline Dairies Limited
MU Distributors Ltd
Meless Group Limited
Swallow Holdings Limited
UK Beer & Soft Drinks Ltd
Woodstar Limited

49410 Freight transport by road
Brands Nexus Ltd
Regal Trade Limited

50200 Sea and coastal freight water transport
Jascera UK Ltd

52101 Operation of warehousing and storage facilities for water transport activities
Artathlon Water Limited

52243 Cargo handling for land transport activities
Sub Enterprises Ltd

52290 Other transportation support activities
Fresh Pal Ltd

53100 Postal activities under universal service obligation
HMH Wholesale Ltd

56101 Licenced restaurants
Eatwell Catering Contractors (Norwich)
Falafel Factory Ltd
Whiskey and Bourbon Club Ltd

56102 Unlicenced restaurants and cafes
Fresh Food Concepts Ltd
S & M (Wholesale Supplies) Ltd

56103 Take-away food shops and mobile food stands
5of5 Juices Ltd
Ferment Revolution Limited
Fresh Food Concepts Ltd
Juicydee Ltd
Nekta Food & Juice Bar Ltd
Ola Acai Ltd
Sweet Caroline Ltd

56210 Event catering activities
After Eight Alcohol Concierge Ltd
Ferment Revolution Limited
Firewater Merchants Ltd
Global Sunshine Distribution Ltd
Onofrei Cash & Carry Ltd
Prestwich Catering & Wholesale Ltd
MD Rahma Ltd

56290 Other food services [33]
ABNN Fresh UK Ltd
ATR Catering Supplies Limited
Acquire Consultancy Limited
Afromax Ltd
Alicia's Coffee House Limited
Ana Express Ltd
Bevtec Services Limited
Budgie Juices Ltd
Cape Crown Global Goods Ltd
Cibo (London) Limited
Cybel Ltd
DSA Frozen Foods Ltd
Debbie and Venky Ltd
Elias Trading Limited
Ewid Ltd
Falafel Factory Ltd
Fruit & Veg 2 U Ltd
Good Gut Guys Ltd
Healthy Food and Drink Online Ltd
Hellenic Agora Limited
Herbs 4 Healthy Living Ltd
Jones Bros. 1877 Ltd
MTS Export Import Ltd
Mane and Rose Limited
Netto Stores Limited
Nile Minar Enterprise Limited
Olsson Logistics Limited
Saapos Ltd

Sub Enterprises Ltd
Symphony Fine Foods Ltd
Tolmid International Ltd
Y Acay Berry Ltd
YummyColombia Ltd

56302 Public houses and bars
Eatwell Catering Contractors (Norwich)

61900 Other telecommunications activities
Suha World Ltd

62020 Information technology consultancy activities
Tomato Tantrum Ltd
Unione Trading Europe Ltd
Yorkshire Enterprise Ltd

62090 Other information technology service activities
Unione Trading Europe Ltd

64204 Activities of distribution holding companies
Global Sports Trade Ltd

64209 Activities of other holding companies n.e.c.
Burlingtown UK Limited
Triple R Industries Limited

64304 Activities of open-ended investment companies
UK Cloud Business PLC

64991 Security dealing on own account
Triple R Industries Limited

68100 Buying and selling of own real estate
Riverroll Limited
Zumi Natural Limited

68209 Other letting and operating of own or leased real estate
Gemini Wholesalers Limited
Loughborough Student Services Ltd
S & M (Wholesale Supplies) Ltd

68310 Real estate agencies
Panopoulos Forest Ltd

68320 Management of real estate on a fee or contract basis
Panopoulos Forest Ltd

69201 Accounting and auditing activities
Global Market Solutions Ltd

69202 Bookkeeping activities
Global Market Solutions Ltd

70210 Public relations and communications activities
Moon Lynx Ltd

70229 Management consultancy activities other than financial management [10]
Acquire Consultancy Limited
Asia Direct Limited
F & T Enterprise Ltd.
H Two Eau International Ltd
Cooray King Holdings Limited
Panopoulos Forest Ltd
RMGL Ltd
Shac International Limited
Tomato Tantrum Ltd
Youngs Vintage Management Ltd

71111 Architectural activities
Cubico Limited

71122 Engineering related scientific and technical consulting activities
Crescent Moon World Project Ltd.

72190 Other research and experimental development on natural sciences and engineering
Riverroll Limited

73110 Advertising agencies
Alpha Aliment Ltd
MD Investgroupp Ltd
Moon Lynx Ltd

73120 Media representation services
Yorkshire Enterprise Ltd

73200 Market research and public opinion polling
Alpha Aliment Ltd

74100 Specialised design activities
Cubico Limited

74901 Environmental consulting activities
Crescent Moon World Project Ltd.

74909 Other professional, scientific and technical activities n.e.c.
Start-Up Drinks Lab Limited

74990 Non-trading company
Waterline (UK) Ltd

77110 Renting and leasing of cars and light motor vehicles
Fast Car Sales Services Ltd

77400 Leasing of intellectual property and similar products, except copyright works
H Two Eau International Ltd

78300 Human resources provision and management of human resources functions
Bri Trade Solutions Limited

79120 Tour operator activities
Caribbean Trade Ltd

79909 Other reservation service activities n.e.c.
Ital World Ltd

82920 Packaging activities
FS Wholesale Distributors (UK) Ltd
MBW Traders Ltd

82990 Other business support service activities n.e.c.
Artisan Drinks Co Ltd
L & D Services UK Limited
Quicklemon UK Ltd
Star International Ltd

85600 Educational support services
CPH Games UK Limited

86900 Other human health activities
Afterall Ltd
Janere UK Limited
Worldwide Essentials Limited

88910 Child day-care activities
Loughborough Student Services Ltd

90010 Performing arts
Tata Trade Ltd

90030 Artistic creation
Sris International Ltd

91040 Botanical and zoological gardens and nature reserves activities
Attila Martocsan Ltd

93120 Activities of sport clubs
Global Sports Trade Ltd

93130 Fitness facilities
Evo Fit Ltd
Fitness Prostar Ltd

93199 Other sports activities
Fitness Prostar Ltd

96090 Other service activities n.e.c.
Ely & Sidney Limited
Kheira Ltd
Mesh Facilities Limited
Netto Stores Limited
Simorgh Limited
Thirsty Work Limited
Tolmid International Ltd

Printed in 8pt Nimbus Sans L

Designed by URW++ Design and Development GmbH

Dellam Publishing Limited

2 Heath Drive, Sutton, Surrey, SM2 5RP

Fax: 020 8770 7478   email: enquiries@dellam.com

SAN: 0177881   EAN/GLN: 5030670177882

www.ingramcontent.com/pod-product-compliance
Lightning Source LLC
Chambersburg PA
CBHW081113080526
44587CB00021B/3580